A Rope of Sand

Benjamin Franklin in 1766, from a portrait by David Martin (from the White House Collection). Franklin served as Pennsylvania's agent from 1757 until 1762 and from 1764 until 1775. He was also agent for Georgia (1768–1774), New Jersey (1769–1774), and the lower house of Massachusetts Bay (1770–1774).

A Rope of Sand

The Colonial Agents, British Politics,
and the American Revolution

~~~~~~~~~~~~~~~~~~~~~~~~~

By Michael G. Kammen

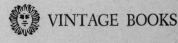 VINTAGE BOOKS

A Division of Random House, New York

Frontispiece, Benjamin Franklin, 1766,
by David Martin

FIRST VINTAGE BOOKS EDITION, February 1974

Library of Congress Cataloging in Publication Data

Kammen, Michael G
  A rope of sand.

  Reprint of the ed. published by Cornell University
Press, Ithaca, N.Y.
  Includes bibliographical references.
  1. Colonial agents. 2. United States—Politics and
government—Colonial period. I. Title.
[E195.K28 1974]   325.3′42′0973   73–13944
ISBN 0–394–71996–4

For My Parents
Blanche L. and
Jacob Merson Kammen

Preface

For almost four decades historians have been intensely concerned with the unsettled circumstances of British politics during the age of the American Revolution. Yet no one has systematically related those unstable conditions to the difficulties of governing an extensive empire at a time of financial and administrative stress. What has been lacking is an account of the disruption of the first British Empire as an entity centered in London, a detailed understanding of the direct impact on colonial affairs made by the tumultuous changes that occurred in British public life during the third quarter of the eighteenth century.[1]

As spokesmen for the colonies and as representatives of colonial concerns, the North American agents felt the effects of British politics personally and as paid lobbyists. They formed the core of the "American interest" in Britain. The deterioration of their institution after 1766 is an extraordinary manifestation of what helped to anticipate and precipitate the disruption of Anglo-American government—the decline of colonial influence "at home." For several generations the American voice had been heard in London through the agents and their allies. Their history in the 1760's and 1770's indicates most clearly how "the hands and servants of power" became impervious to that voice. Consequently I have used the agents and their problematical relationships as a way of focusing on a dimension that has been particularly blurred in our perception of the origins of the American Revolution. Their experiences and observations disclose forcefully

[1] See Edmund S. Morgan, ed., *The American Revolution: Two Centuries of Interpretation* (Englewood Cliffs, N.J., 1965), p. 181; Esmond Wright, ed., *Causes and Consequences of the American Revolution* (Chicago, 1966), pp. 48, 208.

what the revolutionary movement meant at the center of imperial government. Their activities, moreover, form an intricate illustration of the interplay between pressure groups, political action, and policy-making.

The purpose of this book, then, is to describe and analyze the total environment of an interest group during the most crucial generation of its existence. I mean to explain, in terms of the group's activity, the nature and course of a crisis in the affairs of Empire. *A Rope of Sand* is essentially about the decline of American influence in London and is offered as a study in the failure of Anglo-American communications.

The sources of the agents' difficulties are to be found in their relationships to one another, to the progress of the constitutional debate, to their constituents, to their allies in lobbying, and most of all to the British politicians. An examination of these relationships—the substance of this book—reveals the way colonial affairs were handled in London in the years before independence; for the process by which the agencies deteriorated is symptomatic of the way an entire network of formal and informal lines of imperial communication withered under the strain of factional instability, rapid economic growth, and the need for financial and administrative reform.

Sound communications are vital life lines to a far-flung system of dependencies. Hence the importance of the *senado de câmara*, or municipal council, of the old Portuguese empire, equivalent in many respects to the Spanish colonial *cabildo*. Besides having extensive powers in local affairs, these institutions were also influential through their ability to make their voices heard in Lisbon and Madrid, where they kept legal representatives.[2] As Benjamin Franklin wrote to David Hume from London: "I think it of importance to our general welfare, that the people of this nation should have right notions of us." While reading a conservative contribution to the pamphlet literature of the Great Debate in 1769, Franklin corrected the anonymous author in the margins of his copy, remarking at several points upon "the Folly of thinking to make Laws for a Country so unknown." Late in 1774, Dennis De Berdt Jr. wrote his brother-in-law, Joseph Reed, that if Whitehall had "been faithfully inform'd of American Transactions & Situations Things would never have come to this important Crisis."

---

[2] See Bailey W. Diffie, *Latin-American Civilization: Colonial Period* (Harrisburg, Pa., 1945), pp. 747–748; C. R. Boxer, *Portuguese Society in the Tropics: The Municipal Councils of Goa, Macao, Bahia, and Luanda, 1510–1800* (Madison, Wis., 1965), pp. 108–109, 149.

Many years after independence, William Samuel Johnson set about composing his recollections of life in public affairs. Reflecting upon his agency for Connecticut, he especially remembered finding everyone in London "extremely ignorant" of the colonies.[3]

One cause of Britain's remoteness from colonial circumstances lay in the decay of the formal structure of empire. Governors and the complex variety of imperial bureaucrats in America had become weaker as bonds of unity and sources of information than were their unofficial counterparts: merchants, religious organizations, and familial ties. These informal ligaments of the system were by mid-century its substantive and strongest connecting elements. Nevertheless most histories of the American Revolution have examined the formal structure of empire more carefully and completely than the informal. To use Reinhold Niebuhr's generic distinction, the governors and official dignitaries appointed by Whitehall constituted the "vertical" force of cohesion inherent in a central authority. By contrast, the informal bonds were "horizontal" elements of "community" rather than "dominion"—voluntary and nonauthoritative sources of cohesion.[4]

Both community and dominion are necessary components in any successful imperial system. Their collapse leaves the empire without structural supports. The agents occupied a curious place in this schema, because they especially partook of both community and dominion, constituting a kind of bridge between the two. During the later 1760's and 1770's, British administrations destroyed the equilibrium by trying to make the agents greater levers of dominion and less cohesive factors of voluntarism—hence one major cause of the agents' diminished usefulness as mediators.

The work of recent historians in this broad context has been of great importance. Edmund S. Morgan, Jack P. Greene, Charles R. Ritcheson, Bernard Donoughue, and Carl Ubbelohde have analyzed the disruption of the official empire particularly well, while Benjamin W. Labaree, Bernard Bailyn, and Carl Bridenbaugh have done so in the areas of commerce, ideas, and religion. Lawrence H. Gipson has

---

[3] Franklin to Hume, Sept. 27, 1760, Smyth, IV, 83; Franklin's annotated copy of *The True Constitutional Means for Putting an End to the Disputes between Great Britain and the American Colonies* (London, 1769) is in the Rare Book Room, NYPL. De Berdt to Reed, Oct. 8, 1774, Reed MSS, NYHS; Memoirs of Johnson, WSJ MSS (misc. box).

[4] Niebuhr, *The Structure of Nations and Empires* (New York, 1959), pp. 33–34.

attempted to describe comprehensively the undoing of the whole system; and his construct stands as a foundation upon which all others must build. If I have occasionally disagreed with him, I have also profited immensely from the richness of his works. Charles M. Andrews, as part of his last historical testament, observed that "before we can grasp the significance of the critically important events that took place in America, particularly in New England, after 1770, it will be necessary to fathom more clearly the working of the English mind both at Whitehall and at Westminster." [5] Jack M. Sosin and Franklin B. Wickwire have made efforts to remedy the deficiency Andrews noted. Like them, I have been guided by the belief—so closely identified with Sir Lewis Namier—that collective biography can do much to reveal the impulses and tendencies of a period.[6]

The history of the generation prior to the Revolution is certainly one of the most familiar to students of the American past. Another narrative history, even of a particular institution or issue, would be less valuable than a topical and thematic approach that accentuates the particular findings of new research. Consequently I have chosen such an approach, wishing not to retrace the ground already covered by others and hoping to present my own interpretation with greater clarity. The disadvantages, of course, are twofold: an unavoidable measure of internal overlap and the presumption of some familiarity on the part of the reader with the political history of these years.

The book is divided into two sections. The first serves a double purpose: as an introduction to the mechanics of Anglo-American lobbying in the eighteenth century and as a discussion of the agents' relationship to British politics in the decade prior to the Stamp Act crisis. I find that that crisis marked the most significant turning point in the institution's history. Hence its place as the culmination of Part One. Part Two treats the subsequent decade (1766–1775) in terms of the North American interest's declining influence in London. It too concludes with a narrative chapter, demonstrating in this case the agents' ineffectuality during the final imperial crisis. In a separate and forthcoming essay I have attempted to broaden the interpretive per-

---

[5] Andrews, "On the Writing of Colonial History," 3*WMQ,* I (1944), 48.

[6] See Namier's "History," *Avenues of History* (London, 1952), p. 10. Sir Lewis intended to complete a study of the agents, but his Zionist activities prevented him, and the lobbyists remained his *zekher lekhurban*—the unfinished part of his house; see Namier, *England in the Age of the American Revolution* (2nd ed.; London, 1961), pp. 246–254, esp. 251 n. 1.

spective to its logical contextual limits by considering the North American interest in relation to all the other groups competing for power and influence in London at that time.[7] Only through such a perspective, I believe, can one finally hope to appreciate the relationship of interest group politics to the origins of the American Revolution.

Carol Koyen Kammen has shared in several stages of this book's development: research, editorial criticism, and preparation of the manuscript. More important, she has endured both my presence and my absence with calm and patient good humor.

The encouragement and astute critical insights of Bernard Bailyn have continually refreshed my interest in eighteenth-century politics. I can never hope to repay the kindness he has shown me since 1958. Traveling fellowships awarded by Harvard University in 1961 and 1962 made comprehensive research in English and American archives possible.

Aristodimos N. Sofianos and his family were wonderfully gracious while I lived on the island of Hydra, Greece, writing a first draft. They provided me with a quiet study and a memorable exposure to Greek culture. Mrs. Maro Kanavarioti supplied a cottage and, even more, an inspirational view of the Saronic Gulf and the mountains of the Peloponnesus.

Various friends have read the manuscript at different stages and have offered numerous insights: Bernard Bailyn, Alison G. Olson, Fred J. Levy, Richard V. W. Buel, Daniel H. Calhoun, Pauline Maier, John Toye, and Michael Yudkin. I am deeply indebted to them for their thoughtfulness; needless to say, they bear no responsibility for the flaws that remain. I also received valuable suggestions from Verner W. Crane, Jere Daniel III, Malcolm Freiberg, Lawrence H. Gipson, Stanley N. Katz, Walter LaFeber, and Robert J. Taylor. Felix Reichmann of the Cornell University Library took seriously all my bibliographical requests. And the Cornell Faculty Research Grants Committee subsidized final preparation of the manuscript.

The staff of the Institute of Historical Research in London, particularly William Kellaway, were extraordinarily helpful during the months I worked there. Leonard W. Labaree and Helen C. Boatfield

[7] "British and Imperial Interests in the Age of the American Revolution," *Essays on Anglo-American Political Relations, 1675–1775,* ed. Richard M. Brown and Alison G. Olson (New Brunswick, N.J., 1968).

gave me access to the marvelous resources of the Franklin collection at Yale and sent advice as well as copies of unpublished documents in their custody. Mr. and Mrs. F. J. Stitt provided a very gracious reception in Staffordshire: wonderful tales washed down with stout.

For permission to use, cite, or quote from manuscripts in their possession, I am grateful to the following persons and institutions: Earl Fitzwilliam and the Trustees of the Wentworth Woodhouse Settled Estates; Lord Dartmouth and Lady Lewisham; the Trustees of the British Museum; the Officials of the Public Record Office; the Clerk of the Parliaments, House of Lords; the Earl of Malmesbury; Sir John Murray; D. H. Hartley Russell; William C. Coles; the Rosenbach Foundation and Gallery, Philadelphia; the libraries of Harvard, Yale, Brown, Columbia, Duke, North Carolina, Boston, and Bristol Universities; the Haverford College Library; the historical societies of Massachusetts, Connecticut, New York, Pennsylvania, and New Jersey; the Massachusetts and Rhode Island Archives; the Connecticut State Library; the New York Public Library; the Buffalo and Erie County Public Library; the William Clements Library, Ann Arbor, Mich.; the American Philosophical Society; and the South and North Carolina Departments of Archives and History.

In quoting from the sources, I have retained the spelling, punctuation, and capitalization of the originals, except in a few cases where changes seemed necessary in the interest of clarity.

MICHAEL G. KAMMEN

Ithaca, New York
November 1967

Contents

Abbreviations

AAS	American Antiquarian Society, Worcester, Massachusetts
Add MSS	Additional Manuscripts, British Museum, London
AHR	*American Historical Review*
APS	American Philosophical Society, Philadelphia, Pennsylvania
BM	British Museum, London
BPL	Boston Public Library, Boston, Massachusetts
BUL	Bristol University Library, Bristol, England
CC	Committee of Correspondence
CHS	Connecticut Historical Society, Hartford
CRNC	*Colonial Records of North Carolina*, ed. W. L. Saunders (30 vols.; Raleigh, 1886–1914)
CSL	Connecticut State Library, Hartford
CSM	Colonial Society of Massachusetts
DAB	*Dictionary of American Biography*
DNB	*Dictionary of National Biography*
EHR	*English Historical Review*
GLL	Guildhall Library, London
HLHU	Houghton Library, Harvard University, Cambridge, Massachusetts
HLRO	House of Lords Record Office, London
HMC	Royal Historical Manuscripts Commission
HSP	Historical Society of Pennsylvania, Philadelphia
JHC	*Journals of the House of Commons*
LC	Library of Congress, Washington, D.C.
MA	Massachusetts Archives, State House, Boston
MFY	Mason-Franklin Collection, Yale University Library, New Haven, Connecticut

MHM	*Maryland Historical Magazine*
MHS	Massachusetts Historical Society, Boston
NEQ	*New England Quarterly*
NHCHS	New Haven Colony Historical Society, New Haven, Connecticut
NHHS	New Hampshire Historical Society, Concord
NJHS	New Jersey Historical Society, Newark
NYHS	New-York Historical Society, New York City
NYPL	New York Public Library, New York City
PC	Privy Council
PDD	Protestant Dissenting Deputies
PHE	T. C. Hansard, *The Parliamentary History of England from the Earliest Period to the Year 1803*
PMHB	*Pennsylvania Magazine of History and Biography*
PRO	Public Record Office, Chancery Lane, London
PRO CO	Public Record Office, Colonial Office Papers
PRO T	Public Record Office, Treasury Papers
PSQ	*Political Science Quarterly*
RIA	Rhode Island Archives, State House, Providence
RIHS	Rhode Island Historical Society, Providence
SCA	South Carolina Archives, Columbia
SCHGM	*South Carolina Historical and Genealogical Magazine*
SCL	Sheffield City Library, Sheffield, England
Smyth	*The Writings of Benjamin Franklin*, ed. A. H. Smyth (10 vols.; New York, 1907)
VHS	Virginia Historical Society, Richmond
VMHB	*Virginia Magazine of History and Biography*
VSL	Virginia State Library, Richmond
WCL	William L. Clements Library, Ann Arbor, Michigan
1*WMQ*	*William and Mary Quarterly*, first series
2*WMQ*	*William and Mary Quarterly*, second series
3*WMQ*	*William and Mary Quarterly*, third series
WSJ MSS	William Samuel Johnson Manuscript Collection, Connecticut Historical Society, Hartford
WSL	William Salt Library, Stafford, England
YUL	Yale University Library, New Haven, Connecticut

Part One

INSTITUTIONAL OPERATIONS
AND THE IMPERIAL CRISIS,
1756–1766

" 'Tis a kind of Labour in vain to attempt making Impressions on such moveable Materials; 'tis like writing on the Sand in a windy Day."
—BENJAMIN FRANKLIN, 1766

CHAPTER 1

Decades of Development:
The Agencies, 1624–1755

In seventeenth- and eighteenth-century Anglo-America, the genus "agent" included various species. Commercial enterprises and private individuals hired representatives, known as agents, to deal with authorities in London. British ministries maintained diplomatic delegates, also called agents, for missions to other nations, to Indian tribes, and sometimes to colonial governments. In addition, there was a class of crown agents appointed and salaried by the administration to serve as a liaison with the crown colonies—Georgia, the Floridas, and what later became part of Canada. This diverse range of regularly employed agents was broadened by a variety of special agents who undertook particular and temporary commissions. All these species of agents are covered by the definition of an eighteenth-century publicist, Malachy Postlethwayt. An agent, he wrote, "in matters of business, is a person entrusted, or appointed, with the conduct, management, and negotiation of the affairs of other people, or of a corporation." He then noted that "agency-business comprehends any sort of business which is undertaken on the behalf, or on the account, of other persons. To act in this capacity requires suitable natural and acquired talents and abilities; and, in particular, a good knowledge of men and the world." [1]

The agents with whom we are concerned here were the authorized individuals residing in London whose business it was to look after the

---

[1] Herbert L. Osgood, *The American Colonies in the Seventeenth Century* (New York, 1904), I, 113, II, 203, 311, 465; *The Universal Dictionary of Trade and Commerce* . . . (4th ed.; London, 1774), Vol. I, under "Agent" and "Agency-Business."

interests of the North American colonies.[2] The agent was usually empowered to serve as a channel of communication and to arrange matters between his colony's government, or a branch of it, and Britain's officialdom. His activities, as a rule, were limited only by the nature of his instructions, which on occasion "were expressly framed for the purpose of allowing him to refrain from giving an opinion regarding some delicate point involving colonial interests and to plead, instead, lack of authority." [3] But if the agents were usually sources of information, they also were often diminutive ambassadors who could commit their governments to agreements. During the earlier seventeenth century, colonists were sent to England on provincial commissions, or proprietary or company charters, and it was quite natural for the British to regard them as colonial emissaries. As one administrator remarked, it was wise to have "certaine choice ffreinds hiere, who are interested in yore wellfare & who may, as occasion shall serve, time and improve, and perhaps give alterations to such Papers, as you shall transmit, and trust to their Conduct; wch is the continual practice of distant States, by their Agents and Ambassadours, which are resident in their behalf in foreign nations." [4] Within half a century this attitude would undergo significant changes.

As paid lobbyists the agents had various responsibilities: forwarding documents and news, preparing and presenting petitions, securing acceptance of colonial legislation and preventing adverse bills from passing through Parliament, promoting trade, settling land disputes, and handling Indian and military affairs as well as colony finances in London. In short, they were political brokers—extraconstitutional cogs in the machinery of imperial government.[5] As such they might be colonials living in London or especially sent "home" for the purpose, or even Englishmen with interests in America who had never seen the New World. In any case, their primary qualification was familiarity with British political life, especially since the provincial agencies were

---

[2] The West Indian colonies also employed agents similar in function and purpose; see Lillian M. Penson, *The Colonial Agents of the British West Indies* (London, 1924).

[3] Lawrence H. Gipson, *The British Empire before the American Revolution*, I (2nd ed.; New York, 1958), 10–11.

[4] Thomas Povey to Daniel Searle, June 8, 1659, Add MSS 11411, ff. 85–87.

[5] See Ella Lonn, *The Colonial Agents of the Southern Colonies* (Chapel Hill, 1945), ch. 5.

the only offices in Great Britain at the disposal of the colonies. In search of influence, the American assemblies usually selected merchants or politicians—preferably ones trained in the law.

THE AGENTS UNTIL 1690

The agency probably originated in 1624, when Virginia sent John Pountis "to solicite the generall cause of the countrey to the King and the Counciel." Yet the institution developed slowly through the seventeenth century. During these years, colonies chose agents for special missions without fixed salary or term. Even after the position was made permanent, the colonies continued to appoint special agents to aid the regular representative in important matters or even to handle separate issues independently. Although Virginia's agency became partially settled by 1660, it was not fully functional until 1690, along with several of the New England agencies.[6] The northern agencies began later but developed more quickly than their southern counterparts, which frequently became pawns in the recurrent battle between governor and council on the one side and lower house on the other. In the eighteenth century, this problem grew in magnitude and frequently circumscribed the agents' effectiveness when it did not bar the choice of a representative altogether.[7]

Perhaps the most striking characteristic of the earliest colonial agents is their quality. Outstanding men were generally selected, and they gladly accepted the responsibility of defending provincial interests in London. Virginia chose Sir George Yeardley in 1625; the next year he met with considerable success in London in procuring additional supplies and a promise of free importation. Two decades later Maryland sent Governor Leonard Calvert as agent. In 1661, Virginia raised £200,000 in tobacco to meet the expenses of Governor Berkeley, who was sent to quash efforts to revive the old Virginia Company. Berkeley's connections with courtiers, officials, and merchants contributed to his success. That his brother, John Lord Berkeley, was a member of both the Council for Trade and the Council for Foreign

---

[6] "Documents of Sir Francis Wyatt," 2*WMQ*, VII (1927), 128; Lonn, *Agents of the Southern Colonies*, pp. 21–22, 57, 111, and app. 1.

[7] Lonn, *Agents of the Southern Colonies*, pp. 75, 110; Beverly W. Bond Jr., "The Colonial Agent as a Popular Representative," *PSQ*, XXXV (1920), 372–392.

Plantations was also an asset. Virginia's agents in the 1670's were equally well supported and successful.[8]

In New England a similar pattern obtained during the first few generations. Edward Winslow, one of the most important members of the Plymouth Colony, helped to establish the institution by serving in 1634 and 1635. Eleven years later he undertook a second agency on behalf of the Massachusetts Bay Colony, this time to protest charges of intolerance and arbitrary rule in the Puritan commonwealth. He remained in England until his death in 1655—the first colonial to achieve success in public affairs there following a political apprenticeship in America. Winslow came to be regarded as the pre-eminent expert in London on New England life and trade. Whenever the Committee for the Affairs of New England met for business, Winslow was likely to be called upon for advice.[9]

When the Rhode Island plantations sought to rescue themselves in 1643 by procuring a charter in London, they dispatched Roger Williams; the patent was granted after a year through his immense efforts. A decade later he returned to have the charter confirmed; once again he succeeded. In the 1660's the Rhode Island towns recognized the value of well-supported agents and raised funds accordingly. Similarly Connecticut chose Governor John Winthrop Jr. in 1661 and provided him with funds adequate to ensure the success of his mission—procuring the Charter of 1662. When New Hampshire required an agent in 1683, the necessary funds were raised by subscription in order to send Nathaniel Weare, who was also well supplied with supporting documents.[10]

During the last third of the seventeenth century, the agents of Massachusetts Bay were placed on a firmer institutional basis, and *pari passu* began to encounter many of the characteristic problems of the later agencies: insufficient authority, instructions, funds, and appreciation. Only the charter crises of the 1680's brought about a return of the best representatives the commonwealth could appoint: first Joseph Dudley, launching his political career, and then Increase Mather and Sir William Phips during the Glorious Revolution. Their effective-

---

[8] Osgood, *Colonies in the Seventeenth Century*, III, 76, 112–113, 153–154, 202, 252–253.

[9] *Ibid.*, pp. 64–65, 111; W. Sterry-Cooper, *Edward Winslow* (Birmingham, Eng., 1953), pp. 48–49, 55.

[10] Osgood, *Colonies in the Seventeenth Century*, I, 327, 354, 361, 363, III, 109, 356.

ness, based on sound connections, was responsible for the compromise charter of 1691—a milestone in the colony's history.[11]

Following the restoration of Charles II, men responsible for Britain's colonial administration became increasingly eager to have colonial spokesmen available in London. Thus the governor of Virginia was instructed to request that any planters coming to England look after provincial affairs. When the Committee of Trade considered in 1675 how best to curb colonial violations of the Navigation Acts, it decided that each colony ought to keep someone on hand in London to be responsible for the colony's rectitude. After that it was a short step to the view that permanent agents belonged in Britain to transact colonial business. Much of the pressure on the colonists to maintain agents seemed to come from the various governmental committees that arbitrated colonial disputes and that genuinely wanted to hear both sides of any case before rendering a decision.[12] With this in mind, Chief Justice North added a clause to William Penn's charter, requiring him to keep an agent in London who could be held fully responsible for the behavior of subjects in Pennsylvania. If violations of the Navigation Acts were proved, the agent was to pay damages within a year or the colony's government would revert to the crown. For these urgent reasons, perhaps, William Penn served as his own agent for more than thirty years.[13]

Until the end of the seventeenth century, then, agents were appointed largely for temporary missions to handle particular issues. Some eventually remained abroad for a considerable length of time, but most wished to return to their colonies as quickly as possible. After the Glorious Revolution, however, Americans became more aware of the value of permanent agents resident in England. Without them the colonies might be unrepresented in emergencies or for the long cases that could last months or years. At the very least, agents were required

[11] *Ibid.*, 161–162, 317–318, 322, 326–330, 424–440; Herbert L. Osgood, *The American Colonies in the Eighteenth Century*, I (New York, 1924), 123–126; Increase Mather, *A Brief Account Concerning Several of the Agents of New-England, Their Negotiation at the Court of England* . . . (London, 1691).

[12] I am indebted to Dr. Alison G. Olson for permission to read her unpublished manuscript concerning Anglo-American politics and administration in the seventeenth and eighteenth centuries.

[13] Joseph E. Illick, "The Pennsylvania Grant: A Re-evaluation," *PMHB*, LXXXVI (1962), 383–384.

in London once every year when colonial laws arrived and commissions had to be arranged.

After 1690 none of the colonies appreciated the importance of
being well and continuously represented in Great Britain more than
the New England corporate colonies: Massachusetts Bay, Connecticut, and Rhode Island. By the beginning of the eighteenth century,
they, with Virginia, had adopted the agency as perhaps "the most
important, effective, and regular means of maintaining contact with
the various branches of the British government and of guarding both
general and special colonial interests." The practice of retaining permanent agents spread quickly and was especially encouraged by the
reorganized Board of Trade, which found its work greatly facilitated
(in preparing reports and representations to the Privy Council and in
corresponding with the colonial governors) by the presence of men
who could provide reliable information about the colonies.[14]

THE AGENTS FROM 1690 TO 1755

One cannot generalize easily in appraising the activities of the
agents in the eighteenth century. Those from Connecticut, Rhode
Island, and Maryland, for example, were not concerned with one of
the most important responsibilities confronting their colleagues—the
review in Great Britain of colonial legislation. When the royal colonial governments submitted their laws, the agents were expected to
justify them before the crown's legal advisers and secure confirmation.
The agents from the charter colonies, on the other hand, had to be
exceedingly active in order to divert plans formulated at the Board of
Trade for recalling their charters. All the agents, however, appeared
before the Privy Council, met with members of the cabinet, consulted
with the Board of Trade, the attorney general, lords of the Treasury,
the Admiralty, and other administrative branches of government.
They were also granted hearings before parliamentary committees,
and when the occasion demanded, lobbied among the members of
both houses.[15]

[14] Gipson, *British Empire before the Revolution*, I, 11–12.
[15] *Ibid.*, pp. 12–13. Although I have found Professor Gipson's capsule
summary of the agency helpful, I do not agree with his concluding estimate:
"Indeed, it may be said that the influence of the agents was so great that no
decision of importance affecting the colonies was ever arrived at without the
most careful consideration of their informal testimony and arguments as well as

By the turn of the century, most of the colonies then established could claim some experience with agencies; nevertheless the Board of Trade occasionally had to remind neglectful provincials that they lacked a lobbyist to expedite their affairs and supply the administrative boards with information. It is possible, in fact, that the agencies attained institutional maturity early in the eighteenth century in response to a need expressed by the imperial government to have someone do the interoffice errands (and pay fees for the privilege). The burgeoning bureaucracy was sufficiently developed to require agents to overcome its inertia by piloting documents through prescribed channels.[16]

It is not surprising, then, that the Board of Trade attempted to acquire a modicum of regulatory authority over the lobbyists. In 1705 it ruled that any person appearing as agent for any of the plantations should register his credentials in order to ensure against intrusion by unauthorized interlopers. The rule was often honored more in the breach, but the registration order was reaffirmed whenever it became politically expedient. Another aspect of this regulation was the effort to fix a uniform procedure for the appointment of agents. Official preference directed that an agent represent the entire colonial body politic—assembly, council, and governor, with each having a share in his election—instead of being merely the creature of the lower house. This ideal was also violated; but it would become a valuable excuse to disguise ministerial hostility toward the agents after the Stamp Act crisis. Sometimes each branch of the legislature employed its own man, though a dual agency commonly indicated that the regular agent had lost the confidence of his employers, who then supplemented rather than abandoned his services.[17]

The quarter-century following the Treaty of Utrecht was in some respects a notable period in the history of the institution. These were the active days of Sir Henry Ashurst, Jeremy Dummer, Ferdinand

---

their more formal memorials and petitions." The agents were not that influential and were not always regarded thoughtfully by the colonists or by imperial administrators in London.

[16] Edward P. Lilly, *The Colonial Agents of New York and New Jersey* (Washington, D.C., 1936), pp. 65–66; Oliver M. Dickerson, *American Colonial Government, 1696–1765* (Cleveland, 1912), p. 266 nn. 625 and 626.

[17] In 1754, the Board of Trade required all agents to produce their certificates of representation. It provided a special register for the purpose, which is now in the PRO, CO 324/60, Plantations General, Entry Book of Appointment of Agents. See Lilly, *Agents of New York and New Jersey*, pp. 15–17.

John Paris, and Richard Partridge—enterprising and successful agents who illustrate the qualifications requisite for London lobbying at its best.[18] Dummer, for example, from the outset of his agency had access to the larger world of English political society from which most dissenters were barred. In fact, despite his Puritan background, he gained entrance into prominent Anglican circles. That his mistress was Elizabeth, daughter of Bishop Burnet, hardly reduced his prospects. He arrived in London with good letters of introduction; his English relatives held strategic offices in the government; his Old World education won him friends at the Middle Temple and among the military. Dummer had sufficient influence to remove a royal governor and troublesome petty postholders in the colonies, delay parliamentary measures directed against the colonies, obtain patronage for his friends, and get himself elected to the examining board of the South Sea Company.[19]

What manner of friendships other than the ones already mentioned made such a man so powerful? Dummer inhabited a world of intellectuals, court lawyers, secretaries, minor officials, and office seekers. Charles Delafaye and Temple Stanyan, influential secretaries to the Duke of Newcastle, Alured Popple, secretary to the Board of Trade, and Richard West, counsellor to that body, were well known to Dummer, as was William Blathwayt, auditor general of the plantations. On higher levels Dummer acquired the friendship of Lord Treasurer Harley, Speaker of the House Sir Thomas Hanmer, and the Dukes of Newcastle and Hamilton. He gained access to Lord Sunderland through Sir Peter King, recorder of the City of London. And he included Sir Hans Sloane, Dr. William Bray, Addison and Steele, Newton, and Halley in his circle of friends. Finally, Dummer's largest group of intimates were the London merchants trading to America and the land speculators with interests there.[20]

Dummer also indulged in a common eighteenth-century practice—plural officeholding. In addition to his original appointment

---

[18] For Dummer's career, see Charles L. Sanford, "The Days of Jeremy Dummer, Colonial Agent" (unpub. Ph.D. diss.; Harvard University, 1952); for Paris, see Mabel P. Wolff, *The Colonial Agency of Pennsylvania, 1712–1757* (Philadelphia, 1933), pp. 39–41, 57–58, 90–94; for Partridge, see Marguerite Appleton, "Richard Partridge: Colonial Agent," *NEQ*, V (1932), 293–309.

[19] Dummer even became something of a legend and prototype for later agents; see "Stamp Act Papers," *MHM*, VI (1911), 296, and Sanford, "Dummer," pp. 207–214.

[20] Sanford, "Dummer," pp. 207–209, 218–219.

from Massachusetts, he held the Connecticut agency from 1712 until 1730 and was temporary agent for New Hampshire from 1717 until 1720. These multiple agencies earned him the sobriquet "Agent for New England." John Paris also pieced together a patchwork of employments: agent for Maryland's lower house, the Pennsylvania and East Jersey Proprietors, the freeholders of Halifax, Nova Scotia, and the absentee landholders of Jamaica. In 1755, John Sharpe, a London attorney, was agent for Jamaica, Barbados, Antigua, St. Christopher's, and Nevis in the West Indies.[21]

Richard Partridge's record for longevity was unmatched by any other agent. The Quaker served Rhode Island and New Jersey for forty-five years until his death in 1759. Like Dummer, his greatest asset consisted of his circle of acquaintances, and his best hunting ground lay in the personal conference. Partridge was not parsimonious; in 1729 he characteristically spent £1 3s. 4d. for a "treat to a person who was serviceable in giving information in Parliamentary affairs." Partridge's success in acquiring inside knowledge owed much to presents of wine and dinner invitations which secured services from well-placed civil servants. Dummer likewise was a lavish tipper. By recognizing the importance of every doorkeeper and valet, he could dispense £180 in five months. The lobbyists normally had expense allowances to cover such gratuities.[22]

Nonetheless the colonists were not always generous with their agents in the decades after 1690 and thereby undermined the quality of their influence abroad. New York was more careful on this score than many of the colonies, raising funds by subscription or appropriation to underwrite her agents. In 1753 the Virginia Assembly appointed as its agent Peyton Randolph, the colony's attorney general, and voted the extraordinary sum of £2,500 for his support; but this mission involved the famous pistole fee dispute, an issue of great urgency to the burgesses. Ordinarily the London lobbyists complained to their constituents that their salaries were too small, arrived too late, and did not begin to cover the incidental expenses of politicking.[23]

Thus the agencies prior to the Seven Years' War did not constitute a wholly viable institution. During the seventeenth century, failures as well as bright achievements marked their ledger; and in the half-century after the Glorious Revolution, successes were mingled with a

---

[21] *Ibid.*, pp. 222, 225; Ross J. S. Hoffman, *Edmund Burke, New York Agent* . . . (Philadelphia, 1956), p. 19.

[22] Appleton, "Partridge," pp. 295, 305–306; Sanford, "Dummer," p. 221.

[23] Osgood, *Colonies in the Eighteenth Century,* I, 258, 264, IV, 228.

number of lost enterprises. The causes of this mixed record comprise a summary of the agencies before 1755 that is essential to an understanding of their role during the crisis decades preceding the American Revolution. To begin with, agents did not lobby in a vacuum. Variables beyond their control conditioned the quality of their operations. One significant factor was the political climate. As Lewis Morris lamented in 1742, "unless the Court is dispos'd to do us Service, no agent can do us much good . . . ; an agent that will deliver our letters and call for and send the answers to them, & sometimes (but rarely) employ a councill when anything is upon the tap . . . concerning us, seems all that is of use in our present circumstances." [24]

Another variable involved the bureaucracy the agents had to contend with. They continually complained of administrative lethargy. The various boards frequently denied responsibility for some necessary action or document, and lobbyists were shunted off to other offices by underlings anxious to save themselves time and bother. [25] Interminable delays passed from weeks into months and commonly into years. A holiday, a civil servant's gout, the death of a politician, or a prorogation of Parliament made prompt action impossible. [26]

A competent agent, however, could sometimes circumvent the bureaucratic obstacles. Such an expert as Ferdinand John Paris had an uncanny ability to expedite business at the public offices. Using political influence, he could get a document on a docket promptly. Paris also worked rapidly in order to have the proper papers prepared in time for the nearest meeting day. If enough board members were not in London to form a quorum, he dispatched the documents into the countryside to have the requisite number of committee names added. [27]

---

[24] See Lonn, *Agents of the Southern Colonies,* pp. 385, 390–391; Morris to Mrs. Norris, May 14, 1742, NJHS *Collections,* IV (New York, 1852), 145. For a pessimistic appraisal of the agencies in this period, see Morris to James Alexander, Feb. 25, 1736, Rutherfurd MSS, II, 177, NYHS.

[25] John Craig, *A History of Red Tape: An Account of the Origin and Development of the Civil Service* (London, 1955); Philip W. Buck, *The Politics of Mercantilism* (New York, 1942), pp. 133–134; Gipson, *British Empire before the Revolution,* XI, 199 n. 25.

[26] James J. Burns, *The Colonial Agents of New England* (Washington, D.C., 1935), p. 85; Sanford, "Dummer," p. 226.

[27] Paris had great contempt for the efficiency of the Board of Trade. In 1739, he searched for laws of Pennsylvania which had never been acted upon by the Board and found them in a far corner of that office, covered with dust (Wolff, *Agency of Pennsylvania,* pp. 55, 57–59).

Although Paris was unusual in this respect, the other agents learned to accommodate themselves to a stable system which they could at least comprehend if not control. When the machinery of government was tightened after 1766, familiar parts disappeared or were altered, so that the whole administrative apparatus became unpredictable and in certain phases inscrutable.[28]

Among themselves the agents lacked a strong tradition of unity or even professional brotherhood. The agencies developed—and logically so—as extensions of each colony's government in England. The lobbyist was conscious only of a relationship to his particular constituency, and when the interests of two colonies came into conflict, as over a boundary, the agents of those colonies re-enacted the dispute in microcosm in London.[29] This kind of localism was reinforced by the relative absence of questions of common importance upon which they might unite. The joint efforts of the North American agents to prevent a clause requiring the destruction of colonial iron forges in 1729, or to prevent passage of the Molasses Act in 1733 or the Currency Act in 1744 and again in 1748–1749, were unusual and imperfect exercises in cooperation.[30] Thus after 1755, when issues arose of mutual concern to all thirteen colonies, their representatives combined themselves into a monolith with some difficulty. After repeal of the Stamp Act in 1766, divisive parochialism sometimes reappeared with unfortunate results.[31]

This characteristic was accentuated by the colonies themselves, several of which allowed their agencies to lapse into disuse when there was no pressing cause of provincial concern pending in London. Some of the constituencies retarded the development of the agencies in other ways. Throughout the eighteenth century, the lobbyists lamented that a lack of adequate information and instruction kept them from prosecuting their duties. Often action on a given cause was

[28] *Ibid.*, pp. 146–147.

[29] Nicholas Varga, "Robert Charles: New York Agent, 1748–1770," 3*WMQ*, XVIII (1961), 227; Lilly, *Agents of New York and New Jersey*, pp. 194–197.

[30] Lilly, *Agents of New York and New Jersey*, pp. 75, 207–212; Varga, "Charles," p. 225; Arthur C. Bining, *British Regulation of the Colonial Iron Industry* (Philadelphia, 1933), pp. 51–52.

[31] The West Indian colonies had a closer similarity of economic and political interests. Their London lobby was usually able to present a united front, unlike that of the more diverse North American colonies.

balked because the agent had not yet received some crucial document from his employers.[32]

Finally, the calibre of men chosen in the "neglected period" was not always what it might have been. During the seventeenth century, colonial assemblies had usually sent their best men to London, particularly when the objective was important—such as obtaining a provincial charter. Thereafter, when the positions became permanently established, lesser men were frequently chosen, often because the agency had become a political issue in the colonies. Good men were reluctant to accept the office, and the compromise candidates were too often men of inferior ability. The difference was crucial, for a first-rate agent would use all his resources to shape governmental decisions, while a lesser man would be content to handle routine administrative matters and answer questions at the Board of Trade.

By 1755 the condition and quality of the North American agencies were neither excellent nor poor. Their institutional development was complete though discrete. Their potential as an organ of intercolonial cooperation was really untested, and their success was contingent upon forces partially outside their control. The institution was not altogether stable; but so long as politicians, colonial administrators, and colonists were willing to settle imperial problems by compromise, no men were better qualified to arrange these compromises than the agents. Most important, they had built up over three generations experience with a system of British government that was dependable though sluggish, constant though frustrating. When the old order altered during and after the Seven Years' War, the context, conditions, and techniques of lobbying changed.[33] The course of events, issues, and ministries shifted so rapidly that the agents were not always able to adapt adequately to the responses required by each new regime. Only under the unique auspices of the Rockingham ministry in 1765–1766 did the agents, their constituents, and the merchant community come perfectly into alignment. The consequently suc-

---

[32] Lonn, *Agents of the Southern Colonies,* pp. 57 n. 11, 77, 86, 111; Varga, "Charles," p. 216; William R. Smith, *South Carolina as a Royal Province, 1719–1776* (New York, 1903), p. 169; Wolff, *Agency of Pennsylvania,* pp. 52, 61–62.

[33] J. M. Norris, "Samuel Garbett and the Early Development of Industrial Lobbying in Great Britain," *Economic History Review,* ser. 2, X (1958), 450–451.

cessful campaign for repeal of the Stamp Act marked the apogee of the agency. In the subsequent decade that separated repeal from revolution, the agents never repeated the performance of their finest hour.

CHAPTER 2

A Profile of the Agency, 1756-1766

At certain hours of the day, each agent might be found alone, writing to his colonial committee of correspondence perhaps, or preparing a document for presentation. In search of a cluster of North American lobbyists one would probably attend a ministerial levee, an administrative board, or a coffeehouse. The last of these was characteristic of eighteenth-century England and provided a favorite rendezvous for men of affairs. Most of the coffeehouses came to be identified with the particular segment of society that frequented them. The agents visited various establishments, many of which were named for colonies: the Pennsylvania in Birchin Lane, where Franklin received mail; the Virginia and Maryland above Cornhill in Newman's Court; the New York close to the Royal Exchange, patronized by merchants and agents who knew it to be a center of intelligence for people in the American trade; the very popular New England at 60 Threadneedle Street opposite the Exchange; and the Jamaica for the West Indian interest. All these stood only a few blocks apart in the heart of the City. If the agents required a hasty meeting near the Palace of Westminster, they might gather at Waghorn's or at the Parliament Coffee House.[1]

In addition to useful commercial functions—Lloyd's of London began as a coffeehouse—the coffeehouses supplied the domestic and colonial gazettes and served as post offices. They were neither clean nor well-lit nor free from stale smoke. But when the lobbyists conferred around a table, they might enjoy coffee, tea, chocolate, or all

---

[1] Aytoun Ellis, *The Penny Universities: A History of the Coffee Houses* (London, 1956), *passim*.

sorts of hot liquors as well as a variety of solid fare. Some of the agents' ailments, in fact, may have been due to the crapulous quality of their society, and to the fact that colchicum, gout's remedy since ancient times, was largely ignored during the Enlightenment.[2] A number of the lobbyists suffered from problems of ill-health that sometimes hampered or delayed effective operations.[3]

PERSONNEL: A GROUP PORTRAIT

The agents as a group averaged well under fifty years in age at the time of the Stamp Act crisis. Many were relatively young men, and almost all still pursued their professions actively. Roughly half were trained in the law. Another quarter qualified for that broad eighteenth-century rubric "merchant," while most of the rest had made careers of public employment. One fifth did not conform to the Church of England; and not surprisingly, although some had lived in America, all but a few regarded Britain as their home. During the decade prior to 1766, only a handful could be considered colonials—notably Benjamin Franklin, Jared Ingersoll, and perhaps William Bollan.[4]

When the Seven Years' War began, Bollan was one of the most experienced American agents. He had served Massachusetts in that capacity since 1745, and his connections there and in England were considerable. Franklin recalled that "Mr. Bollan was a cautious, exact man," while John Adams thought of him as "a kind of learned man, of indefatigable research and a faithful friend to America." Bollan was officious, continually concocting plans and strategies to offer politicians and placemen. The civil servants occasionally grew weary of

---

[2] E. B. Chancellor, *The Eighteenth Century in London* (London, 1920), p. 136. Dr. Wallace Graham, senior physician at Toronto General Hospital, has recently disputed the traditional view that gout is the result of overindulgence (*New York Times* [City edition], April 29, 1962). See also W. S. C. Copeman, *A Short History of the Gout and the Rheumatic Diseases* (Berkeley, 1964), ch. 6.

[3] *PMHB*, X (1886), 228; William Samuel Johnson's London diary, entries for July 31, Aug. 3 and 7–13, and Oct. 27–31, 1770, WSJ MSS; Esther De Berdt to Joseph Reed, Feb. 3, 1767, Reed MSS, NYHS; Jasper Mauduit to Mass. General Court, March 19, and April 4, 1765, MA, Misc. Letters, 1763–1775, p. 94; MA, XXII, 441–443; Barlow Trecothick to John Pownall, Feb. 1, 1773, *The State of New Hampshire: Miscellaneous Provincial and State Papers 1725–1800*, ed. Isaac W. Hammond, XVIII (Manchester, N.H., 1890), 645.

[4] For biographical data on all the agents, 1755–1775, see the Appendix.

such schemes and had to put the man off, especially since his projects
invariably involved examining "all the records in the kingdom which
relate to the settlement of America, by various searches at the tower,
and the offices wherein the Parliament rolls are kept." [5] Bollan's badg-
ering of bureaucrats at least reflects a positive approach to lobbying.
Most important, he knew the great and petty men of affairs in London. Although he dropped important names readily and always liked
to suggest that "gentlemen of consequence" were seeking his advice,
the fact remains that for a time he had the attention of many major
politicians, including Newcastle and Rockingham. Although Massachusetts' General Court replaced Bollan in 1762, he continued to
lobby informally and maintained close contacts with friends in the
colony.[6]

Bollan was one of two career agents during the prerevolutionary
years—men devoted primarily to their constituents' affairs over a
protracted period and dependent upon them financially. The other
was Robert Charles, who preceded Benjamin Franklin as Pennsylvania's agent and served New York in that office from 1748 until 1770.
Charles was probably born the same year as Franklin, 1706, but in
England. He emigrated to Pennsylvania in 1726 as a penurious private secretary to Governor Patrick Gordon. By the time of his mar-
riage five years later to the Governor's daughter, Charles was regarded
by the leading provincial politicians as capable, responsible, and honest. But they also noted his "haughty and injurious carriage," as well
as his insolent behavior. This strain of instability blended with ambition led to occasional tensions between Charles and some of the men
he had to deal with, particularly British bureaucrats at the public
offices, where Charles was a "conspicuous busybody." [7]

In 1739, he lost his Pennsylvania position and returned to Britain,
where he had important political connections: the Dukes of Newcastle and Argyle, the Earl of Isla, and wealthy Admiral Sir Peter
Warren, whose secretary Charles became about 1743. In 1748, War-

[5] Malcolm Freiberg, "William Bollan: Agent of Massachusetts," *More Books*,
XXIII (1948), 218; Bollan to Andrew Oliver, April 30, 1766, MA, XXII,
468–489.

[6] Bollan to Mass. General Court, June 10, 1762, MA, Letters, 1701–1763,
pp. 358–359; Bollan to Thomas Hutchinson, Jan. 18, [1766?], Hutchinson
TSS, MHS.

[7] Nicholas Varga, "Robert Charles: New York Agent, 1748–1770," 3*WMQ*,
XVIII (1961), 211–235; Charles M. Andrews, *The Colonial Period of American History*, IV (New Haven, 1938), 295.

ren recommended Charles to James De Lancey for New York's vacant agency, and so began a twenty-two-year term on behalf of that constituency. At the same time, Charles served an agent's apprenticeship with a real professional, Richard Partridge. They worked closely together in London, where the senior agent profited from his assistant's knowledge of colonial conditions, especially Indian affairs.[8] Then, in 1754, Pennsylvania rewarded Charles with the rank of coagent and the salary of £100 annually to supplement the £200 he received from New York. His shrewdness as an agent won him the admiration of Proprietor Thomas Penn as well as the grudging respect of his wily opponent, Ferdinand John Paris.[9] During the later 1750's, Charles cooperated with his new colleague, Franklin, but resigned his agency in 1761 following a difference of opinion with his employers over a Pennsylvania supply bill. He remained New York's agent for another decade, however, until 1770, when he "put an end to himself."[10]

With the addition of Franklin in 1757, the agency as a cohesive institution was strengthened immeasurably. Pennsylvania's Assembly wisely sent him to help adjust difficulties with the Penns over the taxation of proprietary estates. Franklin's scientific reputation quickly opened many important doors to him. Membership in the Royal Society put him in contact with Sir John Pringle, the royal physician; and the Doctor was introduced to politicians, high and low, by Robert Charles and Richard Jackson, the barrister. Through the years Franklin's social and intellectual gregariousness brought him many more influential friends as a result of his membership in such organizations as the Honest Whigs. He was close to administration bureaucrats like Treasury Secretary Grey Cooper while trafficking with such an enemy of ministries as John Wilkes, and he maintained simultaneous friendships with Bishop Shipley of St. Asaph and leading dissenters like Joseph Priestley and Richard Price. Franklin's London friend Peter Collinson introduced him to the Hanburys and through them to the important City merchants as well as Lord Granville, President of the Privy Council. Thus a Pennsylvanian visiting London wrote home

[8] Edward P. Lilly, *The Colonial Agents of New York and New Jersey* (Washington, D.C., 1936), pp. 179, 181.

[9] Benjamin Franklin to Isaac Norris, Jan. 19, 1759, *The Papers of Benjamin Franklin*, ed. Leonard W. Labaree *et al.*, VIII (New Haven, 1965), 234–235; Mabel P. Wolff, *The Colonial Agency of Pennsylvania, 1712–1757* (Philadelphia, 1933), pp. 149–150.

[10] *Ibid.*, pp. 124–127, 149–150, 164–165; Varga, "Charles," pp. 213–214.

The North American Agents, 1755–1775 *

Agent	1755	1756	1757	1758	1759	1760	1761	1762
Charles Pinckney	a †	a						
Richard Partridge	a	a	a	a	a			
Benjamin Martyn	a	a	a	a	a			
James Abercromby	a	a	a	a	a	a	a	a
John Thomlinson Sr.	a	a	a	a	a	a	a	i ‡
Robert Charles	a	a	a	a	a	a	a	a
William Bollan	a	a	a	a	a	a	a	a
Alexander Kellet		a						
James Wright			a	a	a	a		
Benjamin Franklin			a	a	a	a	a	
Jared Ingersoll				a	a	a	a	a
Samuel Smith					a	a	a	i
Edward Montagu					a	a	a	a
Joseph Sherwood					a	a	a	a
David Barclay						a	a	a
Richard Jackson						a	a	a
Thomas Life						a	a	a
Peter Cuchet Jouvencal						a	a	
William Knox							a	
Charles Garth								a
Jasper Mauduit								a
Israel Mauduit								a
John Thomlinson Jr.								
John Wentworth								
John Sargent								
Dennys De Berdt								
Barlow Trecothick								
Henry Wilmot								
William Samuel Johnson								
Henry Eustace McCulloh								
Arthur Lee								
Edmund Burke								
Henry Marchant								
Grey Elliott								
Paul Wentworth								
Alexander Elmsley								
Thomas Barker								
Dennis De Berdt Jr.								
Total	7	8	8	9	12	14	14	14

* Because several men held multiple agencies, this table shows the total number of North American agents, rather than the number of agencies held.

1763	1764	1765	1766	1767	1768	1769	1770	1771	1772	1773	1774	1775
a												
i		i	i	i	i	i	i	i	i	i	i	
a	i	i	i	i								
a	a	a	a	a								
					a	a	a	a	a	a	a	a
		a	a	a	a	a	a	a	a	a	a	a
	a	a										
i	i											
a	a	a	a	a	a	a	a					
a	a	a	a	a	a	a	a	a	a			
a	a	a										
a	a	a	a	a	a	a	a	a				
a	a	a	a	a	a	a	a	a	a	a	a	a
a	a	a										
a	a	a										
a	a	a	a	a	a	a	a	a	a	a	a	a
a	a	a										
a	a	a										
a	a	a	a	i								
		a	a									
		a	a									
		a	a	a	a	a	a					
		a	a	a	a	a	a	a	a	a	i	i
			a	a	a	a						
			a	a	a	a	a	a				
					a	a	a	a	a	a	i	
							a	a	a	a	a	a
							a	a	a	a	a	a
										i	i	i
											a	a
											a	a
												a
14	13	18	14	11	13	13	14	11	10	7	9	9

† Active agent.
‡ Agent formally holding office, but inactive.

that "Doctor Franklin looks heartier than ever I knew Him in America and has a most surprising influence here." [11]

The learned Doctor enjoyed his first years as agent. By the year 1762, however, he had grown weary of endless delays and wrangling with the Penns. "I feel here like a thing out of its place," he remarked to William Strahan, "and useless because it is out of its place. How then can I any longer be happy in England? . . . I must go home." Franklin did go home to Philadelphia, but less than three years later he returned to London, where he remained until 1775. [12]

With Partridge's death in 1759, Charles's resignation in 1761, and Franklin's departure in 1762, Pennsylvania's Assembly needed a new man in London. It quite logically turned to Richard Jackson, already Connecticut's agent since 1760, who had worked well with Franklin during his first agency. Jackson was born in 1722 to a wealthy, dissenting English family, [13] entered Lincoln's Inn in 1740, and became a barrister four years later. Although Jeremy Bentham sneered at Jackson's legal capacity, referring to him as "a silk-stocking barrister who never had any briefs," he nonetheless became standing counsel

[11] Leonard W. Labaree, "Benjamin Franklin's British Friendships," APS *Proceedings*, CVIII (1964), 423–428; Verner W. Crane, "The Club of Honest Whigs: Friends of Science and Liberty," 3*WMQ*, XXIII (1966), 210–233; *Letters and Papers of Benjamin Franklin and Richard Jackson, 1753–1785*, ed. Carl Van Doren (Philadelphia, 1947), pp. 89, 96; William Trent to George Croghan, June 10, 1769, HSP.

[12] To Deborah Franklin, Jan. 21, 1758, Labaree, *Papers of Franklin*, VII, 364; to Strahan, July 20, 1762, Smyth, IV, 172.

[13] Jackson's religious persuasion is something of a mystery. Members of his immediate family were nonconformists. Yet he matriculated at Queen's College, Cambridge, and held various offices which theoretically should have been denied to a dissenter. In 1765, his friend Thomas Hutchinson assumed that he belonged to the Church of England. Ezra Stiles, who suspected Jackson's integrity, noted that he was originally a dissenter, but by 1765 "had deeply commenced Courtier, dropped his Religion, & was aiming at Promotion, Preferment & Figure in the Nation." Throughout the 1760's, however, Jackson remained a prominent member of the nonconforming New England Company. Finally, in 1786 he preceded Israel Mauduit as president of the Independent Society for the Propagation of the Gospel (Jackson to Hutchinson, Jan. 9, 1767, MA, XXV, 144–146; "Jackson," *DNB*; Hutchinson to Jackson, Jan. 25, 1765, MA, XXVI, 128; Stiles MSS, VI, 241–242, YUL; New England Co. Letter-book, 1762–1772, f. 5, MS 7927, GLL; Minutes of the General Court of the New England Co., 1655–1816, entry for Dec. 19, 1766, GLL).

for the South Sea Company, Cambridge University, and the New England Company, as well as legal counsel to the Board of Trade in 1770. His abilities, therefore, cannot be so easily despised. He was popularly known as "Omniscient Jackson," referring to his reputed encyclopedic knowledge. His interest in agriculture, in fact, probably initiated his American connections. His written observations on Norfolk husbandry brought him into contact with Franklin (via Peter Collinson) in 1752. At the same time, his desire to purchase a farm in Connecticut called him to the attention of ministers prominent there (via Jared Eliot). Jackson subtly puffed himself to his Connecticut friends and implied that he would not mind having their agency. His correspondence with Franklin developed in the 1750's, so that when the latter arrived in 1757 he depended on Jackson for legal advice. Franklin found him "esteem'd the best acquainted with our American Affairs, and Constitutions, as well as with Government Law in General. He being also thoroughly knowing in the present views of the Leading Members of the [Privy] Council and Board of Trade, and in their Connections and Characters." [14] By 1759, Franklin too sang Jackson's praises, and urged his Pennsylvania correspondent, Joseph Galloway, to consider Jackson as Partridge's replacement. [15]

Not surprisingly, then, Connecticut selected him to succeed Jared Ingersoll [16] as agent in 1760, [17] Pennsylvania to replace Franklin in 1763, and Massachusetts to follow Jasper Mauduit in 1765. He owed his Massachusetts appointment to the influence of his correspondent there, Governor Francis Bernard. Jackson had served as Bernard's liaison with the Board of Trade, prying patronage and perquisites of office from its staff. Bernard had wanted the agency for his friend in 1762, when Mauduit won out instead. Bernard then arranged for Jackson to be a second or "standing" agent to tender the Mauduit

[14] Van Doren, *Franklin and Jackson*, pp. 1–5; *Calendar of Home Office Papers of the Reign of George III, 1760–1775*, ed. J. Reddington and R. A. Roberts (London, 1878–1899), Vol. I, no. 1750; Jackson to Eliot, Sept. 17, 1753, Eliot MSS, YUL; Franklin to Pa. CC, June 10, 1758, Labaree, *Papers of Franklin*, VIII, 88.

[15] April 7, 1759, Labaree, *Papers of Franklin*, VIII, 309.

[16] See the Appendix and Lawrence H. Gipson, *Jared Ingersoll: A Study of American Loyalism in Relation to British Colonial Government* (New Haven, 1920), chs. 3–5.

[17] The colony also appointed Thomas Life, a London attorney, to serve as associate agent.

brothers legal counsel. In January 1765, Jackson finally succeeded Jasper as sole agent, after great contention among factions in the General Court. The other candidates had been Israel Mauduit, Bollan, and Jackson's friend Thomas Hutchinson. One argument urged against Jackson was the evil of pluralism—"that it would be for the advantage of America to have divers[e] agents, & thereby obtain an accumulation of interests and connexions." Despite such objections, Jackson acquired his third concurrent agency; but not before clearing with George Grenville whether "his acceptance of it would be of service to Government." [18] Jackson realized that he had to conciliate his several patrons with their potentially contradictory interests.[19]

The new agent had both shrewd instincts and curious political allegiances. As one colonial observer remarked, "he was absorbed in a System of Politics." The early years of the reign of George III found him "making Court to the Butean Ministry." When a new faction came to power in 1763, Jackson served Grenville as secretary to the Chancellor of the Exchequer and was "generally suppos'd to have considerable influence with him." Jackson assured his American correspondents that his motives in accepting such a situation were honorable, that it might better enable him to help them. As he wrote Franklin: "I have really little interest with Ministers of any kind though I keep a Post that gives me Access to them, perhaps it may be of Service & I may have more." [20] Despite his dual obligation, Jackson retained the respect of many colonists. When Eliphalet Dyer came from Connecticut in 1764 as a private commercial agent, he found

[18] On April 13, 1765, Grenville wrote Charles Jenkinson that "Mr. Jackson's appointment as agent for the Province of Massachusetts Bay is a matter of some delicacy with respect to him and to us. I know his good intentions, but the question is what difficulties it may put him under. Upon the whole I wish to have some conversation with him upon this subject" (*Additional Grenville Papers, 1763–1765*, ed. J. R. G. Tomlinson [Manchester, Eng., 1962], p. 258).

[19] Francis Bernard to John Pownall, Dec. 29, 1763, Bernard to Jackson, Jan. 23, 1763, Jan. 25, 1765, Bernard MSS, III, 120, II, 248–252, III, 277–283, HLHU; Mass. General Court to Dennys De Berdt, Nov. 7, 1765, Lee MSS, Vol. I, HLHU; Charles Jenkinson to George Grenville, April 11, 1765, *The Jenkinson Papers, 1760–1766*, ed. Ninetta S. Jucker (London, 1949), p. 359.

[20] Jackson to Franklin, Jan. 26 and Nov. 18, 1764, Van Doren, *Franklin and Jackson*, pp. 138, 193. See also *The Correspondence of Edmund Burke*, ed. Thomas W. Copeland, I (Chicago, 1958), 211 n.

that his colony's representative was "of more Consequence than all the other Agents for the Continent, as . . . he appears not only most knowing, but heartily Engaged for the Interest of the Colonies." [21]

Although Jackson succeeded Richard Partridge as Connecticut's agent in 1760, Partridge recommended that his assistant and executor, Joseph Sherwood, assume his Rhode Island and New Jersey agencies. [22] A Quaker like Partridge, Sherwood was also an attorney, and like Charles he studied under the master's aegis in the 1750's. He took up his new responsibilities in 1759 with enthusiasm and served his constituencies faithfully, though with mounting frustration. [23]

When the New Jersey and Rhode Island agencies were given over to new hands, Virginia's was also strengthened in 1759 by the appointment of Edward Montagu, a barrister of the Middle Temple who first attracted notice at the bar of the House of Commons in an election case. His younger brother, Admiral John Montagu, had superintended the execution of Admiral Byng in 1757, and from 1771 through 1774 would command the North American station from the St. Lawrence to the Bahamas. [24]

Edward spent the first few years of his agency feuding with his predecessor, James Abercromby. Virginia's Committee of Correspondence expected its new agent to keep an eye on Abercromby to make sure he did not lay his grasping hands on any Treasury money due the colony, and to ascertain as well the commissions charged by other agents in order to determine whether Abercromby's had been exorbitant. [25] After 1761, Abercromby abandoned his attempts at making

[21] Dyer to Jared Ingersoll, April 14, 1764, NHCHS *Papers,* IX (New Haven, 1918), 289; William Allen to Benjamin Chew, Oct. 7, 1763, *PMHB,* XC (1966), 214.

[22] In 1734, Sherwood married a widow worth £15,000, which enabled him to forsake his position as a court clerk in favor of an independent practice in Austin Fryers near the Royal Exchange (*Gentleman's Magazine,* IV [1734], 49; Lilly, *Agents of New York and New Jersey,* p. 128).

[23] Sherwood to Stephen Hopkins, May 11, 1759, Letters, VI, 13, RIA; William Franklin to Benjamin Franklin, Nov. 13, [1766?], APS.

[24] "John Montagu," *DNB.* In 1765, he also became British agent for the King of Poland (Montagu to [Charles Yorke?], April 6, 1765, Add MSS 35637, f. 160).

[25] Abercromby to Lord Loudoun, July 16, and Aug. 29, 1759, Loudoun MSS, Huntington Library and Art Gallery, San Marino, Calif.; CC to Montagu, Dec. 12, 1759, "Proceedings of the Virginia Committee of Correspondence, 1759–1767," *VMHB,* XI (1903), 3.

Montagu's job difficult, and the new agent developed into an efficient, conscientious lobbyist.[26]

One agent with whom Montagu cooperated consistently was his fellow barrister, Charles Garth, agent for South Carolina, briefly for Maryland, and crown agent for Georgia.[27] Garth was born about 1734, attended Oxford, and was called to the bar from the Inner Temple in 1756. Almost annually after that date John Garth, M.P., asked the Duke of Newcastle for a position for his son. Although the Duke regarded Charles as "a very pretty young man; and one who I am persuaded, would make an excellent officer," he never favored him.[28] This was shabby treatment considering Newcastle had received twenty years of parliamentary support from John Garth. Not surprisingly the latter turned elsewhere for patronage. In 1763 he successfully asked George Grenville to appoint his son crown agent of Georgia and commissioner of the salt office. In 1765, Charles followed his father in Parliament as Member for the borough of Devizes.[29]

The Garths had valuable family connections. The Grenville contact had probably been effected through Charles's two cousins in Parliament, James Edward Colleton and Charles Boone. Another cousin, Thomas Boone, held the governorship of South Carolina from 1761 until 1764. Garth was also related to one of the leading families of that colony, and in 1762 Governor Boone persuaded the Assembly to appoint his cousin agent. Despite Garth's connections, however, the most striking aspect of his career was his independence and integrity. He owed his parliamentary seat to none of the great patrons, and he often voted and lobbied counter to the Grenville interest. When he became an M.P., he resigned his crown agency in order to preserve his independence, and when his constituents undertook a bitter fight with Boone in 1763, Garth fulfilled his obligation to his employers by

[26] For Abercromby's career, see the Appendix.

[27] In 1763, the Georgia Assembly persuaded Governor Wright to consent to the appointment of William Knox as a provincial agent to serve concurrently with Garth, the former responsible to the colony and the latter to the crown—a dual arrangement emphasizing the peculiarity of Georgia's place in the Anglo-American political system (Lewis B. Namier, "Charles Garth, Agent for South Carolina," *EHR*, LIV [1939], 642–643).

[28] Numerous letters from John Garth to Newcastle are in Add MSS 32864, 32870, 32916, 32926, 32934, 34713, *passim*; Newcastle to Lord Anson, Feb. 8, 1762, Add MSS 32934, f. 329.

[29] John Garth to Grenville, July 2 and Aug. 22, 1763, Stowe MSS, Vol. CLXIII, ff. 211, 214, BM.

vigorously prosecuting the embarrassing orders sent from Charleston. As he promised, "no tie of friendship will either influence or make me unmindful of the obligation I owe and the duties thence resulting." [30]

He made a fine agent in many respects. While his colleagues often disagreed with one another, he displayed a conspicuous spirit of cooperation. When he confronted a new issue or acquired fresh information about an object of colonial concern, he quickly communicated it to the other agents. When action was required, Garth moved with dispatch.[31] Nevertheless, when he felt his footing unsure or his employers' desires unwise, he could act with deliberation. He was extremely solicitous of the Carolinians' wishes and welfare. His letters to the Committee of Correspondence are fuller and more frequent than those of any other agent his contemporary. His long and lucid accounts of affairs in London suggest a man of infinite patience.[32]

During the crucial period of the Seven Years' War, then, the North American agency was immensely strengthened by the addition in particular of five new men: Franklin (1757), Sherwood and Montagu (1759), Jackson (1760), and Garth (1762). All five were politically astute and skilled in the management of public affairs. Their presence, moreover, could hardly have come at a more important time, for after 1755 the agency assumed larger proportions than ever before. Problems and demands on the agents' time increased as major colonial questions began to come before Parliament. William Bollan noted repeatedly after 1755 that his mission was much more complex and difficult than during his first ten years. In Pennsylvania the outbreak of hostilities in 1756 intensified partisan issues that had seethed for a generation, thereby complicating the work of the colonial agents in London.[33]

In addition to the acquisition of fresh personnel during the war, the institution also profited through pruning old men past their usefulness and younger men who had not shown any warm interest in the colonies. James Wright, subsequently the prerogative-conscious gover-

---

[30] Lewis B. Namier, "Charles Garth and His Connexions," *EHR*, LIV (1939), 445, 452, 457, 465–470; Namier, "Garth, Agent," pp. 632, 643.

[31] Garth to S.C. CC, Sept. 3, 1766, Sept. 26, 1766, Feb. 29, 1768, March 17, 1769, Feb. 5, 1770, *SCHGM*, XXIX, 43–44, 44–48, XXX, 215–217, XXXI, 55–57, 140–142.

[32] Garth to S.C. CC, Dec. 10, 1768, March 12, 1769, *ibid.*, XXX, 233–235, XXXI, 52–54.

[33] Freiberg, "Bollan," pp. 140–143; Wolff, *Agency of Pennsylvania*, pp. 156–157.

nor of Georgia, served as South Carolina's agent until 1760.[34] Benjamin Martyn gave up the Georgia agency in 1763. Although his coagent and successor, William Knox, was fired on the eve of the Stamp Act crisis, Knox was actually the best provincial agent Georgia had had until then, and cooperated with other southern agents on matters of regional interest until the constitutional crisis turned his sympathies away.[35] The removal of James Abercromby in 1759 as agent for Virginia and North Carolina also strengthened the institution. Samuel Smith, an attorney and wealthy London merchant, held Abercromby's Carolina post for two years, until Peter Cuchet Jouvencel took over in 1761. A petty bureaucrat, Jouvencel was connected with men of strength in public affairs and knew the administrative offices well. He was employed as a clerk by the secretaries of state from 1761 until 1767, when he took a similar position at the Privy Seal.[36]

Aging John Thomlinson, New Hampshire's agent since 1734, had been ill for several years, and finally turned the office over to his son in 1763.[37] "Want of Application" made young John basically unsuitable; but he at least held a seat in the House of Commons and was somewhat more vigorous than his father.[38] In 1765, just when fresh strength could make all the difference in the agents' efforts against the Stamp Act, New Hampshire appointed two special agents. One of them was John Wentworth, who would become the colony's governor in 1767, and whose connections with Lord Rockingham were invalu-

---

[34] Labaree, *Papers of Franklin*, VIII, 412 n. 7; "Wright," *DNB*.

[35] As early as 1760, Knox confided to William H. Lyttelton that "the agency for [Georgia] is the thing of all the world that I wish for. . . . I do not so much want the emolument as [much as] the office, as I think that in it, I should be able to recommend myself" (March 5, 1760, Feb. 10, 1762, "Correspondence of William Knox, Chiefly in Relation to American Affairs, 1757–1808," HMC *Report on Manuscripts in Various Collections*, VI [Dublin, 1909], 82, 86). See also Thomas C. Barrow, "A Project for Imperial Reform," 3*WMQ*, XXIV (1967), 108–109.

[36] Samuel J. Ervin, "The Provincial Agents of North Carolina," *Sprunt Historical Publications*, XVI (Chapel Hill, 1919), 70–75; Lewis B. Namier, *The Structure of Politics at the Accession of George III* (2nd ed.; London, 1960), p. 194; *Gentleman's Magazine*, LVI (1786), 999.

[37] James Nevin to Theodore Atkinson, Nov. 14, 1761, Atkinson to Thomlinson, May 13, 1763, Hammond, *New Hampshire Provincial and State Papers*, XVIII, 543, 550.

[38] Thomas Martin to Daniel Rindge, Dec. 24, 1765, Masonian Papers, III, 37, NHHS; Lewis B. Namier and John Brooke, *The History of Parliament: The House of Commons 1754–1790* (London, 1964), III, 522–523.

able during the campaign for repeal in 1766.[39] The other new agent was Barlow Trecothick, a man of tremendous energy and organizational ability.

Born about 1720, Trecothick grew up in Boston. He returned to England at the age of twenty-two after allying himself with Charles Apthorp, a wealthy Boston merchant. By 1755 he was in partnership with John Thomlinson, Apthorp's British correspondent and New Hampshire's agent. Trecothick's commercial interests extended to the West Indies, especially Antigua and Grenada, where he owned considerable property.[40] By 1761 he showed political inclinations and in succeeding years aligned himself with the Rockingham Whigs and Newcastle, serving as their liaison with City politics. From 1768 until 1774 he represented London in the House of Commons, where he was considered a fine speaker. He succeeded William Beckford as Lord Mayor of London in 1770 and saw a great deal of John Wilkes and the City radicals, though his principles lay between theirs and those of the "Old Whigs." [41]

His political experience superbly qualified him for an agency. As early as 1760 he had served Massachusetts informally as a financial agent by handling parliamentary grants distributed to the colony for military outlays. In 1763 the agents of Massachusetts and Connecticut begged Trecothick's assistance in ordering their constituents' finances. He aided them through attendances at the Treasury and interviews with nobles. The high-water mark of his career occurred when he led the campaign for repeal of the Stamp Act. We have Edmund Burke's testimony that Trecothick was "the principal instrument in the happy repeal" movement.[42]

Massachusetts and New York also turned to London merchants in 1765, when they sought to augment the institution's strength. New York employed John Sargent, a director of the Bank of England, to assist Robert Charles during the stamp crisis, but did not maintain

[39] D. H. Watson, "Barlow Trecothick and Other Associates of Lord Rockingham during the Stamp Act Crisis, 1765–1766" (unpub. M.A. thesis; Sheffield University, 1957), pp. 77–86.

[40] Namier and Brooke, *History of Parliament*, III, 557–560.

[41] D. H. Watson, "Barlow Trecothick," *Bulletin of the British Association for American Studies*, N.S., I (1960), 36–49, II (1961), 29–39; *Memoirs of the Marquis of Rockingham and His Contemporaries . . .* , ed. G. T. Keppel (London, 1852), I, 319–320.

[42] MA, XXII, 146–147; Trecothick to Andrew Oliver, Sept. 20, 1763, MA, XXII, 310; Carl B. Cone, *Burke and the Nature of Politics: The Age of the American Revolution* (Lexington, Ky., 1957), p. 95.

him thereafter.[43] Jasper Mauduit, infirm and not always sympathetic to the Bay colonists during his three-year term, resigned in 1765, whereupon the General Court turned to another dissenter, Dennys De Berdt. Recommended for the agency by Dr. Samuel Avery, formerly chairman of the Protestant Dissenting Deputies, De Berdt's credentials were in some respects impressive. After 1748 he had a vital personal stake in the prosperity of North American trade; in 1766 he confessed that he had about £50,000 "lock'd up in America." De Berdt was familiar with the world of British politics. Early in the French and Indian War he prepared advice for Pitt's administration on the pursuit of military operations in America, and in 1763 he appeared before the Board of Trade as a private agent seeking land grants in Canada for a client.[44] Finally, De Berdt had one particularly strong political connection, Lord Dartmouth. Franklin observed that between the evangelical politician and the zealous merchant there was always "an apparently confidential intercourse." [45]

Thus by 1765 the North American agency had expanded its dimensions considerably. Where seven men had served in 1755, there were eighteen a decade later. More than one additional man had been gained almost every year. Vigorous, informed, and concerned personnel had been added, while older and less interested agents had been removed. This does not mean that by 1765 the institution had been totally transformed. But the infusion made an immense difference in the institution's effectiveness during the mid-1760's.[46]

COHESION DEVELOPS

The North American agents lacked a strong institutional tradition of consultation and coordination. Only desultory and irregular cases of

[43] *Documents Relative to the Colonial History of the State of New York,* ed. Edmund B. O'Callaghan (New York, 1853–1887), VII, 908.

[44] *Diary and Autobiography of John Adams,* ed. L. H. Butterfield *et al.* (Cambridge, Mass., 1961), I, 283; De Berdt to Joseph Reed, March 18, 1766, Reed MSS; De Berdt to William Pitt, Feb. 12, 1757, Jan. 3 and 16, 1758, PRO 30/8/19, ff. 347–352; *Journal of the Commissioners for Trade and Plantations from January 1759 to December 1763* (London, 1920–1938), pp. 345–348; "Letters of Dennys De Berdt, 1757–1770," ed. Albert Matthews, CSM *Publications,* XIII (1912), 296–297, 413.

[45] William B. Reed, *Life and Correspondence of Joseph Reed* (Philadelphia, 1847), I, 46.

[46] Max Savelle, *Seeds of Liberty: The Genesis of the American Mind* (Seattle, 1965), p. 577.

cooperative action occurred before 1756. After 1730, for example, they vigorously opposed the vital molasses bill, offering petitions and attending committee hearings with merchants. Their only advantage came in the House of Lords, however, and the bill passed in 1733 despite their efforts. The powerful West Indian lobby and "the commercial theories of the times were against the northern representatives." Fifteen years later, the lobbyists combined to defeat parliamentary efforts to secure prohibition of colonial paper currency. Acting again in concert with the merchants, the agents of six colonies presented remonstrances in 1748–1749. In 1750–1751 they also attempted to thwart stricter administration of the Molasses Act.[47]

The advent of the Seven Years' War, however, brought about more cohesiveness in the institution. Treasury reimbursements to the colonies for their defense expenditures had to be negotiated, apportioned, received, and handled by men in London closely in touch with one another as well as with the colonies. The agents were the obvious persons to serve this function and did so every year after 1756. The experience of regular meetings and personal familiarity formed a pattern for future cooperation when serious issues affecting all the colonies would require joint efforts.

Not that total harmony prevailed among the agents after 1755. The effects of several generations of competitive behavior would not suddenly cease. Occasional arguments preceded certain of the annual financial settlements, for example, because the lobbyists as brokers could not always agree on proper distribution proportions. At the heart of their zealousness was the 2 or 2½ per cent commission each man received from his employers' grant. Massachusetts' agents, especially the Mauduits, usually seemed to be at the core of these disputes. In most cases the disagreements were transitory and gave way to renewed cooperation once the money had been disbursed. But some hard feelings did result, weakening past or potential relationships.[48]

Jasper Mauduit, for example, made snide remarks about the "silence" of his colleagues on a certain issue, and remarked, when unable

[47] Lilly, *Agents of New York and New Jersey*, pp. 207, 211–213; Joseph H. Smith, *Appeals to the Privy Council from the American Plantations* (New York, 1950), p. 601; Ella Lonn, *The Colonial Agents of the Southern Colonies* (Chapel Hill, 1945), p. 327.

[48] Jasper Mauduit to Mass. General Court, Dec. 27, 1962, MA, Letters, 1701–1763, pp. 371–372; William Bollan to Andrew Oliver, July 26, 1763, MA, Misc. Letters, 1763–1773, pp. 8–10.

to call a meeting of the lobbyists, that he had "endeavour'd it in Vain for sometime past." Referring to the revenue bill of 1764, Israel bluntly complained that "it was a great misfortune to us, that the agents of the other Provinces were so slowly disposed to Interest themselves in the affair." The situation was actually not so bleak as the brothers believed, however; though slow getting started, Charles, Sherwood, Thomlinson, and Israel Mauduit himself submitted information and arguments to Grenville in order to counter the pending change in the molasses duty.[49]

Friction also arose when one man wanted another's agency, or when one man succeeded another, thereby making the transition a complicated business that disrupted the smooth functioning of the institution. Tension might also arise between an agent and his newly appointed coagent. Exacerbating bad feeling already extant, the provincial assembly would often ask the new agent to look into the accounts and finances of the older appointee. Massachusetts made such a request of Jasper Mauduit in 1762, when he was appointed to succeed William Bollan; a few years earlier, Virginia's burgesses had given similar instructions to Edward Montagu. In the latter case, the relationship had been poisoned from the start by Abercromby's writing Governor Fauquier that Virginia's affairs were rendered "precarious from the Uncertainty of a Gentleman in Mr. Montagu's Situation in Life, taking upon him the Charge of such Business." Abercromby resented dividing responsibility and commissions with Montagu and Samuel Smith in handling Treasury outlays to Virginia and North Carolina.[50]

The amiable Richard Jackson also had his share of interagency bickering. Jasper Mauduit, who called him "a wholesale dealer in Agencies," tried to obviate Jackson's role as legal counsel for Massachusetts by having Israel made coagent in 1763. Jackson later confided to Thomas Hutchinson that as agent he had little to do with either Mauduit or De Berdt.

[49] Jasper Mauduit to Andrew Oliver, Dec. 30, 1763, Dec. 20, 1764, MA, XXII, 340–341, 421; Israel Mauduit to Mass. General Court, March 23, 1764, MA, Misc. Letters, 1763–1773, pp. 46–47.

[50] Jasper Mauduit to Andrew Oliver, Sept. 23, 1763, May 4, 1764, MA, XXII, 314, LVI, 423–424; Va. CC to Edward Montagu, June 13, 1761, VMHB, XI, 24; James Abercromby to Francis Fauquier, April 14, 1760, to Va. CC, Feb. 21, 1760, Abercromby Letter-book, VSL.

I have always lived upon Terms of Friendship with both Gentlemen as being serious and well disposed Men and of a persuasion that my family has always been connected with, but have very seldom seen them, except I have met them at publick Places of business, and even then that seldom too. . . . As for Mr. Mauduit, I always considered him as a sort of Cypher and therefore advised him myself to make use of his Brother, with whom I have a more external Acquaintance of Civility. Mr. De Berdt is respected as an Honest Active old man (though of no great figure in Life) chiefly by some old Gentlemen that have formerly had some weight, in Publick affairs and besides by Lord Dartmouth the late first Lord of Trade.

Jackson's protest is curious. In 1762 he asked Jasper Mauduit to get him a membership in the nonconformist New England Company. Mauduit complied and the two subsequently attended many of the same meetings.[51] During Jasper's tenure as governor of the organization from 1765 to 1772, Jackson became active in the company's administration, providing legal aid and serving on the committee of estates. Still, Jackson carped at Jasper in letters to Massachusetts, and Hutchinson spread the word that there had been a "difference between him and Mr. Mauduit." [52]

Essentially, however, these examples of divisiveness are confined to a few of the agents and are not characteristic of the decade before the Stamp Act crisis. The two veteran agents, Bollan and Charles, for example, cooperated effectively, as in 1757, when a boundary dispute between New York and Massachusetts produced border disturbances.[53] A year later, Bollan made a serious attempt to bring the North American lobbyists together in support of an important issue. Although he did not gain complete success, the type of action he sought was propitious. At stake were acts passed in Massachusetts to dissolve three marriages there. Bollan recognized that the question might be raised whether *any* colonial assembly had the power to pass laws of

[51] Jasper Mauduit to Thomas Cushing, June 5, 1766, MA, LVI, 479; Jackson to Hutchinson, Jan. 9, 1767, MA, XXV, 144–146; Jasper Mauduit to Andrew Oliver, April 4, 1763, New England Co. Letter-book (1762–1772), f. 5, MS 7927, GLL.

[52] Entry for Dec. 19, 1766, Minutes of the General Court of N.E. Co. 1655–1816, MS 7952, GLL; *ibid.* 1770–1775, Vol. I, ff. 1, 3, 5, 9, 11, 14–15, 21, 23, MS 7920, GLL; Jackson to [Hutchinson?], Feb. 23, 1767, MA, XXV, 167–168; Hutchinson to Nathaniel Rodgers, April 18, 1768, MA, XXVI, 299.

[53] William Bollan to Thomas Hubbard, March 12, 1757, Misc. bound MSS, MHS.

this nature. Therefore he circularized all the agents, "as this matter nearly concerns the power of Legislation in [all] the Colonies." Bollan was thinking along unaccustomed lines for an agent when he wrote to his colleague, James Wright, that "in this as in all other cases relative to the Colonies, I shall ever be ready to promote what may appear for their Interest, and to act as other gentlemen in my Situation do." Such willingness to subordinate localism to the needs of the larger whole was virtually unprecedented.[54]

Bollan hoped that his peers would be alert to the importance of the matter, though he had "learnt by experience the necessity of placing my chief dependance in my own care and assiduity." He was pleasantly surprised, however, by the response he achieved. He conferred with Richard Partridge, who agreed to join him; and he gained the approval of Maryland's agent. Virginia's agreed to "take the opinion of his constituents," and several of the West Indian agents were deeply interested. The Barbados agent even proposed a general meeting of the agents to discuss the issues at stake. Other agents were less favorably disposed; but clearly the institution was moving in a new and unaccustomed direction.[55] In 1761 a group of the agents reached an understanding among themselves as to the timing and methods of lobbying. Initial and mild disagreement within the group gave way to their acceptance of Bollan's proposal on the most effective way to negotiate parliamentary reimbursements. This sort of accommodation was auspicious for the future of the agencies.[56] Even Bollan's successor, Jasper Mauduit, learned to adapt himself to the needs and desires of his fellow lobbyists. By the summer of 1763 he worked with them tolerably well, and during the following year he repeatedly stressed the importance of cooperation.[57]

Benjamin Franklin had recognized the value of unity from the very outset in 1757, and gradually became the core of the American agency. His friendship with Richard Jackson antedated either of their agencies. During the French and Indian War, for example, at Pitt's

[54] Bollan to each of the agents, July 21, 1758, to Wright, July 27, 1758, *ibid.*

[55] Bollan to Thomas Hubbard, Aug. 16, 1758, *ibid.*

[56] Bollan to Andrew Oliver, Feb. 12, 1761, *The Bowdoin and Temple Papers* (MHS *Collections*, ser. 6, Vol. IX [Boston, 1897]), pp. 6–7.

[57] Jasper Mauduit to Andrew Oliver, July 2, 1763, MA, CCLXXXVIII, 5; memorandum of an agents' meeting, Aug. 17, 1763, PRO T 1/423, f. 35; Jasper Mauduit to Andrew Oliver, Aug. 25 and Dec. 20, 1764, MA, XXII, 410, 421.

request, they jointly drafted military advice on North American operations. In the 1760's they conferred on numerous matters other than those involving the Pennsylvania agency.[58] Franklin so enjoyed the lawyer's company and influence that even when he later felt a considerable constitutional gap separated them he continued to maintain cordial relations. Similarly Franklin early developed and sustained firm relationships with Partridge, Charles, Jared Ingersoll, and John Thomlinson.[59]

In the later 1750's the southern colonial agents also began to discover the virtues of joint action on matters of regional importance. In 1758 several of them united to oppose the granting of a salt monopoly in the Commons; and Abercromby and Wright collaborated on a joint application to Parliament for the privilege of importing Bay salt, a boon already allowed the northern provinces. The partial success of these efforts spurred the southern agents on, and in 1759–1760 three of them, in conjunction with British merchants, appeared before a committee of the House of Commons to oppose a petition. After the agents had been heard five times, the petition was dismissed.[60]

William Knox, during the period of his service to Georgia from 1762 to 1765, worked willingly with his colleagues, particularly Charles Garth. At the beginning of Knox's agency, they had jointly sought a renewal of the plantation bounty on indigo. Early in 1764 they offered an alternative to the pending currency bill. Later that year they also discussed the state of the silk culture in Georgia with the Board of Trade; and, with some interested merchants, they successfully petitioned Parliament to permit South Carolina and Georgia to expand their markets by exporting rice directly to the French West Indies and Spanish colonies in Africa, subject to the same duty paid on rice shipped to places south of Cape Finisterre in Europe.[61]

Cooperative leadership characterized Garth from the beginning of his agency in 1762 until about 1770. Early in 1765 he began a four-year period of mutual assistance with Virginia's Edward Mon-

---

[58] PRO 30/8/96, ff. 13–14; Van Doren, *Franklin and Jackson*, pp. 25–26; Franklin to Joseph Galloway, Aug. 22, 1766, MFY.

[59] Labaree, *Papers of Franklin*, VII, 248–249; Franklin to Pa. CC, May 13 and June 10, 1758, *ibid.*, VIII, 68, 87–89; *Journal of Commissioners for Trade, 1759–1763*, pp. 59–63, 109; Gipson, *Ingersoll*, p. 77.

[60] Lonn, *Agents of the Southern Colonies*, pp. 246, 327–328.

[61] Namier, "Garth, Agent," pp. 642, 648–649; Garth to S.C. CC, Sept. 26, 1766, *SCHGM*, XXIX, 44–48; PRO T 1/424, ff. 298–299.

tagu. Garth offered the House of Commons Montagu's memorial against the mutiny bill in 1765, and the two petitioned the Treasury Board for permission to import salt from any part of Europe to Virginia and South Carolina. Montagu reciprocated in 1768, when he placed Garth's petition from Maryland to the crown in Lord Hillsborough's hands. Finally, fifteen months later, these two, joined by North Carolina's agent, memorialized the Board of Trade against efforts then current to reduce the bounty granted on the exportation of tar, pitch, and turpentine from the southern colonies.[62]

By the later 1750's, the North American agents had even begun to cooperate occasionally with their West Indian counterparts, an undertaking quite contrary to their past experience. As recently as the early fifties, the continental pressure group had split the "sugar lobby," thereby delaying action on the sugar and trade laws until the 1760's. But by 1754, Bollan was meeting with a West Indian agent who suggested "that a few of the Chief of us concern'd shou'd meet, in order to settle among ourselves the Disputes about the Molasses Trade." Bollan was convinced of the man's sincerity, but remained skeptical of the possibility of rapprochement between the two lobbies. By 1758, however, agents from New England, the southern *and* West Indian colonies were cooperating on the question of salt production, a good omen for the crisis of 1765, when the West Indian and North American interests would combine in force.[63]

Various factors helped to increase cohesiveness among the agents after 1756. The pressure of legislative circumstance was perhaps only the most obvious; such pressure, for example, produced vigorous and effective opposition to the currency bill in 1757. William Pitt, as wartime leader of Newcastle's ministry, was also a factor. His circular letter of December 1758 to the colonial governors stressed the importance of dispatching documents relating to colonial military expenditures to the duly authorized agents in London. Pitt thereby helped to accentuate the agents' role as Anglo-colonial brokers.[64] Direct coopera-

---

[62] Entry for April 4, 1765, Harris Debates, Malmesbury MSS, Christchurch, Hants.; PRO CO 5/1331, ff. 38–39; Garth to Hillsborough, Oct. 1, 1768, PRO CO 5/1281, ff. 155–156; Montagu to Va. CC, March 3, 1770, *VMHB*, XII, 166–167; Garth to S.C. CC, March 10, 1770, *SCHGM*, XXXI, 233–235.

[63] Varga, "Charles," p. 227; Bollan to Josiah Willard, Aug. 12, 1754, Price MSS, MHS; Henry Tucker to his brother, March 21, 1758, PRO CO 37/18.

[64] William Pitt to the Governors of North America, Dec. 29, 1758, O'Callaghan, *Documents Relative to the Colonial History of New York*, VII, 355.

tion among the agents was advocated by the offices responsible for colonial administration, which requested from time to time that the agents assemble in order to settle particular issues, usually financial.[65] Between 1757 and 1764, the experience of regular and frequent meetings to arrange reimbursement divisions was invaluable, and carried over into other matters to provide momentum toward united efforts.[66]

By 1764 the Virginia Committee of Correspondence could inform its representative as follows: "Since we find, upon other Occasions, that you have met with a ready Disposition in the Agents of the other Colonies to Cooperate with you, whenever the general Interest of the Continent of America seems to have been concern'd, we are of Opinion that their Aid & Assistance, in all Probability can never, upon any Occasion whatever, be more seasonably ask'd than in the present Conjuncture." [67] By 1764 all the committees of correspondence had picked up the cadence, and were instructing their delegates similarly. Massachusetts Bay took the lead, as James Otis, Thomas Cushing, and others circularized all the colonies, urging them to stress that the agents "might be directed by the Representatives of the People on the Continent of North America to unite in the most serious Remonstrance against measures so destructive of the Liberty, the Commerce and Property of the Colonists." Meanwhile, southern agents were admonished to unite with their colleagues on behalf of the northern colonies, all toward the preservation of *American* freedom.[68] This new wave of pressure did, in fact, succeed in many respects,

---

[65] Samuel Martin to Jasper Mauduit, June 21, 1762, *Jasper Mauduit: Agent in London for the Province of the Massachusetts-Bay, 1762–1765* (MHS *Collections,* Vol. LXXIV [Boston, 1918]), p. 55; Richard Partridge to Stephen Hopkins, Dec. 16, 1755, *The Correspondence of the Colonial Governors of Rhode Island, 1723–1775,* ed. G. S. Kimball (Boston, 1902–1903), II, 175–176.

[66] Jasper Mauduit to ?, Dec. 31, 1762, MA, Letters, 1701–1763, p. 373; Richard Jackson to Thomas Fitch, April 13, 1765, CHS *Collections,* XVIII, 342–343; John Thomlinson Jr. to his father, March 26, 1764, *Records and Letters of the Family of the Longs of Longville, Jamaica . . . ,* ed. R. M. Howard (London, 1925), I, 226.

[67] Va. CC to Montagu, July 28, 1764, *VMHB,* XII, 10.

[68] Otis *et al.* to Franklin, June 25, 1764, Franklin to Otis *et al.,* Franklin MSS, nos. 42–43, LC; James Habersham to William Knox, April 15 and July 18, 1765, *The Letters of Hon. James Habersham, 1756–1775* (*Collections of the Georgia Historical Society,* Vol. VI [Savannah, 1904]), pp. 30, 32, 40–41

though not so completely as some historians have imagined;[69] and by 1765 a mature pressure group had been formed. By the time the campaign to repeal the Stamp Act unfolded, the agents were well acquainted with the techniques and advantages of a united front. Putting their parochial and divisive tendencies aside, they waged a successful battle.[70]

Until 1756 the agents had been institutionally parochial and were individually concerned with the affairs of one colony or even one party within that colony. Men of wider vision were needed and gradually acquired thereafter. Their handling of colonial reimbursements and finances during the Seven Years' War helped familiarize them with one another and with mutual problems. The agents themselves gained a fresh awareness of the role they might play in imperial government. Their heightened experience, familiarity with Whitehall and Westminster, and sound contacts were positive gains. When the Sugar Act presented them in 1764 with their first major challenge as a unified pressure group, their response, while imperfect, was not the failure historians have generally assumed. Aware of the mood of Parliament and of the plans of the administration, they "wasted no time objecting to the passage of the act and concerned themselves only with calculating appropriate sizes for the duties."[71] The agents knew that parliamentary lobbying had to be the art of the possible. Although they occasionally misread the temper of politics in Great Britain, their sensitivity to public issues in the mid-1760's was gradually achieving its keenest edge. It remained to be seen whether their constituents would fully recognize the potential inherent in the institution.

[69] Jack M. Sosin, "Imperial Regulation of Colonial Paper Money, 1764–1773," *PMHB*, LXXXVIII (1964), 183. Cf. James J. Burns, *The Colonial Agents of New England* (Washington, D.C., 1935), p. 130; Lawrence H. Gipson, *The British Empire before the American Revolution*, I (2nd ed.; New York, 1958), 13.

[70] Franklin to Richard Jackson, Sept. 1, 1764, Van Doren, *Franklin and Jackson*, p. 177.

[71] *Pamphlets of the American Revolution, 1750–1776*, ed. Bernard Bailyn, I (Cambridge, Mass., 1965), 358.

CHAPTER 3

The Agents and Their Constituents

Paradoxically the greatest difficulties the agents had to overcome in the years before 1766 were created by their employers. Since the late seventeenth century the colonists had not been consistently prudent where their London lobbyists were concerned. Consequently, by the middle of the eighteenth century, the institution was burdened with unnecessary handicaps that would affect the Americans' understanding of its uses and purposes. While easing briefly in the 1760's, these handicaps subsequently became more damaging to the agency and to the strength of Anglo-American ties. Before 1766 such vexations sometimes slowed the functioning of the pressure group, but rarely impeded operations altogether.

AUTHORITY, COMMUNICATIONS, FINANCES, AND FRICTION

An agent normally found himself bound by written instructions from his constituents that defined and circumscribed his freedom of discretionary action. As a rule Massachusetts and Pennsylvania, for example, "strictly enjoined" the Mauduits, Bollan, and Jackson to guard against specific dangers or achieve particular aims. Sometimes the requisite instructions did not arrive in time to be of service, however, thereby adding to transoceanic misunderstanding.[1] An unfortunate impasse occurred between Massachusetts and her lobbyists

[1] Mass. House of Representatives to Jasper Mauduit, June 13, 1764, Dartmouth MSS, Vol. II, no. 51, WSL; Pa. CC to Jackson, Nov. 1, 1764, Franklin MSS, no. 44, LC. Drafts of the letters instructing Massachusetts' agents from 1765 until 1773 are conveniently grouped in one MS letter book, designated MA, Letters, 1765–1773.

in 1763–1764. While the sugar bill was pending, Jasper Mauduit curtly and frequently reminded his employers that he had not "received any objections to this scheme," and therefore did not think himself "at Liberty to make any." When Mauduit did finally receive directions to oppose the bill, they arrived too late to activate him prior to passage of the act.[2]

On those occasions when the lobbyists were allowed a few degrees of latitude, they revealed a quality of responsibility that accentuated what the institution might have achieved. Trecothick, Jackson, and De Berdt were permitted some discretion in timing their petitions. New Hampshire accompanied a memorial for Trecothick's handling with the permissive reminder that *he* could most accurately judge "the fittest time of presentation or whether it will be best wholly to suppress it," since he most accurately knew "the Temper of the Parliament, ministry, & of his Majesty." Richard Jackson's relationship with Pennsylvania and Connecticut gradually became equally relaxed. He wisely withheld petitions in Parliament when the prospect of success seemed dim. His Massachusetts colleague, De Berdt, also took minor liberties both in the moment and methods of submitting his remonstrances; and he was "at Liberty to strike out the offensive Parts" where necessity required.[3]

By contrast, Charles Garth deviated from his instructions with diffidence, even when his doing so redounded to the benefit of South Carolina, as in 1766, when he begged their "forgiveness in not literally carrying" their "Commands into Execution forthwith upon the Rece'pt thereof." On occasions when time did not permit his consulting them beforehand, he drafted and inserted clauses where he felt the petitions of his constituents required them. If at all possible, however, he would "beg the favour" of their sentiments to know whether he might be authorized to offer an application for a certain

[2] Jasper Mauduit to Timothy Ruggles, Dec. 30, 1763, Feb. 11, 1764, MA, XXII, 340–341, and MHS *Collections*, ser. 1, VI (Boston, 1800), 194; Allen S. Johnson, "The Passage of the Sugar Act," 3*WMQ*, XVI (1959), 512.

[3] N.H. Assembly to Trecothick, Nov. 17, 1768, *Documents and Records Relating to the Province of New Hampshire, from 1764 to 1776*, ed. Nathaniel Bouton, VII (Nashua, N.H., 1873), 188; Jackson to Pa. Assembly, Nov. 9, 1765, Misc. MS Collection, APS; De Berdt to Thomas Cushing, Dec. 21, 1767, Aug. 26 and Nov. 19, 1768, "Letters of Dennys De Berdt, 1757–1770," ed. Albert Matthews, CSM *Publications*, XIII (1912), 329, 338, 345.

end.[4] Franklin gradually acquired the complete confidence of the colonists. Consequently he had the broadest discretionary powers of all the agents. Even early in his London career, he assumed liberties lesser men would have shied away from.[5] Read continuously from 1764, his instructions from Pennsylvania reveal the steady transmutation of his agency into an ambassadorship-at-large.[6]

Some of the agents commonly had to contend with an absence of authorization altogether. In 1762, three years after his appointment, Joseph Sherwood lamented to the New Jersey Committee of Correspondence that he still had not received his power of agency.[7] The agents' operations at the Treasury also were impeded on occasion by insufficient authority from their respective colonies, causing proposals and settlements offered by Treasury secretaries to go a-begging.[8]

An especially complicated problem arose when an agent's instructions expressed privately a point of view inconsistent with the colony's public utterances. This occurred particularly before 1766, when the colonists were reasonably discreet (and uncertain) about their developing constitutional views. The agent was then obliged to lobby according to his instructions, while mouthing publicly the sentiments then in use for good imperial relations—sentiments often out of phase with the real feelings of Americans. The ambiguities inherent in such a situation not only made the agent's work difficult but also desensitized the British to the growth of colonial radicalism.[9]

[4] Garth to S.C. CC, Jan. 19 and June 6, 1766, May 17, 1767, May 14, 1770, *SCHGM*, XXVI, 88, XXVIII, 230–234, XXIX, 223–230, XXXI, 283–288.

[5] See James Hamilton's address to the Pennsylvania Assembly, Jan. 18, 1763, *Pennsylvania Colonial Records . . .* , IX (Harrisburg, 1852), 10.

[6] *Pennsylvania Archives*, ed. C. F. Hoban and Gertrude MacKinney (Philadelphia, 1852–   ), ser. 8, VII, 5643–5645, 5793–5794, 5884–5885, 5946–5947, 6069–6071, 6104–6106, 6168–6169, 6277–6281, 6290, 6451–6452, 6658–6659, VIII, 6728, 6901.

[7] Sherwood to Samuel Smith *et al.*, Sept. 16, 1761, Jan. 1, 1762, Sherwood Letter-book, NJHS.

[8] Richard Partridge to Stephen Hopkins, July 12, 1756, Sherwood to Stephen Hopkins, Jan. 31, 1760, *The Correspondence of the Colonial Governors of Rhode Island, 1723–1775*, ed. G. S. Kimball (Boston, 1902–1903), II, 224, 303.

[9] Mass. House to Jasper Mauduit, Nov. 3, 1764, *Speeches of the Governors of Massachusetts from 1765 to 1775 . . .* , ed. Alden Bradford (Boston, 1818), pp. 24–25.

In still other circumstances the precise extent of an agent's authority might be unclear, thereby throwing negotiations into confusion. In 1758–1759, for example, Franklin and the Penns' agent foundered over the issue of the proprietor's estates. Paris declared that the business was stalled because of Franklin's "Want of Power to conclude proper Measures." Franklin explained, however, that he refused "to take upon me to settle a Money Bill with the Proprietors, as having no Power to do an Act of that kind that should be obligatory on the Assembly, for that they neither had given nor could give me such a Power." [10]

Some colonies dispensed information and documents required by the agents no more sensibly than they did instructions and authority. Perhaps the most recurrent theme in the communications from lobbyist to employer was the plea for more frequent and fuller correspondence. Otherwise the agent would perpetually be delayed and his mission debilitated. In 1755, the New York Assembly finally created a Committee of Correspondence to communicate with Robert Charles. Nevertheless, in 1763, John Watts of New York wrote General Richard Monckton a characteristic note: "The lazy Committee I find have neither wrote to you nor the Agent, representing the State of the Colony." [11]

Massachusetts lapsed continuously in this respect. The efforts of both Bollan and Jasper Mauduit to gain extra compensation on account of the Bay Colony's Nova Scotia garrison were complicated by the failure of the colonists to provide muster rolls, copies of General Amherst's certificate, and adequate accounts. Yet, by 1764, there were indications of a favorable change.[12] In 1755 and 1756, Richard Partridge complained to Rhode Island that he was receiving inadequate information too slowly; but the colony's communications gradually improved, particularly when necessary for prosecution of the war.[13]

[10] Jan. 19, 1759, *The Papers of Benjamin Franklin,* ed. Leonard W. Labaree *et al.,* VIII (New Haven, 1965), 194, 233–234.

[11] Nicholas Varga, "Robert Charles: New York Agent, 1748–1770," 3*WMQ,* XVIII (1961), 230; *Letter Book of John Watts* (NYHS *Collections,* Vol. LXI [New York, 1928]), p. 211; Ross J. S. Hoffman, *Edmund Burke, New York Agent . . .* (Philadelphia, 1956), pp. 78, 108.

[12] *Pamphlets of the American Revolution, 1750–1776,* ed. Bernard Bailyn, I (Cambridge, Mass., 1965), 474, 723–724.

[13] Partridge to Stephen Hopkins, July 4 and Dec. 16, 1755, May 7, 1756, Kimball, *Correspondence of Governors of Rhode Island,* II, 153, 175–176, 213–214.

Franklin found Pennsylvania erratic when it came to a steady supply of data. In 1757–1758 the province was delinquent on this score, and in 1759 Franklin complained accordingly. But by this time Isaac Norris had been alerted to the importance of a well-supplied agent, and took action.[14]

Ironically the provincials invested extensive financial authority in the very men they treated costively in terms of political responsibility and information. But here they had no alternative. Each colony maintained an account in London in order to expedite the deposit of parliamentary grants and have a ready fund to satisfy British creditors. Some broker had to be appointed, and normally the colony lobbyist was chosen. Beginning in 1757, the secretaries to the Treasury negotiated colonial claims directly with those agents who furnished security and were properly accredited. Until the end of the Seven Years' War, an agent's success was measured by his ability to procure his province's reimbursement; for a colony was inclined to blame its representative for procrastinations by the British bureaucracy. Once granted, the funds would be banked or invested, sometimes as bills of exchange drawn upon the agent by provincials.[15]

The agents were quite eager to have the broker's commission of 1½ to 2½ per cent allowed on each amount they handled. Where the grant ran to several thousand pounds, the commission constituted a considerable increment to the agent's income. The fee sometimes even exceeded his salary. Therefore any lobbyist deprived of access to this perquisite felt aggrieved and alienated from his constituents. At one time or another almost half the colonies managed to disappoint their delegates, which invariably led to recriminations.

New Jersey bypassed Joseph Sherwood, for example, and employed a special financial agent, the firm of Andrew and Henry Drummond, bankers in Charing Cross. No wonder Sherwood wrote to the Committee of Correspondence in anguish: "When I received Advice of my Appointment to the Agency I expected it was part of my Business to

[14] Franklin to Joseph Galloway, Feb. 17, 1758, to Isaac Norris, March 19, 1759, to David Hall, April 8, 1759, Labaree, *Papers of Franklin*, VII, 376–377, VIII, 291, 321–322.

[15] James J. Burns, *The Colonial Agents of New England* (Washington, D.C., 1935), pp. 16, 67, 84–85; Dora Mae Clark, *The Rise of the British Treasury* (New Haven, 1960), pp. 95, 181; Joseph Sherwood to Stephen Hopkins, June 14, 1760, Letters, VI, 38, RIA.

receive this money; the rest of the Agents in General receive it for
their respective Provinces and so do I for Rhode-Island." [16] Despite his
repeated pleas, however, the committee continued to rely on the
Drummonds.[17] Sherwood must have wondered whether his constituents believed him unworthy of their trust. Nor had his position as
Rhode Island's broker been so easily achieved as he implied. He had to
entreat that colony's authorization in order to receive its war expendi-
ture repayment. Although the Assembly unofficially permitted Sherwood to accept and deposit sums due the colony, it would not bother
to provide him with the letter of attorney each agent was obliged to
produce at the public offices. Not surprisingly a bitter tug of war arose
between province and agent over the latter's commission. Sherwood
charged 2 and sometimes 2½ per cent for receiving the gross sum,
investing it in the exchequer, purchasing foreign coin, shipping insur-
ance, and other pains. He informed Rhode Island that 2½ per cent
was the customary amount and that he had not charged any interest
on money advanced to pay the colony's processing fees. Then he
waited anxiously for a reply.[18]

After seven months Sherwood expressed astonishment at his employers' lethargy. After two years he again reminded them of his
commission, suggestively pointing to his meager salary in vindication.
Finally the stunned lobbyist learned from the treasurer of Rhode
Island that the colony had drawn on him for the entire amount of the
parliamentary grant, "leaving not one farthing for the great Expences
I was at, Fees at the offices, my Salary or any other allowance whatsoever. This I think is SHAVING TOO CLOSE." Nevertheless Sherwood
honored all the province's debts.[19]

James Abercromby ran a similar course with Virginia. He had been
apprehensive at the prospect of a coagent appointed by the burgesses,
for at best the two would have to share the lucrative brokerage fees. "I

[16] June 6, 1761, "Letters of Joseph Sherwood," NJHS *Proceedings*, V
(Newark, 1851), 134-135.

[17] Andrew Drummond and Co. to Samuel Smith, July 14, 1764, Feb. 9,
1765, Simon Gratz MSS, HSP.

[18] Sherwood to Stephen Hopkins, July 14, 1759, June 14, Aug. 8, Oct. 24,
1760, Letters, VI, 17, 38, 41, 42, RIA; MS Accounts of the Agents (1760),
no. 32, RIA.

[19] Sherwood to Hopkins, March 3, 1761, Aug. 20, 1762, Nov. 25, 1763,
Sherwood to Samuel Ward, March 9, 1763, March 13, 1766, Letters, VI, 44,
88, VII, 8, VI, 106, VII, 37, RIA.

run a risk of being cut out of the usual allowance for transacting this affair," Abercromby confessed. More likely, the newcomer would handle the finances altogether, since the colony was outraged by the 2½ per cent commission Abercromby charged. The Committee of Correspondence deputized Edward Montagu to investigate his colleague's scrupulousness, thereby driving a firm wedge between the two lobbyists. And Montagu did, in fact, displace his peer as the Old Dominion's financial executor in London.[20]

New York apparently trusted Robert Charles no more than New Jersey did Sherwood or the Virginia burgesses did Abercromby. The Assembly arranged to have the agent manage the parliamentary grants in partnership with Sir William Baker. They were to set up a joint account at a reliable London bank and then invest the grants in safe but profitable notes and pay all drafts drawn against their account by the New York treasurer. For serving New York as cobroker, Baker divided a 3 per cent commission with Charles.[21] A comparable situation helped to precipitate the break in Charles's relations with Pennsylvania. In 1760 that colony's share of the annual grant was administered by coagents Franklin and Charles, yet the £60 commission was made out in the Doctor's name only. He graciously offered half to Charles, who refused, preferring to ask his employers for a separate commission equal to Franklin's. The assembly stood firm, and Charles shortly requested his release from further duties.[22]

During his first mission, Franklin handled his employers' funds in Britain—investing here, selling stocks there, though not always wisely. His commission amounted to only half of 1 per cent of the colony's parliamentary grant.[23] After his return to Philadelphia in 1762, the agency stood vacant until Richard Jackson's appointment

---

[20] Abercromby to Lord Loudoun, July 16 and Aug. 29, 1759, Loudoun MSS, Huntington Library, San Marino, Calif.; Abercromby to Francis Fauquier, April 14, 1760, Abercromby Letter-book, VSL; Va. CC to Montagu, June 13, 1761, "Proceedings of the Virginia Committee," *VMHB*, XI, 24.

[21] *New York Mercury*, Jan. 2, 1764; Varga, "Charles," p. 229.

[22] Mabel P. Wolff, *The Colonial Agency of Pennsylvania, 1712–1757* (Philadelphia, 1933), pp. 209–211.

[23] Franklin to C. Norris and T. Leech, Nov. 17, 1761, Bamberger Autograph Collection, NJHS; G. S. Eddy, ed., "Account Book of Benjamin Franklin Kept by Him during His First Mission to England as Provincial Agent, 1757–1762," *PMHB*, LV (1931), 128; James H. Hutson, "Benjamin Franklin and the Parliamentary Grant for 1758," 3*WMQ*, XXIII (1966), 575–595.

and Franklin's reappearance in London late in 1764. When it became necessary to authorize an interim broker, the Pennsylvania Assembly chose two politically prominent merchant houses: Sargent and Aufrere, and the Barclays.[24] Jackson had power of attorney to manage Connecticut's funds and did so admirably, paying bills of exchange drawn on him by the governor, banking Treasury funds, and keeping the colony accounts neatly in order.[25]

Massachusetts had a penchant for developing divisive quarrels with her agents over their functions as bankers and brokers. In 1759 the Bay Colony conferred on John Pownall, secretary to the Board of Trade, power of attorney to receive and remit funds jointly with William Bollan. The latter promptly went into a frenzy at the prospect of fee-splitting. In 1760, Pownall gracefully declined, contending that his work occupied him fully.[26] Jasper Mauduit, authorized to succeed Bollan as broker as well as agent, also encountered difficulties.[27] Perhaps Charles Garth had the best solution. He simply in-

---

[24] The three Lower Counties of Newcastle, Kent, and Sussex (later Delaware) had their own London agent, although he received operating expenses from a general fund appropriated by Pennsylvania. David Barclay Jr. served from 1760 until 1765, when Dennys De Berdt replaced him. An interested and sincere friend of America, Barclay was born in 1728, the son of a prosperous Quaker merchant of the same name who exported to the colonies. David Jr. assumed the reins of the business upon his father's death in 1769, adding the export trade to his Lombard Street banking establishment and a prosperous brewery. After William Beckford and Barlow Trecothick, Barclay may well have been the most influential merchant of his time in London. In addition to his Delaware agency, Barclay acted as Pennsylvania's broker. He contributed to the campaign for repeal of the Stamp Act by writing a lengthy plea, which his friend, Lord Hyde, communicated to George Grenville. Barclay thereby repeated a lobbying technique he had employed earlier against the Mutiny Act (*A History of the Barclay Family,* comp. C. W. Barclay [London, 1924], III, 249–250; H. R. Fox Bourne, *English Merchants* [London, 1866], II, 134–137; Barclay to Hyde, Dec. 13, 1765, Grenville MSS in the possession of Sir John Murray, London).

[25] MS designation "War," X, 388, 398, 404, CSL; see also Theodore Atkinson to Trecothick and Thomlinson, June 7, 1765, *The State of New Hampshire: Miscellaneous Provincial and State Papers 1725–1800,* ed. Isaac W. Hammond, XVIII (Manchester, N.H., 1890), 568.

[26] Bollan to Andrew Oliver, March 20, 1760, Pownall to Bollan, July 12, 1760, Bollan to James Otis, Aug. 8, 1760, MA, CCLXXXVII, 175, 177, 179.

[27] Mauduit to Timothy Ruggles, April 8, 1763, to Andrew Oliver, Nov. 25, 1763, MA, CIV, 249–252, XXII, 318.

formed his constituents that "most of the Colonies have granted to their Agents . . . from one to two and a half per cent.; whatever the Assembly shall think right upon this or any other head I have no doubt will be satisfactory to me."[28]

The colonists could be equally shortsighted about agents' salaries and operating expenses. After the outbreak of the Seven Years' War, the Bay Colony's costiveness alienated a succession of agents. It reduced William Bollan, accustomed to receiving £330 annually, to £200 in 1758. The chagrined lobbyist bluntly notified his constituents that his services were being grossly undervalued; but they paid no heed. Then, between 1760 and 1762, the agent was subjected to sharp inquiry on account of the excessiveness of his expenses.[29] Jasper Mauduit's quarrel with Massachusetts became even more bitterly contested than Bollan's. The trouble began in 1764, when Mauduit harmlessly left it "to the General Court to Determine what they think right to allow for the Agency." When the legislature decided upon a salary of £100 annually, Mauduit's wrath and reply could not have been more explosive. "What have I done? or wherein have I been deficient in my duty to the Province, to deserve so publick an affront, as the Voting me a Salary of a hundred a year?"[30] The General Court required a year and a half to muster a defense, and then stood unyielding behind the initial sum appropriated.[31]

It was difficult to persuade capable colonials to leave family and friends for inadequately rewarded service in London. New Hampshire paid her agents only £50 annually, with no allowance whatever for expenses. For John Wentworth's efforts as special agent during the campaign against the Stamp Act he received nothing. John Watts's stricture against the New York Assembly applied equally to many of the colonies: "The Evil is, the Majority of the House are so narrow minded, they cannot be prevail'd upon to allow a Stipend worth a Persons Acceptance of any Note or Weight." Fortunately, a year

[28] Garth to S.C. CC, Aug. 25, 1764, Sir Lewis Namier, "Charles Garth, Agent for South Carolina," *EHR*, LIV (1939), 635.

[29] Bollan to Andrew Oliver, Aug. 20, 1760, April 30, 1766, MA, CCLXXXVII, 181–181a, XXII, 488.

[30] Mauduit to [Andrew Oliver?], April 5, 1764, to Timothy Ruggles, April 5, 1764, *ibid.*, LVI, 419, CCLXXXVIII, 13; Mauduit to Samuel White, Sept. 4, 1765, AAS.

[31] Mass. House to Mauduit, March 18, 1767, Adams MSS, NYPL.

before the Stamp Act crisis, New York raised Robert Charles's salary from £200 per annum to £500.[32]

Benjamin Franklin, despite his eminence, was not always properly rewarded. When he left Philadelphia in 1757, the Assembly voted him £1,500 sterling "to defray the expense of [his] voyage and nego-tiations in England." Thereafter he received "nothing more," though he remained sanguine. "They will, I make no doubt, on winding up the affair, do what is just." [33] Edward Montagu received £500 a year from the burgesses of Virginia, including expenses, a reasonable sum and the envy of many agents, including Charles Garth. Even so, Garth accepted his financial relationship with South Carolina cheer-fully. The Committee of Correspondence in Charleston allowed the agent £200 annually, and encouraged him in addition "to make out a bill of all actual disbursements, and also of other reasonable charges in the prosecution of their affairs." Occasionally the Commons House was dilatory about appropriating Garth's funds; but for the most part they remained on good terms. Garth generously even suggested that his father's purse would always be at the command of the province.[34]

The colonists were also prone to commit public and private indiscre-tions that made professional life difficult for the agents. In 1764, for example, Richard Jackson discovered "articles in the papers from America" which alluded to his political connections. Jackson notified Franklin quickly that he had little enough influence in London, "& perhaps the less for such Publications." De Berdt as well as Franklin cautioned their constituents continuously against "the inconvenience in imediately putting every thing into print." [35] This was a problem of

[32] Wentworth to Lord Hillsborough, May 2, 1769, John Wentworth Letter-book, p. 230, NHHS; Watts to Sir William Baker, March 30, 1765, *Letter Book of John Watts*, p. 341; *Historical Memoirs from 16 March 1763 to 9 July 1776 of William Smith . . .*, ed. W. H. W. Sabine (New York, 1956), I, 70.

[33] Hoban and MacKinney, *Pennsylvania Archives*, ser. 8, VII, 6427, VIII, 6899; Franklin to Josiah Quincy, April 8, 1761, Smyth, IV, 99–100.

[34] Va. CC to Montagu, Dec. 12, 1759, *VMHB*, X, 342; Garth to Maryland Assembly, Feb. 14, 1767, Namier, "Garth, Agent," p. 636.

[35] Jackson to Franklin, Aug. 11, 1764, *Letters and Papers of Benjamin Franklin and Richard Jackson, 1753–1785*, ed. Carl Van Doren (Philadelphia, 1947), p. 175; De Berdt to Thomas Cushing, Nov. 19, 1768, Matthews, "Letters of De Berdt," pp. 346–347; *Boston Gazette and Country Journal*, April 9, 1764.

particular delicacy for Franklin during his first agency, for in 1758 the Penns acquired copies of his letters to the Assembly which offended them deeply. In consequence Franklin needed to be "cautious how I speak freely of Persons and Measures here, lest [Penn] should have a Handle to create me Enemies." Nevertheless, the agent had to remind his correspondents again and again about the confidential nature of his letters, a problem that would reach crisis proportions after 1766.[36]

These points that sparked antipathies between agent and employers generated more heat than light. Too often recriminations led to damaged relationships. Such was the case in 1764, when the distraught Massachusetts House of Representatives rebuked Jasper Mauduit for the "timid character of his communications with the Ministry." They chided him for his mild opposition to the Sugar and Mutiny Acts and upbraided him simultaneously for adhering inflexibly to his instructions and for exceeding them as well: "No Agent of this Province has Power to make express Concessions in any Case without express Orders." When the infirm woolen draper responded tartly, the infuriated assembly—threatening to expose Mauduit's "indecent" letter—reminded him of its "fondness for publications." [37]

The agents were vulnerable and in most cases highly sensitive to adverse criticism originating in the colonies.[38] Franklin's stature and lifetime of involvement in provincial politics made him an inevitable object of opprobrium in America. Some of his political enemies in Pennsylvania believed he had taken liberties with his expense account during his first mission to London, and they encouraged pamphleteers who attempted to sabotage the Doctor's second appointment in 1764. A year later these antagonists began to circulate all sorts of untruths, some even suggesting that Franklin fomented the Stamp Act. These caused him much anguish and plagued him during the following decade.[39] Jared Ingersoll underwent vilification in Connecticut be-

[36] Franklin to Joseph Galloway, Sept. 16, 1758, April 7, 1759, Labaree, *Papers of Franklin*, VIII, 151, 313.

[37] Mass. House to Mauduit, June 13, 1764, Feb. 19, 1766, Add MSS 35910, ff. 302–307, and MA, Letters, 1765–1773, p. 6.

[38] James Abercromby to George Grenville, Jan. 6, 1764, Add MSS 38204, ff. 9–10.

[39] William Tryon to Board of Trade, June 24, 1765, Dartmouth MSS, Vol. II, no. 78, WSL; J. Phillip Gleason, "A Scurrilous Colonial Election and Franklin's Reputation," 3*WMQ*, XVIII (1961), 75; *The Writings of John Dickinson*, ed. Paul L. Ford (*Memoirs of the Historical Society of Pennsylvania*, Vol. XIV [Philadelphia, 1895]), pp. 151–154.

cause he accepted a stamp distributorship in 1765. For two years thereafter, his special agency (1764–1765) became suspect, and like Franklin he was charged with responsibility for preparing and executing the ignominious act.[40]

THE AGENTS AND PROVINCIAL POLITICS

The focus of this volume is confined to the agents as London lobbyists rather than the institution as an object of provincial politics. The latter concern has dominated most previous studies of the colonial agency and, as an integral part of the political history of each colony, comprises a discrete field for investigation. There is a point, however, at which the two complementary subjects intersect—that moment when the exigencies and excesses of provincial life reverberated across the Atlantic to restrict the lobbyists' maneuverability. As Thomas Hutchinson remarked with reference to his colony's agent, "the more respect shown him the greater weight he will have; but our misfortune is that we are influenced by party personal views more than by a regard for the public interest." The increasingly common quarrels between governor and lower house, for example, often served to involve, distract, and even discredit the representative. Such a situation existed with perhaps most striking intensity in the case of Massachusetts.[41]

When James Otis and his supporters successfully ousted Bollan in favor of Jasper Mauduit in 1762, they threw down a gauntlet to the Hutchinsonians. Thereafter, the opposing forces engaged each other continuously until the coming of the Revolution. In the process the scene of battle shifted from Boston to London, where the agents were charged with responsibility for deposing first Francis Bernard and then his successor. Ironically the personnel involved changed attitudes and identities so readily that relationships became malleable. The

[40] Edmund S. and Helen M. Morgan, *The Stamp Act Crisis: Prologue to Revolution* (Chapel Hill, 1953), ch. 13.
[41] Harold W. Currie, "Massachusetts Politics and the Colonial Agency, 1762–1770" (unpub. Ph.D. diss.; University of Michigan, 1960); Jack P. Greene, *The Quest for Power: The Lower Houses of Assembly in the Southern Royal Colonies, 1689–1776* (Chapel Hill, 1963), ch. 13; Hutchinson to Ebenezer Silliman, Nov. 1764, *Jasper Mauduit: Agent in London for the Province of the Massachusetts Bay, 1762–1765* (MHS Collections, Vol. LXXIV [Boston, 1918]), p. 161 n. 1.

Mauduits soon were found too cautious by the Otis faction, while Bollan gradually shed his connections with the "oligarchs" in favor of the more radical circle represented by Samuel Danforth and James Bowdoin. To complicate the struggle, Governor Bernard had his own candidate for the agency, though Bernard gradually and reluctantly withdrew from direct participation in selecting the agent, trusting to his "negative to keep out Improper & disagreeable men." Bernard had the prescience to envision the inevitable outcome of this tripartite tension: "The Consequence will be to separate the Agency of the Governor and Council from that of the House & so the Importance of that Office will be destroyed & the value of it will make it not worth acceptance." [42] Thus there was justice in Barlow Trecothick's bitter remark in 1762: "Indeed I am truly ashamed to see the Dignity & Welfare of the Province thus prostituted to [?] motives of sect & party. It needs a person of weight & knowledge of public business as well as of leisure to attend it." [43]

Provincial politics in Pennsylvania had a similar though less severe effect on its agents. One of the grievances Franklin was to present in 1757 claimed that the proprietors wished to deprive the Assembly of the power and means of supporting an agent and hence of prosecuting their complaints before the crown and Parliament. Several years later, Richard Jackson subtly chided the Assembly for *its* divisiveness, hoping a new-found harmony would free him and Franklin from the burden of petitioning for a change of government. The instructions of the agent from year to year depended very much upon "the Complexion of the next assembly." In fact Franklin's return to England in 1764 was one result of an election triumph by the antiproprietary party in the legislature. The winning group quickly voted to send him as a special agent to seek royal status. [44]

Popular control of the agency became an object of contention most

[42] Currie, "Massachusetts Politics," p. 6; Bernard to John Pownall, Feb. 22, 1763, to Richard Jackson, July 26, 1763, Oct. 6, 1766, to Thomas Pownall, March 15, 1766, Bernard MSS, II, 264–265, III, 82–84, V, 159–164, 91–94, HLHU.

[43] Trecothick to John Temple, July 10, 1762, Bowdoin-Temple MSS, Vol. I, MHS.

[44] John J. Zimmerman, "Benjamin Franklin: A Study of Pennsylvania Politics and the Colonial Agency, 1755–1775" (unpub. Ph.D. diss.; University of Michigan, 1956), *passim;* William S. Hanna, *Benjamin Franklin and Pennsylvania Politics* (Stanford, 1964); Jackson to Pa. Assembly, Nov. 9, 1765, Misc. MS Collection, APS.

prominently in the proprietary colonies. There the people had no available means to bring their grievances before the crown without some independent medium of representation. For this reason the proprietor opposed the appointment of an agent even more vigorously than a royal governor would. Maryland never had a regular agent after 1746. The lower house tried repeatedly in the 1760's—but without success.[45] In 1765, when the legislature defied the Calverts by selecting a special agent, it chose neither Jackson nor Franklin (whom the proprietors feared was the object of the Assembly's approaches), but Charles Garth, already agent for South Carolina.[46] The Council, meanwhile, vetoed Garth's selection and refused to appropriate funds for an agent instructed by the lower house alone. The popular party was unable to raise sufficient money to sustain Garth independently; and he, in turn, would not have accepted another permanent constituency without power of discretion in executing its instructions: "He wished to choose the time and opportunity of acting, and to be free to act or not, according to his own best judgment." [47]

On numerous occasions Garth's South Carolina constituents embroiled him in their domestic controversies, particularly between governor and assembly. Like De Berdt and Franklin, Garth was called upon to apply the necessary leverage to have a governor removed, an awkward task that diverted the agent's energies from issues of intercolonial interest. In North Carolina the assembly and chief executive also fought for control of the provincial agency—to the detriment of the institution. Peter Cuchet Jouvencel found himself caught in the enmity between governor and lower house. His tenure remained so uncertain that he stood in continual dread of replacement. To forestall dismissal when he anticipated it, the agent threw himself on the mercy of newly appointed Lieutenant Governor Tryon, enabling that politician to boast: "I had an agent sealed up in my Pocket." When Jouvencel's office fell vacant, Tryon proposed William Knox, the representative house nominated Thomas Barker, and the Council

[45] Beverly W. Bond Jr., "The Colonial Agent as a Popular Representative," *PSQ*, XXXV (1920), 372–392; Charles A. Barker, *The Background of the Revolution in Maryland* (New Haven, 1940), pp. 337–339.

[46] Barker, *Revolution in Maryland*, pp. 304–305; *MHM*, XII (1917), 377–381.

[47] Garth to Hillsborough, Oct. 1, 1768, PRO CO 5/1281, f. 155; Barker, *Revolution in Maryland*, pp. 337–339.

backed a third candidate. As a result of this stalemate no agent was chosen for three years.[48]

In Virginia the appointment of an agent stirred up somewhat less strife than in Maryland and the Carolinas. In 1718 the Council first rejected the burgesses' demand for an agent of their own choosing. At mid-century the struggle began in earnest; and by 1759, the lower house succeeded in appointing Montagu its own representative, thereby creating a dual agency. For a few years thereafter, Abercromby and Montagu played out in London the tensions between rival factions in Virginia, like marionettes responding magically to some remote manipulators.[49]

As politics in New Hampshire became polarized between the popular element and the aristocratic Wentworth clan, the agency suffered accordingly. John Thomlinson's initial position as lobbyist in the 1730's had depended upon his business relationship with Benning Wentworth and his brother Mark Hunking, colonial mast agent. Thomlinson had applied pressure in England to have Benning Wentworth displace Jonathan Belcher as governor. But with the establishment of the Wentworth-dominated officialdom (which excluded most Assembly members), Thomlinson found himself in an awkward position, particularly when the elected speaker of the house engineered a plot to remove the Governor (1748–1752). Only the collapse of the cabal and restoration of Benning Wentworth's hegemony over the Assembly eased Thomlinson's delicate situation.[50]

In New York, provincial dynasties also contended for power emanating from London—to which one avenue was the colony agent. When the Assembly chose Robert Charles in 1748, the Governor felt betrayed. "I have lately discovered the spring of all my disappointments in England," Clinton wrote, "by Mr. Charles (upon whome I

---

[48] W. R. Smith, *South Carolina as a Royal Province, 1719–1776* (New York, 1903), ch. 4; Samuel J. Ervin, "The Provincial Agents of North Carolina," *Sprunt Historical Publications*, XVI (Chapel Hill, 1919), 73–77; Tryon to Board of Trade, June 24, 1765, Dartmouth MSS, Vol. II, no. 78, WSL.

[49] Bond, "Agent as Popular Representative," pp. 390–391; Abercromby to ?, Feb. 19, 1760, PRO T 1/400, ff. 106–107; Francis Fauquier to Board of Trade, Sept. 1, 1760, PRO CO 5/1330, ff. 28–31; E. I. Miller, "The Virginia Committee of Correspondence, 1759–1770," 1*WMQ*, XXII (1913), 6–10.

[50] Jere R. Daniell, "Politics in New Hampshire under Governor Benning Wentworth, 1741–1767," 3*WMQ*, XXIII (1966), 76–105.

depended) acting in confidence with Sir Peter Warren." [51] By 1761, Charles faced the first of four attempts by politicians in New York to remove him from office. Cadwallader Colden offered Charles's job to John Pownall, secretary to the Board of Trade, in exchange for the lieutenant governorship. Pownall discreetly avoided a precarious situation (though Colden got his commission anyway). Then William Alexander, Earl of Stirling, unsuccessfully urged New York's merchants to appoint an English friend as Charles's coagent, claiming that a person of greater importance was needed to communicate with M.P.'s and ministers. [52] Early in 1764 his nemesis was Colden again; for the Lieutenant Governor informed the Board of Trade that Charles had "no authority from this Government to appear as Agent, he had no instruction from the Governor or Council, the design of the Assembly being that he should Act independently of them." Frequently thereafter the agent encountered unexpected difficulties at Whitehall on account of Colden's "irregular interposition." [53]

Quite obviously one of the most unfortunate aspects of the agency's being an issue in provincial politics was that men unsuited for the office were occasionally chosen. Although some unfortunate selections occurred in the decade before the Stamp Act crisis, the worst effects would be felt between 1766 and 1775. With the opening of the Seven Years' War, most Americans in public life did begin to think more seriously about the caliber of their agents. As a result a prolonged discussion began as to what an agent was, what he might do, and how he should be chosen. One Pennsylvanian observed in 1755 that the agents "may & no doubt do everything in their power"; yet he was sure that "they cannot have that [same] weight as a solemn deputation of the House of Representatives." Others also urged the selection of a group of assemblymen for special missions to London; but it was finally agreed that men already "upon the Spot must be sure to know more minutely the particular circumstances of matters than any one"

[51] Stanley N. Katz, "An Easie Access: Anglo-American Politics in New York, 1732–53" (unpub. Ph.D. diss.; Harvard University, 1961), p. 373.
[52] William A. Duer, *The Life of William Alexander, Earl of Stirling* (NJHS *Collections*, Vol. II [New York, 1847]), p. 66 n.; Varga, "Charles," pp. 230–234.
[53] Colden to Board of Trade, Jan. 21, 1764, *Documents Relative to the Colonial History of the State of New York*, ed. Edmund B. O'Callaghan, VII (Albany, 1856), 607; John Watts to Robert Monckton, Dec. 13, 1764, *Letter Book of John Watts*, p. 315; Hoffman, *Burke*, pp. 94–95.

in the colony. In Connecticut several years later the same ambivalence prevailed, though by 1760 the general assumption was that only someone permanently resident in London could adequately serve as agent.[54]

By the time of the Stamp Act crisis, almost every colony had become persuaded of the value of agents properly accredited and supported. His brief tenure as New Hampshire's coagent in 1765–1766 impressed upon John Wentworth the peculiar problems of the office as well as its possibilities. Annoyed that £7,000 which Parliament owed the colony had not been applied for by the Thomlinsons, and annoyed by their neglect of New Hampshire's affairs, Wentworth remarked that the agent's illness "must for ever prevent our Affairs from being properly urg'd." The young provincial felt very strongly that New Hampshire should appoint a new agent and pay him as much as £1,000 sterling each year, "whereby he may be independent of People here and have it his Duty to exert his utmost attention, in the colony's service." The thousand pounds would include all commissions, fees, and expenses. Since these normally amounted to several hundred pounds, the proposed salary was not exorbitant. Better to have a man well paid and the province's servant, Wentworth remarked, than "only a Merchant . . . you rather think yourselves under." Wentworth clearly recognized the urgent necessity for a devoted, vigorous agent at a "time when the Provinces need friends to be watchful for their dearest rights." [55]

Yet for a variety of reasons it was difficult if not impossible for the agents to become all they might have been. From the changing perspective of their American employers, lobbyists were regarded as unfortunate necessities. While the political and constitutional ideas of Americans were in flux, particularly regarding the complex problem of representation, what place was there for colonial agents? As early as 1764, James Otis repudiated any consideration of the agents as true representatives of the colonies, a view that would deepen with each succeeding year.[56] From 1624 until 1755 the agents had been their

[54] Wolff, *Colonial Agency of Pennsylvania*, pp. 194–195; Jared Ingersoll to Thomas Fitch, Aug. 10, 1761, *The Fitch Papers* (CHS *Collections*, Vol. XVIII [Hartford, 1920]), pp. 137–142.

[55] Wentworth to Daniel Peirce, Jan. 15, 1766, Peirce Papers, Portsmouth Athenaeum, N.H. I am grateful to Jere R. Daniell for bringing this letter to my attention.

[56] Bailyn, *Pamphlets of the American Revolution*, I, 170, 417, 466.

constituents' lobbyists, as well as handymen to the colonial administration in London. During the Seven Years' War their role as brokers
took on added dimensions that helped sustain them through the
Anglo-colonial crisis which immediately followed the war. Thereafter
still other functions and roles might have been open to the agents.
Their capacity to fill these roles would depend upon whether they
could transcend their past limitations.

CHAPTER 4

The Agents and
Colonial Administration

In 1762 an acute political observer described the process of government in Georgian England as the "detail and manner of passing business through the public offices," in which practice "the constant clerks and servants of these offices are the greatest proficients." [1] Because the daily routine of lobbying in London brought the agents into close contact with the great boards and their officials, it becomes essential to understand the bureaucratic nature of eighteenth-century imperial administration. What was it like to maneuver a bill through Westminster or a petition through the chambers of Whitehall? What mutations did the bureaucracy undergo after midcentury? And what impact would these changes have on lobbyists, their influence, and the bonds of empire?

BUREAUCRACY AND THE MECHANICS OF LOBBYING

Some of the many definitions of bureaucracy are objectively dispassionate, while others are overtly pejorative. All, however, seem to share certain common attributes. There is the element of structured authority and the concomitant set of informal relationships without which a formal administrative hierarchy cannot function. A bureaucracy is a system of government managed by officials jealous of their power yet often reluctant to accept responsibility. Civil servants are

[1] Anonymous, *A Political Analysis of the War,* quoted in Leslie Scott, "Under Secretaries of State, 1755–1775" (unpub. M.A. thesis; Manchester University, 1950), p. 104.

organized into departments executing decisions commonly made by others. In some cases, however, the officials may even become so influential that they share in formulating policy. Inflexibility, sluggishness, conservatism, and the development of a hereditary caste are commonly associated with bureaucracy in its historical context.[2]

Most authorities would agree that a bureaucracy in the modern sense did not exist in Britain before the nineteenth century. Really professional administrators and the dimensions of depth were lacking.[3] Nevertheless the central government had been bureaucratic in character for centuries. During the reign of Henry VIII, a system of great departments came into being capable of carrying on the management of the state largely independent of the personal action and capacity of the monarch. Early in Elizabeth's reign the absence of vigorous royal direction forced the administrative class to assert itself; and under the first Stuarts the burden of court and government so increased that resentment against the king's servants became a major factor in the crisis of 1640–1642 initiating the Civil War. "The bureaucratic setting of the Hanoverian governmental world was even now becoming visible," one scholar has suggested.[4]

[2] *Reader in Bureaucracy*, ed. Robert K. Merton *et al.* (Glencoe, Ill., 1952), *passim*; Harold J. Laski, "Bureaucracy," *Encyclopedia of the Social Sciences*, III, 70–73.

[3] See Lewis B. Namier, *Conflicts: Studies in Contemporary History* (London, 1942), pp. 198–199; but cf. Franklin B. Wickwire, *British Subministers and Colonial America, 1763–1783* (Princeton, 1966), ch. 1.

[4] Only recently have students in the field of British administrative history come to appreciate the early development of bureaucratic characteristics and their influence on government. T. F. Tout, *The Place of the Reign of Edward II in English History* (2nd ed.; Manchester, Eng., 1936), suggests a bureaucracy in embryo early in the fourteenth century. In *The Tudor Revolution in Government* (Cambridge, 1953), G. R. Elton found a transition from "household government" to "national bureaucratic government" occurring in the 1530's. G. E. Aylmer, in *The King's Servants: The Civil Service of Charles I, 1625–1642* (London, 1961), and David Mathew, in *The Social Structure of Caroline England* (Oxford, 1948), examine the emergence of a bureaucratic class in the seventeenth century. For its continued development in the eighteenth century, see E. E. Hoon, *The Organization of the English Customs System, 1696–1786* (New York, 1938), esp. ch. 2; J. G. A. Pocock, "Machiavelli, Harrington, and English Political Ideologies in the Eighteenth Century," 3*WMQ*, XXII (1965), 582; W. R. Ward, "Some 18th Century Civil Servants: The English Revenue Commissioners, 1754–1798," *EHR*, LXX (1955), 25–54; Franklin B. Wickwire, "Admiralty Secretaries and the British Civil Service," *Huntington Library Quarterly*, XXVIII (1965), 235–254. Sir Ernest

Among the characteristics fully in evidence by the eighteenth century were clearly formalized procedures, copious written records,[5] interdepartmental jealousies, and specialization. Lethargy had overcome numerous officials in strategic positions. By 1763, for example, the revenue commissioners met only in June. Because they all lived far from London, a solicitor largely maintained the work of their office.[6] During the period of "salutary neglect"—the reigns of Anne and the first two Georges—a sluggish quality developed in imperial administration. At times this worked to the advantage of the provincials. In the 1740's and 1750's, for example, Robert Charles successfully prevailed upon the Board of Trade to put off consideration of New York's Boundary Act. Finally the New Jersey proprietors who opposed it gave up in disgust.[7]

The excessive length of time required to prosecute colonial problems suggests another bureaucratic tendency potentially detrimental to Anglo-American union. Lobbying in London could be very costly, for as William Bollan remarked in 1754, "the Expences necessarily attending the negotiation of Business here, are in proportion to the Business to be done, to the number & kind of persons with whom it is to be negotiated & the manner of doing it. . . . It is impossible to drive about the wheels of Business without a considerable Expence."[8] In addition to high legal fees, lobbyists had to contend with a system of gratuities and bribes. At every turn—the lobby of Commons, the chambers of Whitehall, the anterooms of noble homes—agents found themselves obliged to dispense money in order to expedite their busi-

---

Barker, *The Development of Public Services in Western Europe, 1660–1930* (Oxford, 1944), pp. 32–33, is also valuable.

[5] By the middle of the eighteenth century the rooms of the Board of Trade had become inadequate to house the great quantities of records—some 2,000 bound volumes of papers—that had accumulated (Arthur H. Basye, *The Lords Commissioners of Trade and Plantations . . . 1748–1782* [New Haven, 1925], p. 194).

[6] Ward, "Some 18th Century Civil Servants," pp. 25, 52. By contrast, the chief merit of the bureaucracy in eighteenth-century Prussia was its relative efficiency; under Frederick the Great, matters that did not require special investigation were dispatched rapidly (see Walter L. Dorn, "The Prussian Bureaucracy in the Eighteenth Century," *PSQ*, XLVI [1931], 412).

[7] Nicholas Varga, "Robert Charles: New York Agent, 1748–1770," 3*WMQ*, XVIII (1961), 222–223; John Pownall to Robert Charles and Joseph Sherwood, Oct. 22, 1763, PRO CO 5/1130, p. 221.

[8] Bollan to Josiah Willard, April 19, 1754, Price MSS, MHS.

ness. Perquisites presented to menials to assure their discretion in matters relating to their masters were known as "vails." [9]

Every service performed at a governmental agency had its price, both above and below board. By 1714 the clerks at the plantation office became so greedy that the lords commissioners found it necessary to establish a rule that no clerk should "presume to demand any money from any person for any business done in the office." An informal system of fees continued nevertheless. As one scholar has observed, "the line between accepting a gratuity for doing a service which should be done without one, and the accepting of one for a service which should not be rendered at all, is a shadowy one; but that is the line which separates tipping and bribery." The situation was so out of hand by 1730 that the Board of Trade prohibited subalterns from demanding or accepting gratuities for ordinary services. This led in 1731 to the establishment of fixed fees. A schedule of gratuities was drafted and posted at the Board, all others being outlawed. Simultaneously the House of Commons institutionalized a similar table for its clerks, but based on an earlier list first set in 1700. These required sums, printed and hung in the speaker's chamber, the lobby, and the clerk's office, were all paid to the chief clerk-without-doors, who then distributed them to the various officers of the House. Altogether such fees constituted a tidy income for the recipients. [10]

Because every action performed by the governmental hierarchy cost the interested party substantial amounts, the agents had expense accounts. At the end of each fiscal year—and sometimes quarterly— they sent their annual charges to their constituents for reimbursement. These documents reveal a great deal about the modes of lobbying in London. The more effective agents were careful to disperse extra sums at the Board of Trade, Treasury, Privy Council, and offices of the secretaries of state. At Christmas, for example, Charles Garth distributed two guineas among the menials at each of these locations. When Shelburne took over the Southern Department in 1766, Garth was

[9] E. S. Turner, *What the Butler Saw* (New York, 1962), p. 49; William Samuel Johnson to Eliphalet Dyer, Sept. 12, 1767, *The Susquehannah Company Papers: Memorial Publications of the Wyoming Historical and Genealogical Society*, ed. Julian P. Boyd (Wilkes-Barre, Pa., 1930–1933), II, 321.

[10] Oliver M. Dickerson, *American Colonial Government, 1696–1765* (Cleveland, 1912), pp. 69, 71–72; O. C. Williams, *The Clerical Organization of the House of Commons, 1661–1850* (Oxford, 1954), pp. 301–304; John Hatsell, *Precedents of Proceedings in the House of Commons . . .* (London, 1776–1796), II, 276, 281–282, 286–288.

careful to tip the new minister's porter ten shillings and six pence. Dennys De Berdt's presents to the doorkeeper and messengers of Parliament, the Board of Trade, Privy Council, and offices of the secretaries of state, as well as servants of M.P.'s and nobles ran to £40 a year. In addition, De Berdt left a £10 retaining fee with the clerk of the Commons so that he would be immediately notified whenever any matter affecting the colonies came before the House.[11] His predecessor, Jasper Mauduit, distributed two guineas each to the doorkeepers at the Board of Trade, the Treasury, and the House of Commons, plus five shillings to the porters at the Treasury—expedient since he was seeking to recover his colony's wartime outlays, a process involving a parliamentary grant approved by the Treasury. As Pennsylvania's agent, Robert Charles annually dispensed five guineas to messengers and doorkeepers at the public offices and House of Commons. Joseph Sherwood charged Rhode Island and New Jersey each £30 per year for such outlays and coach hire about London.[12]

Office in eighteenth-century Britain, then, was a property for which a consideration was paid at the time of acquisition. Officials so recruited were not so much professional administrators after the Prussian pattern as *rentiers* anxious to profit by their investment. Every department had a "fund" consisting of the fees it received. The "patenter" at the head of the office, acting as a sort of entrepreneur, took his share of the profits and left the underlings to fare as best they could. The secretary to the Board of Trade, for example, absorbed 40 per cent of all fees taken by his office.[13]

Most of the departments were boards that met with varied frequency around baize-covered tables. They manifested all the attributes commonly associated with such bodies: legalism, ceremonialism,

[11] Garth's accounts are to be found in *SCHGM*, XXIX, 117–119, XXX, 172–175, 226–228, XXXI, 129–131, XXXIII, 228–230, 267–268; Jackson's are printed in CHS *Collections*, XIX (Hartford, 1921), 43–45; De Berdt's are in the Dartmouth MSS, Vol. I, ii, no. 974, WSL, and MA, XXII, 572–579.

[12] *Jasper Mauduit: Agent in London for the Province of the Massachusetts-Bay, 1762–1765* (MHS *Collections*, Vol. LXXIV [Boston, 1918]), pp. 102, 154–157; Mabel P. Wolff, *The Colonial Agency of Pennsylvania* (Philadelphia, 1933), pp. 204–211. Sherwood's New Jersey accounts are in his MS letter book at the NJHS and in the Franklin MSS, LXVII, 131, APS; his Rhode Island financial papers are in the MS accounts of the agents, nos. 30, 32, 36, 39, RIA.

[13] Barker, *Development of Public Services*, p. 32; Dickerson, *American Colonial Government*, p. 76.

and departmentalism. Each of them deliberated. They continually referred issues to each other, thereby losing efficiency.[14] More significantly, they usually lacked a real power of direct action. Although they issued warrants or instructions, they were not themselves the instruments of action. Departmentalism in Georgian England appeared in various ways. The agents had to pursue their requests through a maze of offices and boards that were remarkably parochial. In order to procure reimbursement for their employers' wartime outlays, the agents were obliged to carry warrants from office to office for approval. Meanwhile they had to tip the ever expectant civil servants and underlings. All too often lobbyists were put off by the tendency of one administrative unit to shunt responsibility onto another. An agent might be told at the Treasury that he must see the Board of Trade. Meeting with a negative response there he would go to the secretary of state and then often right back to the Treasury again.[15]

The process of presenting a colonial petition is characteristic, for the procedure stretched from one office to another. First the agent submitted his memorial to the secretary of state. He in turn could consult the cabinet or direct it to the president of the Privy Council, who then referred it to the Board of Trade. Their lordships would relegate the memorial to legal counsel for consideration; and then the process operated in reverse until the bureaucracy discharged the document in one form or another.[16] With so many chambers in the nautilus it was difficult for lobbyists to know exactly where to seek help, and potentially easy for the administration to evade embarrassing questions and petitions. But until the later 1760's, the agents' freedom to petition

[14] George III to Bute, March 1763, *Letters from George III to Lord Bute, 1756–1766,* ed. Romney Sedgwick (London, 1939), pp. 202–203; XI Lawrence H. Gipson, *The British Empire before the American Revolution,* XI (New York, 1965), 38.

[15] William Bollan to Thomas Hubbard, April 12, 1759, MHS *Collections,* ser. 1, VI (Boston, 1800), 44–46; see also Bollan to Hubbard, May 12, 1758 (Misc. bound MSS, MHS), where the agent reports having to go from Treasury, to Paymaster General's Office, to War Office, to the house of the Secretary at War, to the Duke of Newcastle's house, back to the Treasury, the House of Commons, the Treasury again, the Commons again, and then to the Chancellor of the Exchequer, who placed the petition before the House!

[16] Dennys De Berdt to William Smith, May 18, 1766, "Letters of Dennys De Berdt, 1757–1770," ed. Albert Matthews, CSM *Publications,* XIII (1912), 316; Charles Garth to S.C. CC, May 31, 1767, SCHGM, XXIX, 128–129.

was largely uncomplicated by administrative niceties, and often the petitioner even found his efforts accelerated by cooperative civil servants.[17]

By the middle of the eighteenth century, the civil service could exert a significant influence upon both policy and legislation.[18] Because the King in Council could not possibly read and evaluate all the laws and petitions that came from the colonies, they had to be processed by the Board of Trade's secretary, clerks, and solicitor. Even then neither the commissioners nor the privy councillors could have digested the reports of their legal counsel. At best they could only consider aspects, otherwise relying on the judgment of subordinates.[19]

Colonial laws sent to England for approval reached the Board of Trade in several ways. They could be delivered to one of the secretaries of state, who would then either transmit them to the Board or place them before the Privy Council. In the latter case they were referred to the committee of the Council, which in turn passed them on to the Board of Trade. Because it was advantageous to get laws to the Privy Council as quickly as possible, the agents usually delivered them directly to the senior clerk there. Laws might also be taken directly to the Board of Trade; but this path was usually avoided because the commissioners could swallow and forget a law that had not first been to the Privy Council. If a law did not affect a particular department—customs, admiralty, Bishop of London—it was sent to a crown lawyer for his opinion, where it usually remained until someone paid him a fee and saw that he made his report. Otherwise it might remain in his hands for years. This was especially true of private bills.[20]

In 1718 a crown counsellor became the Board of Trade's legal adviser, and thereafter received all colonial legislation for appraisal before final consultation by the commissioners. Consequently an agent lobbying for confirmation of a law might begin his campaign

---

[17] *Acts of the Privy Council of England (Colonial Series)*, ed. W. L. Grant and J. Munro (London, 1908–1912), IV, 612.

[18] See Franklin B. Wickwire, "King's Friends, Civil Servants, or Politicians," *AHR*, LXXI (1965), 18–42.

[19] Richard Jackson to Jonathan Trumbull, Feb. 6, 1770, Trumbull MSS, III (i), 6a-d, CSL; Ross J. S. Hoffman, *Edmund Burke, New York Agent . . .* (Philadelphia, 1956), p. 78.

[20] Dickerson, *American Colonial Government*, pp. 264–266.

with the king's counsel; for the fate of an act depended very much upon his report. The Board of Trade, however, was too often dilatory, its legal adviser too slow in submitting his reports, and the time involved in communicating with agents or their colonies exasperatingly long. Matthew Lamb assumed the position in 1746 and held it until his death in 1768. The agents found him irascible on more than one occasion. Seeking approval for Massachusetts legislation in 1762, Jasper Mauduit waited on Lamb "to quicken his report upon those acts." The solicitor informed the agent that nothing could be done until the long Christmas holiday ended. Other representatives experienced interminably long operational delays on account of Lamb.[21]

Finally, a degree of incompetence must be included among the characteristics of Georgian bureaucracy. When Treasury grants were made to the colonies in 1761, the agents discovered so many mistakes in the warrants that it became necessary to issue new ones, which delayed the disbursement. All sorts of impediments arose to hinder the harried lobbyists: failure of a certain office to prepare a necessary letter, the loss of a document, the obstinacy of imperious nobles, or a lack of cooperation among governmental agencies.[22]

Nevertheless, in the later 1750's and early 1760's, the distribution of governmental positions for purposes of political influence probably did not reduce efficiency in the civil service as much as has been supposed. In many offices a great deal of work was accomplished, "even if it was not done by those who held the titular and highly paid responsibility." Although appointments were ordinarily made on the basis of influence rather than merit, large-scale changes did not usually follow political shifts. On the contrary, continuity of service was sometimes a problem, since a man customarily kept his place, "short of scandalous misbehavior, though he might grow too aged to write or to attend the office."[23]

---

[21] Charles M. Andrews, "The Royal Disallowance," AAS *Proceedings,* XXIV (1914), 342–362; Jasper Mauduit to ?, Dec. 27, 1762, MA, Letters, 1701–1763, p. 372; Joseph Sherwood to Samuel Smith, Sept. 7, 1763, Sherwood Letter-book, NJHS; "Matthew Lamb," *DNB.*

[22] William Bollan to Andrew Oliver, June 13 and July 11, 1761, MA, Letters, 1701–1763, pp. 333–336, 343; Richard Jackson to Andrew Oliver, Aug. 17 and Nov. 21, 1766, MA, Misc. Letters, 1763–1773, p. 146.

[23] J. Steven Watson, *The Reign of George III, 1760–1815* (Oxford, 1960), pp. 60–61.

A case in point is John Pownall, who served the Board of Trade for three decades, wielding considerable influence there by the 1760's. As secretary to the Board, he opened and read correspondence, prepared the agenda, drafted letters or representations, and prepared commissions and instructions for governors. Thus, in 1760, Cadwallader Colden maintained contact with Pownall because from him "the inclinations of the Board of Trade may be more easily learn'd than otherwise." [24] In 1745, Pownall, age twenty, became clerk of reports for the Board. By 1758 he achieved the secretaryship he coveted, and was regarded as the chief "back stair" access to Lord Halifax. He received considerable information and advice on the colonies from his "fraternal connection" Thomas Pownall, though during these years the two did not always share similar opinions about problems of colonial management. An American lobbyist reported in 1764 that Thomas' "Brother, Secretary pownal, Seems to be a very Good kind of a Man and has a Much Beter Carrector than the Governor." [25] John exemplified several of the characteristics of Sir Raffle Buffle, the civil servant caricatured by Trollope in *The Three Clerks*. Like Sir Raffle he was a bit pompous and—at times—inclined to inertia.

Pownall was undeniably important and often quite efficient. In 1763 he had a hand in drafting the Proclamation Line that would keep American settlers east of the Alleghenies. William Knox, who joined Pownall in the American Department in 1770, remarked that his colleague had "established the office so extremely well" that he found little room for subsequent improvement. In the years before and during the Stamp Act crisis, the agents found Pownall pliable. While he was not in full agreement with many colonial positions, Bollan, Thomlinson, Jasper Mauduit, Garth, and Jackson all reported Pownall's willingness to cooperate and dispense information relating to colonial business. In the decade after 1766 he became decreasingly

[24] Dickerson, *American Colonial Government*, pp. 76–78; Colden to Peter Collinson, Nov. 11, 1760, *Colden Letter Books* (NYHS *Collections for 1876*, Vol. I [New York, 1877]), p. 38; Wickwire, *British Subministers*, pp. 69–71, 73–76.

[25] Franklin B. Wickwire, "John Pownall and British Colonial Policy," 3*WMQ*, XX (1963), 543–554; John A. Schutz, *Thomas Pownall: British Defender of American Liberty* (Glendale, Calif., 1951), p. 233; George Croghan to Sir William Johnson, March 10, 1764, *The Critical Period, 1763–1765*, eds. C. W. Alvord and C. E. Carter (Springfield, Ill., 1905), pp. 223–224.

tractable and remained in office despite legs so crippled that he had to be helped from his chair.[26]

As a rule, then, governmental changes only meant that new appointments would be filled by friends of the new administration. A significant exception occurred in 1763, however, when a purge took place in the tax office. Although the men ousted were first given a chance to demonstrate loyalty, their dismissal seems to have been as much designed to eliminate useless men as to remove Newcastle's spies. In either case the event is significant, for it was part of a major overhaul of the Treasury Department's handling of colonial administration. In September 1763 the Treasury approved the appointment of a special clerk at the Customs House to receive dispatches from America, prepare replies, supervise the conduct of colonial officers, and make quarterly reports to the Treasury. The next month a new series of Treasury office records was established, called the "America Book." It brought together copies of documents that had previously been distributed among other classes of papers, and represented an attempt at tightening up the handling of colonial affairs in London.[27]

Significantly it was in the subsequent eighteen months that the agents encountered so much difficulty in opposing measures for America prepared at the Treasury. Partly the causes lay in new policy considerations, partly in the determination of a different ministry, and partly in a major shift in responsibility for provincial government from Whitehall to Parliament. Nonetheless, points of contact and methods of proceeding that had been familiar for decades disappeared at the Treasury in 1763, thereby complicating the task of lobbyists just when political changes were beginning to do so as well. The results would be far-reaching.

At the Board of Trade a similar change occurred in 1764, when an unusual directive required employee punctuality, attendance at John Pownall's behest, careful protection of books and papers, and scrutiny

[26] William Knox, *Extra Official State Papers* (London, 1789), I, 24; Bollan to James Otis, May 8, 1761, *Jasper Mauduit*, p. 18; James Nevin to Theodore Atkinson, Nov. 14, 1761, *The State of New Hampshire: Miscellaneous Provincial and State Papers 1725–1800*, ed. Isaac W. Hammond, XVIII (Manchester, N.H., 1890), 543; Richard Jackson to Francis Bernard, March 15, 1766, MA, XXII, 459.

[27] Dora Mae Clark, *The Rise of the British Treasury* (New Haven, 1960), pp. 126–127, 131; W. R. Ward, *The English Land Tax in the Eighteenth Century* (Oxford, 1953), pp. 118–119.

of all visitors to the clerk's room.[28] While this may have inconvenienced lobbyists somewhat, their duties were essentially unimpaired so long as the Board remained casual about the agents' credentials. Early in the eighteenth century, the commissioners had attempted to regulate the agents by requiring them to register their authorizations. Going a step farther, Whitehall then sought to fix a uniform procedure for the appointment of lobbyists. But for decades such controls were ignored or honored according to the dictates of convenience and the composition of the Board of Trade. In 1754 the Board reviewed the credentials of all the agents and called New York's method of appointing Robert Charles into question. Upon examination Charles responded with equivocal answers that nevertheless proved acceptable. The commissioners preferred not to notice the fact that Charles was agent for the Assembly and not the whole colony.[29]

In 1760 the Board reaffirmed its theory of the agent as a creature of the entire legislature; yet a year later it responded permissively to the confused circumstances in North Carolina surrounding the highly irregular selection of Cuchet Jouvencel. In 1765, Dennys De Berdt "was admitted, without the least question, as agent," although his credentials were from the House of Representatives only. William Bollan, dismissed by Massachusetts in 1762, continued to appear unimpeded at all the public offices with no authority whatever.[30] Soon after the Stamp Act crisis, however, the Board and the American Department showed a new and officious concern for the sanctity of some agents' appointments.

Three bureaucrats offered a characteristic and revealing observation in 1759: "In our practice we have not experienced any Inconveniency from the Laws as they now stand, and considering How long they have subsisted, We are apprehensive that any attempt to alter them for the sake of Correcting small Inaccuracies may be hazardous and attended with dangerous consequences not to be foreseen by Us." [31] As the Seven Years' War ended, the system of colonial administration

---

[28] *Journal of the Commissioners for Trade and Plantations from January 1764 to December 1767* (London, 1920–1938), pp. 107–108.

[29] Hoffman, *Burke*, pp. 20–21; Varga, "Charles," pp. 219–220.

[30] Board of Trade to Arthur Dobbs, April 14, 1761, Colonial Documents, 1761–1764, Bancroft Transcripts, NYPL; Bollan to Andrew Oliver, April 18, 1763, Dana MSS, 1764–1769, MHS; De Berdt to Edward Sheafe, Oct. 21, 1767, Matthews, "Letters of De Berdt," p. 327.

[31] G. Metcalfe, J. Tyton, H. Simon to ?, April 5, 1759, PRO T 1/392, ff. 41–43.

resembled a gnarled tree that had taken curious forms through decades of neglect. It may not have been symmetrical or elegant, but it
thrived. Belated attempts at pruning in the wrong season might simply kill the unruly branches and sap life from the trunk.

ACCESS, INFLUENCE, AND THE AGENTS

In the middle of the eighteenth century there was considerable
concern in Anglo-American thinking with political and governmental
equilibrium. This was the aim of "mixed government," and toward
achieving such an equilibrium men recognized that "certain modes of
non-legal influence were proper and necessary to maintain the balance." [32] Hence the important role of lobbyists, for example, and their
involvement in a system of public management that thrived on "connexion" and "interest." This circumstance of course placed the agent
in a delicate predicament, for he had to cultivate influence without
being compromised or sacrificing his independence. Especially in a
bureaucratic context, reliable acquaintances were required as sources
of information. Without them a lobbyist could hardly expedite the
passage of business through channels of government.

Fortunately for the agents, contacts before and during the Seven
Years' War might be found in any unit or level of the governmental
hierarchy. Edward Montagu relied on one of the Treasury lords, and
while Jasper Mauduit did too, he, Sherwood, and some of their colleagues also depended upon the secretaries to that board, senior clerks,
and subordinates. Similarly the lobbyists sought the assistance of
many different persons in Westminster. Bollan received information
and suggestions from the doorkeepers of both houses of Parliament,
from senior and assistant clerks in the Commons, as well as from
Members themselves. [33]

Most agents—particularly those properly considered Englishmen

---

[32] Samuel H. Beer, *Modern British Politics: A Study of Parties and Pressure
Groups* (London, 1965), p. 10.

[33] Montagu to Va. CC, Jan. 18, 1770, *Journals of the House of Burgesses of
Virginia*, ed. H. R. McIlwaine and J. P. Kennedy (Richmond, 1905–1913),
XII, xvii; Jasper Mauduit to Andrew Oliver, Aug. 8 and Dec. 10, 1763, MA,
XXII, 303–305, 332; Sherwood to Stephen Hopkins, Dec. 3, 1759, Jan. 31,
1760, May 30, 1761, *The Correspondence of the Colonial Governors of Rhode
Island, 1723–1775*, ed. G. S. Kimball (Boston, 1902–1903), II, 298, 303, 320;
William Bollan to Samuel Danforth, March 23 and June 23, 1769, May 19,
1770, *The Bowdoin and Temple Papers* (MHS *Collections*, ser. 6, Vol. IX
[Boston, 1897]), pp. 134, 147, 187.

—recognized the importance of cultivating connections at the lower and middling levels of the hierarchy. Seeking special compensation for Massachusetts in 1763, Jasper Mauduit went first to John Pownall, then to a member of the Board of Trade, then to George Grenville, and finally to Lord Halifax, the Secretary of State for the Southern Department.[34] The handful of agents who were truly colonials behaved somewhat differently and sometimes thoughtlessly. Coming from America they expected to go directly to the top, to what they regarded as the ultimate sources of political authority. They also wished to bypass departments they looked upon as corrupt. In some cases they seemed not to realize the significant role played by the civil servants. Whatever the cause they made a mistake. The administrative class had become a privileged caste with considerable power and access to the aristocracy. The "servants of power" were watchful of their status and resentful of attempts by provincials to circumvent the prescribed procedural paths. Ignoring the middle echelons could only serve to alienate potentially useful men.

Franklin was initially guilty of this myopia when he first arrived in 1757 and 1758. Having served as clerk of the assembly during his earlier career in Pennsylvania politics, he should have known where to solicit support. When Franklin first reached London, he immediately sought Pitt's friendship and favor, "but without Success. He was then too great a Man, or too much occupy'd in Affairs of greater Moment. I was therefore oblig'd to content myself with a kind of non-apparent and unacknowledged Communication thro' Mr. Potter and Mr. Wood, his Secretaries, who seem'd to cultivate an acquaintance with me by their Civilities, and draw from me what Information I could give." [35] Franklin's miscalculation may have been partially responsible for his initial lack of success, for as his friend John Fothergill noted in 1758: "B. Franklin has not yet been able to make much progress in his affairs. . . . Such is the unhappy turn of mind of most of those, who constitute the world of influence in this country." [36]

[34] Mauduit to Timothy Ruggles, Dec. 10, 1763, MHS *Collections*, ser. 1, VI (Boston, 1800), 189–191.

[35] William Samuel Johnson to Jedediah Elderkin, Jan. 23, 1768, Emmet Collection, NYPL; Franklin to William Franklin, March 22, 1775, Smyth, VI, 320; Franklin to Edward Tilghman *et al.*, Nov. 26, 1761, *The Papers of Benjamin Franklin,* ed. Leonard W. Labaree *et al.,* IX (New Haven, 1966), 389–390.

[36] Labaree, *Papers of Franklin,* VIII, 67 n. 9; Fothergill to Israel Pemberton, June 12, 1758, Etting Collection, Pemberton MSS, HSP.

Franklin learned a great deal about London lobbying merely by studying his opponents' tactics.[37] Hence he began to cultivate good working relationships with John Pownall and John Clevland, secretary to the Admiralty, and remarked that "by working with a Friend who has great Influence at the Board, [an agent] can serve the Province as effectually as by an open Reception and Appearance." By 1759, Franklin's access at the offices of the Board of Trade was quite free, so that he was "allow'd to search in the Press, containing the Plantation Acts, for the New-England Indian Trade Laws." His freedom of search, so important to an American lobbyist, would remain unimpaired for almost a decade.[38]

Franklin's predecessor and coagent, Richard Partridge, found his influence among men concerned with colonial administration quite strong in the 1750's. He too had no difficulty procuring documents and affidavits, partially because of his good relationship with clerks and secretaries at the Privy Council, the attorney general's office, and the offices of the secretaries of state. Partridge developed cordial ties with secretaries Henry Fox and Thomas Robinson, as well as with Halifax at the Board of Trade. And finally, his ability to work through strategically placed private individuals was also unimpaired until his death in 1759.[39]

The influence of Partridge's colleague William Bollan was equally strong in this period. His access to documents at the great boards was quite open, and his "researches" in state papers at the public offices were never impeded, in part because of his friendships with almost every civil servant whose work concerned the colonies. What is so striking, however, is the quality of Bollan's connections. These men notified him informally of information he might need and advised him on the best course of action to pursue. Moreover they sought and took his advice on matters involving the colonies.[40] At the higher levels

[37] Franklin to Isaac Norris, March 19, 1759, Labaree, *Papers of Franklin*, VIII, 294–296.

[38] Franklin to Joseph Galloway, April 7, 1759, to Isaac Norris, June 9, 1759, *ibid.*, VIII, 314–316, 397–400.

[39] Partridge to Stephen Hopkins, Aug. 8, 1755, to Jonathan Nichols *et al.*, Aug. 28, Sept. 6, and 10, 1755, to William Greene, Oct. 7, 1757, Kimball, *Correspondence of the Governors of Rhode Island*, II, 156, 161, 163–164, 169, 259; Partridge to Henry Fox, Nov. 18, 1755, to Thomas Fitch, Nov. 4, 1758, CHS *Collections* (Hartford, 1919), XVII, 183, 361.

[40] Bollan to Thomas Hubbard, March 12, 1757, Misc. bound MSS, MHS; Bollan to James West, Nov. 5, 1759, MA, CCLXXXVII, 173; Bollan to

Bollan's influence also was notable. He could rely particularly on the Speaker of the Commons, the Chancellor of the Exchequer, and Lord Sandys, who succeeded Halifax as First Lord of Trade in 1761.[41]

Bollan's successor, Jasper Mauduit, as we have seen, utilized connections at every level in the hierarchy, dispensing retainers in order to keep useful men favorably disposed to the Massachusetts interest. Their contemporaries, Jared Ingersoll, Edward Montagu, and John Thomlinson experienced similar ease of access until the Stamp Act crisis. For none of these men were there serious obstacles to obtaining documents, information, or advice from those who decided or managed the processes of colonial administration.[42]

Between 1755 and 1765 the agents generally improved their connections within the civil service. The latter, in turn—with the notable exception of the Treasury purge in 1763—remained relatively stable in these years despite the political tumultuousness that followed the rise of Pitt in 1757. The lobbyists' sources of authority and friendship were perhaps slightly stronger in Parliament than in Whitehall.[43] But that imbalance would be rectified with the accession of the Rockingham Whigs; so that in 1765–1766 the agents remained influential in Westminster and had even more authority with His Majesty's government. In this sense, the decade that followed the outbreak of the Seven Years' War witnessed a steady improvement in the agents' relations with those responsible for colonial administration.

Andrew Oliver, Nov. 16, 1759, March 20, 1760, *ibid.*, 174–175; Bollan to Joshua Sharpe, Jan. 11 and Feb. 16, 1760, Sharpe MSS, YUL; Bollan to ?, June 10, 1762, MA, Letters, 1701–1763, 356–359; and see Wickwire, *British Subministers*, p. 57.

[41] PRO T 1/392, ff. 41–43; Bollan to Thomas Hubbard, May 12, 1758, Misc. bound MSS, MHS; *Jasper Mauduit*, p. 15.

[42] Mauduit to James Bowdoin, Dec. 24, 1762, *Bowdoin and Temple Papers*, p. 12; Jared Ingersoll to William Pitt, March 4, 1760, PRO T 1/400; Ingersoll to Thomas Fitch, Aug. 10, 1761, CHS *Collections*, (Hartford, 1920), XVIII 137–142; Montagu to John Pownall, Nov. 17, 1763, PRO CO 5/1330, f. 133; James Nevin to Theodore Atkinson, Nov. 14, 1761, Hammond, *New Hampshire Provincial and State Papers*, XVIII, 543.

[43] Benjamin Franklin to Isaac Norris, March 19, 1759, Labaree, *Papers of Franklin,* VIII, 294–296.

CHAPTER 5

The Agents and Their Allies

If successful lobbying requires dependable connections within the formal structure of government, it also stands in need of informal allies. Such allies may be other interest groups currying favor, or private, nonpolitical elements in the society at large, or certain media of public communication—the press, for example. The colonial agents found all three of these types vital to their work; for in combination with the merchants trading to North America, the British dissenting societies, and the London publishers they might bring far more pressure to bear on government than they could alone.

COMMERCIAL COOPERATION

Colonial lobbyists traditionally sought—with varying degrees of success—a working relationship with the commercial classes at home. A number of the provincial representatives were themselves members of that community and at times provided an interlocking leadership for the combined groups. Each valued the other's cooperation. The merchants might work through the agents to settle accounts and ascertain colonial needs, while the agents enlisted their allies in pressuring Westminster or Whitehall. In colonial matters, eighteenth-century parliaments and governmental boards were quite sensitive to the views of the merchants. Where their interests came into conflict with those of the colonies, the agents sought to persuade the merchants that greater advantages would accrue from freer trade. Accommodation was reciprocally beneficial, since commerce formed a common bond between them, "the welfare, the paying capacity, and the goodwill of the colonial customers being an obvious concern of the British merchants." [1]

The North American agents and merchants had developed a sound relationship during the eighteenth century. Following 1715 a number of merchants seemed willing to serve as agents, and after the third decade of the century, agents were increasingly associated with the newly formed merchant clubs. The one enduring difficulty faced by the agent-merchant coalition was the occasional conflict of mercantile and colonial interests. British merchants might favor the regulation of colonial commercial development; but as individuals sympathetic to the economic health of America their position became ambivalent. The lobbyists' most serious challenge in this respect before 1764 was to reconcile the merchants to colonial acts spawning paper currency. The merchants feared losses from payment of debts in paper, which by depreciating the currencies effected unfair reductions in the claims of British creditors. In 1763–1764 a sufficient proportion of the mercantile community exerted influence that resulted in the restrictive Currency Act; the Board of Trade supported their complaint against quantities of paper money issued without provision for sufficient sinking and discharging funds.[2]

In 1764 the agents also encountered some difficulty persuading the merchants that Anglo-American trade could not tolerate the Sugar Act. The provincial representatives pointed out the impact the measure would have on colonial purchases in Britain and how it would spur American efforts at achieving self-sufficiency. But the merchants trading to North America did not fully cooperate until the effects of the subsequent colonial boycott were revealed on the countinghouse ledgers.[3]

[1] Ella Lonn, *The Colonial Agents of the Southern Colonies* (Chapel Hill, 1945), ch. 10; James J. Burns, *The Colonial Agents of New England* (Washington, D.C., 1935), pp. 136–145; Lewis B. Namier, "Charles Garth, Agent for South Carolina," *EHR,* LIV (1939), 637–638.

[2] Lawrence H. Gipson, "Virginia Planter Debts before the American Revolution," *VMHB,* LXIX (1961), 259–277; Burns, *Agents of New England,* pp. 136–137; Joseph H. Smith, *Appeals to the Privy Council from the American Plantations* (New York, 1950), p. 601. For the differences in 1764 between the agents and merchants on the question of paper money as legal tender for debts, see Jack M. Sosin, "Imperial Regulation of Colonial Paper Money, 1764–1773," *PMHB,* LXXXVIII (1964), 185.

[3] Burns, *Agents of New England,* p. 138; Alan Hardy, "The Duke of

Nevertheless, a basis for helpful interaction had developed during the Seven Years' War. The colonists acquired confidence in the reliance their representatives might place on the merchants, and such confidence was warranted. At war's end, when Charles Garth and other agents petitioned the Treasury and Board of Trade for a bounty on hemp grown in the colonies, each approached the merchants trading to his constituent colony. Cooperation ensued and the administration granted the request. Even the Currency Act as it finally appeared contained a compromise imposed upon Grenville's ministry by the agents in conjunction with a partial but powerful group of merchants trading to North America. The statute would prevent colonial legislation establishing paper bills with legal-tender status, but would not set a time limit to any issues then in circulation. During these months, Massachusetts's agents began cultivating a good relationship with the merchants trading to New England, as did the southern agents with merchants trading to the South. In the latter case, the key issue was the exportation of rice from the colonies to non-British ports. Garth and his associates gained the merchants' consent and maneuvered the desired bill through Parliament.[4]

In 1765, Grenville's administration prepared a mutiny bill that provided for billeting troops in private homes in America. Such a threat to their liberty agitated the colonists and their agents. Hence Franklin, Trecothick, Ingersoll, and Garth engaged the merchants' support, "leaving it to their discretion what steps they will choose to take." Garth met with a committee appointed by the merchants and explained the nature of the bill to them. In consequence, the merchants delegated one of their body, M. P. Richard Glover, to join the agents in interviewing the Secretary at War. Under the pressure of a two-hour session he agreed to act with Grenville to have the bill modified. Thus Shelburne remarked to Chatham a few years later that the mutiny bill "was altered by the merchants and agents, who substi-

---

Newcastle and His Friends in Opposition, 1762–65" (unpub. M.A. thesis; Manchester University, 1956), p. 252.

[4] Va. CC to Edward Montagu, Dec. 12, 1759, "Proceedings of the Virginia Committee of Correspondence, 1759–1767," *VMHB*, XI (1903), 3; Lewis B. Namier, *England in the Age of the American Revolution* (2nd ed.; London, 1961), pp. 251–253; Jasper Mauduit to Timothy Ruggles, Feb. 11, 1764, MA, XXII, 350–352; W. R. Savadge, "The West Country and the American Mainland Colonies, 1763–1783, with Special Reference to the Merchants of Bristol" (unpub. B.Litt. thesis; Oxford University, 1951), pp. 166–167; *JHC*, XXIX, 958, 980, 982, 1004, 1014.

tuted empty houses, provincial barracks, and barns." [5] Joseph Sherwood proclaimed to his constituents both the potency of a unified North American pressure group and its potential for the future. Taking note of the merchant-agent alliance to lower the molasses duty and abridge the powers of the vice-admiralty courts, he revealed that "the Agents, with the assistance of the Merchants of London, have made Strong and Vigorous Opposition, to the Unconstitutional and illegal measure of Quartering Troops in Private Familys." [6]

Early in 1765, Richard Jackson and coagent Jared Ingersoll separately remarked to Connecticut's Governor Fitch that the London merchants were alarmed at the strains recently placed on Anglo-American trade. As a result they had agreed to meet with the agents to "petition Parliament upon the Acts that respect the trade of North America." Jackson reported that he had "concerted some Measures for that purpose with some of the Principal Merchants of London, who all agree that their Returns from America are fallen very short." The winter of 1764–1765 had seen numerous instances of cooperation between agents and the committee of London merchants trading to America.[7]

The merchant community of Bristol was similarly active during the later fifties and early sixties. The Society of Merchant Venturers there had been relatively unconcerned about colonial problems until its members discovered that adverse ministerial measures were seriously affecting their profits. The stagnation of colonial trade prompted them to act vigorously in 1765 and 1766, so that the Bristol merchants played a major role in agitating for repeal of the Stamp Act. One of the key links in organizing both the London and Bristol merchants to support the colonies at this time was David Barclay, who obtained the help of the Linen Traders of London as well as the Society of Merchant Venturers.[8]

[5] *Lloyd's Evening Post and British Chronicle*, Aug. 16, 1765; Trecothick to Welbore Ellis, [1765?], Franklin MSS, APS; Jack M. Sosin, *Agents and Merchants: British Colonial Policy and the Origins of the American Revolution, 1763–1775* (Lincoln, Neb., 1965), p. 35; Edmond Fitzmaurice, *Life of William, Earl of Shelburne* (London, 1875–1876), II, 43.

[6] Sherwood to Stephen Hopkins, April 11 and May 2, 1765, Letters, VII, 12–13, RIA.

[7] Ingersoll to Fitch, Feb. 11, 1765, NHCHS *Papers*, IX (New Haven, 1918), 314, 332, 335; Jackson to Fitch, Feb. 9, 1765, CHS *Collections*, XVIII (Hartford, 1920), 317.

[8] *Politics and the Port of Bristol in the Eighteenth Century*, ed. W. E.

The narrative of the repeal movement is a familiar one, as is that of the merchant-agent coalition responsible for its success.[9] The intensive series of consultations in January 1766 prompted Joseph Sherwood to commend "the Vigorous application and Interest of the London Merchants." In February and March agents and merchants continued to meet together and confer with prominent politicians. Out of these sessions emerged a profusion of petitions and accommodations, including the support of the West Indians, whose cooperation at a crucial moment was graphically recorded in a note from one of Newcastle's subordinates in the Commons. James West reported watching "Tregothick [*sic*], Hanbury & a great number of merchants with the agents full of thanks in the Lobby." The merchant members of the House of Commons were prominent among the advocates of repeal; only six out of fifty-two voted against abolishing the Stamp Act.[10]

POLITICS AND DISSENT

The legal status of dissenters in Britain changed gradually during the eighteenth century. The Toleration Act of 1689 allowed Trinitarians willing to accept thirty-five of the Thirty-nine Articles to preach and teach freely if they obtained a license. These conditions were not carefully enforced, however, and were abolished in 1779. Similarly, nonconformists were, at least theoretically, excluded from public office and the universities; but these restrictions were also ignored when expedient. The more ardent dissenters—a minority—resented their role as second-class citizens, built up a life and culture of their own, and sought to change their condition by legal means. The majority, however, increasingly prosperous and respectable, were anxious to minimize their reputation as radicals. Only a few were of such delicate conscience that largely theoretical discriminations would bother them. Therefore a great many dissenters did not support the politically active minority.[11]

Minchinton (*Bristol Record Society Publication*, Vol. XXIII [Bristol, 1963]), pp. xxx–xxxi; Anne T. Gary, "The Political and Economic Relations of English and American Quakers (1750–1785)" (unpub. D.Phil. thesis; Oxford University, 1935), p. 244 and n. 2.

[9] Allen S. Johnson, "British Politics and the Repeal of the Stamp Act," *South Atlantic Quarterly*, LXII (1963), 169–188.

[10] Sherwood to Samuel Smith, Jan. 11, 1766, NJHS *Proceedings*, V (Newark, 1851), 150; PRO 30/8/97, ff. 47–48; West to Newcastle, Feb. 7, 1766, Add MSS 32973, f. 377.

[11] Caroline Robbins, *The Eighteenth-Century Commonwealthman: Studies*

Nevertheless that minority attracted considerable attention, largely because of its publications and organizations, especially the Protestant Dissenting Deputies. Through pamphlets, membership ties, and mutual assistance, many colonial dissenters became involved in the activities and concerns of their British brethren. During the first half of the eighteenth century, a trans-Atlantic community of interest developed that flourished unevenly during the fifth, sixth, and seventh decades. Provincial Congregationalists, Presbyterians, and Baptists might seek money, books, or advice from the Dissenting Deputies or the New England Company, or assistance in licensing dissenting meeting-houses in Virginia or in preventing the establishment of an American bishop. London groups were willing to help as best they could, although in actual fact their influence was not as strong in the 1750's and 1760's as Americans thought. The fifties were fairly quiet years for English dissent, and the subsequent decade, while more active, was perhaps superficially so.[12] It is true that many leaders of the reform movements were dissenters and that they had learned techniques of political agitation and lobbying. But they were largely intellectuals: readers, writers, and subscribers to journals and societies. "Industry and commerce could absorb their energies," Caroline Robbins has shown, "and charitable foundations their largesse." Their influence was not considerable, especially when politics were unstable.[13]

Given the various successes that British nonconformists did achieve for their American friends, however, and given the Whiggish allegiance they shared, it was not surprising that colonists and their agents began to turn increasingly to prominent dissenters for influence in

---

in the *Transmission, Development, and Circumstance of English Liberal Thought from the Restoration of Charles II until the War with the Thirteen Colonies* (Cambridge, Mass., 1959), pp. 223, 232; J. Steven Watson, "Dissent and Toleration," *Silver Renaissance,* ed. Alex Natan (London, 1961), p. 9.

[12] Norman C. Hunt, *Two Early Political Associations: The Quakers and the Dissenting Deputies in the Age of Sir Robert Walpole* (Oxford, 1961); Maurice W. Armstrong, "The Dissenting Deputies and the American Colonies," *Church History,* XXIX (1960), 298–320; Richard B. Barlow, *Citizenship and Conscience: A Study in the Theory and Practice of Religious Toleration in England during the Eighteenth Century* (Philadelphia, 1962), p. 131.

[13] Robbins, *Eighteenth-Century Commonwealthman,* p. 258; William Kellaway, *The New England Company, 1649–1776: Missionary Society to the American Indians* (Glasgow, 1961), pp. 171–172, 177, 181–195.

London.[14] Like the cooperation of agents and merchants, the representatives of the Meeting for Sufferings combined with such Quaker agents as Partridge and Sherwood provided a coordinated pressure group. The Hanburys, Barclays, and Collinsons, all dissenting merchants in London, cooperated with the lobbyists and were invaluable because of their experience in dealing with the Treasury, the Board of Trade, and even Parliament directly.[15]

By midcentury the two institutional elements had joined hands. Alarm at the prospect of an American bishop in 1749 caused the Protestant Dissenting Deputies to combine with the colonial agents "to prevent the said Scheme taking Effect." In 1750, in response to a letter from the Committee of Ministers at Boston, the Deputies set up a special committee, including Israel Mauduit and Dennys De Berdt, "to prevent all Encroachments upon the Religious Rights of the people there." By the later fifties this alliance had been firmly welded and the threat of episcopacy temporarily averted. Throughout the decade the Mauduit brothers and De Berdt remained publicly active on behalf of colonial dissenters and developed reputations, particularly in Massachusetts.[16]

Ever since Increase Mather's agency in 1689 and 1690, when the Puritan was endorsed by English dissenters and acquired strong attachments to them, the Bay Colony had cultivated religious bonds in London. By 1762 the Congregationalists urgently wished to achieve two major goals: prevent Governor Bernard from chartering a new college in Hampshire County, and gain incorporation for the new Society for the Propagation of Christian Knowledge among the Indians of North America. Therefore they gave serious consideration to replacing Bollan with an influential dissenter, especially since the advocates of a western college were already working through dissenters in London. In July 1762, Thomas Hollis, a wealthy dissenter and publicist, wrote to his friend Jonathan Mayhew in Boston, recommending Jasper Mauduit as the best person to oppose the plan for an

---

[14] See Leonard J. Trinterud, *The Forming of an American Tradition: A Re-examination of Colonial Presbyterianism* (Philadelphia, 1949), p. 232.

[15] Bernard Manning, *The Protestant Dissenting Deputies* (Cambridge, 1952), pp. 408, 410, 417, 420–421; G. H. Guttridge, *English Whiggism and the American Revolution* (Berkeley, Calif., 1942), p. 3; Gary, "Relations of English and American Quakers," p. 52.

[16] Carl Bridenbaugh, *Mitre and Sceptre: Transatlantic Faiths, Ideas, Personalities, and Politics, 1689–1775* (New York, 1962), pp. 91–92, 95–99, 110, 133.

American bishop as well as the college in Hampshire County. Hollis regarded Mauduit as "a leader among the dissenters, and in connection with people in power." [17]

It is not too surprising, then, that in 1762 the General Court voted to replace Bollan with Mauduit. Although it represented a factional victory, the decision seemed sensible in many respects. While Bollan had been a good agent, he was an Anglican. With the threat of a colonial bishop and the newly active Society for Propagation of the Gospel moving swiftly in New England, the fear arose that Bollan would be unable to defend colonial rights if they conflicted with the designs of the Church. Jasper Mauduit, on the other hand, seemed the perfect alternative. Acting chairman of the Dissenting Deputies and treasurer of the New England Company, he was the father-in-law of Thomas Wright, also a politically active and important dissenter, and brother of Israel Mauduit, well-known pamphleteer, well-connected placeman, and prominent among nonconformists as well. [18]

Within a year the Otis faction in Massachusetts realized it had made a mistake. Jasper presided over a meeting of the P.D.D. in 1762, when the letter from Boston seeking help against the Church of England was read. Yet he could not bring himself to support the provincials' plans. Instead he wrote to his constituents of the "impropriety of my Solliciting Subscriptions [for incorporation of the S.P.C.K.I.N.A.], when I am myself not only a member, but Treasurer of another more antient Society [the New England Company], founded on a Royal Charter, and established for the promoting the very same end and purpose with this new one." Incorporation was in fact not achieved, but more perhaps because of the Mauduits' lack of enthusiasm, rather than—as Israel claimed—the mild opposition of the bishops. [19]

[17] Cotton Mather, *Parentator* (Boston, 1724), pp. 159–160; Henry Lefavour, "The Proposed College in Hampshire County in 1762," MHS *Proceedings*, LXVI (Boston, 1942), 53–79.

[18] Robert E. Brown, *Middle-Class Democracy and the Revolution in Massachusetts, 1691–1780* (Ithaca, 1955), p. 184; Robert J. Taylor, "Israel Mauduit," *NEQ*, XXIV (1951), 208–230; Jasper Mauduit to Andrew Oliver, Nov. 19, 1762, MA, Letters, 1701–1763, p. 422.

[19] P.D.D. Minute Book, Vol. I, f. 460, MS 3083, GLL; Jasper Mauduit to H. Gray, Oct. 27, 1762, MA, LVI, 407–408; Israel Mauduit to Jonathan Mayhew, April 8, 1763, Mayhew Papers, no. 67, Bortman MSS, Boston University. For Jasper Mauduit's assessment of the reasons for failure, see his letter to James Bowdoin, April 7, 1763, *The Bowdoin and Temple Papers* (MHS *Collections*, ser. 6, Vol. IX [Boston, 1897]), pp. 14–16.

Mauduit's constituents soon became uneasy about their agent. John Adams observed in his diary in 1763 "the unfitness of Mr. Mauduit to represent this Province at the British court, both in point of age and knowledge. He is . . . seventy years old; an honest man, but avaricious; a woolen draper, a mere cit." Thomas Hutchinson confided to Richard Jackson later that year that "from what I had heard of Mr. Mauduit for several years past I had formed the same opinion with you that he was a very honest man but had no other qualifications for an Agent." [20]

Although Jasper had been recommended to Jonathan Mayhew in 1762 by Thomas Hollis, the great benefactor changed his mind a year later when he cryptically requested "that in the future You do not put me into any sort of connection *whatsoever,* with Mr. Agent Mauduit, or with his Brother once the Reverend Mr. Israel Mauduit," a request he emphatically repeated the following year.[21] In 1763 the General Court had empowered Israel to act as agent whenever his brother was unable to. On the surface Israel's credentials were excellent. Jeremiah Dyson, one of the lords of trade, was his "intimate Acquaintance," along with Charles Jenkinson, secretary to the Treasury. Mauduit was also close with Jenkinson's Treasury colleague, Thomas Whately, and their counterpart at the Board of Trade, John Pownall. In addition, Israel was in contact with the Yorke-Hardwicke connection, and with Charles Townshend. Despite Mauduit's dissenting activities, he even had close friends prominent in the Anglican S.P.G., who kept him informed in minute detail of conferences and strategies fomented there.[22]

But one so well connected found it too easy to use his abilities and friendships for personal gain. The famous attack on Pitt in 1760, *Considerations on the Present German War,* was "written by one

[20] *The Works of John Adams,* ed. Charles F. Adams (Boston, 1850), II, 141; Hutchinson to Jackson, Aug. 3, 1763, MA, XXVI, 64–66.

[21] Hollis to Mayhew, July 28, 1762, Dec. 6, 1763, Aug. 28, 1764, "Thomas Hollis and Jonathan Mayhew, Their Correspondence, 1759–1766," ed. Bernhard Knollenberg, MHS *Proceedings,* LXIX (1956), 131, 142, 155; Francis Blackburne, *Memoirs of Thomas Hollis* (London, 1780), I, 252–253.

[22] Israel Mauduit to [Andrew Oliver?], March 3, 1764, MA, LVI, 412–413; Jasper Mauduit to [Oliver?], March 13, 1764, MA, XXII, 359; Jasper Mauduit to ?, Dec. 31, 1762, MA, Letters, 1701–1763, p. 373; Israel Mauduit to Mayhew, April 8 and Aug. 8, 1763, Mayhew Papers, nos. 67, 72, Bortman MSS, Boston University.

Mauduit, who when Lord Bute came into power, was rewarded with a good place for his services." [23] When Bute's ministry gave way to others, Israel continued to accumulate sinecures. In addition to being customer of Southampton, he acquired from Grenville the crown agency for Newfoundland, Cape Breton, and Nova Scotia, worth £300 annually and requiring no work. He retained this place through most of his remaining years. In short, Israel Mauduit was compromised as a lobbyist even before he began as coagent. This is surely what Hollis discovered during the winter of 1763, when his principle of apolitical behavior prevented him from communicating his mistrust explicitly to his friends in Massachusetts.[24]

Despite its difficulties with the Mauduits, the General Court kept them almost two years longer. There was still "a great hankering after a dissenter for an Agent," however, and in 1765, De Berdt and Jackson were named.[25] De Berdt's qualifications were almost as imposing as Mauduit's, for he too was deeply involved in the activities of the Dissenting Deputies and the New England Company. More important, De Berdt would use his religious persuasion to benefit his employers, for his faith brought him close to an enthusiast of considerable importance, Lord Dartmouth.[26]

The accession of De Berdt and Jackson augmented Massachusetts' interest in London when it counted most—the months before the Stamp Act crisis reached its climax. Jackson's parallel agencies for Massachusetts, Connecticut, and Pennsylvania linked the three colonies that relied most heavily on nonconformists in London for political assistance.[27] In all three cases the support was quite often substantial but at other times illusory. The Penns, for example, were as capable of

---

[23] [John Almon], *The History of the Minority; During the Years 1762, 1763, 1764, and 1765 . . .* (London, 1766), p. 13; Horace Walpole, *Memoirs of the Reign of King George III*, ed. C. F. Bucker (New York, 1894), I, 25.

[24] *Gentleman's Magazine*, XXXIII (1763), 98; PRO T 60/22, Order Book (1762–1767), p. 221; PRO T 60/23, Order Book (1766–1772), p. 25; PRO T 60/24, Order Book (1772–1780), p. 90; *The Royal Kalendar & Court & City Register* (London, 1774), p. 278; *JHC*, XXXII, 552, 561, 569, 578.

[25] Francis Bernard to Richard Jackson, Dec. 18, 1762, Bernard MSS, II, 240–243, HLHU; Bernard to Jackson, Jan. 23, 1763, *ibid.*, pp. 248–257.

[26] P.D.D. Minute Book, Vol. I, ff. 444, 467, 497, MS 3083, GLL; Dartmouth to Dennis De Berdt, July 22, 1766, HMC *14th Report, Appendix, Part X, The Manuscripts of the Earl of Dartmouth*, II (*American Papers*) (London, 1895), 47.

[27] See Chapter 2, note 13, above.

working through English Presbyterians as their opponents were of working through London Friends.[28]

The English community of nonconformists before 1766 was an elusive interest that might help or hinder the colonists and their representatives. In the middle decades of the century, effective engines of political action developed in London among the dissenters. But by the early sixties, with Dr. Benjamin Avery ill, the Deputies no longer played an active and positive part in colonial affairs. Moreover their energies were now absorbed by a long and costly litigation before the House of Lords which won them exemption from serving in "burdensome offices in corporations." Fortunately for colonial nonconformity, "other and more useful means of intelligence and sturdy support came from England at critical times in the 1760's." [29] The successes achieved in Anglo-American ecclesiastical lobbying in the 1750's would not easily be continued in the subsequent decade. The major reason is clear—"during the early part of the reign of George III . . . political activity for and by dissenters was negligible." Professor Robbins' remark may be overstated, but it is correct in its essentials. Fortunately for the colonists, the middle and later sixties witnessed a resurgence of nonconformist strength in politics. By no coincidence, these were also among the agents' most effective years.[30]

THE FOURTH ESTATE

The newspapers and pamphlets that proliferated in the eighteenth century were useful in promoting colonial attitudes in Britain. Franklin, one of the greatest controversialists of his age, recognized the tremendous power of the pen in a neat apothegm: Through the instrument of the press one could not only "strike while the iron is hot," but "heat it continually by striking." Because lobbyists were propagandists, it becomes necessary to examine the uses they made of the press as well as the nature of their relationship to the publishers and booksellers of London. First one ought to consider the gazettes, for "at least ninety-nine hundredth parts of the people," remarked one agent, "take their opinions from the papers." [31]

[28] Mabel P. Wolff, *The Colonial Agency of Pennsylvania, 1712–1757* (Philadelphia, 1933), pp. 181, 185.

[29] Bridenbaugh, *Mitre and Sceptre*, pp. 183–184; Barlow, *Citizenship and Conscience*, p. 135.

[30] Robbins, *Eighteenth-Century Commonwealthman*, p. 258; Barlow, *Citizenship and Conscience*, ch. 4.

[31] Arthur M. Schlesinger, *Prelude to Independence: The Newspaper War on*

In the third quarter of the eighteenth century, English journalism underwent a transition of significance to contemporary publicists. Until the 1760's, His Majesty's government had exercised a strict authority that pervasively dulled the printed word as a weapon for political minorities. To keep an eye on the London journalists, administrations employed various clerks, spies, and coffeehouse runners known as "messengers of the press." The Treasury hired several to secure all political pamphlets, magazines, and broadsides. These men provided a direct link between the government and contemporary channels of communication. Together with the king's messengers-in-ordinary, they scrutinized masks of anonymity in order to arraign audacious writers and printers.[32]

Publishers with a taste for security, therefore, "were very chary of placing their imprints" imprudently. They had to guard carefully against libel suits; and no one could be perfectly certain what the administration and law courts would consider improper. "There is such a backwardness, or rather shyness, in the others who can write," John Almon reported in 1764, "that nothing has been done." He added that a "terrible panic" had "seized all the printers and publishers both in and out of the City." Pamphlets continued to appear against the budget, general warrants, and other issues of ministerial policy; but the opposition weeklies were virtually ended.[33] Soon, however, a thaw became apparent.

The Gazetteer and New Daily Advertiser, published by Charles Say, was the first daily paper to print speeches and accounts of parliamentary debates with some regularity. It was considered a liberal organ, and Franklin favored it during the sixties with many of his essays.[34] *The Public Advertiser* may have been the finest paper of its day. Editor Henry Sampson Woodfall called it "a Cockpit for Political Spurring," and Franklin and later Arthur Lee used it a great deal as a

Britain, 1764–1776 (New York, 1958), p. 46; Robert R. Rea, "Bookseller as Historian," *Indiana Quarterly for Bookmen*, V (1949), 76–77.

[32] Robert R. Rea, *The English Press in Politics, 1760–1774* (Lincoln, Neb., 1963), p. 9; H. R. Fox Bourne, *English Newspapers* (London, 1887), I, 177–178, 234.

[33] R. A. Austen-Leigh, "William Strahan and His Ledgers," *Transactions of the Bibliographical Society*, ser. 2, III (1923), 262; Almon to Lord Temple, Nov. 12, 1764, *The Grenville Papers*, ed. W. J. Smith (London, 1852–1853), II, 457–460; Walpole, *Memoirs of the Reign of George III*, II, 3–9.

[34] R. L. Haig, *The Gazetteer, 1735–1797* (Carbondale, Ill., 1960), 89, 143; *American Archives*, comp. Peter Force (Washington, D.C., 1837–1846), ser. 4, II, 848–849.

forum. Caleb Whitefoorde, a wine merchant and one of the proprietors of this daily, lived close by Franklin in Craven Street. Often the Doctor passed his essays through his neighbor's hands en route to Woodfall's desk.[35] *St. James's Chronicle,* an opposition evening journal utilized by the agents, was printed by Henry Baldwin at the Britannia Printing Office in Fleet Street.[36]

In search of American news, reprints from the colonial gazettes, and the controversies stimulated by the agents, one might conveniently go to a coffeehouse to pick up any of these newspapers. On the first page, amidst a clutter of advertisements, the layout always provided some political "Letters to the Printer"—a customary vehicle for the lobbyists. Turning to the second or third page, one found the vital pulse of the paper—"London Intelligence"—where all manner of information, notices, and rumors appeared. Merchants, agents, and others interested in American affairs might be advised that their petition would be ready for signing at a notary's in Cornhill on a certain day at a given time.[37]

Among all the agents Franklin was supremely successful in utilizing the newspapers. During the years of his first agency, in fact, he was almost the only one to do so to any significant extent. Even then he showed an awareness of the larger issues that would increasingly trouble the colonies and the Empire. His first essay in 1758 treated the question of Pennsylvania's proprietorship; but the next seven were more general, concerning the war, colonial defense efforts, British peace advocates, the Canadian question, and related problems. Beginning in 1758, Franklin cooperated with coagent Robert Charles and with Richard Jackson in preparing pieces for the newspaper.[38]

William Strahan, the round-faced Scot who printed the *Chronicle,* was one of Franklin's most important connections in London. In addition to influencing the contents of a major paper for which Franklin wrote, he also printed Ralph Griffith's *Monthly Review,* the literary magazine most sympathetic to America and to Franklin personally.

[35] *Benjamin Franklin's Letters to the Press, 1758–1775,* ed. Verner W. Crane (Chapel Hill, 1950), pp. xvi, xx; *The Whitefoord Papers . . . ,* ed. W. A. S. Hewins (Oxford, 1898), pp. 141–142.

[36] Verner W. Crane, "Certain Writings of Benjamin Franklin on the British Empire and the American Colonies," *Papers of the Bibliographical Society,* XXVIII (1934), 14; Stanley Morison, *The English Newspaper* (Cambridge, Eng., 1932), p. 153.

[37] Morison, *The English Newspaper,* pp. 148, 163; *St. James's Chronicle,* Feb. 1–3, 1770.

[38] Crane, *Franklin's Letters to the Press,* pp. xi–xix; Smyth, III, 443–445.

No wonder the Scot found that his work afforded him "many Opportunities of Information with respect to what is doing at home as well as in America." While Franklin was still in Philadelphia in 1764, he sent documents to Strahan for publication, such as the Assembly Resolves that had been published in the *Pennsylvania Gazette*. When the Doctor returned to London for his second mission, he and Strahan resumed their close professional and personal association.[39]

Because of pressures from Whitehall, the agents were restricted in stating the American case in English newspapers before 1765. The campaigns of that year and 1766, however, helped usher in a new era in political journalism wherein liberties previously unknown would be allowed to opponents of governmental policy.[40] Franklin, of course, was partly responsible for this change. Lobbying against the Mutiny Act early in 1765, he probably authored the anonymous protest of the North American agents that appeared in the *Gazetteer*, as well as two expostulations signed "An American" that ran in *St. James's Chronicle* in April. That fall he began a hectic publicity campaign against the Stamp Act. Through Strahan's assistance he published in the *London Chronicle* excerpts from his colonial correspondence (with identities suppressed). During the subsequent winter, Franklin emitted a barrage of his own material as well as extracts of letters from articulate provincials.[41] His colleagues among the agents also began to use the press increasingly in the early sixties, although many of them preferred the pamphlet—a more sustained effort that might attract wider attention.

The printers and booksellers of London were a social group vitally important to those lobbyists engaged in propagandizing through the journals and ephemeral books of the day. Which publishers then

[39] J. A. Cochrane, *Dr. Johnsons' Printer: The Life of William Strahan* (Cambridge, Mass., 1964), pp. 105–106; Strahan to Franklin, May 4, [1765?], Pierpont Morgan Library, New York City; Franklin to Strahan, May 16, 1767, Pierpont Morgan Library; John E. Pomfret, "Some Further Letters of William Strahan, Printer," *PMHB*, LX (1936), 478.

[40] The change was notable, but hardly warrants James Burns' exaggeration that "the agents flooded the papers and presses . . . with a series of letters and pamphlets" (*Agents of New England*, p. 115). P. D. G. Thomas, "The Beginning of Parliamentary Reporting in Newspapers, 1768–1774," *EHR*, LXXIV (1959), 623–636.

[41] *Gazetteer*, May 2, 1765; Crane, *Franklin's Letters to the Press*, pp. xlviii, 294; Franklin to Charles Thomson, Feb. 27, 1766, Smyth, IV, 411; Strahan to David Hall, Jan. 11, 1766, *PMHB*, X (1886), 92.

would undertake the writings of the agents? Where could they be found? How dependable were they? And how effective were the lobbyists as pamphleteers?

The Chapter Coffee-house was sacred to London's booksellers and publishers. They met there to buy and sell copyrights and stock, or arrange to share the risk of a new venture. An agent anxious to disseminate his pamphlet or have one from America reprinted would go to the Chapter in search of a printer absent from his shop. Franklin might send an errand boy there to find James Brotherton or John Sewall, partners who undertook several books dealing with the colonies. William Bollan or Jasper Mauduit might inquire after William Nicoll, who did work for these two agents in 1765 and 1766. Bollan, however, most preferred his neighbor, Samuel Baker, located nearby in Covent Garden. A book auctioneer and publisher, Baker handled essays for Bollan in 1762, 1764, and 1766. Thereafter Bollan relied on William Owen at Homer's Head, near the Temple Bar, or John Williams, next to the Mitre Tavern in Fleet Street. Williams supported John Wilkes, sold copies of the *North Briton*, and was perpetually in legal perplexities between 1765 and 1774. In 1766 he reprinted and sold James Otis' *The Rights of the British Colonies Asserted and Proved*.[42]

In the 1760's, Franklin turned to Thomas Becket's printing house at Tully's Head in the Strand, as well as John Wilkie's at "the Bible" in St. Paul's Church Yard. Wilkie, publisher of the *London Chronicle* and *The Bee*, did work for Franklin in 1765 and after. Becket brought before the public essays by Franklin in 1760, 1764, and 1766.[43] For much of their contact with the public, Franklin and Bollan relied on John Almon, one of the most important publishers of his day. Beginning as a journeyman printer in 1759, he quickly made a reputation in London. During the Seven Years' War, Almon published a review of Pitt's administration which he dedicated to Lord Temple. An introduction and patronage ensued for Almon, and through Temple he came to know Newcastle, Rockingham, and other Whig leaders. By

[42] Walter Besant, *London in the Eighteenth Century* (London, 1902), p. 315; H. R. Plomer, *A Dictionary of the Printers and Booksellers Who Were at Work in England . . . from 1726 to 1775* (Oxford, 1932), pp. 36, 187–188, 264–265; Fox Bourne, *English Newspapers*, I, 177–178.

[43] Plomer, *Dictionary of the Printers*, pp. 20, 264; Franklin to Becket, Dec. 17, 1763, Columbia University Library; Franklin's MS Ledger, 1764–1775, *passim*, APS.

the war's end, trusted implicitly by Temple, Almon visited frequently at Pall Mall. In 1761 the printer of the *Gazetteer* engaged him to run that paper. Two years later Almon established himself opposite Burlington House in Piccadilly and received the blessing of the opposition club, the "coterie," as their bookseller.[44]

He was also quite cordial to the American agents, publishing for Franklin in 1765 and after, as well as for Bollan. William Knox recognized that Almon was "an excellent fellow at circulating a work, and understands all the mystery of raising its character and exciting purchasers." The Piccadilly printer had standing orders from many Members of Parliament to send them whatever appeared during the parliamentary recess. He also had an uncanny eye for the proper moment to distribute an essay in order to make it most effective. "Mr. Almon, who is a thorough judge of times and seasons for publication, does not intend to publish . . . 'till the return from Newmarket races," Knox noted, "when many persons from different parts of the Kingdom pass through London." Like most contemporary lobbyists, Knox knew the best time to publish—just before Parliament opened.[45] Almon apportioned quite a few essays by colonials to William Strahan for printing, such as the order for 1,250 copies of the *Farmer's Letters*. Strahan independently contracted to publish other works produced by the agents.[46]

When Charles Dilly completed his apprenticeship in 1764, he sailed for America to establish connections with colonial booksellers for his brother Edward. Located in the City near the Mansion House, the Dillys gained prominence through their colonial trade. Before the Revolution they republished or sold a large number of provincial books on the British market. Edward, a supporter of Wilkes, was known in America as a publisher for nonconformist writers, particularly those from Boston and Philadelphia. Whereas Charles was interested in Americans for business reasons, Edward welcomed their ac-

---

[44] Almon to Lord Temple, Aug. 14 and Nov. 12, 1764, June 15 and 23, 1765, Grenville MSS in the possession of Sir John Murray, box B-1; Plomer, *Dictionary of the Printers*, p. 4; Rea, "Bookseller as Historian," pp. 75–95.

[45] Knox to George Grenville, Oct. 18, 1769, *Grenville Papers*, IV, 469; Knox to Grenville, July 23 and Oct. 4, 1768, Add MSS 42086, ff. 70–71, 369.

[46] Small Ledger and Commonplace book of William Strahan, 1752–1768, Add MSS 48802, ff. 34, 38, 66, 71, 76; Quarto Ledger of Strahan, 1768–1785, Add MSS 48803, ff. 20, 26, 47; entries for March 30 and June 4, 1765, Franklin's MS Ledger, 1764–1775, APS.

quaintance out of political inclination. He often received the agents in his home as guests.[47]

As important as these printers and sellers were, however, it was still the lobbyists who were responsible for preparing the basic materials. As early as 1731, when the molasses bill was under consideration in the Commons, each M.P., upon entering the House, received a copy of *The Case of the British Sugar Colonies,* drafted by the Barbados agents, and a copy of *The Case of the British Northern Colonies,* prepared by the North American agents.[48] Nevertheless the custom of pamphleteering by agents developed slowly. Friends of Pennsylvania in London lamented the fact that no one in the earlier 1750's answered the proprietary pamphlets critical of the Quaker Party and the Assembly.[49] Franklin's arrival in 1757 marked a significant change in this respect. Cooperating with Strahan, he secured the publication of Charles Thomson's *Enquiry into the Causes of the Alienation of the Delaware and Shawanese Indians,* a sharp attack on proprietary injustices to the Indians, which received wide circulation in England.[50]

Franklin, Charles, and Jackson were well aware of the value of publicity and the importance of timing it properly.[51] Soon after he reached London, Franklin joined with Jackson to prepare a major work designed to eliminate the Penns and proprietary government from Pennsylvania. In June 1759 it appeared, produced by Strahan, under the title *An Historical Review of the Constitution and Government of Pennsylvania.* Though Jackson wrote the large volume in its final form, Franklin, Charles and even William Franklin contributed necessary information about Pennsylvania's history. It was expedient that the authorship not obviously be that of the Pennsylvania agent; but for political reasons Jackson did not want to have sole responsibility for the work either. Hence the uncertainty associated with its authorship. In part it was intended as a reply to William Smith's *Brief State of the Province of Pennsylvania,* which had successfully aroused

---

[47] S. H. Bingham, "Publishing in the Eighteenth Century with Special Reference to the Firm of Edward and Charles Dilly" (unpub. Ph.D. diss.; Yale University, 1937), pp. 4, 7, 9, 100–101.

[48] Wolff, *Agency of Pennsylvania,* p. 45.   [49] *Ibid.,* p. 195.

[50] William S. Hanna, *Benjamin Franklin and Pennsylvania Politics* (Stanford, 1964), p. 128.

[51] Franklin to Thomas Leech *et al.,* June 10, 1758, *The Papers of Benjamin Franklin,* ed. Leonard W. Labaree *et al.,* VIII (New Haven, 1965), 88–89.

English opinion against the Quaker government in Pennsylvania. Jackson's work was equally partisan, and Franklin hoped it would "put a finishing stroke to the Prejudices that have prevailed against us and set the Proprietary Character and Conduct in their proper Lights."[52]

The next year Franklin and Jackson continued their collaboration, preparing *The Interest of Great Britain Considered*, which Thomas Becket undertook to print. During the movement for repeal of the Stamp Act, Franklin recast the arguments of this essay to suit the needs of the new campaign. Becket and De Hondt brought out the second edition on January 16, 1766—perfectly timed for maximum effectiveness.[53] Franklin's shrewd instincts also enabled him to utilize to fullest advantage the work of other writers favorable to the colonies. That same month of January, Strahan printed on Franklin's order the first and second English editions of Daniel Dulany's widely read *Considerations on the Propriety of Imposing Taxes in the British Colonies* and, in February, the first English edition of John Dickinson's *The Late Regulations Respecting the British Colonies*. Almon published both. The Doctor also reprinted one of Dickinson's speeches in 1765, prefaced by his own thirty-five-page introduction, "of itself a very considerable tract."[54]

The author of an essay ordinarily received nothing but publicity for his work, and many were published anonymously or pseudonymously. Perhaps because pamphleteering was not remunerative, or perhaps because it was politically perilous, or because it was so time-consuming, only a few agents actively attempted to reach the public and politicians in this way. One of the most industrious, if not always successful, was William Bollan. (Dennys De Berdt assumed that any screed Bollan produced must inevitably "be a tedious performance.")[55] In the spring of 1763, during peace negotiations with the French, Bollan felt Massachusetts' interest required his solicitousness, even though he was no longer officially an agent. Between eleven and midnight he would go out and with the assistance of his

[52] *Ibid.*, p. 361; Hanna, *Franklin and Pennsylvania Politics*, pp. 128–129.
[53] Labaree, *Papers of Franklin*, IX, 47–100; *London Chronicle*, Jan. 16, 1766.
[54] Crane, *Franklin's Letters to the Press*, p. xlix; *Monthly Review*, XXXII (1764), 67; Franklin to Joseph Galloway, Jan. 9, 1769, WCL.
[55] De Berdt to Edward Sheafe, Sept. 11, 1769, Letters of Dennys De Berdt, 1757–1770," ed. Albert Matthews, CSM *Publications*, XIII (1912), 378.

bookseller, Samuel Baker, get the printer to set type. The resulting pamphlet was not influential, and its publication put the author £150 out of pocket.[56] In the year of the Stamp Act he did a more effective job, answering Soame Jenyns' contentions for virtual representation and American taxation.[57] In 1766 he undertook an ambitious project, an important examination of *The Freedom of Speech and Writing upon Public Affairs.*[58]

Charles Garth wrote practically nothing of his own, though in 1762 he executed his constituents' instructions by having published the *Full State of the Dispute between the Governor and the Commons House of Assembly of . . . South Carolina.* During the Stamp Act crisis, Garth informed the colonists that some pamphlets sent him duplicated others he "had received before from several parts of America; they have long since been reprinted in London." [59]

The Mauduits did most of their writing before and after their employment by Massachusetts, unfortunate for the colonies because Israel was one of the most accomplished polemicists of his generation. Early in 1764 he prepared a memorial to the Treasury lords for his brother and Massachusetts Bay. A few months later he purportedly designed a pamphlet for distribution in the lobby of Westminster, but thought better of it for dubious reasons. Later that year, obliged to publish the English edition of Jonathan Mayhew's *Remarks* against New England episcopacy, Mauduit tried to have the tract abridged and printed at a disadvantageous time.[60] In 1764 *The Rights of the British Colonies* by James Otis was sent to Jasper Mauduit "to be improved as he may judge proper." Before the Stamp Act crisis concluded, it had been reprinted four times in London and advertised as "highly necessary for the perusal of the members of both houses and

---

[56] Bollan to Andrew Oliver, April 18, 1763, Dana MSS (1674–1769), MHS; *The Ancient Right of the English Nation to the American Fishery . . .* (S. Baker, 1764).

[57] *The Mutual Interest of Great Britain and the American Colonies Considered . . .* (W. Nicoll, 1765).

[58] See Leonard W. Levy, *Legacy of Suppression: Freedom of Speech and Press in Early American History* (Cambridge, Mass., 1960), pp. 157–159.

[59] Lewis B. Namier, "Charles Garth and His Connexions," *EHR*, LIV (1939), 465 n. 1, 466; Garth MS fragment dated Feb. 22, 1766, NYHS.

[60] Worthington C. Ford, "The Mauduit Pamphlets," MHS *Proceedings*, XLIV (1911), 144–175; Jasper Mauduit to Timothy Ruggles, Feb. 11, 1764, MHS *Collections*, ser. 1, VI, 195; Thomas Hollis to Jonathan Mayhew, Oct. 10, 1764, Knollenberg, "Hollis and Mayhew," p. 157.

of such who choose to make themselves masters of an argument so little understood." [61]

Interestingly enough, one of the most successful instruments of colonial propaganda was not an agent, but one of their best allies—a dissenting philanthropist who disdained involvement in the political maelstrom about him. Thomas Hollis financed many reprints in London, particularly the secular tracts of the leading New England divines. By the later 1760's, Hollis "had become . . . the busiest English literary agent for American writers against the 'usurpations' of George III's ministers." One of the few times Hollis breached his insistence upon political aloofness occurred during the movement to repeal the Stamp Act, when he undertook a private campaign to inundate Lord Rockingham with colonial opinions. [62]

By 1765 various allies of the North American lobbyists had converged into a cooperative pressure group, with the agents at their core. The dissenting community became politically active once again, strengthened by its successes and experiences in the 1740's and 1750's. At least some of the agents had discovered the uses of the press and had overcome the reluctance of many of the printers and editors to handle material in opposition to administration policies. Most of all, the merchant community, suffering from the postwar depression and hurt by American trade boycotts, solidly united with the agents to oppose new measures affecting the colonies. What remains to be seen is the agents' relationship to the political changes responsible for those measures. The years of the war and its aftermath would find British politics transformed—and the agency as well.

[61] *Pamphlets of the American Revolution, 1750–1776*, ed. Bernard Bailyn, I (Cambridge, Mass., 1965), 409.

[62] Caroline Robbins, "The Strenuous Whig, Thomas Hollis of Lincoln's Inn," 3*WMQ*, VII (1950), 429–430, 433, 435, 440.

CHAPTER 6

The Agents and British Politics

One of the agents' most important responsibilities was keeping Britain's men of affairs well informed about the colonies. This was a difficult task because most of those men had for generations managed to avoid familiarity with America. They were unaware of colonial conditions, needs and aspirations—a deficiency that would plague the agents increasingly. This was equally true of Whitehall and Westminster. William Bollan, lobbying in 1759, reported that he found officials "either wholly strangers to the nature of the colonies (one of the chief of them having frankly told me he was shamefully ignorant of them) or under some prejudice concerning them." Henry Cruger Jr. spent three weeks in London in 1766, "every Day with some one Member of Parliament, talking as it were for my own Life. It is surprising how ignorant some of them are of *Trade* and *America*." [1] Scholars who have examined parliamentary debates on American questions during this period have firmly noted "the extent of Parliament's ignorance of the people over whom it claimed to exercise supreme authority." [2]

Partial responsibility for this condition may rest with shortsighted American visitors to London who would report nearly anything in order to accomplish their narrow purposes. As John Wentworth re-

[1] Alison G. Olson, "The British Government and Colonial Union, 1754," 3*WMQ*, XVII (1960), 28; Bollan to Thomas Hubbard, April 12, 1759, MHS *Collections*, ser. 1, VI (Boston, 1800), 42; Cruger Jr. to Cruger Sr., Feb. 14, 1766, *Commerce of Rhode Island, 1726–1774* (MHS *Collections*, Vol. LXIX [Boston, 1914]), I, 139–140; see also William Allen to Benjamin Chew, Oct. 7, 1763, "William Allen–Benjamin Chew Correspondence, 1763–1764," *PMHB*, XC (1966), 214.

[2] Sir Lewis Namier and John Brooke, *The History of Parliament: The House of Commons, 1754–1790* (London, 1964), I, 161.

marked, important Britons "rec'd. too much encouragmt and information from many of our Countrymen who have been here upon hasty visits . . . and have been expecting some preferment." But the problem also arose from a subtly growing difference of opinion over the role and importance of colonies within the imperial structure. Countering the effects of this divergence continually engaged the agents and their allies.[3]

THE AGENTS, POLITICIANS, AND PARLIAMENT

In attempting to surmount these opinions, the agents relied upon various techniques and channels to inform and correct the views British politicians held of colonial circumstances. The simplest arrangement and the one most commonly employed was the transmission of a letter from America to an agent who in turn submitted it for some minister's perusal. In this manner the agents supplied Rockingham with provincial correspondence during the campaign to repeal the Stamp Act, as De Berdt did for Dartmouth, then First Lord of Trade. Franklin and Montagu kept Lord Shelburne so informed while he was Secretary of State for the Southern Department (and hence the colonies) from 1766 until 1768. In some cases, the letter was posted from agent to politician; on other occasions the lobbyist delivered it personally, with polemical accompaniment or supplication.[4]

The agents also had informal methods of relaying public information from America to public figures, one being to keep copies of colonial gazettes before their eyes.[5] Efforts such as these were relatively easy. Several of the most enterprising lobbyists, however, did more, at least until 1770. Barlow Trecothick acted as a communications liaison between the New England colonies and the Rockingham-Newcastle connection. Trecothick dispatched letters back and forth from provincials to politicians and served the Old Whigs as

[3] Wentworth to Daniel Rindge, Nov. 29, 1765, Masonian Papers, III, 3, NHHS; Franklin to Isaac Norris, March 19, 1759, *The Papers of Benjamin Franklin*, ed. Leonard W. Labaree *et al.*, VIII (New Haven, 1965), 293.

[4] Mr. Russel to De Berdt, Nov. 11, 1765, Dartmouth MSS Vol. II, 110, WSL; Montagu to Lord Shelburne, Sept. 8, 1766, Shelburne MSS, CXI, 317, WCL; Franklin to Joseph Galloway, Feb. 17 and March 13, 1768, Smyth, V, 97, 112.

[5] William Bollan to Lord Rockingham, Nov. 4, 1765, Feb. 7, March 26, and April 19, 1766, Fitzwilliam MSS, R 24–28, R 24–66, R 24–74, R 24–78, SCL.

adviser on American affairs. Bollan used the personal interview to fill Rockingham's mind with news of colonial conditions. When word of the Boston massacre reached London, Bollan "directly drew up a memorandum . . . for the use of the Lord Mayor" and other friends of the colonies, giving them the American version of what had occurred.[6]

After passage of the Stamp Act in 1765, De Berdt wrote lengthy, informative letters to Lord Halifax and Lord Dartmouth, explaining the adverse effects of the new legislation on the imperial economy. De Berdt made a practice of drafting his constituents' grievances into memorials which he presented to various ministers, accompanied by affidavits and other pertinent documents. He spent considerable sums each year to have copies made of the General Court's letters, which he then delivered to Members of Parliament and various nobles. Massachusetts had earlier made a practice of sending packets of colonial books for Jasper Mauduit to distribute in Westminster. Charles Garth also provided Members with printed arguments against the pending currency bill in 1764.[7]

Franklin, as we have seen, was the master publicist of the colonies, employing every conceivable technique including the intimate luncheon or dinner as a means of projecting American opinion. Administrations even tended to use Franklin as a sounding board for colonial opinion and various *ballons d'essai* of their own. Whitehall would prevail upon a mutual friend to write the Doctor a letter designed to elicit his "Sentiments in writing on the then State of Affairs." Franklin took advantage of such opportunities to compose answers he knew would be "immediately communicated, and a good deal handed about among them."[8]

The more formal presentation of information or complaints was

[6] Newcastle to Trecothick, Sept. 13 and 20, 1766, Add MSS 32977, ff. 77, 111; Trecothick to Newcastle, Sept. 15, 1766, *ibid.*, f. 83; Trecothick to Rockingham, Nov. 4, 1768, Fitzwilliam MSS, R 1–1112, R 1–1113a-b, SCL; Bollan to Samuel Danforth, April 28, 1770, *Bowdoin and Temple Papers* (MHS *Collections*, ser. 6, Vol. IX [Boston, 1897]), p. 177.

[7] "Letters of Dennys De Berdt, 1757–1770," ed. Albert Matthews, CSM *Publications*, XIII (1912), 335–336, 428–441; De Berdt's letter and memorial to Shelburne, 1767, Large MSS, MHS; "Aspinwall Papers, Part II," MHS *Collections*, ser. 4, X (Boston, 1871), 717; Mauduit to H. Gray, April 9, 1764, MA, LVI, 420; Sherwood to Moses Brown, Sept. 22, 1770, *The Correspondence of the Colonial Governors of Rhode Island, 1723–1775*, ed. G. S. Kimball (Boston, 1902–1903), II, 427.

[8] *Boston Gazette and Country Journal*, April 14, 1766; Franklin to William

usually handled by means of petitions. Lobbyists had traditionally presented American memorials to the King in Council, a procedure requiring that documents be submitted through the Secretary of State for the Southern Department. The royal reply came down through the appropriate governor, who duly transmitted it to the provincial assembly.[9] Owing to the onset of changes in colonial administration by legislative fiat during the Seven Years' War, however, petitions for redress of grievances were increasingly directed at Parliament. There the process was somewhat different and much less familiar, since the colonists had petitioned Parliament very little since 1734.

Only a member could offer the House of Commons a petition. Hence an agent had to seek some favorably disposed M.P., usually selected for his influence on groups interested in the question at issue. If the House consented to listen, he read the substance of the document. If it contained nothing objectionable, it was received—brought to the table and read in its entirety by the clerk of the House. In the Lords, on the other hand, an agent might be heard at the bar or else be represented there by counsel.[10]

Quite clearly all these modes of presenting information and requests depended for their success upon what contemporaries called "interest," but which we usually refer to as the exertion of influence. The interest or influence of the American colonies was reasonably secure in the years after the outbreak of the Seven Years' War. The agents' sound and increasing connections in the cabinet and Parliament were partially responsible for their heightened success in these years.[11]

At mid-century Parliament played a curious role in politics, for its activity had reached low ebb. The session beginning in 1754, for example, saw the enactment of sixty-nine bills. While thirty-five were classified as private acts and thirty-four as public, nearly all of them would be regarded as private by modern standards. This does not

Franklin, Aug. 28 and Nov. 25, 1767, March 22, 1775, Smyth, V, 45–46, 67, VI, 349; Franklin to Pa. CC, April 16, 1768, Smyth, V, 120; Franklin to Samuel Cooper, June 8, 1770, Smyth, V, 259.

[9] The process is explained by Henry Eustace McCulloh in a letter to the N.C. CC, *CRNC*, VIII, 55.

[10] See Franklin's superb description to Joseph Galloway, Jan. 9, 1769, *Benjamin Franklin's Autobiographical Writings*, ed. Carl Van Doren (New York, 1945), pp. 186–187.

[11] Namier and Brooke, *History of Parliament*, I, 46 ff.; Ella Lonn, *The Colonial Agents of the Southern Colonies* (Chapel Hill, 1945), p. 245; William Bollan to Newcastle, Nov. 26, 1755, Add MSS 32861, f. 98.

mean they were insignificant, for many had considerable effect in
terms of social and economic change. What is notable, however, is the
limited role played by public issues in parliamentary conduct, discussion, and elections.[12] On the eve of the Seven Years' War, the agents
found that the House of Commons deferred almost entirely to Whitehall, where matters of colonial policy were concerned. When William
Bollan attempted to present a petition against extending the Mutiny
Act to America in 1755, the Commons would not even enter it upon
their minutes, "for that wou'd be speaking out to the people in
America," a function properly done by the crown through its governors.[13]

   This outlook began to change with some rapidity during the war,
largely owing to Pitt's initiative and recognition of the need for new
colonial legislation. Between 1756 and 1763 a dramatic shift took
place—one which made the peers and the 558 Members of Parliament more important for the colonies than they had ever been before.
Fortunately the agents had friends in both houses, particularly the
Commons, and developed many new ones during and immediately
after the war. Richard Partridge, for example, could depend upon
"two considerable Members who were distinguished for their abilities
in the house," and Jared Ingersoll had ready access to the gallery of
the House of Commons, a privilege denied the agents after 1767.
Franklin and Jackson, in addition to the usual connections, were
extremely friendly with the speakers of the House. Even William
Knox provided Georgia with invaluable parliamentary friends prior to
the Stamp Act crisis.[14] With at least thirteen stages for full debate on
any bill, no lobbyist could hope for success without such friends.[15]

---

[12] Richard Pares, *King George III and the Politicians* (Oxford, 1953), p. 3;
Samuel H. Beer, *British Politics in the Collectivist Age* (New York, 1965), p.
25.

[13] Bollan to Josiah Willard, March 5, 1755, Misc. Bound MSS, MHS.

[14] *Ibid.*; Partridge to Stephen Hopkins, April 6, 1756, Kimball, *Colonial
Governors of Rhode Island*, II, 206; Lawrence H. Gipson, *Jared Ingersoll* (New
Haven, 1920), p. 75; Bollan to Andrew Oliver, Feb. 12, 1762, *Jasper Mauduit:
Agent in London for the Province of the Massachusetts-Bay, 1762–1765*
(MHS *Collections*, Vol. LXXIV [Boston, 1918]), pp. 24–25; Jackson to Frank-
lin, April 4, 1763, *Letters and Papers of Benjamin Franklin and Richard
Jackson, 1753–1785*, ed. Carl Van Doren (Philadelphia, 1947), p. 98; James
Habersham to William Knox, July 27, 1764, *The Letters of Hon. James
Habersham, 1756–1775*, (Collections of the Georgia Historical Society, Vol.
VI [Savannah, 1904]), p. 25.

[15] J. Steven Watson, *The Reign of George III, 1760–1815* (Oxford, 1960),
p. 58.

Most important of all, beginning in 1761, a succession of agents was elected to Parliament, giving them a dual status potentially invaluable to the colonists. As early as May 1758, Franklin had observed that "almost every Thing is granted Members of Parliament, the Ministry being extreamly unwilling to disoblige them lest they should join in some Opposition, and therefore I think it would be Prudence in our Assemblies hereafter to chuse their Agents among the Members of the House of Commons." Franklin repeatedly urged such a choice upon his constituents, arguing that if they continued "to employ two Agents, one should be a Member of Parliament, whose Weight and Influence with the Ministry may stand us in good Stead on Occasion." [16]

In 1761, Abercromby and John Thomlinson Jr. won seats, followed by Jackson in 1762, Garth in 1765, and Trecothick in 1768. When Edmund Burke was named New York's agent in 1770, he had been an M.P. for five years. Including John Sargent, re-elected in 1765 (the same year he became New York's special agent), the colonists had five agents in the Commons during the Stamp Act crisis—three of them active lobbyists. What difference did their presence make? How was their membership an asset to their trans-Atlantic constituents? These questions cannot be answered unequivocally, because having agents with parliamentary seats was a mixed blessing to the provincial assemblies. For example, only a Member might present petitions in the House. But to do so restricted the freedom of an agent-M.P. to participate forcefully in debate on the particular issue at hand. [17] Thus Franklin could have a memorial submitted by Jackson, but the latter thought "what he had to say in support of it would have more weight if it were *offered* by another." [18]

Many obvious advantages, however, accrued from employing men within Westminster. The colonies acquired potential spokesmen in the supreme legislature. [19] Having two constituencies could reinforce

[16] Franklin to Thomas Leech *et al.*, May 13, 1758, to Isaac Norris, March 19, 1759, to Joseph Galloway, April 7, 1759, Labaree, *Papers of Franklin*, VIII, 63, 297, 309–310.

[17] In addition, an M.P. could not present a petition that he had signed (Garth to S.C. CC, Feb. 8, 1765, Lewis B. Namier, "Charles Garth, Agent for South Carolina," *EHR*, LIV [1939], 650).

[18] Franklin to Joseph Galloway, Oct. 11, 1766, WCL; Jackson to Mass. General Court, Dec. 27, 1765, MA, *Letters, 1764–1774*, p. 13.

[19] D. H. Watson, "Barlow Trecothick and Other Associates of Lord Rockingham during the Stamp Act Crisis, 1765–1766" (unpub. M.A. thesis; Sheffield University, 1957), p. 59.

the agent's zeal for eliminating objects of Anglo-American antagonism. By mingling daily with various other members, the agents could achieve a special sensitivity to the Commons' receptiveness on a given issue, as well as accumulate high priority information affecting the timing and techniques of lobbying. As one colonist remarked to Jasper Mauduit, "Mr. Jackson . . . being a member of Parliament, will be able to advise" the best time and manner for presenting petitions.[20]

As ministerial stringency after 1766 struck upon the device of excluding lobbyists from the galleries, those agents within Parliament could report to their colleagues and constituents what had transpired in debate.[21] Even more important, agents with places in the Commons would actually expedite the functioning of parliamentary machinery where it involved American bills. Jackson and Garth sat on influential committees that markedly affected the process and progress of legislation.[22] One way or another they might amend pending statutes and even take the speaker's chair when the House sat as a committee of the whole. In 1768, for example, Garth sought renewed permission for the colonies to export rice to Great Britain without charge. Sir John Cust left the chair; Garth presided over the committee of the whole and then turned the chair back to the speaker. Garth then reported the bill from the committee, and the House agreed to the amendments and ordered that the document be engrossed the following day. The bill passed promptly, and Garth personally carried it to the Lords to seek their concurrence.[23]

Thus the agency made a singularly important institutional gain in the early sixties by acquiring new voices in Parliament.[24] The added

---

[20] Namier, "Garth, Agent," p. 642; Jackson to Franklin, Nov. 12, 1763, Van Doren, *Franklin and Jackson*, pp. 113–114; Mauduit to Mass. General Court, Feb. 9, 1765, MA, XXII, 434; John Cotton to Mauduit, Nov. 3, 1764, MA, LVI, 427–431; Franklin to Pa. CC, June 10, 1766, *PMHB*, V (1881), 354.

[21] Charles Garth to S.C. CC, May 17, 1767, *SCHGM*, XXIX (1928), 229–230.

[22] Jackson to Thomas Fitch, April 19, 1765, CHS *Collections*, XVIII (Hartford, 1920), 343; Garth to S.C. CC, April 11, 1770, *SCHGM*, XXXI, 254; Kenneth Mackenzie, *The English Parliament* (London, 1950), p. 48.

[23] *JHC*, XXXI, 291, XXXII, 89, 91, 94, 383, 421, 885, 916.

[24] See Namier and Brooke, *History of Parliament*, I, 161–162. Writing of the seventy-year period after the Glorious Revolution, Lawrence H. Gipson states that "while Connecticut and other colonies were not technically represented in Parliament, in practice the vital interests of these dependencies were doubtless given almost every protection that might have been expected had

strength would prove essential, for British politics had been undergoing tumultuous change, with significant effects upon all pressure
groups in London.

POLITICAL CHANGE, COLONIAL ADMINISTRATION, AND THE AGENTS

Within the constitutional arrangements of eighteenth-century Britain, two conditions were essential for the stability of an administration. It had to be led by a politician who enjoyed the confidence of the
king; and this leader had to command a majority in the Commons.
These criteria also indicate that he required the support of the "Court
and Treasury" members while not alienating too many independents.
As head of the Treasury he would control patronage, and he would
also want to hold a seat in the Commons to facilitate personal management.[25] Robert Walpole and Henry Pelham had enjoyed just such
conditions, as would Lord North later; but with Pelham's death in
1754, the stability of British politics began to fail. The advent of war
produced functional coalitions, thereby mitigating some of the worst
effects of factionalism. With the accession of George III, however,
instability became the dominant fact of public life, and for a decade
every other consideration was contingent upon it.[26]

In 1756, Horace Walpole warned a confidant that men of affairs
paid too little attention to the French problem. "We are engaged in a
civil war—not between St. James's and Leicester House, but between
the Dukes of Grafton and Bedford, about a new turnpike road on the
back of the town—as you may imagine, it grows politics; and if it is
not compromised during the recess, the French may march deep into
the Kingdom before *they* become greater politics." [27] If the French
threat could be overlooked in the face of partisan politics, the colonial

---

these colonies enjoyed representation in the House of Commons, under the
given conditions. This situation was made possible through the efficient work of
their influential agents, some of them members of Parliament." Although
Gipson has considerably overstated the case, it is true that the institution
reached peak effectiveness during the 1765–1766 crisis (*The British Empire
before the American Revolution*, III [2nd ed.; New York, 1960], 100).

[25] Bernard Donoughue, *British Politics and the American Revolution: The
Path to War, 1773–1775* (London, 1964), p. 14.

[26] Namier and Brooke, *History of Parliament*, I, 1; Herbert Butterfield,
"Some Reflections on the Early Years of George III's Reign," *Journal of British
Studies*, IV (1965), 97.

[27] *Horace Walpole's Correspondence With Sir Horace Mann*, ed. Wilmarth
S. Lewis *et al.*, IV (New Haven, 1960), 549.

agents were bound to find _their_ operations retarded. This became particularly noticeable in 1757, when Abercromby, Partridge, and Franklin all complained of "the Confusion of Publick Affairs" to their constituents. Whenever ministerial regroupings were in progress, effective lobbying was curtailed.[28]

The problem was exacerbated by the accession of George III in 1760. He resented the whole notion of "connexion," and wished to break up the system by which aristocratic leaders formed coalition governments and, as it seemed to George, forced the crown to accept their nominees for the ministry. The alliance between Pitt and Newcastle which George inherited was shaky enough. When it came apart in 1761, the King proceeded to act on his principles and turned to Bute, his mentor and favorite. The abrasive personal politics of the next ten years was intensified by the relative absence of normal stabilizing conditions. Each successive first minister fashioned and enlarged his own faction while in office. Under these conditions, major issues which might be debated and settled were limited to two or three per parliamentary session. While the harsh and persistent maneuvering for power dragged on, pressure groups and private interests waited impatiently on the sidelines.[29]

Given the disturbed state of domestic politics, colonial affairs were bound to suffer. Agents attempting to function found their task progressively more difficult. For sixty years the operations of their institution had been facilitated by connections that were reliably situated. Suddenly all aspects of political life became uncertain. As Franklin complained to the Pennsylvania Committee of Correspondence, " 'tis a kind of Labour in vain to attempt making Impressions on such moveable Materials; 'tis like writing on the Sand in a windy Day." [30] The permutations of British ministries can be seen quite clearly through the eyes of frustrated agents whose lobbying haphazardly stopped and started again at the mercy of destructive political conflicts.

[28] Abercromby to Va. CC, May 13, 1757, Lonn, _Agents of the Southern Colonies_, p. 157; Partridge to William Greene, Oct. 7, 1757, Kimball, _Colonial Governors of Rhode Island_, II, 259; Franklin to Deborah Franklin, Nov. 22, 1757, Labaree, _Papers of Franklin_, VII, 275.

[29] Watson, _Reign of George III_, pp. 7–8; Namier and Brooke, _History of Parliament_, I, 197–198; Archibald S. Foord, _His Majesty's Opposition, 1714–1830_ (Oxford, 1964), p. 359.

[30] June 10, 1766, _PMHB_, V (1881), 355.

Between the death of George II in 1760 and the conclusion of the war in 1763, the governments of Newcastle and Pitt gave way to the Earl of Bute's administration, and his in turn to Grenville's. Still there was no expectation of stability, and in September, Jasper Mauduit reported the Treasury lords had adjourned owing to political confusion. When Eliphalet Dyer arrived in November as a private lobbyist, Richard Jackson warned him against making hasty "applications, as it is very uncertain at present who will be the persons in Power after the Sitting of the Parliament . . . as the present Ministry are not Supposed to be permanent." Seven weeks later the situation was no more settled, and Jackson informed Franklin that "affairs here were never so mutable." In July 1765, Franklin found colonial "affairs are at a total Stop here, by the Present unsettled State of the Ministry." As the Grenvillites gave way to the Rockinghams, Jackson observed that "one hardly knows who to apply to on any occasion in any department except the Treasury which is the only one fixed, and even there the hurry of business yet so new to Gentlemen little acquainted with business in general leaves little leisure for new subjects of application." [31]

During the very years when British politics was undergoing rapid and unpredictable changes, the locus of responsibility for imperial policy was also shifting. Through the war years, especially with Pitt at the helm, the Commons began to respond to issues of colonial government. Franklin first noticed this in 1759 and reported that the Privy Council should have brought the Pennsylvania proprietary issue into the House, "but they are afraid the Parliament would establish more Liberty in the Colonies than is proper or necessary, and therefore do not care the Parliament should meddle at all with the Government of the Colonies." [32]

This strain intensified until after the Peace of Paris in 1763, when problems of American government required a major relocation of responsibility for colonial policy. The New World became an engross-

[31] Jasper Mauduit to Andrew Oliver, Sept. 6, 1763, MA, XXII, 309; Dyer to Jared Ingersoll, Nov. 3, 1763, NHCHS *Papers*, IX (New Haven, 1918), 287; Jackson to Franklin, Dec. 27, 1763, Van Doren, *Franklin and Jackson*, pp. 121–122; Franklin to Hugh Roberts, July 7, 1765, Smyth, IV, 386; Franklin to Cadwallader Evans, July 13, 1765, APS; Jackson to Andrew Oliver, July 26, 1765, MA, Misc. Letters, 1763–1773, pp. 100–101.

[32] Franklin to Isaac Norris, March 19, 1759, Labaree, *Papers of Franklin*, VIII, 295–296.

ing concern of Commons and Lords, who hitherto had viewed it as
merely part of a mercantile system overseen by the Secretary of State
for the Southern Department and the Board of Trade. As legislative
decisions surpassed executive administration in importance, opportunities for individual negotiation and favor faded.[33]

For nearly a century the agents had institutionalized accommodating relationships with the various governmental boards and civil servants. Suddenly the traditional lobbying apparatus in Georgian London was wrenched into new and unfamiliar forms.[34] The measure of
an agent's capacity and shrewdness swiftly became his ability to discern the proper points and persons where pressure could best be
applied. As never before, the place was Westminster. And in the
eighteenth century the House of Lords was quite as important as its
elected counterpart. The nobility had to be buttonholed and cajoled as
much as the Members across the way. Often dependents and relatives
of powerful lords sat in the Commons. Bills were frequently initiated
in the upper house, their early form taking shape there. Politicians
usually formed opinions of pending legislation at this stage. In many
respects Parliament was one body with two interacting parts which
often arranged for an issue to be handled in the Lords. Thus the
lobbyists' field of operations broadened immensely after 1763, and
with it the complexity of achieving Anglo-American understanding.[35]

Not surprisingly the agents who displayed the greatest sensitivity to
the importance of the House of Lords were the handful with seats in
the Commons, particularly Jackson, Garth, and Trecothick. They
reduced the obstacles blocking repeal of the Stamp Act in the upper
house in 1766; and Garth carefully managed with Lord Dartmouth
"the Introduction and Patronage . . . of the Applications to the
House of Peers" during that same campaign. When a bill for abolishing the Currency Act was slated to come before the Lords early in

---

[33] Stanley N. Katz, "An Easie Access: Anglo-American Politics in New York,
1732–1753" (unpub. Ph.D. diss.; Harvard University, 1961), p. 448.

[34] Dora Mae Clark, *The Rise of the British Treasury: Colonial Administration in the Eighteenth Century* (New Haven, 1960), pp. 126 ff.; cf. Watson,
Reign of George III, pp. 60–61.

[35] A. S. Turberville, *The House of Lords in the Eighteenth Century* (Oxford, 1927), *passim*. I am indebted to Mr. Maurice F. Bond, Clerk of the
House of Lords Record Office, Victoria Tower, Westminster, for stimulating
and helpful discussions.

1767, Benjamin Franklin drafted some "Hints of Argument" for Lord Grafton's use in supporting the bill before the assembled nobles.[36]

As petitions increasingly became the concern of Parliament, lobbyists had to acquaint themselves with unfamiliar patterns of operating. This heightened importance of Parliament gradually elicited several manuals institutionalizing procedures hitherto casual and flexible.[37] In consequence, the agents had signposts to guide them. But these same aids would also eliminate the traditional detours that had made an inscrutable system functional.[38]

Political instability also wrought important changes in the handling of colonial administration at the great boards. At the accession of George III, the Board of Trade was composed almost entirely of fresh faces. Of the previous commissioners only Soame Jenyns continued, and he would remain until 1780. Lord Sandys replaced Halifax as chairman, but with the powers of that office much reduced. All the Board's importance, however superficial, accumulated over a decade was suddenly lost, particularly control of colonial correspondence and patronage. As before, the Board could only act on matters brought to its attention by the Privy Council, a secretary of state, or one of the other offices. The Order in Council of May 1761 had no effect on the nature of routine business, however, and the traditional patterns of lobbying remained unaltered. The other departments continued to seek advice and information; the agents continued to petition and confer there.[39]

When the Seven Years' War ended, an American Department was badly needed to handle the accumulated problems of colonial government. Instead there occurred only the sequence of replacements that

[36] Garth to Thomas Ringgold *et al.*, March 5, 1766, *MHM*, VI (1911), 288; Franklin to Jackson, Feb. 13, 1767, Van Doren, *Franklin and Jackson*, p. 197.
[37] *The Liverpool Tractate: An Eighteenth Century Manual on the Procedure of the House of Commons*, ed. Catherine Strateman (New York, 1937), pp. xxiii–xxiv, xxix, 34–35; *The Method of Proceedings in Order to Obtain a Private Act of Parliament* (London, 1767), pp. 5–24; John Hatsell, *Precedents of Proceedings in the House of Commons . . .* (London, 1776–1796), II, 144, 189 n., 203.
[38] See Jasper Mauduit to Timothy Ruggles, April 8, 1763, *Jasper Mauduit*, p. 100; Mauduit to Ruggles, Dec. 10, 1763, MHS *Collections*, ser. 1, VI, 192.
[39] William Bollan to James Otis, May 8, 1761, *Jasper Mauduit*, p. 15; Arthur H. Basye, *The Lords Commissioners of Trade and Plantations . . . 1748–1782* (New Haven, 1925), pp. 106–112, 118.

saw Sandys replaced by Charles Townshend, he in a month by Lord
Shelburne, and he in five months by Hillsborough. Thus more than
two decades of stability gave way to confusion and mutability. In
1763, just when it became most important for agents to smooth the
troubled imperial waters, strong political winds made the going very
rough. All the reliable qualities of permanence gave way to an inscru-
tability that made effective operations difficult.[40]

Political and personal prejudices contributed to the increasing com-
plexity of dealing with the bureaucracy and heightened Whitehall's
difficulties in handling American issues judiciously. Halifax, now
Lord Lieutenant of Ireland, and Egremont, Secretary of State for the
Southern Department, were very jealous of the ambitious Shelburne.
John Pownall, secretary to the Board of Trade, despised Egremont and
persuaded Shelburne to undercut him by keeping the business of the
Board of Trade a secret from the Southern Department. Welbore
Ellis, Secretary at War, upon whom Egremont relied for advice in
colonial affairs, in turn incited his colleague to thwart the First Lord
of Trade. When Halifax shifted to the Northern Department later in
1763, he used his influence to have Hillsborough appointed in Shelburne's place. The real victims of this fluctuation and jealousy in
colonial administration were the colonists and their London representatives.[41]

Most important of all for the lobbyists' institution and trans-
Atlantic government was the effect of these changes on the agents
themselves. In the decade after 1756, despite many handicaps, they
achieved a new status in imperial politics. Their gain, not surprisingly,
came at the expense of the colonial governors. Those individuals had
long been the formal and official link between London and the colonies. In 1702, for example, when Virginia's burgesses circumvented
the governor and petitioned the Queen directly through their agent,
they were advised that they must proceed through orthodox channels.
Actually, the heightened role the agents played in the eighteenth
century was partially made possible because the governors commonly
neglected their duty of keeping the home government informed.[42]

Perhaps it was for this reason that between 1752 and 1766 the

[40] Basye, *Lords Commissioners of Trade*, pp. 120, 122, 124, 128.

[41] *Ibid.*, 132–133; Jasper Mauduit to ?, March 12, 1763, MA, Letters,
1701–1763, p. 385.

[42] William Byrd, *The London Diary (1717–1721) and Other Writings*, ed.
Louis B. Wright and Marion Tinling (New York, 1958), p. 14.

colonial governors were de-emphasized in the Anglo-American system, facilitating the quiet rise of the agents. Until 1752 governors had been directed to correspond both with the Board of Trade and with one of the secretaries of state. In that year a new order was issued making the Board of Trade responsible for the governors and other provincial officers. In all ordinary matters the governors were to correspond with the lords commissioners alone. (Not surprisingly this order was reversed in 1766.) Similarly, the governors had traditionally been responsible for handling Indian relations in their respective colonies. But in 1754–1756 a system of regional superintendents was initiated, further diminishing the executives' role.[43] Moreover, the presence of the British army in any colony, particularly after 1756, introduced a center of authority external to the political structure of the colony. The development of an American military establishment under a commander-in-chief reduced the importance of governors, who were essentially local politicians. Still another reason for these institutional changes may have been the slipping prestige of the governors in provincial politics and the loss of influence several of them suffered in London in the fifties.[44]

In any case the governors' decline exactly paralleled the agents' augmented status in the structure of Anglo-American government. Significantly, in 1756 the Secretary at War sought the agents' opinion on a proposal to encourage the enlistment of foreign Protestant colonists.[45] At a time when the Treasury sought to systematize in London administration of the crown colonies, it seized upon the device of the crown agent—a new creation of the later fifties—indicatively patterned after the older institution of North American agents. The new

[43] Evarts B. Greene, *The Provincial Governor in the English Colonies of North America* (New York, 1898), pp. 65–71; *Sources and Documents Illustrating the American Revolution, 1764–1788 and the Formation of the Federal Constitution,* ed. Samuel Eliot Morison (2nd ed.; New York, 1965), pp. 63, 66; Gipson, *British Empire before the American Revolution,* XI, 430.

[44] John Shy, *Toward Lexington: The Role of the British Army in the Coming of the American Revolution* (Princeton, 1965); John A. Schutz, *William Shirley, King's Governor of Massachusetts* (Chapel Hill, 1961), pp. 225, 232–233, 242, 245; Jack P. Greene, *The Quest for Power: The Lower Houses of Assembly in the Southern Royal Colonies, 1689–1776* (Chapel Hill, 1963), p. 359; W. L. Morton, "The Local Executive in the British Empire, 1763–1828," *EHR,* LXXVIII (1963), 436–457.

[45] Nicholas Varga, "Robert Charles: New York Agent, 1748–1770," *3WMQ,* XVIII (1961), 228.

crown agents handled their colonies' finances and received instructions from the Treasury and Board of Trade. This was another sign that Whitehall was cognizant of the agency and its potential uses.[46]

In 1757 the Treasury selected the colonial agents to expedite Anglo-colonial financial arrangements for the French and Indian War. In 1764, Grenville met with the agents a number of times to discuss his program for America. This was true of the stamp duties, as we shall see, and of the American mutiny bill. With Grenville's approval Charles Jenkinson met with Franklin and Thomas Pownall, and as a result there were changes in the billeting of soldiers advantageous to the colonies.[47] This sort of consultation between agents and ministers would become less frequent after 1766, and rare after 1770.

The decade following 1756 was a momentous one for the agents. Despite the handicaps attendant upon political instability, the North American pressure group sought influence systematically and achieved it in partial measure. Its members recognized that political change would significantly affect colonial administration and they adapted accordingly, especially through the services of several agents in the House of Commons, a new source of influence after 1761. They were also assisted by the Board of Trade's decision to stay out of the agency selection process in the colonies and to forbid the governors' interfering. A case in North Carolina in 1761 induced the Board to declare that "the Representatives of the People are and ought to be free to chuse whom they think proper to act, in whatever concerns the affairs and interest of the Colony here, and with whom they & the Council only can correspond." [48] This policy would undergo radical change by 1768.

Obviously the colonial agents were not uniformly successful in the years before 1765. Legislation disadvantageous to the colonies passed despite their efforts. But all interest groups are fallible; and the agents' most egregious lapses occurred in 1763–1764, just when the Treasury

[46] Lillian M. Penson, "The Origin of the Crown Agency Office," *EHR*, XL (1925), 199–200; Clark, *Rise of the British Treasury*, p. 98. In 1761, the Postmaster General appointed a resident agent in New York (*ibid.*, p. 101).

[47] *Ibid.*, pp. 95–96, 120–124, 127, 130; Franklin to Samuel Rhoads, July 8, 1765, Smyth, IV, 388. Edward Montagu of Virginia also opposed this measure successfully in 1765.

[48] Franklin to Joseph Galloway, Sept. 6, 1758, to Isaac Norris, March 19 and June 9, 1759, Labaree, *Papers of Franklin*, VIII, 146, 292, 398; Board of Trade to Arthur Dobbs, April 14, 1761, Colonial Documents, 1761–1764, Bancroft Transcripts, NYPL.

—administrative source of the new colonial measures—underwent an unsettling political upheaval. The London representatives were transforming their institution while coping with an almost impossible period in British public life and colonial management. Given these difficulties they—or at least many of them—acquitted themselves well between 1756 and 1766.[49]

[49] See *Pamphlets of the American Revolution, 1750–1776*, ed. Bernard Bailyn, I (Cambridge, Mass., 1965), 358; Shy, *Toward Lexington*, pp. 185–186.

CHAPTER 7

The Agents and the
Stamp Act Crisis, 1765–1766

On March 4, 1766, when the bill for repeal of the Stamp Act passed the House of Commons, jubilant colonial agents gathered in the lobby to celebrate the culmination of a long campaign. When the act received royal assent four days later, the triumphant lobbyists chartered the brig *Minerva* to carry the news to America. They had gradually overcome their traditional limitations and transformed their uncertain initial responses into vigorous opposition. For when a stamp bill had been in preparation at the Treasury, during the winter of 1763–1764, the colonial agents had not all acted with a sense of urgency.[1]

PASSAGE

George Grenville rose in the Commons on March 9, 1764, to speak about the precarious financial situation of his government. He suggested that colonial stamp duties might be necessary, but requested no parliamentary action until the next session, ostensibly to allow the colonies an opportunity to offer objections or an alternative method of raising the required funds. Actually Grenville's subordinates needed

---

[1] Lawrence H. Gipson, "The Great Debate in the Committee of the Whole House of Commons on the Stamp Act, 1766, as Reported by Nathaniel Ryder," *PMHB*, LXXXVI (1962), 39–40; William B. Reed, *The Life of Esther De Berdt . . .* (Philadelphia, 1853), p. 76. My interpretation of attitudes and events differs in a number of places throughout the chapter from Jack M. Sosin's in *Agents and Merchants: British Colonial Policy and the Origins of the American Revolution, 1763–1775* (Lincoln, Neb., 1965), pp. 49–72.

more time to accumulate information about taxable items and documents used in America in order to facilitate their writing a bill. Meanwhile the colonial agents, several of whom had reported the "Gentle Shepherd's" budget speech to their constituents, wondered what possible alternatives might be acceptable to the administration. They requested a conference with Grenville which took place on May 17, 1764—the most important and controversial conference in the history of the agencies.[2]

The agents asked the minister for a copy of the proposed bill so that their "respective constituents might have the whole, both substance and form under their deliberation." But Grenville could not oblige them as the bill was still in rough form. Then, without repudiating his offer made on the floor of the Commons ten weeks earlier, Grenville retreated. He conceded that for the colonies "the raising it within themselves and appropriating it would have been attended with very many difficulties." He warned proleptically that colonial refusals to pay would go unheeded by an unsympathetic Parliament. When the agents sought the objects and rates of the tax, they were informed that "everyone knew the stamp laws here, and that this Bill is intended to be formd upon the same plan." Grenville then departed from orthodoxy and the terms of his budget speech by suggesting that the agents should assent in advance to the uncertain new tax, thereby setting a precedent for consultations about future levies. The agents did not follow the First Lord's advice, for some of them at least realized that he was gently closing off the alternatives he had mentioned earlier.[3]

Ambiguity characterized the conference. By evading the agents' desire to know the amounts required of the colonies, Grenville made it

---

[2] Jasper Mauduit to Mass. General Court, March 13, 1764, MA, XXII, 359; Edward Montagu to Va. CC, April 11, 1764, *Virginia Gazette* (Purdie and Dixon), Oct. 3, 1766; Eliphalet Dyer to Jared Ingersoll, April 14, 1764, NHCHS *Papers*, IX (New Haven, 1918), 291; Edmund S. and Helen M. Morgan, *The Stamp Act Crisis: Prologue to Revolution* (Chapel Hill, 1953), pp. 53–60.

[3] There are three accounts by contemporaries—two by agents present at the conference and the third by Jasper Mauduit, whose brother attended (Jasper Mauduit to Mass. General Court, May 26, 1764, MA, XXII, 375; Lewis B. Namier, "Charles Garth, Agent for South Carolina," *EHR*, LIV [1939], 646; William Knox, *The Claim of the Colonies to an Exemption from Internal Taxes* [London, 1765], pp. 31–33). Narratives which appeared in subsequent years are unreliable because the episode became a political football during the Great Debate. The more important pieces in this polemic are William Knox, *The Controversy between Great Britain and Her Colonies Reviewed* (London,

impossible for them to consider a substitute tax themselves.[4] It is not clear from accounts of the interview whether Grenville held open the possibility of utilizing the conventional requisition system as a viable alternative to stamp duties. Had he done so it would have been insincere, for as he admitted a few years later:

It will be extremely difficult, if not impracticable, for the colonies to apportion a certain sum by a convention of deputies from each colony. They would, therefore, never do it, and the convention of deputies would quarrel, which would probably be attended with very bad consequences. . . . The difficulty of assessing the specific sums on each colony would then fall upon the Parliament. . . . And as the various circumstances of the colonies would render it extremely difficult, if not impossible, to establish any permanent rate for the several quotas, the consequence would be that none would be established.[5]

Grenville's position was awkward. He deeply believed that the colonies were obliged to share in supporting a North American military establishment. Recognizing the inadequacy of traditional means of raising provincial funds, he also believed that a parliamentary tax was

1769), 198–199; Edmund Burke's speech "On American Taxation," delivered April 19, 1774; and Israel Mauduit, *Mr. Grenville's Offer to the Colony Assemblies to Raise the Supply Themselves Instead of Having It Done by a Parliamentary Stamp Act* (Feb. 1775). John Almon later reprinted Mauduit's version with the comment that "this paper is insidious. The insinuation is obvious; it is this, that America refused to give any aid or assistance to Great Britain: no insinuation could be more unjust" (*Biographical, Literary, and Political Anecdotes*. . . . [London, 1797], II, 86–92). Finally there is Benjamin Franklin's "True History of the Difference Between the Colonies and the Author of the Stamp Act," written in 1778 (Smyth, VII, 118–120).

[4] Grenville privately suggested the sum of £80 to £100,000 to Israel Mauduit (*The Jenkinson Papers, 1760–1766*, ed. Ninetta S. Jucker [London, 1949], p. 307).

[5] Grenville to William Knox, July 15, 1768, "Correspondence of William Knox, Chiefly in Relation to American Affairs, 1757–1808," HMC *Report on Manuscripts in Various Collections*, VI (Dublin, 1909), 97. On July 2, 1764, Charles Jenkinson, secretary to the treasury, wrote Grenville as follows: "In the last session of Parliament you assigned as a reason for not going on with the Stamp Act, that you waited only for further information on that subject. This having been said, should not Government appear to take some step for that purpose? I mentioned this to you soon after the Parliament was up. I remember your objections to it; but I think the information may be procured in a manner to obviate those objections, and without it we may perhaps be accused of neglect" (Jucker, *Jenkinson Papers*, p. 305). See also Dora Mae Clark, *The Rise of the British Treasury* (New Haven, 1960), p. 120.

the only satisfactory solution. But that involved a dangerous departure from constitutional precedents cherished in North America. A stamp tax would be an innovation transposing authority from colonial legislatures to an imperial assembly in which no colonial as such participated. By broaching the idea of a stamp bill a year before it would be ready, Grenville hoped to win the consent of the colonial legislatures as well as gain time to complete what he considered an equitable table of duties. At worst the colonists would do nothing and the Stamp Act would appear as the inevitable outcome of colonial indecision. Shrewdly he tried to soften the blow for the Americans by holding out the possibility of some alternative they might invent. But when the agents made an effort to discern suitable substitutes, he became evasive. In the process he exposed himself to charges of bad faith.[6]

Grenville had been deluded in hoping for colonial consent to his stamp tax. Still he stood pledged to collect an American revenue and knew he had parliamentary support. Moreover, Parliament's authority over the colonies had been questioned. The best way to assert that authority was to exercise it. Therefore he pressed his bill to completion in the autumn and had it prepared for presentation to the House of Commons early in 1765. The agents meanwhile proceeded with uncertain resolve. They were promptly instructed by their colonies to oppose the act and offer petitions against it. If that did not succeed they were to "have them [the petitions] printed and dispersed over the Nation, or the substance of them, at least, published." The colonies denied that Parliament had the right to tax them, though they informed their agents that they would contribute by requisition if only the ministry would suggest quotas.[7]

[6] The recent literature surrounding this affair is extensive. Edmund S. Morgan and Frederic J. Ericson are Grenville's harshest critics (Morgan, *Stamp Act Crisis*, ch. 5, and "The Postponement of the Stamp Act," 3*WMQ*, VII [1950], 353–392; Ericson, "The Contemporary British Opposition to the Stamp Act," *Papers of the Michigan Academy of Science, Arts and Letters*, XXIX [1943], 489–505). Charles R. Ritcheson takes a middle position in "The Preparation of the Stamp Act," 3*WMQ*, X (1953), 543–559, while Jack M. Sosin defends Grenville in *Whitehall and the Wilderness: The Middle West in British Colonial Policy, 1760–1775* (Lincoln, Neb., 1961), ch. 4, and *Agents and Merchants*, pp. 52–53.

[7] Va. CC to Edward Montagu, Dec. 20, 1764, "Proceedings of the Virginia Committee of Correspondence, 1759–1767," *VMHB*, IX (1902), 354. For the various colonial instructions to the agents see Morgan, "Postponement of the Stamp Act," 370 n.

The worried agents realized that owing to their constituents' declarations of right the issue was fast becoming a test of Parliament's authority. They also knew Parliament would not hear remonstrances tending to question its legislative supremacy; so a few agents, led by William Knox,[8] urged that they unite in a petition of their own, stressing expediency rather than right. Such a petition was drafted but never presented because most of the agents—constrained by their instructions—did not feel free to sign it. Instead they sought assistance from the merchants, many of whom opposed the idea of an American stamp tax. But the merchants had not yet "become sufficiently alarmed to mobilize and concert their opposition." As one agent wrote, "the merchants talk much, but [we] cannot bring them to Act." [9]

As 1764 ended, unhappy prospects loomed ahead for the agents. Despite considerable propaganda there was no organized opposition in Parliament to Grenville's bill. The discouraged agents agreed with Edward Montagu of Virginia that "the House appeared so unanimous in [its] opinion that America should ease the revenue of this annual expense that I am persuaded they will not liken to any remonstrance against it." [10] After several tactical meetings the lobbyists decided upon one last effort to "ward off the intended blow" by renewing their interview with Grenville. They delegated Garth and Jackson, both Members of Parliament, as well as Franklin and Ingersoll to wait on the Chancellor of the Exchequer. The group met on February 2, 1765.

The agents opened by seeking for the colonies a self-imposed tax rather than duties levied in London. When Grenville asked them for a better device, they reverted to requisitions "as being a Method the people had been used to." The Chancellor raised his thick eyebrows

[8] Georgia's legislature reappointed Knox annually until November 1765, when it instructed the Committee of Correspondence to fire him because he had advised the colony to submit to the stamp duties. Knox's performance during the Stamp Act crisis is as confusing as the communications he received from his constituents. He defended the measure in pamphlets, opposed it in petitions, and arranged to be examined before the House of Commons (*Brief State of Mr. Knox's Case*, broadside, HLHU; *PHE*, XVI, 137; Knox to George Grenville, [Jan. 1766?], Grenville MSS in the possession of Sir John Murray, box B-2).

[9] Knox, *Claim of the Colonies*, p. 35; Morgan, *Stamp Act Crisis*, p. 63; Jasper Mauduit to Mass. General Court, Jan. 16, 1765, MA, XXII, 426.

[10] Montagu to Va. CC, April 11, 1764, *Virginia Gazette* (Purdie and Dixon), Oct. 3, 1766.

and "warmly rejected the thought," curtly asking the foursome whether they "could agree upon the several proportions Each colony should raise." They conceded that they could not. Grenville, in turn, admitted that his civil servants lacked adequate information from which to assign quotas. Having reached an impasse, the first minister stated that nothing could be done to dissuade him anyway, for "he had pledged his Word for offering the Stamp Bill to the house, [and] that the house would hear all [the agents'] Objections & would do as they thought best." [11]

Apart from Grenville's fixed commitment to a stamp bill, his behavior at the conferences was less than candid. His request that the agents decide what proportion each province should pay was indeed rhetorical. As head of the Treasury he knew very well that for several years the agents had encountered problems when called upon to divide parliamentary grants. He also knew that he was departing from precedent by asking the agents for information which the administrative offices should provide. The Secretary of State for the Southern Department, the Treasury Board, and the Board of Trade ought primarily to have supplied the data Grenville lacked, since they traditionally accumulated such information through inquiries sent to various officials in America. Grenville surprised the lobbyists when he asked them to set requisition quotas. He knew they would be unauthorized and unable to do so. Finally, Grenville's concession that "he did not think anybody here [in his government] was furnished with Materials" to apportion the required sum among the colonies was a tacit recognition of his administration's inadequate knowledge of colonial conditions. [12]

As the unsuccessful conference concluded, Grenville shifted any further lobbying on the part of the agents from his own office to Parliament, where he introduced his stamp proposals on February 6, 1765. [13] The ensuing debate was a singular success for the administra-

[11] Ingersoll's narrative of the conference, written on Feb. 11, 1765, is printed in NHCHS *Papers*, IX, 312–314; Garth's account, dated Feb. 8, 1765, is in Namier, "Garth, Agent," p. 649.

[12] Lawrence H. Gipson, *The British Empire before the American Revolution*, X (New York, 1961), ch. 2; Franklin B. Wickwire, *British Subministers and Colonial America, 1763–1783* (Princeton, 1966), 83 n.

[13] The agents were not without initiative while the Stamp Act was in preparation. Franklin later claimed that he had presented Grenville with a plan for a general loan office in America—one that would issue interest-bearing bills of credit with parliamentary safeguards to prevent depreciated currency. "Mr.

tion. Even those most ardently opposed to the new duties merely argued that they were inexpedient, but did not deny Parliament's authority. This point was so generally accepted that when Connecticut's Jared Ingersoll "advised the Agents if possible to get that point Canvassed that so the Americans might at least have the Satisfaction of having the point Decided upon a full Debate," he found "it could not be done." The only bright moment occurred when Colonel Isaac Barré made his memorable equation of colonial patriots with "Sons of Liberty." The next day the House of Commons passed the fifty-five resolutions which formed the basis of the Stamp Act. Having secured parliamentary approval, Grenville introduced the actual bill on February 13.[14]

The agents meanwhile had been busily trying to circumvent the restriction placed upon their freedom of action by the shackles of constitutionality. Assisted by Garth, Ingersoll pressed his friend, Secretary to the Treasury Thomas Whately, who was responsible for preparing the duties, and succeeded in having some duties lowered and three items dropped from the list altogether. The agents persuaded a committee of London merchants that the stamp duties would have deleterious effects on North American commerce. In consequence the merchants agreed to prepare a petition. Garth procured one signed by South Carolinians in London which he planned to present on February 15, but with little hope of success.[15]

His fears were justified. He submitted his petition while Sir William Meredith presented Virginia's for Edward Montagu. Rose Fuller offered one "in behalf of the Merchants in London trading to America." But the House objected to hearing the merchants in support of the colonies, so Fuller withdrew his petition rather than see it rejected outright. The American remonstrances became objects of warm debate; but the Commons refused by a large majority to listen,

Grenville paid little attention to it, being besotted with his Stamp Scheme, which he rather chose to carry through" (Franklin to Joseph Galloway, Oct. 11, 1766, WCL). An anonymous writer, probably Edward Montagu, drafted a table showing "a computation of the number of inhabitants in each colony, and a proportion of duties which might be raised in each, as an equivalent in lieu of the Stamp Duties" (*Virginia Gazette* [Purdie and Dixon], July 11, 1766).

[14] Morgan, *Stamp Act Crisis*, pp. 66–69; Ingersoll to Thomas Fitch, Feb. 11, 1765, NHCHS *Papers*, IX, 306; *The Correspondence of the Colonial Governors of Rhode Island, 1723–1775*, ed. G. S. Kimball (Boston, 1902–1903), II, 383 n. 2.

[15] Ingersoll to Fitch, Feb. 11, 1765, NHCHS *Papers*, IX, 314; Namier, "Garth," pp. 650, 652.

claiming they violated that body's tradition against hearing petitions opposed to money bills. When Richard Jackson's memorial for Connecticut met the same fate, he pocketed a similar one from Massachusetts; "& seeing which way the same would be governed he told the house he would defer it till another Time. . . . The other Agents seeing the point thus ruled, thought it to no purpose to offer any more." [16]

Robert Charles had received a petition from New York "which was conceived in terms so inflammatory that he could not prevail on any one Member of the House to present it." This difficulty foreshadowed a problem which dogged the agents in the following decade and constricted their utility as a pressure group. Garth warned his employers that more Members would be won with the honey of expediency than with ideological vinegar: "Some of the petitions that were framed in America and sent over from some of the Colonies to their agents, questioned the power of Parliament in very high tones, phrases inserted that Members very well inclin'd to serve the Colonies could not be prevailed with to offer them to the House from a certainty of incurring the censure of Parliament." [17]

Some of the opposition, led by Henry Seymour Conway, castigated Parliament's refusal to hear the petitions—a prelude to many similar denials before 1776. The bill nevertheless passed the second division without even a reading, and by March 22 the Stamp Act was a British statute. Thomas Ruston wrote with some validity that Grenville had secured its passage "merely by browbeating our agents, and suppressing Remonstrances which were ordered by his Majesty to be laid before the House." That the act would not become effective until November, at least, resulted from the agents' request for delay. The behavior of the colonists in the interim is well known. They rioted, organized a boycott of British goods, and ostracized the stamp distributors. [18] The behavior of the agents is less familiar.

[16] Ingersoll to Fitch, March 6, 1765, NHCHS *Papers*, IX, 315–318; Harris Debates, Feb. 15, 1765, Malmesbury MSS, Christchurch, Hants.; Garth to S.C. CC, Feb. 17, 1765, Namier, "Garth, Agent," pp. 650–651; *JHC*, XXX, 147–148.

[17] Ingersoll to Thomas Fitch, March 6, 1765, NHCHS *Papers*, IX, 317; Namier, "Garth, Agent," pp. 650–651. See also Walter E. Minchinton, "The Stamp Act Crisis: Bristol and Virginia," *VMHB*, LXXIII (1965), 149–150.

[18] Alan Hardy, "The Duke of Newcastle and His Friends in Opposition, 1762–1765" (unpub. M.A. thesis; University of Manchester, 1956), pp. 251–253; Thomas Ruston to J. Ruston, March 3, 1766, WCL; Lawrence H. Gipson, *Jared Ingersoll* (New Haven, 1920), p. 141.

In certain respects it was disappointing, for they seemed to have capitulated. Richard Jackson's sentiments were shared by several agents. After the act passed he wrote that "the Stamp Duty is some heavier than I thought it, when I opposed the first Motion, yet I hope it will not be intolerable. . . . I hope therefore that the Tax will be cheerfully, or at least patiently submitted to." [19] Early in April, Grenville maneuvered shrewdly. He needed to appoint stamp distributors for the colonies, but preferred to ease the pain by naming colonials of good standing rather than alien Britons. He therefore summoned the agents to a conference where Whately persuaded Franklin and Barlow Trecothick to recommend distributors for Pennsylvania and New York, and Jared Ingersoll to accept the job in Connecticut. As Ingersoll related it, "the offer was made generally to those who had appeared as the Agents or friends of the Colonies, to take it themselves or nominate their friends." [20]

Five years later Grenville boldly used this incident to vindicate his Stamp Act. Speaking in the House in 1770, he claimed that before proposing the act he had sought the advice of "men of the first respectability. . . . Far from thinking the tax impracticable, some of the assemblies applied to me, by their agents, to collect this very tax. . . . Many, almost all, of those persons have since been active against it. . . . Did they [not] apply to me to appoint their relations, their sons, their best friends?" [21] Grenville's tales had grown tall in the interval, or else his memory had grown short.

The unfortunates who so compromised themselves found that their reputations suffered greatly in the colonies, and they quickly regretted an imprudence that permanently obliterated from many memories all their efforts of the preceding and even subsequent years. During the spring of 1765, the agents redirected their efforts, lobbying strenuously against the mutiny bill with a group of interested North American merchants. In this endeavor they achieved greater success.

---

[19] Jackson to Thomas Fitch, March 9, 1765, CHS *Collections*, XVIII (Hartford, 1920), 341–342. See also Jared Ingersoll to Fitch, March 6, 1765, NHCHS *Papers*, IX, 319, 332.

[20] *Connecticut Gazette*, Sept. 10, 1765, in NHCHS *Papers*, IX, 332–333; Franklin to Josiah Tucker, Feb. 26, 1774, Smyth, VI, 200; James McEvers to Trecothick, Aug. 26, 1765, Main Papers, HLRO.

[21] *Sir Henry Cavendish's Debates of the House of Commons during the Thirteenth Parliament of Great Britain*, ed. John Wright (London, 1841–1843), I, 494–496.

(Through the labors of Franklin, Montagu and Ingersoll, the act included elaborate rules for preventing abuses as the result of quartering soldiers or impressing horses and wagons in the colonies. At Montagu's initiative the clause was eliminated that would have permitted billeting in private homes.) [22] But the agents could do little about the Stamp Act until they heard from the colonies and until the winter session of Parliament opened later in the year. When news did arrive of their constituents' response, they reacted with alacrity. [23]

REPEAL

The story of the campaign to repeal the Stamp Act during the fall and winter of 1765–1766 is a familiar one and has been the subject of various monographs. The important role the agents played has also been scrutinized, so that only the highlights need be reviewed here. It is the nature and success of the agents' participation rather than the detailed narrative that is significant. [24]

While the agents awaited word from America during the summer of 1765, George III dismissed Grenville in a fit of pique over a regency bill. The King's preferred replacement, William Pitt, could not merge his small following into the coalition necessary for some semblance of ministerial stability. As a result the monarch resorted to an administration headed by the Marquess of Rockingham and including the old Duke of Newcastle, General Conway, and the Duke of Grafton. These young and Old Whigs took office early in July, and for the next five months resembled nothing so much as a newborn colt

---

[22] Gipson, *British Empire before the American Revolution*, XI, 44–45.

[23] Namier, "Garth, Agent," p. 642; Nicholas Varga, "The New York Restraining Act," *New York History*, XXXVII (1956), 236; Benjamin Franklin to Lord Kames, April 11, 1767, Smyth, V, 18.

[24] For general accounts of repeal, see John C. Miller, *Origins of the American Revolution* (2nd ed.; London, 1959), ch. 7; Charles R. Ritcheson, *British Politics and the American Revolution* (Norman, Okla., 1954), ch. 2; Morgan, *Stamp Act Crisis*, ch. 15. The more important special studies are Allen S. Johnson, "British Politics and the Repeal of the Stamp Act," *South Atlantic Quarterly*, LXII (1963), 169–188; D. H. Watson, "Barlow Trecothick and Other Associates of Lord Rockingham during the Stamp Act Crisis, 1765–1766" (unpub. M.A. thesis; Sheffield University, 1957); B. R. Smith, "The Committee of the Whole House to Consider the American Papers (January and February 1766)" (unpub. M.A. thesis; Sheffield University, 1956); Gipson, "The Great Debate," pp. 10–41.

deserted by its mare, standing shakily in need of support. By keeping himself aloof and refusing to aid the Rockinghams, Pitt left the ministry in distress. Then news of the American riots arrived in autumn to present the newcomers with the problem of calming an agitation their opponents had called into being. Lacking any weighty backing within Parliament, Rockingham accepted assistance outside Westminster from the merchants.[25]

Their alliance depended upon a common repugnance to the Stamp Act. Several of the Marquess' supporters were friends of America and had opposed the passage of Grenville's duties. The merchants trading both to North America and the West Indies had many differences, but they found that this measure of the previous ministry affected them both adversely—a fact they had not fully appreciated earlier in 1764 and 1765. They were financially troubled by the depression that followed the end of the Seven Years' War, and colonial agreements not to import British goods until the Stamp Act was repealed compounded their fretfulness.

On December 4, 1765, the London merchants, led by Barlow Trecothick, formed a committee of twenty-eight to organize mercantile sentiment and arrange a publicity campaign directed at Parliament and advocating repeal. Trecothick, just appointed New Hampshire's agent and previously an informal political broker for Massachusetts, headed the committee and served as liaison between merchants and agents on the one hand and the Rockingham Whigs on the other.[26] Trecothick met with Rockingham and some of his subordinates to draft a circular letter which they dispatched to thirty trading and manufacturing towns throughout the kingdom, seeking their support. In consequence Parliament received petitions from twenty-six commercial centers as well as from London. Most important, these documents adhered closely to the argument that if American trade was allowed to deteriorate, Britain's prosperity would rapidly decline. They never mentioned parliamentary authority.

Although Parliament met briefly on December 17, it adjourned on the twentieth to permit vacancies to be filled so that a full house would be present when the American problem was offered for debate on January 14. During the interlude Trecothick kept busy conferring

---

[25] G. H. Guttridge, *English Whiggism and the American Revolution* (Berkeley, 1942), p. 65.

[26] Cooperation between Trecothick and Rockingham really began during the second week in November at a dinner initiating tactical meetings.

with ministers, merchants, and agents alternately. Nor had the latter been idle. From October onward, William Bollan, acting as agent without portfolio, began to deluge Rockingham with letters urging repeal. Franklin "was extreamly busy attending Members of both Houses, informing, explaining, consulting, disputing, in a continual Hurry from Morning to Night." In November he had an audience with Lord Dartmouth, the new president of the Board of Trade, in which the agent suggested that stamp taxes be suspended for a number of years and then conveniently dropped when a favorable opportunity arose, without the question of right even having been raised.[27]

All the while the merchants and agents met to coordinate their petitioning and collect materials for presentation to Parliament when it reconvened.[28] Nevertheless the prospects for repeal at this point were uncertain. Richard Jackson wrote confidentially on January 11 that he doubted the act would be repealed, though "every other Relief may be, I think, expected, & even this Law will probably be reduced to nothing more, than a Proof of the Power of Parliament to impose taxes as well as make other Laws for America."[29]

On the same day William Strahan sent an American friend a detailed description of Franklin's efforts to discredit the Stamp Act:

The Assiduity of our Friend Dr. Franklin is really astonishing. He is forever with one member of Parliament or another (most of whom by the bye seem to have been deplorably ignorant with regard to the Nature and Consequence of the Colonies) endeavouring to impress them; first, with the Importance of the present Dispute; then to state the Case clearly and fully, stripping it of every thing foreign to the main Point; and lastly, to answer objections arising either from a total Ignorance, a partial Knowledge, or a wrong Conception of the matter. To enforce this repeatedly, and

[27] Watson, "Barlow Trecothick and Other Associates," pp. 15, 234–244; Franklin to Lord Kames, Feb. 25, 1767, Abercairny Collection, no. 562, Scottish Record Office, Edinburgh; Franklin to Deborah Franklin, Feb. 22, 1766, Smyth, IV, 408; Franklin to Galloway, Oct. 11, 1766, WCL.

[28] Marguerite Appleton, "The Agents of the New England Colonies in the Revolutionary Period," *NEQ*, VI (1933), 376. For the mass of evidence accumulated by the lobbyists preparatory to inundating Parliament, see the 190-item bundle in the Main Papers, reference for Jan. 14, 1766, HLRO.

[29] Jackson to Thomas Fitch, Jan. 11, 1766, CHS *Collections*, XVIII, 383; for a running commentary on the repeal campaign, see the extracts from Jackson's letters to Francis Bernard, Nov.–March 1765–1766, printed in *Speeches of the Governors of Massachusetts from 1765 to 1775 . . .* , ed. Alden Bradford (Boston, 1818), pp. 69–73.

with Propriety, in the manner he has done these last two months, I assure you is no easy Task. By this means, however, when the Parlt. reassembles, many members will go into the House properly instructed, and be able to speak in the Debates with Precision and Propriety, which the Well-wishers of the Colonies have hitherto been unable to do. —This is the most necessary and essential Service he could perform on this Occasion. . . . All this while, too, he hath been throwing out Hints in the Public Papers, and giving answers to such Letters as have appeared in them, that required or deserved an answer. —In this manner is he now employed, with very little Intermission, Night and Day.[30]

It was just at this time also that Franklin invented his famous cartoon, "Magna Britannia her Colonies Reduc'd" (which is reproduced as Plate VIII), to suggest what would happen if Britain used force on the colonies. He had many copies reproduced on cards and used them to send messages during the period of crisis, especially "to men in power in Great Britain"; he also "employed a Waiter," it was reported, "to put one of them in each Parliament Mans hand as he entred the house the day preceding the great debate of the Stamp Act."[31]

Meanwhile Rockingham's government faced a serious dilemma: how to redress the grievances of the colonists without diminishing the honor of Parliament. At the end of 1765 the administration still lacked a definite policy. But within a fortnight the young Marquess united his ministers in favor of repeal—rather than mere revision preferred by the crown. The solution that fused the government was reached on January 17 and closely resembled that advocated by Pitt on the fourteenth when he rose in the Commons to applaud the rebellious Sons of Liberty. Rockingham wrote that "the ideas we join in are . . . a declaratory act in general terms,—afterwards to proceed to considerations of trade, etc., and finally determination on the stamp act, i.e., a repeal." He introduced the resolution for the Declaratory Act on February 3, and one for repeal on February 21. During the intervening weeks, his administration tendered the agents every encouragement in their program of promoting and publicizing popular demands for repeal.[32]

[30] To David Hall, Jan. 11, 1766, quoted in J. A. Cochrane, *Dr. Johnson's Printer: The Life of William Strahan* (Cambridge, Mass., 1964), p. 113.

[31] Edwin Wolf II "Benjamin Franklin's Stamp Act Cartoon," APS *Proceedings*, XCIX (1955), 388–390. See Plate VIII.

[32] Watson, "Barlow Trecothick and Other Associates," p. 50; Gipson, "The Great Debate," p. 10.

Petitions perhaps proved to be the pressure group's most effective weapon. Most of the twenty-six petitions from the commercial centers arrived between January 17 and 27. Their coordination and simultaneous presentation was due largely to Trecothick's efforts. These petitions' complaints of economic stagnation were reinforced by the obvious fact of continued depression. High unemployment and disquieting reports of unrest in the colonies inclined Parliament to give a careful hearing to proposals of the administration, petitions of the agents, and the testimony of various witnesses called before the House of Commons sitting as a committee of the whole.

In addition to petitions from British merchants and manufacturers, Parliament heard memorials from lobbyists Montagu and Knox, presented by Garth, carefully phrased to avoid any affront to the supreme legislature. Nearly all of the agents of the North American and West Indian colonies were invited to attend the committee of the whole house on February 4 in order to testify against the Stamp Act.[33] Those agents, merchants, and visiting Americans who were called to the bar of the House were not casual witnesses. Their testimony had been carefully rehearsed beforehand with their inquisitors. Trecothick and Franklin were the featured performers, each holding the stand for four hours, on the eleventh and thirteenth respectively, and eloquently offering statistics and views calculated to impress their jury.[34] The overall presentation of oral and documentary evidence was structured to emphasize the disastrous economic consequences of the Stamp Act and minimize the colonists' denial of Parliament's authority to tax them. Following this strategy, Rockingham did not utilize the memorials of the Stamp Act Congress in New York. Charles Garth, for one, knew that their not being properly signed was only a pretext.[35]

At eleven o'clock on the night of February 7 the agents crowded into the lobby of the Commons at the moment of victory over Grenville's proposed address to the King urging enforcement of the Stamp

[33] Garth to S.C. CC, Jan. 19, 1766, *SCHGM*, XXVI, 68–92; *JHC*, XXX, 513.

[34] Trecothick's testimony was probably rehearsed the morning of his performance with the Duke of Newcastle (Add MSS 32973, f. 411). The questions Richard Jackson asked one witness were patently prepared in advance (Smith, "Committee of the Whole," pp. 27–29). For Franklin's prearrangements, see Smith, "Committee of the Whole," pp. 26, 33.

[35] "Stamp Act Papers," *MHM*, VI (1911), 285. Franklin had worked hard to give the impression that the colonists objected only to internal, not external taxes (Morgan, *Stamp Act Crisis*, p. 272).

Act. But the outcome was still far from clear. One agent wondered as late as February 16: "What will become of the stamp act, I dare not guess; no labor of mine has been spared to obtain its repeal; which is however strongly opposed, and at present by an apparent majority in the House of Lords." With Trecothick assisting in the presentation of petitions to the Lords, that body eventually came around. Parliament passed the Declaratory Act first and then agreed to repeal on February 22. On March 18 the King added his assent.[36]

The process had been exhausting. Debates continued night after night till the early hours of morning, requiring the agents to attend continuously. Jackson found "carrying the repeal . . . miraculous. . . . I have never been a minute out of the House of Commons for above six weeks whilst it has been on, often till ten at night, not seldom till three in the morning." Many of the other agents wrote similarly to their friends and constituents abroad.[37]

In addition to hard work and concerted effort, other factors had spurred repeal along. The political kaleidoscope had turned briefly to allow just the right pieces to fall into place. The lobbyists had almost the full cooperation of Rockingham's administration. Moreover, two long-conflicting interest groups—North American and West Indian—briefly joined hands against a measure inimicable to both; and these trading interests had gained political influence since the accession of George III. The postwar depression coupled with an effective American boycott made those involved in the American trade unusually susceptible to friendly persuasion in 1765–1766. Trecothick's intimate knowledge and adroit control of ministerial support was a circumstance entirely new to movements of this kind. Furthermore, one Scot wrote in 1766 that the "true Reason . . . for the Repeal was the great sums owing by Americans to great Britain." Lacking stamps, the American courts had closed, and alarmed British creditors feared they would be unable to bring suits to recover their debts.[38]

[36] Bradford, *Speeches*, p. 71; Richard Jackson to Samuel White, March 12, 1766, MA, Letters, 1764–1774, p. 19; Trecothick to Newcastle, March 3, 1766, Add MSS 32974, f. 133; Smith, "Committee of the Whole," pp. 95–96; *JHC*, XXX, 451, 601–602. See also Thomas H. D. Mahoney, "Edmund Burke and the American Revolution: The Repeal of the Stamp Act," *Burke Newsletter*, VII (1965–1966), 518.

[37] Bradford, *Speeches*, p. 72; Benjamin Franklin to Lord Kames, Feb. 25, 1767, Scottish Record Office.

[38] Dr. John Fothergill wrote that "America owes the Repeal of the Stamp Act to the assiduous Endeavors of Alderman Trecothick, Capel Hanbury & Dr.

The successful movement for repeal had partially resulted from reinforcement that the agents had received from unofficial auxiliaries. George Folliott, a New York merchant visiting London in 1765–1766, was warmly received by Rockingham. The Marquess and his political deputy, Dowdeswell, asked endless questions of the visitor, ranging from North American commerce to attitudes behind the Boston riots. Thomas Hollis had also intensified Rockingham's impressions on the colonial question, and Pitt's as well. Dennis De Berdt Jr. and Joseph Reed had done the same for Dartmouth.[39]

Still another important factor played a part, a military consideration—the danger that France and Spain might aid the colonies in the event of rebellion. Charles Garth suggested that one of the chief arguments for repeal was "the impracticability of enforcing this Law throughout the Continent without a Military Force, [and] the impending and sure Ruin from a conflict of that Nature." In the secret parliamentary debates certain members anticipated the seriousness of potential military involvement as well as danger to their commercial system. In addition, the accidental removal of staunch political die-hards helped. Thomas Hutchinson Jr. wrote his father that he heard "Mr. Jackson in Conversation give it as his Opinion that if the Duke of Cumberland had not died, instead of a repeal of the Act, there wou'd have been a number of Regiments in America before this."[40]

The agents had been able to overcome their parochial tendencies and for the moment forge a new conception of their office. In 1765, Franklin found the agents "have been of late so much engaged in our general American affairs that it was necessary to let what particularly related to [Pennsylvania] sleep awhile for the present." Such concerted operations were unusual when set against the full history of the agency. The lobbyists had produced the most remarkable achievement

Franklin" (*The New Régime, 1765–1767*, ed. C. W. Alvord and C. E. Carter [Illinois State Historical Library *Collections*, Vol. XI (Springfield, 1916)], p. 220). Lucy S. Sutherland, "Edmund Burke and the First Rockingham Ministry," *EHR*, XLVII (1932), 49–50, 63–66; Emory G. Evans, "Planter Indebtedness and the Coming of the Revolution in Virginia," 3*WMQ*, XIX (1962), 528.

[39] MS diary of George Folliott, Edward Hall MSS, No. 67, Wigan Central Public Library, Lancashire, England; Diary of Thomas Hollis, p. 443, Colonial Williamsburg; De Berdt Jr. to Joseph Reed, Feb. 15, 1766, Reed MSS, NYHS.

[40] Gipson, "The Great Debate," pp. 36–37 n., 40; William Bollan to Hutchinson, March 1, 1766, MA, XXV, 63; Hutchinson Jr. to Hutchinson, July 1, 1766, MA, XXV, 85.

in their institution's annals.[41] The momentum of their triumph carried forward until early May, when the ministry appreciably altered the Sugar Act of 1764. The North American agents and merchants argued that a lower duty was essential to a restoration of imperial trade, and they deserve substantial credit for this change as well.[42]

[41] Franklin to John Ross, Feb. 14, 1765, Smyth, IV, 361; Bernard Donoughue, *British Politics and the American Revolution: The Path to War, 1773–1775* (London, 1964), pp. 4, 146, 289.

[42] *JHC*, XXX, 783–808; Allen S. Johnson, "The Political Career of George Grenville, 1712–1770" (unpub. Ph.D. diss.; Duke University, 1955), pp. 442–443.

Part Two

INSTITUTIONAL DECLINE
AND IMPERIAL DETERIORATION,
1766–1775

"*Juncta juvant,* and when vested with ample authority I have gone in to the Lords of the Treasury at the head of seven or eight agents of so many colonies, but now they seem a rope of sand."
—WILLIAM BOLLAN, 1773

CHAPTER 8

A Profile of the Agency, 1766–1773

As Rockingham's administration gave way to the Grafton-Chatham coalition in 1766, the agents had no way of knowing that their pinnacle of success had just been passed. The coming decade would bring immense strains to bear on their institution and would finally cause its demise; but this was not immediately apparent. At least until 1770, the North American pressure group retained many of the appearances of vigor and some of the reality.

PERSONNEL: A GROUP PORTRAIT

De Berdt, Jackson, and Robert Charles all remained active until 1770, though with diminishing success. Charles had never been financially secure. The vicious factionalism of New York politics in the later 1760's added to his personal instability and lessened his effectiveness until he took his own life in 1770.[1] Richard Jackson's political stature also suffered on account of provincial politics. Some in Massachusetts had always been suspicious of his integrity; and at the end of 1766 the Bay Colony dismissed him, contending that the "general Interests of the Colonies cannot be so effectually Served by uniting the Agency of several of them in the Same person, as by each having its own Separate agent." Its appointment of Franklin a few years later would belie this pretext.[2]

[1] Charles to Newcastle, Sept. 19, 1760, Add MSS 32911, f. 413; Nicholas Varga, "Robert Charles: New York Agent, 1748–1770," 3WMQ, XVIII (1961), 213.
[2] *The Works of John Adams*, ed. Charles F. Adams (Boston, 1850–1856), II, 151; Dec. 8, 1766, MA, XXII, 499, 501.

While he remained agent for Pennsylvania and Connecticut, Jackson continued to disclaim having any political influence. The summer of 1766 found him in the country recovering his health. He despaired that it had suffered from his exertions during the campaign for repeal the past winter and announced that he was "quite giddy with looking on, and heartily tired with the share I have had in attending upon Great Men." Jackson insisted to friends that he wanted to abandon his House membership and depart for Italy. He claimed, to certain correspondents, that he was politically "disengaged: —I look on myself as totally unconnected." [3] But to other political associates Jackson revealed a different picture, one supported by external evidence. He seemed to have connections everywhere rather than nowhere. Late in 1766 he boasted that he was "fortunate in a particular friendship with Lord Shelburne who is at the Head of the American Department, as well as with his friend Col. Barre." A few months later he told Jared Ingersoll that he was "on Terms of Friendship to almost all the Administration." Although Lord Halifax—a well-informed politician—referred to him in 1768 as one of Grenville's men, Jackson was in fact returned to Parliament that year for a borough at the disposal of the Treasury. [4]

In April 1769, Jackson made his last recorded speech in Parliament on America, supporting Thomas Pownall's motion for repeal of the Townshend Duties. That same year he resigned his Pennsylvania agency. When he became legal adviser to the Board of Trade in 1770, honor compelled him to relinquish Connecticut's commission to his colleagues Thomas Life and William Samuel Johnson. [5] His new role as king's counsel required that he pass judgment on colonial legisla-

---

[3] Jackson to Mass. General Court, Aug. 17, 1766, MA, Misc. Letters, 1763–1773; Jackson to Thomas Hutchinson, July 15, 1767, MA, XXV, 186–188; Jackson to Francis Bernard, March 15, 1766, MA, XXII, 462; Jackson to Jonathan Trumbull, Sept. 18, 1768, Jonathan Trumbull Sr. MSS, CHS.

[4] Jackson to William Pitkin, Nov. 8, 1766, CHS *Collections*, XIX (Hartford, 1921), 50; Jackson to Ingersoll, Feb. 20, 1767, NHCHS *Papers*, IX (New Haven, 1918), 403; "Analysis of Personnel of Commons," Dec. 20, 1766, Fitzwilliam MSS, R-86, SCL; Halifax to Grenville, April 18, 1768, Grenville MSS in the possession of Sir John Murray, box A-3.

[5] Lewis B. Namier and John Brooke, *The History of Parliament: The House of Commons, 1754–1790* (London, 1964), II, 669–672; *Boston Evening Post*, Oct. 30, 1769; William Samuel Johnson to Jonathan Trumbull, Aug. 20, 1770, "Letters of William Samuel Johnson to the Governors of Connecticut," *The Trumbull Papers* (MHS *Collections*, ser. 5, Vol. IX [Boston, 1885]), p. 449.

tion; and on occasion he made recommendations to Hillsborough and Dartmouth contrary to the wishes of his former constituents and friends. Jackson took his job very seriously in the 1770's. The Privy Council even had to rebuke him now and again for being overly officious.[6]

The services of Jackson's colleague, Dennys De Berdt, proved to be a mixed blessing in the later 1760's. His home in Artillery Row became a meeting place for Americans in London, two of whom, Arthur Lee and Stephen Sayre, attached themselves to him, forming a kind of cabal and serving the old man as assistant agents.[7] De Berdt's great asset during the Stamp Act crisis had been his connection with Rockingham's First Lord of Trade, Dartmouth. The latter was replaced by Hillsborough later in 1766, however, and was never long enough in a position of authority to be really useful until after De Berdt's death in 1770. Ironically, by the time Dennis De Berdt Jr. became New Jersey's agent in 1775, Dartmouth was just concluding his three year tenure as Secretary of State for the American Department.[8]

While American visitors to London in the later sixties found De Berdt friendly and obliging, there were indications that either his judgment was slipping or else that he was not so well informed as he had been earlier in the decade. One source observed that De Berdt filled his constituents' "ears with what he picks up, from one Coffee House and another or at one great man's levee or another and interprets every civil word, every squeeze *by the hand and come tomorrow* as proofs of the sentiments and inclinations of those who act the farce, all [of] which keep up the hopes of the party and even make them arrogant."[9] De Berdt deluded himself and his constituents by overestimating their political credit.

[6] Charles Garth to S.C. CC, Nov. 24, 1770, *SCHGM*, XXXIII, 117–123; Jack P. Greene and R. M. Jellison, "The Currency Act of 1764 in Imperial-Colonial Relations, 1764–1776," 3*WMQ*, XVIII (1961), 503, 508; *Acts of the Privy Council of England (Colonial Series)*, ed. W. L. Grant and J. Munro (London, 1908–1912), Vol. IV, no. 651, Vol. V, no. 222.

[7] F. L. Lee to De Berdt, Lee, and Sayre, June 5, 1770, Virginia MSS, Group II, Bamberger Signers Collection, NJHS.

[8] William B. Reed, *The Life of Esther De Berdt* (Philadelphia, 1853), pp. 96, 178.

[9] Thomas Coombe Jr. to Coombe Sr., Jan. 4, 1769, Coombe Papers, HSP; Nathaniel Rodgers to William Samuel Johnson, April 8, 1769, Johnson Letter-book, Vol. II, Bancroft Transcripts, NYPL.

The agent's ability to prosecute his duties vigorously was contingent upon his American clients' paying their debts so that he could afford the expense of Sayre's active assistance. Moreover De Berdt's capacity to cooperate with the other agents was restricted by a running feud between Franklin and himself. Finally, he did not stand well with the administration—Hillsborough "hates his very name"—so that after his death one nonconforming minister wrote from London that "the agency of the colonies which was in his hands can [not] come into worse. . . . If the colonies had greater men agents, they would have been treated in a very different manner." [10] In short, this kindly old man might have been adequate in quieter times. But between 1768 and 1770, Massachusetts was the object of controversy in London, a result of the Circular Letter and efforts to expel Governor Bernard. Such storms were too great for the harried shipper to weather and he went under. [11]

When Benjamin Franklin was chosen as De Berdt's successor in 1770, he acquired his fourth concurrent agency. In 1768, Georgia had asked him to represent her interests, and the next year New Jersey did also. [12] Paradoxically, for all his influence and exertion, the foremost agent's performance has not won him the unanimous applause of either his contemporaries or historical observers. One may quickly discount the cant of Franklin's political enemies in Britain and America who rumored that he helped effect the Stamp Act; there are the more accurate observations of William Strahan and others to the contrary. Yet in the decade after 1766, Franklin faced illness and discouraging frustrations courageously if not always with equanimity, a fact noticed by his friends. In 1769, James Boswell observed that "Franklin again is all jollity and pleasantry." Two years later Strahan wrote to William Franklin that his father had changed again: "His Temper is grown so very reserved, which adds greatly to his *natural Inactivity*, that there is no getting him to take part in *anything*." Another Pennsylvanian visiting London at this time found Franklin "the most cautious Man I have ever seen" after spending an evening

[10] Esther De Berdt to Joseph Reed, Nov. 7 and Dec. 12, 1766, Reed MSS, NYHS; John Stafford to Jeremy Belknap, April 10, 1770, MHS *Collections*, ser. 6, IV (Boston, 1891), 41.

[11] De Berdt also succeeded David Barclay Jr. as Delaware's agent in 1765, and held that position for five years.

[12] Alfred O. Aldridge, "Benjamin Franklin as Georgia Agent," *Georgia Review*, VI (1952), 161–173.

in his company.[13] The contrast with 1765–1766 is extraordinary. But Franklin's energies and abilities had not suddenly deserted him. His diminished success as a lobbyist after the Stamp Act crisis was less the result of chill London winters and gout than of his colleagues' and constituents' imprudence.

Barlow Trecothick, Franklin's great ally during the Stamp Act crisis, would remain an agent until 1773; yet owing to changing economic conditions, Trecothick never again exerted so much pressure on the government for repeal of legislation restricting commerce with America. His willingness to cooperate with other agents in the late 1760's[14] to secure repeal of the Currency Act was understandably lessened by an unhappy experience with watered-down money tendered him by a New Hampshire debtor. Nevertheless, in April 1770, he moved repeal of the tea duty in the Commons, making a speech on behalf of Anglo-American commerce reminiscent of his fiery efforts four years earlier.[15] From 1766 onward the locus of his political concern became subtly diverted from colonial issues, and his participation in public affairs was gradually restricted by waning interest and health.[16] The turning point came late in 1770, when his preoccupation with City and national politics totally absorbed him. The issues of the great constitutional debate, moreover, impaled him on the horns of a dilemma which he neatly put in 1771: "I will support the privileges of the House; but in supporting them, am I to overturn the privileges of mankind?"[17] In 1771, Trecothick petitioned Parliament for New Hampshire's 1758 defense reimbursement. The account had been

---

[13] *Boswell in Search of a Wife, 1766–1769,* ed. Frank Brady and F. A. Pottle (New York, 1956), p. 292; Strahan to William Franklin, April 3, 1771, APS; Thomas Coombe Jr. to Coombe Sr., June 6, 1770, Coombe Papers, HSP.

[14] William Samuel Johnson's London diary, 1767–1771 (WSJ MSS), indicates that Trecothick did not attend the coffee-house strategy meetings of the agents during these years.

[15] Samuel Wentworth vs. Trecothick, Add MSS 36218, ff. 151–153; William Samuel Johnson to Jonathan Trumbull, April 14, 1770, MHS *Collections,* ser. 5, IX, 430. In 1767, Trecothick led the North American merchants and agents in a movement to prevent an American salt duty (MHS *Collections,* ser. 5, IX, 229).

[16] William Samuel Johnson to Robert Temple, Feb. 12, 1768, Johnson Letter-book, I, Bancroft Transcripts, NYPL.

[17] Trecothick to Selectmen of Boston, May 10, 1770, MS no. 224, Rare Book Room, BPL; *Sir Henry Cavendish's Debates of the House of Commons during the Thirteenth Parliament of Great Britain,* ed. John Wright (London, 1841–1843), II, 439.

transmitted long before but illness prevented his making proper application for payment. The very next month he notified a relative that
henceforth he intended to spend most of his time in the country, a
decision reinforced in 1772 by the purchase of a manor in Surrey
which was "held by the singular tenure of presenting the Sovereign at
his coronation dinner with a mess of pottage." In 1774, when Trecothick's palsy worsened, he admitted that he had "been long on the edge
of the grave." He died the next year.[18]

One other experienced New England agent remained after 1766.
Although Joseph Sherwood's New Jersey constituents dismissed him
in that year, he remained Rhode Island's agent—despite the fact that
his relations with that colony were little more cordial than with New
Jersey.[19] In both cases his plaintive appeals for money dominate. The
thirteen years of his Rhode Island agency were largely taken up by
efforts to obtain parliamentary reimbursement for the colony's 1756
expedition against Crown Point. Predictably then, the efficiency and
dispatch with which Sherwood managed the agency business in 1765
gave way by 1770 to apathy. During these years Sherwood wrote with
decreasing frequency, casually handled political pamphlets sent him
from Rhode Island for reprinting and distribution in London, and
resignedly advised his constituents not to expect him to attempt to
counter any measure resolved on by the administration.[20] A faction in
the Rhode Island legislature reacted by attempting in 1769–1770 to
oust him. It did not succeed and Sherwood subsequently poured out
his resentment toward this and his constituents' financial ingratitude.
Although he felt "the assembly have used me very unkindly," Sherwood remained nominal agent until his death in 1773. His wife
claimed arrearages from the colony of £323, and his brother John, a
notary public, served Rhode Island informally and badly for another
year.[21]

[18] *JHC*, XXXIII, 333, 337; PRO T 60/23, p. 449; Trecothick to James Ivers,
May 8, 1771, Misc. Bound MSS, Vol. XIV, MHS; John Temple to James
Bowdoin Jr., March 15, 1774, *The Bowdoin and Temple Papers* (MHS
Collections, ser. 6, Vol. IX [Boston, 1897]), pp. 358–359; Trecothick to
Rockingham, Aug. 10, 1774, R 1–1501, Fitzwilliam MSS, SCL.

[19] William Franklin to Benjamin Franklin, Nov. 13, [1766?], APS; Sherwood to Samuel Ward, March 29, 1766, Letters, VII, 38, RIA.

[20] Letters, VI and VII, *passim*, RIA; Sherwood to Moses Brown, Sept. 22,
1770, Moses Brown MSS, I, 115, RIHS.

[21] Joseph Sherwood to Moses Brown, Sept. 15, 1770, *The Correspondence of
the Colonial Governors of Rhode Island, 1723–1775*, ed. G. S. Kimball

Among agents for the southern colonies, two provided continuity after the Stamp Act crisis: Edward Montagu and Charles Garth. In 1770, Arthur Lee, who coveted the Virginia agency, castigated "E.M." in the public press through the guise of Junius Americanus:

A man who sells his Country, is to them a Monster; a character almost beyond their Conception. You are an Agent; they suppose you an Advocate for that Province; they have no other Representatives at the Court of Great Britain; they have relied on you with Confidence, and rewarded your professed (I wish I could say real) Services, with Liberality; By infinite Art, you have for many Years succeeded in imposing on their unsuspecting Temper; Accident has discovered your Principles and Connections, or they might much longer have cherished a Serpent to sting them. How infinite must be their Astonishment, when they find of a Truth, that you are in close Union with their Enemies, their unrelenting Persecutors.[22]

Had Montagu really been such a treacherous agent? His connections were useful but not exceptional: a friend on the Treasury Board, and the Earl of Eglintoun, Lord of the Bedchamber in Waiting, who would introduce Montagu's memorials to George III. During the movement to dispose of the Stamp Act, the lobbyist dutifully presented Virginia's petition and cooperated closely with Garth.[23] But Montagu's remonstrances soon became brief and in some cases less knowledgable than those of other agents. He seemed dilatory about presenting the ministry with documents sent by his constituents, many of which he regarded as nugatory. Finally, while he operated in concert with most of the agents on issues of consequence from 1766 to 1770, he was also obliged to devote many hours to requesting patronage for provincial politicians. All in all, he was neither so useless as some of his fellows, nor so feckless as his severest critics suggested.[24]

(Boston, 1902–1903), II, 425; Ann Sherwood to Rhode Island, June 26, 1773, Letters, VII, 98, RIA; John Sherwood to Joseph Wanton, Aug. 13, 1774, Letters, VII, 113, RIA.

[22] *Maryland Gazette*, Jan. 15, 1770.

[23] William Bollan to Edmund Trowbridge, May 12, 1765, photostat, MHS.

[24] John Almon, *A Collection of . . . Papers Relative to the Dispute between Great Britain and America . . . from 1764 to 1775* (London, 1777), p. 236; *Journal of the House of Lords*, XXI, 297; PHE, XVI, 136–137; Montagu to Va. CC, Jan. 18, 1770, *Journals of the House of Burgesses of Virginia*, ed. H. R. McIlwaine and J. P. Kennedy (Richmond, 1905–1913), XII, xvii; *Virginia Gazette* (Purdie and Dixon), July 9, 1767.

The Virginia burgesses grew disenchanted with him, however, and in 1770 dropped him without replacement. The next year Colonel Richard Bland asked a friend in England: "Pray what is become of Mountague our late agent? I suppose he takes his removal in great dudgeon. I confess I had some share in displacing him. I cannot recollect a single Instance in which he was serviceable to this Country and I think it useless & unjust to our selves, to continue him longer in office." [25] Montagu's dismissal occurred just as he was attempting to guard Virginia's western lands against speculative encroachment. Victimized by provincial factionalism, he went his own way, eventually substituting for his Virginia constituency the agency of Granada. [26]

By 1770 the position of Charles Garth as South Carolina's agent was changing. A year earlier his constituents had rebuked him for assenting to a petition originated by the agents which appeared to make too many constitutional concessions. Thereafter Garth's daily operations became more perfunctory, and his value as a point of contact waned. He did not enjoy the confidence of the opposition, and on the eve of the 1774 election John Robinson listed him as pro-administration. By August of the following year, Garth was regarded as dependant upon the ministry. [27]

Fortunately the agency after 1766 did not rely entirely upon veterans. There would be eleven new faces, though only seven of them in any way invigorated the institution. Henry Wilmot, for example, who replaced Sherwood as New Jersey's agent in 1766, was an eminent

[25] E. I. Miller, "The Virginia Committee of Correspondence of 1773–1775," 1*WMQ*, XXII (1913), 100; Bland to Thomas Adams, Aug. 1, 1771, *VMHB*, VI (1898), 133–134.

[26] *Virginia Gazette* (Purdie and Dixon), Oct. 8, 1772; Montagu to Dartmouth, April 30, 1774, Dartmouth MSS, Vol. I, ii, no. 972, WSL.

[27] Namier and Brooke, *History of Parliament*, II, 483–485; Garth to S.C. CC, Jan. 20 and May 27, 1775, Garth Letter-book, SCA. When Georgia's Assembly sought to appoint Garth as its permanent agent in 1767–1768, a wrangle arose, pitting commons against council and governor. The result was a compromise candidate, Franklin, who served from 1768 until 1774. The lower house felt it wise in 1773 to assure the colony of representation in the event of Franklin's absence or demise, so it chose Grey Elliott as assistant agent. A Georgia planter resident in London, Elliott had been a councillor and deputy auditor of the colony. He did nothing as agent, accepted an office at the Board of Trade, and remained in England after the outbreak of revolution (W. W. Abbot, *The Royal Governors of Georgia, 1754–1775* [Chapel Hill, 1959], pp. 109, 136, 142–144, 160).

London solicitor and private secretary to Lord Chancellor Camden. Known as "the Giant of Grays Inn," Wilmot had served the Leeward Islands as agent since 1749. After 1760, Pennsylvania's proprietors hired him as their private agent. So did William Alexander, Earl of Stirling, who had political and property interests in New Jersey. As early as 1761, Sherwood had observed that Stirling "is not pleased with my Appointment to the Agency, having perhaps some Particular Friend of his own to Introduce." Once Wilmot became agent for the East Jersey Proprietors (to settle their boundary differences with New York), it was relatively easy for Stirling to obtain the position for his man.[28]

Sherwood's surrogate promptly proved that he had been a poor choice. He instructed his new employers to "consider me as at present in some Degree a Stranger to your Colony. . . . I am agent for the four Leeward Islands, and if ever any contest shall arise wherein their Interests and yours come in Competition . . . you must allow me to preserve my allegiance to them." Wilmot neglected his correspondence with the New Jersey committee, and by 1767 there were "no tidings of any thing's being done by their own agent," William Franklin reported to his father; "the Assembly having some resentment for their being surprised into the appointment of him, will probably remove him at this sessions." Actually it took until 1769 for them to dismiss Wilmot in favor of Benjamin Franklin.[29]

Henry Eustace McCulloh, who became North Carolina's agent in 1768, was also an attorney and as unsuitable as Wilmot for the agency. Shrewd, unscrupulous, and salacious, he wanted the position in order to further his career. Born in London, he was taken to North Carolina in 1740 as an infant, but returned to England, where he was

---

[28] William Alexander Papers, III, 11, NYHS; Sherwood to Samuel Smith, June 6, 1761, "Letters of Joseph Sherwood," NJHS *Proceedings*, V (Newark, 1851), 134–135; Wilmot to Earl of Stirling, Sept. 25, 1766, William A. Duer, *The Life of William Alexander, Earl of Stirling* . . . (NJHS *Collections,* Vol. II [New York, 1847]), pp. 84–85.

[29] Wilmot to Cortlandt Skinner, Sept. 25, 1766, "Documents Relating to the Colonial History of the State of New Jersey, 1757–1767," *New Jersey Archives,* ser. 1, IX (Newark, 1885), 571–572; William Franklin to Benjamin Franklin, June 10, 1767, *ibid.,* p. 625. In 1774, Arthur Lee took over informally for Franklin, and during the final year the agency was held by Dennis De Berdt Jr. (Lee to Dartmouth, April 10, 1775, Dartmouth MSS, Vol. II, no. 1214, WSL).

admitted to the Middle Temple in 1757 and subsequently called to the bar.[30] He went back to his childhood home in 1761, remaining there six years as a councillor, customs collector for the Port of Roanoke, and agent for his father, whose land speculations had amassed a vast empire in Carolina. The senior McCulloh, a London merchant politically dependent upon Bute, first suggested a stamp bill to the administration in 1757 and actually helped to shape Grenville's duties.[31]

From the moment Henry McCulloh reached London in 1767, he made it clear to his Carolina correspondents that he and the agency were simultaneously available. He particularly offered himself on account of his father's "knowledge & extensive Connections with almost every distinguished Character of Business in the Kingdom." In 1768 he received the appointment, largely through the efforts of Colonel John Harvey, speaker of the Assembly. McCulloh's public letters, read at face value, suggest that he took his responsibilities seriously. But private letters to his close friends reveal him as dissimulating. He wrote Harvey in 1769, for example, that his spirit as well as his "Circumstances are independent." Yet he admitted to intimates that he "had always much ambition as to my Connections." In 1770 he took pride in having "a friend in a corner with Lord North." [32]

McCulloh devoted much of his time to seeking patronage for those friends who would pay him well enough for his efforts—and to sampling the wiles of London's women: "The Charms of female attraction are here irresistibly bewitching." Hence he has been fairly evaluated as "a man of more than ordinary ability and culture, cun-

[30] E. A. Jones, *American Members of the Inns of Court* (London, 1924), pp. 143–147; *Life and Correspondence of James Iredell . . .* , ed. Griffith J. McRee (New York, 1857–1858), I, 8.

[31] Charles G. Sellers, "Private Profits and British Colonial Policy: The Speculations of Henry McCulloh," 3*WMQ*, VIII (1951), 535–551; John Cannon, "Henry McCulloch and Henry McCulloh," 3*WMQ*, XV (1958), 71–73; James High, "Henry McCulloh, Pro-Genitor of the Stamp Act," *North Carolina Historical Review*, XXIX (1952), 24–38; cf. " 'A Dress of Horror!': Henry McCulloh's Objections to the Stamp Act," ed. Jack P. Greene, *Huntington Library Quarterly*, XXVI (1963), 253–262.

[32] McCulloh to Harvey, Sept. 13, 1767, July 24, 1769, *CRNC*, VII, 516, VIII, 58; McCulloh to Edmund Fanning, May 20, 1768, *ibid.*, VII, 752–753; N.C. CC to McCulloh, Dec. 12, 1768, *ibid.*, VII, 878–879; McCulloh to Fanning, Sept. 12, 1767, Jan. 26, 1768, Fanning-McCulloh Papers, no. 252, Southern Historical Collection, University of North Carolina Library; McCulloh to James Iredell, May 5, 1770, Nov. 5, 1771, McRee, *Iredell*, I, 63, 102.

ning rather than wise. Of loose morals, with a decent regard for appearances, he veiled his vices from the public eye." Nevertheless, in 1771, North Carolina reappointed him for another two years.[33] When the roué returned there in 1773 to inspect his extensive real estate, he left the agency in his father's hands, prompting one wag to remark that "the old man is the best agent of the two." Back in London in 1774, his constituency curtailed, he tried to replace it by standing as a parliamentary candidate in support of Lord North, but failed. After the outbreak of hostilities he became a loyalist, lost his North Carolina lands by confiscation, and retired to a country seat near London.[34]

A number of the newcomers, however, were more sensibly chosen than Wilmot and McCulloh, and proved to be weightier additions to the North American pressure group. Connecticut's controversy with the heirs to the Mohegan Indian lands dated back to 1705, but had been dormant since 1743. When claimants reopened the case against the colony in 1766, it sent William Samuel Johnson as special agent to assist Jackson in defending the provincial interest.[35] Litigation moved forward so slowly, however, that Johnson found himself with free time which he used to expedite favors for friends at home and cooperate with the other colony agents. Johnson had anticipated a speedy return home, but remained until 1771, when the interminable "cause" drew to a close before the Privy Council. At issue concurrently were the Susquehanna lands disputed by Connecticut and the proprietors of Pennsylvania. Johnson assisted in these proceedings reluctantly because he felt they might endanger his colony's charter. The case lingered on through the outbreak of the Revolution, well after his departure.[36]

[33] McCulloh to Iredell, July 14, 1769, Aug. 26, 1773, McRee, *Iredell*, I, 9, 45, 177; McCulloh to Harvey, March 3, 1770, *CRNC*, VIII, 184; McCulloh to Fanning, Sept. 12, 1767, Fanning-McCulloh Papers, University of North Carolina; Samuel J. Ervin, "The Provincial Agents of North Carolina," *Sprunt Historical Publications*, XVI (Chapel Hill, 1919), 76.

[34] Alexander Elmsley to Samuel Johnston, May 17, 1774, *CRNC*, IX, 999; McCulloh to James Iredell, Oct. 2, 1775, MSS Department, Duke University Library; Petition of Sundry American Loyalist Agents, PRO T 1/518.

[35] For the Mohegan case, see C. W. Bowen, *Boundary Disputes of Connecticut* (Boston, 1882), ch. 5.

[36] *The Public Records of the Colony of Connecticut*, ed. C. J. Hoadly and J. R. Trumbull (Hartford, 1850–1890), XII, 501. The most recent biography is by G. C. Groce, *William Samuel Johnson* (New York, 1937). For the Susquehanna case, see Oscar Zeichner, *Connecticut's Years of Controversy, 1750–1776* (Chapel Hill, 1949), chs. 5 and 8.

Johnson was a staunch Anglican and son of the cofounder and first president of King's College.[37] His moderate political position enabled Johnson to deal freely in London with men of every opinion; and he accordingly cultivated a broad field of associates. He dined and met impartially with Thomas Whately, Israel Mauduit, John Pownall, the De Berdt clan, and Benjamin Franklin. When Johnson arrived early in 1767, Richard Jackson introduced him to the Speaker of the House of Commons and took him through the Palace of Westminster and all the courts of law. Despite his high church ties and some questionable political friendships, Johnson was a thorough patriot. His disgust with the venality of British politics even restricted his lobbying activity. He proudly admitted that he "might have obtained very good things by deserting the interests of the country that gave me my birth, by abusing and misrepresenting it, or by licking the dust of the feet of ministers or of the slaves of ministers." [38]

Richard Jackson and solicitor Thomas Life were grateful for Johnson's assistance in the Mohegan cause. Life wrote Governor Trumbull that Johnson's knowledge had been invaluable to Connecticut's counsellors. They presented the case with such skill that in 1771 the Privy Council reaffirmed the decision of the Royal Commission of 1743 in favor of Connecticut and the eastern landholders.[39] After Jackson's resignation in 1770 and Johnson's return to Stratford in 1771, Life became sole agent. He had considerable legal experience as recommendation. As early as 1751 he had dealt with that professional among agents, Ferdinand Paris, and during the 1760's Jackson preferred to present many of his agency memorials through Life as solicitor. He had, however, a lawyer's cautious instincts and lacked personal commitment to the colonies. His constituents were clients and employers, no more and no less. He must, nevertheless, have been a credit to his profession, for his services were much in demand. Franklin hired him to handle a case involving Georgia, and the two worked together from time to time.[40]

[37] Johnson's church affiliation helped him politically. Dr. Berkeley, Prebendary of Canterbury, gave him a letter of introduction to Berkeley's parishioner, Lord Dartmouth.

[38] Johnson's London diary, entry for Feb. 9, 1767, and *passim*, WSJ MSS; Zeichner, *Years of Controversy*, 310 n. 43.

[39] Life to Trumbull, July 25, 1771, Trumbull MSS, III (1), 76a-c, CSL; Groce, *Johnson*, p. 90.

[40] MS Category "War," X, 392–394, CSL; Life to Jonathan Trumbull, July 25, 1771, Trumbull MSS, III (1), 76a-c; Franklin's account with Life is in the Franklin MSS, LXIX, 108, APS.

In 1768, two years after William Samuel Johnson's appointment, William Bollan formally rejoined his erstwhile colleagues in the agency. In that year, having been appointed special agent by the now radical Council, he helped procure incriminating letters sent by Governor Bernard and returned them to friends in Massachusetts. This action so delighted the Council that it appointed Bollan officially its agent—a decision that would complicate Anglo-American politics in succeeding years and call into question the very nature of the agency.[41] An American visitor to London reported in 1770 that Bollan "tires the patience of a great man when near one, yet I think he Loves America, and am sure he had great merrit in Transmitting Some Late papers." He would perform many valuable, and many futile, services for the colonies after 1768.[42]

Two years after Bollan's accession, two other newcomers received agency appointments: Arthur Lee and Edmund Burke. The youngest and most brilliant of a group of talented Virginia brothers, Lee recognized his own limitations in public life: "impatience . . . impetuosity and imprudence," coupled with an unusually suspicious nature. His education in Britain had been thorough, ranging from medicine to law; and when he returned there in 1768 he set about cultivating a catholic assortment of political relationships, ranging from Lord Hillsborough, Barré, and Shelburne to Wilkes and the radicals.[43] From the moment Lee reached London he coveted an agency, writing to his brother in Virginia that he would be happy to serve either the burgesses or the Council in that capacity. Having been commercial agent for the Mississippi Company, he did not lack experience. Thus when Massachusetts named Franklin its agent in 1770, the General Court asked the newly prominent Junius Americanus to assist him.[44] Lee worked hard at his apprenticeship, but chafed at the lack of an agency fully his own. He continually chided his brother about Virgin-

---

[41] Malcolm Freiberg, "William Bollan, Agent of Massachusetts," *More Books*, XXIII (1948), 176–179; Samuel Cooper to Thomas Pownall, July 12, 1769, "Letters of Samuel Cooper to Thomas Pownall, 1769–1777," ed. Frederick Tuckerman, *AHR*, VIII (1903), 309.

[42] ? to William Cooper, 1770, Sam Adams MSS, NYPL.

[43] Burton J. Hendrick, *The Lees of Virginia* (Boston, 1935), pp. 137–150; Lee to Hillsborough, Nov. 13, 1768, Lee-Ludwell MSS, VHS; Lee to [Richard Henry Lee?], Dec. 27, 1768, Lee MSS, no. 16, APS.

[44] Not all contemporaries were so impressed. Lee went with Wilkes to a dinner attended by Dr. Samuel Johnson. When the latter was told that one of the strangers present was Junius Americanus, Johnson muttered, "Too, too, too" (*Boswell's Life of Johnson*, ed. George B. Hill [Oxford, 1934], III, 68).

ia's vacant agency after Edward Montagu's demise, freely admitting he wanted the status he might gain from official authorization. He also hoped to use the agency as a step toward securing a parliamentary seat. Virginia never replaced Montagu, but when Franklin returned to America the remnant of his agency became Lee's.[45]

The New York Assembly appointed Edmund Burke its agent late in 1770 upon learning of Robert Charles' death.[46] The powerful James De Lancey had wanted one of the Rockingham Whigs for New York's agency. Selecting Burke, however, was perhaps unwise. A recent biographer has shown that Burke "did not understand the nature or the depth of American discontent, and in subsequent debates [after 1769] he continued to underestimate the importance the Americans attached to constitutional rights." Burke never believed that Parliament lacked constitutional authority to tax the colonies; he had defended American views and interests when it suited the tactics of his party. He was not well acquainted with the contemporary colonial scene and, so far as is known, had no regular correspondents in North America until after 1770. Why then did Burke accept the agency? It was worth £500 annually which he badly needed. He regarded the job lightly and felt it would require very little time or effort.[47]

His employers found his letters to the Committee of Correspondence unsatisfactory. They tended, in fact, to be perfunctory and infrequent. Sometimes Burke did not even mention New York acts for which the committee was especially anxious to secure crown approval. In addition, his foresight often failed him. The bill allowing the East India Company to export tea to America in its own ships (with a

[45] Lee to [Richard Henry Lee?], Dec. 27, 1768, Lee MSS, no. 16, APS; Lee to Mass. General Court, Dec. 29, 1770, Sept. 22, 1771, MA, Letters, 1764–1774, pp. 85, 91; Lee to Richard Henry Lee, May 20, 1770, Aug. 17, 1772, Lee MSS, nos. 22, 28, APS; Lee to Richard Henry Lee, Feb. 14 and Oct. 20, 1773, Lee MSS, Vol. II, HLHU, and Lee-Ludwell MSS, VHS.

[46] Ross J. S. Hoffman, *Edmund Burke, New York Agent* . . . (Philadelphia, 1956), pp. 15–193.

[47] Carl B. Cone, *Burke and the Nature of Politics: The Age of the American Revolution* (Lexington, Ky., 1957), p. 179; Hoffman, *Burke*, pp. 73–74, 108, 121; Dennys De Berdt to Edward Sheafe, Sept. 11, 1769, "Letters of Dennys De Berdt, 1757–1770," ed. Albert Matthews, CSM *Publications*, XIII (1912), 378. In one sense it is unfair to be excessively critical of Burke's agency. As M.P. for Bristol he interpreted his responsibilities broadly and never visited there. Even so, Burke's conception of constituency was hardly to be desired in an agent.

drawback of the duty paid on importation first into England) led directly to the 1773–1774 crisis. But Burke had no apprehension and did nothing to oppose it. Not once in 1773 did he even mention the Tea Act to his constituents. Increasingly Burke became anxious at the prospect that his responsibilities as M.P. and agent might conflict. As early as 1771 he wondered how long it would be "consistent with the Duties of my situation to continue my little Offices to the Province." After 1770, Burke's enemies used his agency to attack him in the popular press, accusing him most often of being compromised.[48]

The last agent to be appointed before the ultimate crisis developed was Henry Marchant, sent by Rhode Island in 1771. When the effort to replace Sherwood failed, the Assembly selected Marchant, the colony's attorney general, to plead with the Privy Council for Rhode Island's 1756 expedition expenses. The ardent dissenter and son of liberty arrived in London "armed with a host of letters and a kind of pocket Baedecker which [Ezra] Stiles had written for him." Marchant's portfolio was indeed impressive. It included letters to Trecothick, Franklin, Jackson, William Samuel Johnson, Bollan, Sherwood, Arthur Lee, Stephen Sayre, the Barclays, William Meredith, and John Pownall. He took lodgings across from Franklin's in Craven Street. With such credentials it is not surprising that when he returned to Rhode Island in 1772, Franklin—noting the difficulty of Marchant's negotiations—observed that the patriot's perseverance, assiduity, and address had accomplished more than the Doctor would have expected of any man. More the pity his colony only kept him a year as agent.[49]

PERSONAL AMBITIONS AND PUBLIC IMPRESSIONS

Many colonial agents, like other London lobbyists, were personally opportunistic. This was inevitable in Georgian England, given the vague distinctions made between public and private sectors in finance,

[48] Burke to James De Lancey, Aug. 20, 1772, *The Correspondence of Edmund Burke,* ed. Lucy S. Sutherland, II (Chicago, 1960), 328–329; Hoffman, *Burke,* pp. 120–121, 123–124, 127, 155; Cone, *Burke,* I, 256–257; P. T. Underdown, "Edmund Burke as a Member of Parliament for Bristol . . ." (unpub. Ph.D. diss.; University of London, 1955), pp. 192–193.

[49] David S. Lovejoy, "Henry Marchant and the Mistress of the World," 3*WMQ,* XII (1955), 375–398. The major source is Marchant's London diary, owned by Miss Alice Clarke, copy in the RIHS. Marchant's bound booklet of introductory letters is in the vault, M-331, RIHS. See also Franklin to Ezra Stiles, July 28, 1772, MFY.

job-holding, and relations between the state and social groups. Under ordinary conditions, however, petty and grasping traits in the agents as individuals were not especially harmful to the colonies' welfare. Indeed there had been times when advancing an agent's individual fortune might also benefit his constituents. After 1766, however, when Anglo-American stability was under duress, personal ambitions became a hazard, both to the institution's cohesiveness and to the imperial relationship it sought to sustain.[50]

The extent to which even Franklin suffered from conflicts of interest has been questioned by contemporaries as well as historians. One observer in 1770 was "not a Litle surprised that the assembly of Massachusett's Bay should make choice of Benjamin Franklin for their Agent. That Gentleman holds a Lucrative place in the Post Office for which he is intirely dependant on the Ministry. Can he therefore, dare he support the claims of His Constituents against the Claims of the British Parliament?" This colonial assumed that if Franklin were completely devoted to America, the administration would surely deprive him of his office. Six weeks later, Franklin wrote his sister in Boston that his steadfast rule was "never to turn aside in public affairs through views of private interest; but to go straight forward in doing what appears to me right at the time."[51]

At that very moment, however, late in 1770, Franklin was affiliated with a number of land speculators seeking control of 2,400,000 acres on Virginia's Ohio River frontier. His participation in the Illinois and Grand Ohio Companies involved lobbying of vast proportions throughout the later sixties and beyond. Politically prominent members of these organizations were obliged to enlist the influence of ministers in each administration as well as the support of influential civil servants. Although Franklin later insisted that he had never obligated himself to anyone while seeking land grants, one scholar has

---

[50] One of the most acerbic indictments of the agents on this score came from Dr. John Fothergill in 1769: "The agents are unknown, unconnected, no witnesses of their behavior. For the most part they are pensionaries, or wish to be so, and are either inactive or false to your interests. I except Dr. Franklin, but even it is possible that desparation of succeeding may lessen his assiduity" (Fothergill to William Logan, May 8, 1769, Gilbert Collection, College of Physicians, Philadelphia, Pa.).

[51] Alexander McDougall to Nathaniel Niles, Nov. 6, 1770, Bortman MSS, Boston University Library; Franklin to Jane Mecom, Dec. 30, 1770, *The Letters of Benjamin Franklin and Jane Mecom*, ed. Carl Van Doren (Princeton, 1950), p. 123.

suggested that the Doctor's activity in this respect may have caused politicians to regard him as a self-seeking speculator-scientist, rather than a respectable political representative.[52] Franklin also sought patronage favors for friends. When he occasionally balked at engaging in such applications, it was because he feared antagonizing particular factions in the colonies, and not because the activity might reduce his leverage for other more important issues.[53]

Richard Jackson was closely associated with several of Franklin's speculative ventures, and like his coagent requested jobs for friends.[54] He acquired 20,000 acres in Nova Scotia for himself and later joined Franklin in solicitations for the Illinois and Grand Ohio syndicates. Several other lobbyists engaged in the madcap scramble for land in North America as well.[55] A majority of the agents also acted as patronage intermediaries for colonial office-seekers.[56] Through the seventeenth and eighteenth centuries this had developed as one of an agent's accepted functions; but by 1770 the injection of first principles into a system previously untroubled by them made it impossible for a scrupulous colonial to expect favors of this sort from ministers he otherwise opposed.[57]

In addition to simple job-seeking, some of the agents were burdened by a miscellany of personal requests. When William Samuel Johnson was appointed in 1766, all sorts of people in Connecticut decided to

[52] "William Trent Calls on Benjamin Franklin," ed. William E. Lingelbach, *PMHB*, LXXIV (1950), 43–50; Franklin to William Franklin, Oct. 7, 1772, Craven Street Letter-book, 1772–1773, Franklin Papers, LC; Bernhard Knollenberg, letter in 3*WMQ*, IV (1947), 549.

[53] Franklin to George Read, June 12, 1766, W. T. Read, *Life and Correspondence of George Read . . .* (Philadelphia, 1870), p. 24; Franklin to William Franklin, March 19, 1767, Pierpont Morgan Library, New York City; William Franklin to Benjamin Franklin, June 10, 1767, *New Jersey Archives*, ser. 1, IX, 626–628.

[54] Jackson to Charles Jenkinson, June 17, 1765, Add MSS 38204, f. 273; Jackson to Jared Ingersoll, Sept. 8 and Nov. 30, 1767, NHCHS *Papers*, IX, (New Haven, 1918), 414, 418.

[55] *Journal of the Commissioners for Trade and Plantations from January 1764 to December 1767* (London, 1936), p. 64; Grant and Munro, *Acts of the Privy Council (Colonial Series)*, IV, 816; PRO PC 2/111, pp. 125, 332, 347, 478, 496, 510, 646, 676; Hoffman, *Burke*, p. 84.

[56] Edward Montagu to Shelburne, Sept. 8, 1766, Shelburne MSS, CXI, 317, WCL; William Samuel Johnson to Jared Ingersoll, Feb. 18, 1767, WSJ MSS; Henry Eustace McCulloh to John Harvey, March 30, 1770, *CRNC*, VIII, 184.

[57] Arthur Lee to Richard Henry Lee, Oct. 20, 1770, Lee MSS, I, 121, APS.

take advantage of his presence in London. He was swamped by endless requests to manage real estate, collect debts, buy watches, and so forth. Pursuing only a part of these errands occupied a fair portion of the agent's time.[58]

The lobbyists themselves were hardly reluctant to advance their own careers and accounts. Even those agents warmest in behalf of the colonies often compromised their offices by seeking or accepting another. The boundary dispute between South Carolina and Georgia, for example, caught Charles Garth in a curious crossfire. When the issue first developed in 1763, Garth was employed by South Carolina and served Georgia as crown agent. By 1766, when the Georgia legislature determined to win royal approval for a land law governing a tract on the River Altamaha, Garth was under obligation to the assemblies of both colonies, though his Georgia appointment lacked official confirmation. Throughout the controversy he took the part of South Carolina, his first employer.[59]

William Bollan, during his agency, also held the office of advocate general of Massachusetts. This entailed the responsibility of prosecuting offenders against the Acts of Trade. But "he could ill afford publication of the fact that he was attempting to suppress Massachusetts' trade at the same time that he was representing her interest in Britain." After Bollan lost his absentee advocacy, he pleaded with several administrations for personal consideration while unsuccessfully remonstrating against their measures as agent for the Massachusetts Council.[60]

Even William Samuel Johnson revealed an ambiguous attitude toward problems of pluralism and patronage. In 1767 he hoped the Susquehanna Company would not offer him its agency because he feared provincial critics would regard it as incompatible with his colony office. Yet as his provincial agency drew to a close, he catered to those he felt might help him acquire the New York chief justiceship that he coveted. Johnson was even willing to serve as Cadwallader Colden's private agent while in London, working to obtain the perquisites of office for New York's lieutenant governor. Doing so, how-

---

[58] Johnson to John Broadhurst, May 24, 1768, WSJ MSS (box 1); Johnson to Ebeneezer Silliman, Feb. 24, 1767, *ibid.*

[59] Garth to Shelburne, June 3, 1763, Shelburne MSS, LXIX, 173, WCL; Garth to S.C. CC, June 6, 1766, *SCHGM*, XXVIII, 230–234.

[60] Freiberg, "Bollan," pp. 51–53; Bollan to Hillsborough, May 25, 1772, Dartmouth MSS, Vol. II, no. 366, WSL.

ever, meant antagonizing powerful and well-connected politicians, which the colonial lobbyists could ill afford.[61]

Becoming instruments for special interests reduced the likelihood of the agents' achieving success on those public issues that were driving a wedge into the Anglo-American political world; for "it was not wise to have 'too many irons in the fire' and run the risk of failing 'to bring any to maturity,' an excessive number of applications being liable to create an ill impression in the house of commons." [62] All too often the pursuit of private hopes estranged one agent from another, damaging their cohesiveness.

THE DECLINE OF COHESION

A famous Franklin cartoon that first appeared in 1754 depicted a segmented serpent above the caption "join or die." The agents were not the particular object of this lesson but might well have been; for cooperation among them declined gradually during these years, undermining their effectiveness as a pressure group. This does not mean that either they or their constituents were unaware of the importance of a monolithic appearance. On the contrary, committees of correspondence invariably instructed their representatives to unite in support of causes important to the colonies generally. The agents themselves—even those most guilty of quarreling—recognized its deleterious effects.[63]

The year 1770 clearly seems to have marked a significant watershed in the capacity and willingness of the agents to cooperate among themselves. From 1763 until 1770, the lobbyists averaged one joint consultation per month (exclusive of the holiday and adjournment seasons of government). During the next three years (1771–1773)

---

[61] Johnson to Eliphalet Dyer, Sept. 12, 1767, *The Susquehannah Company Papers: Memorial Publications of the Wyoming Historical and Genealogical Society*, ed. Julian P. Boyd (Wilkes-Barre, Pa., 1930–1933), II, 321; Johnson to Alexander Wedderburn, Oct. 25, 1771, Oct. 5, 1772, Johnson Letter-book, II, Bancroft Transcripts, NYPL; Colden to Arthur Mairs, Nov. 12, 1770, *Colden Letter Books*, II (NYHS *Collections for 1877* [New York, 1878]), 235–236; Colden to Johnson, Nov. 12, 1770, April 2 and May 8, 1771, *Colden Letter Books*, II, 237, 318–319, 322.

[62] Lewis B. Namier, "Charles Garth, Agent for South Carolina," *EHR*, LIV (1939), 637.

[63] Arthur Lee to Thomas Cushing, Dec. 6, 1774, PRO CO 5/118, ff. 92–93.

they do not appear to have conferred once.[64] "The agents think it their duty," Charles Garth wrote in 1768, "to meet Weekly to consult together, and to Act as Exigencies offer." Their assiduousness was rewarded early in 1769, when the North American interest succeeded in averting more stringent application of the act for quartering troops in America. Yet at that very time, March 1769, Garth's letters begin to reveal a dissidence resulting from the agents' inability to agree on whether to support an application Franklin had drafted for repeal of the Townshend duties. The petition argued along expedient lines, mostly sidestepping the issues agitating the constitutional debate. Garth felt that

nothing is waived, conceded or given up, but rather cautiously reserved. . . . But the Agents of some of the Colonies to the Northward, doubting what Construction might be put upon it both in Great Britain and America, thought it not right to afford any Handle for an undue Construction of Concession or otherwise on our parts, and the rather, as the Matter of right was so much an Object with their Constituents, that they would not even apply by Petition to the House of Commons.[65]

One of the most important projects undertaken by the agents following revocation of the Stamp Act was the campaign to repeal the Currency Act. It occupied them intensely after 1766, and their difficulties form a striking contrast to their united effort in 1765–1766. Even before repeal was an objective, several of the agents revealed misgivings about "the great Sin of paper money making." Jackson candidly conceded to Franklin that he had "been always inclined against a Paper Currency." De Berdt, like Trecothick, preferred "a good & solid Coin to a precarious & pernicious currency." Although Franklin had conceived a plan for a general loan office in America as a stamp tax surrogate in 1765, by 1767–1768, when it appeared that Parliament with merchant backing would take the plan seriously, Franklin had lost his enthusiasm for it. Nor had the colonies developed a concerted campaign against the measure. The consequences

[64] This calculation, based upon references in letters, diaries, and public documents, discounts those occasions when administrative boards required the presence of the agents at a hearing. Only meetings initiated by the agents and attended by more than three have been included.

[65] Garth to S.C. CC, Nov. 10, 1768, March 12 and 17, 1769, *SCHGM*, XXX, 232, XXXI, 52–54, 56; Franklin to Joseph Galloway, March 21, 1769, WCL. See also Gipson, *British Empire before the American Revolution*, XI (New York, 1965), 257.

frustrated those agents in the repeal vanguard. Garth, for example, informed South Carolina that he had begun "to ruminate whether it may not be practicable for you to go on without any further Application for a Repeal of the late Act." His constituents passed a modified money measure anyway, which Jackson recommended that the Board of Trade have disallowed.[66]

One cause of this failure was the reappearance and intensification of the agents' old nemesis—parochialism. In 1767, when hope of abolishing the Currency Act appeared uncertain, Franklin "proposed to Mr. Jackson the putting our colony [Pennsylvania] foremost, as we stood in a pretty good light, and asking the favour for us alone." That same year, Massachusetts instructed Dennys De Berdt not to cooperate with his colleagues, as the colony was not then interested in a paper currency. Two years later, Robert Charles sought a special dispensation for New York to set up a land bank and issue £120,000 in bills to be legal tender at the loan office and colonial treasury.[67]

When the agents conferred in these years on matters of common interest, they would "lay down a plan to be pursued by each individual in their *several applications.*" In executing strategy they "repeatedly, *but separately* waited upon" the Secretary of State for American affairs. They thereby neglected their own practice and their constituents' advice of 1764–1766 that all the agents united behind one strong remonstrance created the most powerful effect. The revival of colonial boundary disputes after 1769 heightened this parochialism and the agents' sense of disparate identities. The uncertain delineation between New York and New Jersey and between North Carolina and South Carolina set Charles, Franklin, Wilmot, McCulloh, and Garth in opposition just when such controversies should have been minimized. Moreover, a land dispute between New York and settlers west of the Connecticut River brought Edmund Burke and Paul Wentworth, New Hampshire's agent, into conflict.[68]

[66] Jackson to Franklin, April 13, [1764?], APS; De Berdt to ?, Oct. 21, 1767, Matthews, "Letters of De Berdt," p. 453; Greene and Jellison, "Currency Act of 1764," pp. 492–493; Garth to S.C. CC, July 5, 1767, Nov. 24, 1770, *SCHGM*, XXIX, 298–301, XXXIII, 117–123.

[67] Franklin to Joseph Galloway, June 13, 1767, Smyth, V, 27; Mass. House to De Berdt, June 1767, MA, Letters, 1765–1773, pp. 51–53; Greene and Jellison, "Currency Act of 1764," p. 513.

[68] Italics mine. William Samuel Johnson to William Pitkin, Oct. 20, 1768, Jan. 3, 1769, MHS *Collections*, ser. 5, IX, 198, 304–305; New Jersey CC to Benjamin Franklin, Dec. 7, 1769, MS Collections, NJHS; PRO CO 5/380, ff.

In the later sixties a variety of troublesome tensions developed between individual agents. By 1770 even Jackson's ties with Garth weakened under the strain of the former's opposition to a law passed by the South Carolina Assembly for which Garth had been instructed to gain crown confirmation. Jackson's successors in the Massachusetts agency could be remarkably insensitive to the need for cooperation. In 1770, Bollan suggested that the agents who sat in the House of Commons did not defend the colony with sufficient vigor in debate.[69] In 1773 he regretted the absence of other agents at the administrative boards when colonial legislation was under scrutiny. After his reappointment by the Massachusetts Council in 1768, Bollan and his coagent, Dennys De Berdt, had little to do with each other. When Bollan offered to collaborate in petitioning the House of Commons, De Berdt declined, enabling his colleague to boast later that he "never acted in conjunction with Mr. De Berdt in any one matter." [70]

De Berdt's coterie did not enjoy cordial relations with many of the agents. They particularly mistrusted Franklin, believing that in 1765 "he stood entirely neuter till he saw which way the cause would be carried, and then broke out fiercely on the side of America." By 1768, Franklin could no longer endure the jibes being fired from Artillery Court. He blasted the Massachusetts agent in a letter signed "The Public" carried by the *Public Advertiser* and reprinted in Boston. Their enmity lingered even after De Berdt's death, largely because the merchant's son-in-law Joseph Reed, De Berdt Jr., Lee, and Sayre all wanted agencies while Franklin occupied four simultaneously. Nor had De Berdt cared for Franklin's friend, Richard Jackson. Because the merchant suspected that Massachusetts paid his coagent a salary five times his own, he avoided consulting Jackson whenever possible.[71]

9–13; Garth to S.C. CC, April 18, 1771, April 21, 1772, *SCHGM*, XXXIII (1932), 131–134, 236–237; *Journal of the Commissioners for Trade and Plantations from January 1768 to December 1775* (London, 1937), pp. 421–422.

[69] Jackson to Board of Trade, June 5, 1770, PRO CO 5/379, ff. 93–94; Garth's petition dated Nov. 29, 1770, PRO CO 5/380, ff. 5–7; Bollan to Samuel Danforth, April 28, 1770, *Bowdoin and Temple Papers*, p. 177.

[70] Bollan to Samuel Danforth, April 25, 1773, Bowdoin-Temple MSS, Vol. II, MHS; De Berdt to Edward Sheafe, Sept. 11, 1769, Matthews, "Letters of De Berdt," 378; Bollan to Danforth, March 6, 1770, *Bowdoin and Temple Papers*, p. 165; Bollan to Thomas Hutchinson, April 15, 1771, Bowdoin-Temple MSS, Vol. II, MHS.

[71] Esther De Berdt to Joseph Reed, Dec. 12, 1766, Reed MSS, NYHS;

When Lee and Sayre attacked their enemies, they preferred to shower grape on all the agents rather than fire at them individually. In 1770, under the signature "A.S." (for their combined first names), they released a volley that echoed in several colonial newspapers. After praising De Berdt, dead just a month, they referred to Bollan's "monstrous and most unreasonable Account unsettled with his Constituents." Then they scored Jackson for serving as Grenville's secretary during the preparation of the Stamp Act, for opposing John Wilkes in 1769, and for seeming "inclinable still to become a dependent Placeman." Charles, Wilmot, Garth, Abercromby, and Montagu were each roasted in turn as servile placemen; and Franklin—treated ambiguously—received criticism because his son's governorship had been acquired through Bute's influence. Only Johnson and Sherwood warranted cordial words from "A.S." [72]

Perhaps owing to mutual mistrust between Franklin and the Artillery Court cabal, when the Doctor toured greater Britain for two months in 1771 with Jackson, he left the agency in the hands of his grand-nephew, Jonathan Williams Jr., rather than his assistant, Arthur Lee. After 1770, Franklin discovered that other relationships, hitherto cordial and accommodating, were becoming tense and tenuous. In that year Montagu entered a caveat at the Board of Trade on Virginia's behalf against the Grand Ohio Company, for which the Doctor lobbied. The previous year Franklin had even recognized that he and Jackson stood well apart in their views of the nature of imperial government. Once the latter was ensconced at the Board of Trade as king's counsel, Franklin found that his old friendship meant little if Jackson disapproved of colonial laws submitted for confirmation.[73]

Particularly important was the interplay after 1770 between Franklin as agent for the Massachusetts Assembly and each of his two colleagues, the Council's representative William Bollan and deputy

---

Esther De Berdt to Dennys De Berdt, Sept. 12, 1766, to Dennis De Berdt, March 14, 1775, Reed, *Esther De Berdt*, pp. 99, 210; Dennys De Berdt to Samuel White, Dec. 14, 1765, Matthews, "Letters of De Berdt," p. 308.

[72] The *Virginia Gazette* (Rind), April 26, 1770, and the *New York Journal or the General Advertiser*, June 7, 1770, carried the piece, first printed in London on April 10, 1770. I am indebted to Professor Verner W. Crane for his thoughtful analysis of the authorship.

[73] PRO CO 5/1332, f. 154; PRO T 1/475, ff. 246–248; *Journal of the Commissioners for Trade and Plantations, 1768–1775*, p. 394.

agent Arthur Lee. Franklin respected Bollan's fund of knowledge and
had occasionally consulted him before they came to share the constituency of the General Court.[74] After several meetings early in 1771
between the two, Franklin reported that "there is a good Understanding between us which I shall endeavour to cultivate." [75] By 1772 the
Doctor tactfully began to take the lead. As agent for four colonies he
was accustomed to a certain latitude in action and responsibility. As a
result he began to find Bollan too cautious "and not easily persuaded
to take Steps of . . . Importance without Instructions or Authority." [76]

Arthur Lee's role as a junior agent was rather ambiguous. The
Massachusetts Assembly disappointed him by selecting Franklin as its
regular agent in 1770. While Lee genuinely admired Franklin's abilities, the tension between these two shortly produced hasty accusations
springing from jealousy. In 1771, Lee wrote Sam Adams that he had
read

lately in your papers an assurance from Dr. Franklin that all designs
against the charter of the colony are laid aside. This is just what I expected
from him; and if it be true, the Dr. is not the dupe but the instrument of
Lord Hillsborough's treachery. . . . His duplicity would not impose on
one possessed of half Dr. F's sagacity. . . . The possession of a profitable
office at will, the having a son in high post at pleasure [Governor of New
Jersey], the grand purpose of his residence here being to effect a change in
the government of Pennsylvania, for which administration must be cultivated and courted, are circumstances which, joined with the temporising
conduct he has always held in American affairs, preclude every rational
hope that in an open contest between an oppressive administration and a
free people, Dr. F. can be a faithful advocate for the latter. . . . By
temporising I mean consulting the inclination of ministers and acting
conformable to that, not to the interests of the province.

Lee suggested that Franklin had been "totally inactive" since 1767,
working craftily to please both colonists and administration. The
young Virginian concluded by protesting how disagreeable he found
such backbiting, especially "as your generous confidence has placed

[74] Bollan was initially uneasy at the prospect of a coagency (Bollan to Samuel
Danforth, Jan. 28, 1771, *Bowdoin and Temple Papers*, p. 258).
[75] Franklin to James Bowdoin, Feb. 5, 1771, Smyth, V, 297. Yet when
Franklin made his tour with Jackson in 1771, he did not bother to notify Bollan
of his departure or intended absence from London (Bollan to Samuel Danforth,
Oct. 18, 1771, Dartmouth MSS, Vol. II, no. 350, WSL).
[76] Freiberg, "Bollan," pp. 217–218.

me in the light of a rival to him. But I am so far from being influenced by selfish motives, that were the service of the colony ten times greater, I would perform it for nothing." [77]

By 1773, if not before, Franklin thoroughly understood his assistant's motives, remarking that "a young one impatient for the Succession" caused him some discomfort. Nevertheless the veteran of many political wars took Lee's impetuosity in his stride, regarding the young lawyer as "a Gentleman of Parts and Ability; and tho' he cannot exceed me in sincere Zeal for the Interest and Prosperity of the Province, his Youth will easily enable him to serve it with more Activity." [78]

Appropriately enough, that same year, 1773, elicited William Bollan's poignant utterance: *"Juncta juvant,* and when vested with ample authority I have gone into the Lords of the Treasury at the head of seven or eight agents of so many colonies, but now they seem a rope of sand." [79] The agents' cohesiveness as a pressure group had lessened. Partially private interests, the loss of personnel, and unstable personal relationships were responsible. But these were minor factors compared with the impact of the Great Debate.

[77] Lee to Thomas Cushing, Feb. 18, 1771, PRO CO 5/118, ff. 88–89; Lee to Sam Adams, June 10, 1771, Richard H. Lee, *The Life of Arthur Lee* (Boston, 1829), I, 216–218.

[78] Franklin to Thomas Cushing, July 7, 1773, Smyth, VI, 85. Others among Lee's colleagues were less patient and tolerant. Infuriated by an attack from Junius Americanus, Robert Charles inserted a denunciation of Lee in the public press. Referring to Lee's "rancorous dart of malice," Charles indicated that he would settle for no less than a personal apology (*Gazetteer and New Daily Advertiser,* Oct. 9, 1769). Writing to Jared Ingersoll, William Samuel Johnson remarked that Lee "delights in the fire and fury of a Party, & is perfectly well adapted to please the Bostonians" (June 15, 1772, NHCHS *Papers,* IX, 436).

[79] Bollan to James Bowdoin, Sept. 29, 1773, *Bowdoin and Temple Papers,* p. 320.

CHAPTER 9

The Agents and the Great Debate

Because the agency provided a form of colonial representation in Britain, it is extremely important to establish the relationship of its members to the constitutional controversy known as "The Great Debate." How did it involve and appear to them? Since the agents' attitudes fed back into America as well as into British public opinion, these views are important. Many of the lobbyists had a unique vantage point from which to view the chasm separating Britain and her colonies. The agents had commitments to both sides. Consequently the majority were subjected to an uncomfortable kind of neutrality. They were well situated to differentiate between the primary and more superficial issues agitating pamphleteers and politicians. A number of them took positions representative of views along the ideological spectrum. As intellectual considerations rather than expediency became the only satisfactory basis for conciliation in colonial minds, the prospect of reunion lessened and the lobbyists found their work more difficult. Simultaneously the agents faced the problem of whether they were or could become political representatives at a time when the very nature of the institution was coming into question: whose creature was the agent and to whom was he responsible? As solutions to these problems became increasingly elusive, a sense of futility—barely visible by 1770—was manifested on both sides, especially by the winter of 1773–1774.

THE AGENCY AND COLONIAL REPRESENTATION

Earlier in the eighteenth century, when a man permanently resident in England held an agency, it had usually been a straightforward professional arrangement. A solicitor might even work for a colony in one case and oppose it in another. By the close of the Seven Years' War, however, many agents had, and indeed were selected for, strong political allegiances. Meanwhile the lower house in quite a few colonies became assertive, demanding exclusive control over the agent. The steadily intensified aggressiveness of the popular legislative body vis-à-vis governor and council naturally produced this insistence.

The power struggle for control of the London lobbyist quickly acquired in several colonies an Anglo-American dimension as Whitehall sought to curb what appeared to be a dangerous tendency. The Secretary of State for the new American Department, Lord Hillsborough, contended in 1769 that agents should be approved by all three parts of the provincial government. He refused to accept the credentials of men not so chosen.[1] To the colonists this seemed to be another invidious attempt to restrict their rights; and the agency itself became a component of the Great Debate. Uncertainty followed, constricting the capacity of certain agents to operate. Hence Franklin's complaint that he wished "the public character of a colony agent was better understood and settled, as well as the political relation between the colonists and the mother country." [2]

As agents for the Massachusetts Assembly and Council, Franklin and Bollan were most affected,[3] although owing to his established reputation the Doctor felt less anxiety than his colleague. He assured his constituents that "he should always be heard when they had anything to transact." Nevertheless he was quite sensitive to the new dilemma.

The Doctrine that no Agent ought to be received or attended to by Government, who is not appointed by an act of the General Court to which the Governor has given his assent, if established, must be attended with very ill Consequences: For . . . if whatever is to be transacted

---

[1] The requirement that an agent's proper credentials be registered at the Board of Trade had been ignored for some years past; see Joseph Sherwood to Samuel Smith, Sept. 16, 1761, "Letters of Joseph Sherwood," NJHS *Proceedings,* V (Newark, 1851), 135.

[2] To Thomas Cushing, Feb. 5, 1771, Smyth, V, 294–295.

[3] Franklin also had difficulty because the New Jersey Assembly claimed "the Sole right of appointing an agent" (Edward P. Lilly, *The Colonial Agents of New York and New Jersey* [Washington, D.C., 1936], p. 137). Burke's agency too was endangered by Hillsborough's dictum (N.Y. Assembly to Burke, May 31, 1774, Burke MSS, SCL).

between the Assemblies of the Colonies and the Government is to be done by agents appointed by and under the Direction of the three Branches, it would be utterly impracticable for an Assembly ever to lay before the Sovereign their Complaints or Grievances occasioned by the corrupt and arbitrary administration of a Governor. . . . So that we are reduced to a choice of difficulties: either to have no Agent at all, but such as shall be under the Influence of the Minister, or to find some other way to support an agent than by Grants of the General Assembly.

By 1772, Hillsborough still sought to ignore the improperly authorized agents, causing Franklin to comment that if the minister persisted the unacceptables would be reduced to promoting Massachusetts' "Interests by Conversation as private Gentlemen or by Writing." [4] Both Franklin and Bollan searched for colonial precedents to vindicate their appointments, and looked closely at the puzzling Virginia agency. Although Virginia had a dual arrangement with Abercromby and Montagu, the latter had been regarded as representing the whole colony. By the time Bollan called the peculiar situation to Hillsborough's attention, Virginia had dropped Montagu, and the Secretary of State insisted that such an appointment would never be allowed again anyway. [5]

Franklin believed that no agents at all would be preferable to ones burdened by Hillsborough's restrictions. Better to "leave the crown, when it wants our aids, or would transact business with us, to send its ministers to the colonies." The whole controversy, eased but not resolved by Hillsborough's resignation in 1772, elicited from Franklin recognition that agents potentially had adhesive qualities for the deteriorating Anglo-American system of government. In his opinion, agents had always been as valuable to the administration "as to the colonies from whence they come, and might still be so, if properly attended to, in preventing, by their better information, those disgraceful blunders of government, that arise from its ignorance of our situation, circumstances, abilities, temper, &c." Some of his colleagues,

[4] Thomas Hutchinson to John Pownall, July 17, 1771, MA, XXVII, 199; James J. Burns, *The Colonial Agents of New England* (Washington, D.C., 1935), p. 14 n. 31; Edward J. Fisher, *New Jersey as a Royal Province, 1738–1776* (New York, 1911), p. 97; Franklin to James Bowdoin, Jan. 13, 1772, Smyth, V, 359.

[5] *Ibid.*; Bollan to Thomas Hutchinson, April 15, 1771, Bowdoin-Temple MSS, Vol. II, MHS; Bollan to Samuel Danforth, Oct. 18, 1771, Dartmouth MSS, Vol. II, No. 350, WSL.

however, such as Arthur Lee—in a fit of jealous rage—thought less in terms of potential than of reality. To Lee it appeared that

the only duty an American agent has to do, is to make a very formal and humble visit to Whitehall, with any paper his assembly sends him. He leaves it to the pleasure of the minister, and thinks his duty is done. 'Tis not all who will do even this paltry service. . . . What reason has America to expect anything farther, when by far the greater number of her agents are unknown here, of no abilities, no rank, or if any, of a bad character; some of them menials, all of them servile expectants.[6]

Richard Jackson believed that Massachusetts should "employ a discreet and able Man from among themselves, if not as Agent, to look out for one here." Burke, on the other hand, when he submitted his own qualifications for New York's perusal, rejected, as potentially effective agents, not only colonials but many Britons as well.

I am near to the scene where your business is finally transacted; I have an opportunity of knowing something of the temper, the disposition, and the politics of people here; and not being so deeply and warmly engaged as yourselves, I may be able sometimes to give you hints, on which your maturer sense may build something useful to you in your affairs.

Otherwise he argued as Lee did that "any merchant in the City, or any active clerk that can rummage public offices and wait in the ante-chambers of Ministers" could serve just as well. Like Franklin and Bollan, Burke rejected Hillsborough's notion that an agent ought to represent the colony as a corporate whole. Rather the agent should be the creature of the elected legislature only, "that is, a person appointed by them to take care of the interests of the people of the province as contradistinguished from its executive government."[7]

When the House of Commons refused to accept a petition from Bollan because it regarded his appointment as inadequate, Burke stood to challenge such imprudence. He argued that not to admit an agent was to deny justice, and he asked his brethren "by whom shall we hear the colonies, if not by agents?" Yet Burke explicitly rejected any

[6] Franklin to Thomas Cushing, April 13, 1772, Smyth, V, 392; *Benjamin Franklin's Letters to the Press, 1758–1775*, ed. Verner W. Crane (Chapel Hill, 1950), p. 266; Arthur Lee to [Richard Henry Lee?], Sept. 18, 1769, Richard H. Lee, *The Life of Arthur Lee* (Boston, 1829), I, 192.

[7] Jackson to Thomas Fitch, Nov. 15, 1765, CHS *Collections*, XVIII (Hartford, 1920), 377; Ross J. S. Hoffman, *Edmund Burke, New York Agent . . .* (Philadelphia, 1956), pp. 104–107.

suggestion that the agents were or might become political delegates of the colonies. Positive that America could not participate viably and directly in Parliament, he also ignored the question of those lobbyists who also happened to be Members of Parliament. Burke conceived of himself as an agent, not a representative; "he had employers at New York, not constituents." As early as 1769 he attacked the idea of American members.[8] Consequently when Francis Maseres wrote *The Canadian Freeholder,* he cited Burke's objections but still asserted the feasibility of colonial inclusion in Parliament.

I mean, in the appointment of agents for the American Colonies residing in Great Britain. . . . The difference of these agents from their constituents in America is found to be no impediment to their transacting the business entrusted to them to the satisfaction of their constituents. . . . Nor is it found to be necessary that these agents should be perpetually crossing the seas to and from America in order to receive these instructions. . . . The same may therefore well be supposed concerning any representatives. . . . In short, admit these agents into parliament, with a reasonable increase of their number; and the business is done.[9]

Other agents had mixed feelings about the desirability of American representation and the usefulness of agents in that capacity. Jackson thought Parliament should "give a Right of sending Members [to the House of Commons] to the American parts of the British Dominions." Like Charles Garth, he clearly did not regard the few agents in the Commons as colonial delegates.[10] William Bollan agreed. In an essay published in 1766 he approved of colonial representation while flatly rejecting the conception of America's being virtually included in Westminster either through agents as then constituted or through British Members.[11]

[8] Entry for April 28, 1774, Matthew Brickdale's parliamentary debates, MS minute book no. 11, BUL; Edmund Burke, *Speeches and Letters on American Affairs* (London, 1908), p. 122; Hoffman, *Burke*, p. 181; Burke to Rockingham, Aug. 23, 1775, *The Correspondence of Edmund Burke,* ed. G. H. Guttridge, III (Chicago, 1961), 196.

[9] Maseres, *The Canadian Freeholder: A Dialogue* . . . (London, 1776), I, 186–187.

[10] Jackson to Thomas Fitch, June 5, 1765, CHS *Collections,* XVIII, 350; Jackson to Francis Bernard, Nov. 26, 1765, MA, XXII, 456. For Garth's view, see his part in the Commons debate of Feb. 15, 1765, Harris Debates, Malmesbury MSS, Christchurch, Hants.

[11] Bollan, *A Succinct View of the Origins of Our Colonies* . . . (London, 1766), pp. 23–24; Bollan to Samuel Danforth, March 18, 1769, *The Bowdoin and Temple Papers* (MHS *Collections,* ser. 6, Vol. IX [Boston, 1897]), p. 132.

Franklin considered these questions from time to time during his agency, and his reflections are useful because they reveal much about the views of the colonists, most of whom after 1764 rejected the idea of parliamentary representation. That circumstance, of course, would have obviated their classic protest against taxation.[12] At the height of the Stamp Act crisis Franklin recognized that "the time has been, when the colonies would have esteemed it a great advantage, as well as honour to be permitted to send members to Parliament; . . . The time is now come when they are indifferent about it, and will probably not ask it, though they might accept it if offered them."[13] Two years later, continuing in the same vein, Franklin exposed the position of the agencies and the true reason why Whiggish colonials had no desire to send delegations to England: "We have all the advantage in the argument of taxation, which our not being represented will continue to give us. . . . And to be sure such an important business would never be treated of by agents unimpowered and uninstructed."[14]

THE AGENTS VIEW THE IMPERIAL CRISIS

The North American agents viewed themselves as their constituents' only spokesmen in Britain. A number of them, at least, also regarded the colonies as the asylum where British liberties would ultimately be preserved. They said as much in a notice probably inserted by Franklin in the *London Gazetteer* and subsequently reprinted in provincial journals. As a participant in the Great Debate, however, Franklin was notable for his pragmatic rather than dogmatic or theoretical approach. He eschewed controversy based upon natural law, the rights of man, and the social contract because he foresaw the fissure such issues would widen. Instead he concentrated on arguments devoted to proving the inexpediency of British policy for the economic health of the Empire. But his public approach should not

[12] Samuel Cooper confided to Thomas Pownall on New Year's Day, 1770: "It is now I find, consider'd as dangerous, by some men of Influence to have any Provincial Agent at all with such Pow'r as formerly given—They say it is inconsistent to object against Representatives in Parliament, and yet put the Province into the Pocket of one man, upon whom the Governor has a negative" ("Letters of Samuel Cooper to Thomas Pownall, 1769–1777," ed. Frederick Tuckerman, *AHR*, VIII [1903], 313).

[13] Jan. 6, 1766, Smyth, IV, 456, V, 16–17.

[14] To John Ross, Dec. 13, 1767, *ibid.*, V, 74. See also Verner W. Crane, "Franklin's Marginalia, and the Lost 'Treatise' on Empire," *Papers of the Michigan Academy of Science, Arts and Letters*, XLII (1957), 167.

obscure the fact that from 1764 onward he was deeply concerned with such questions as sovereignty, the nature of the imperial system, and the colonies' place in it. His attitudes toward these problems are revealed much more candidly and clearly in his correspondence and marginalia than in public documents. Nevertheless all three are important as indicators of American sentiment during the years before the rupture.[15]

In 1764, when Franklin was still in Philadelphia, he agreed with Richard Jackson in objecting to what both identified as internal taxes. "Two distinct Jurisdictions or Powers of Taxing cannot well subsist together in the same Country," the Doctor wrote. The power of taxation could not reside simultaneously in the colonial assemblies and Parliament. So long as America was unrepresented in the House of Commons, that body would lack the authority to levy rates in the New World. Two years later, Franklin still acknowledged the advantage of having colonials in Parliament, but cited British reluctance to allow "equitable participation in the government of the whole." In the absence of a truly imperial legislature, he urged the continuation of "requisitorial letters from the crown (according to the long established custom) to grant such aids as [American] loyalty shall dictate, and their abilities permit." At this point he still conceded that Parliament was in the best position to regulate imperial commerce.[16]

As late as 1767, Franklin continued to distinguish between internal and external taxation, indicative of the fact that his views on the constitutional problems were still developing. By 1768, however, he saw the problem whole, namely, "that no middle doctrine can be well maintained. . . . Something might be made of either of the extremes; that Parliament has a power to make *all laws* for us, or that it has a power to make *no laws* for us." The Doctor confided to his son that he found "more numerous and weighty" arguments for the second extreme. Adopting that position, it followed that "the colonies would

[15] *London Gazetteer,* May 2, 1765; *Newport Mercury,* July 8, 1765; Clinton Rossiter, *Seedtime of the Republic* (New York, 1953), p. 290; Verner W. Crane, "Franklin's Political Journalism in England," *Journal of the Franklin Institute,* CCXXXIII (1942), 205–224.

[16] Franklin to Jackson, May 1, 1764, *Letters and Papers of Benjamin Franklin and Richard Jackson, 1753–1785,* ed. Carl Van Doren (Philadelphia, 1947), p. 157; Crane, *Franklin's Letters to the Press,* p. 173; "Letter concerning the gratitude of America," Jan. 6, 1766, Smyth, IV, 400–402; Verner W. Crane, *Benjamin Franklin, Englishman and American* (Baltimore, 1936), p. 129.

then be so many separate states, only subject to the same king, as England and Scotland were before the union." [17]

Franklin adhered to this position, essentially without change, from 1768 forward. It would be six years, however, before he admitted it publicly. In 1769 he read and annotated Allen Ramsay's *Thoughts on the Origin and Nature of Government Occasioned by the Late Disputes between Great Britain and Her American Colonies*. Franklin's essential observation was that colonials were not British, but rather American subjects of the king. Hence they were outside Parliament's power. A year later he inscribed even more heretical observations in the margins of another pamphlet, *Reflections Moral and Political on Great Britain and Her Colonies*. By this time "British Empire" seemed a vague expression to Franklin, disguising the fact that "it consists of many States under one Sovereign." Only those parliamentary statutes that the colonists saw fit to adopt had any validity in America, for the colonists "owed no Obedience to the British Legislature. Its Jurisdiction did not extend out of the Realm." [18]

By 1770, Franklin had dropped the distinction between internal and external taxation altogether. In the third "Colonist's Advocate" he argued that the British could not tax America "without previously new-modelling their whole internal Constitution." The provincial assemblies, he felt, had always assessed taxes "for bearing the Expences of each respective Government." To sustain this contention Franklin appealed to "the prime Maxim of all free Government, viz. That no Subject is to be deprived of any Part of his Property, but by his own Consent." Thereafter he merely embellished ideas he had refined between 1768 and 1770: that parliamentary statutes were not binding on the colonists, that the king alone was America's sovereign, and that local assemblies were autonomous. [19]

The progress of Richard Jackson's thinking forms an instructive contrast to Franklin's, since both began by holding the same view, yet after a decade had veered off onto alternative paths. Their differences reflect those that finally separated American patriots and British

[17] Crane, *Franklin's Letters to the Press*, p. 170 n. 2; Franklin to William Franklin, March 13, 1768, Smyth, V, 115.

[18] The two pamphlets are in the Rare Book Room, LC. In the first, see p. 50; in the second, pp. 29, 33, 41, 44, 49–50, 53.

[19] Crane, *Franklin's Letters to the Press*, pp. 170 n. 2, 174, 254; *Benjamin Franklin's Autobiographical Writings*, ed. Carl Van Doren (New York, 1945), pp. 295, 308.

moderates. In 1763 and 1764, Jackson contended that "the Mother Country is mistress of the Trade of its Colony" and therefore could tax foreign trade but not the provinces internally. The latter might create a dangerous precedent.[20]

By the time of the parliamentary debates on the Stamp Act in 1765, Jackson found himself in a quandary common among colonial sympathizers. His response was characteristic of most of his contemporaries so perplexed. As America presented protests the problem became one of reconciling the sovereignty inherent in Westminster with denials of its power to tax overseas possessions.[21] When Jackson spoke in the Commons on February 6, 1765, he asserted that "Parliament is undoubtedly the universal, unlimited legislature of the British dominions, but it should voluntarily set bounds to the exercise of its power." Either American members must be elected or, short of that remote possibility, funds ought to be raised exclusively by the provincial assemblies. He did not doubt the need for a supreme legislature or its constitutional right "to impose Taxes of every sort on every part of the British Dominions." Nevertheless "the Right cannot be exercised without great Publick & Private Mischiefs and therefore should not be." Jackson advised his constituents to pressure the administration along lines of expediency. Otherwise "arguments against the Power of Parliament prove too much because they prove that not a single Act of Parliament binds the whole Kingdom of Great Britain."[22]

During and after 1766, Jackson juggled the two incompatible ideas: parliamentary sovereignty and taxation by consent. He argued that our "future Rule in America may be that we have used in Ireland," suggesting that the authority to tax be left dormant. He even hinted to Thomas Hutchinson that Parliament did not have a general power over the colonies since legislation was not an essential part of government—much less so the power of raising money. Most of all, however, the "Omniscient" solicitor yearned for a united empire. He moved steadily away from the colonial angle of vision, admitting that he dreaded "innovations in Constitutions." By 1774 he was reluctantly devoted to Parliament's supremacy. There had to be a general legisla-

---

[20] Jackson to Franklin, Dec. 27, 1763, Jan. 26, 1764, Van Doren, *Franklin and Jackson*, pp. 123, 138–139.

[21] Crane, "Franklin's Marginalia," p. 168.

[22] Jackson's arguments "On Internal Taxes in America," [1765?], Van Doren, *Franklin and Jackson*, pp. 193–196; Jackson to Thomas Fitch, Feb. 9 and June 5, 1765, CHS *Collections*, XVIII, 316, 350–351.

ture, and for such a role only Westminster, even unreformed, was best suited.[23]

Charles Garth followed a course remarkably parallel to Jackson's. At the end of 1764, South Carolina's lobbyist believed the colonists could oppose particular acts without "disputing the general superintending power of Parliament over every part of the Dominions." During the debates that took place early in 1766, Garth found himself persuaded by Pitt's position that taxation was inseparable from representation. He argued, moreover, that a constitution which cannot be exercised with justice and equity is worthless. If Parliament should not tax North America, it seemed silly to search for precedents to justify such action. As late as 1769, Garth sought recognition in the House of Commons for colonial legislative powers and requisition as the legitimate means of raising supplies.[24]

Edmund Burke, like Jackson and Garth an M.P., was less troubled than they by the perplexing progress of the Great Debate. Not that he failed to regret the divisive effect of constitutional discourse, for he did. The fundamental questions, he felt, "ought forever to be buried in silence." But Burke was not burdened by the question of consistency. From 1766 to the end of his agency, his essential contention remained constant and lucidly expressed in his speech before the Bristol election.[25] He upheld "the just, wise, and necessary constitutional superiority of Great Britain," but believed "that this superiority is consistent with all the liberties a sober and spirited American ought to desire." In effect this meant abandoning parliamentary taxation as a means of supply. Parliament was both the local legislature of Great Britain and the imperial congress overseeing the various inferior legis-

[23] Jackson to Mass. General Court, Aug. 15, 1765, to Francis Bernard, Nov. 9, 1765, MA, XXII, 447, 455; Jackson to Pa. Assembly, Nov. 9, 1765, Misc. Collections, APS; Jackson to Thomas Hutchinson, March 3 and Nov. 18, 1766, MA, XXV, 64–66, 101–107; Jackson to William Samuel Johnson, April 15, 1774, WSJ MSS Vol. II.

[24] Lewis B. Namier, "Charles Garth, Agent for South Carolina," *EHR*, LIV (1939), 649; Garth to S.C. CC, Jan. 19, 1766, March 17, 1769, *SCHGM*, XXVI, 72, 85, XXXI, 55–57.

[25] "As for my American Measures," Burke wrote in 1775, "they have one thing to recommend them; a certain Unity of Colour, which has stood wearing for upwards of nine years; and which every day appears more and more fresh" (to Richard Champion, Jan. 10, 1775, Guttridge, *Burke Correspondence*, III, 96). Cf. Edmund Burke, *Selected Writings and Speeches on America*, ed. Thomas H. D. Mahoney (Indianapolis, 1964), p. xviii.

latures. The provincial bodies, he urged, were legally competent to sustain their governments in peacetime. Unrealistically and unhistorically he added that this competence extended to military expenses during war years. Consonant with Rockingham's Declaratory Act, Burke saw no reason why Parliament should not make occasional use of the taxing power to prove its right to do so, provided men well informed on the colonial situation were at the helm. Clearly that situation might only occur when the Rockingham faction returned to power. Therein lay the importance of the colonial question for Burke. It provided another excuse to castigate North's administration in hopes of toppling it.[26]

Dennys De Berdt also opposed the administrative policies that followed 1763 more for practical than intellectual reasons. It seemed to him that the measures Grenville initiated would upset the smooth flow of trans-Atlantic trade and undermine imperial commerce. Nevertheless De Berdt responded to the constitutional issues of the decade, and his attitudes are representative of the most liberal wing in British public life—the merchants and dissenters bound to America by commerce and religious affiliation.[27] De Berdt's views were shaped by those of his provincial correspondents. He assumed the first colonists had been driven from Great Britain by oppression and had later offered to make a contract with the crown upon conditions formalized in the colonial charters. These documents gave the transplanted Britons the right to tax themselves. In 1770, the year of his death, De Berdt reaffirmed at some length that the colonists had historically and constitutionally been allowed to tax themselves and regulate their own "internal affairs." This view claimed a decreasing number of adherents in Britain after 1770, however outspoken those few may have been.[28]

De Berdt's coagent after 1768, William Bollan, wrote extended essays so heavily weighted with classical references and historical data that he scarcely sustained a systematic consideration of the nature of

---

[26] Burke to John Cruger, April 16, 1773, *The Correspondence of Edmund Burke, 1768–1774*, ed. Lucy S. Sutherland, II (Chicago, 1960), 430; Burke to James De Lancey, Jan. 5, 1774, *ibid.*, pp. 505–506; Burke, *Speeches and Letters on American Affairs*, pp. 60–65, 107; *Burke's politics*, ed. Ross J. S. Hoffman and Paul Levack (New York, 1949), pp. 60, 85.

[27] De Berdt to Thomas Cushing, Dec. 21, 1767, March 18, 1768, "Letters of Dennys De Berdt, 1757–1770," ed. Albert Matthews, CSM *Publications*, XIII (1912), 329, 331.

[28] De Berdt to Sam Adams, June 27, 1768, *ibid.*, pp. 333–334, 455–461.

imperial government or the fabric of English constitutionalism. As late as 1769, Bollan would go no farther than rejecting the concept of virtual representation as specious.[29] In 1766 he published several essays marginally related to the issues of the Great Debate. In these he contended that a supreme legislative jurisdiction must exist for the Empire, vested in Parliament according to the British constitution and leaving the colonists with subordinate powers. Yet under Parliament's aegis the North Americans were part of a commonwealth and entitled to British rights and benefits. To maintain this point of view in another pamphlet three years later Bollan relied on natural law. After 1770 his radicalism grew alongside that of his constituents, and his letters to Boston continually reinforced their inclination to root America's defense in "nature, reason, & the common law."[30]

William Samuel Johnson's attitudes are typical of the colonial moderate whose sense of patriotism and alienation from Britain enlarged as the debate developed. Like Bollan, he saw "a superintending supreme power in the British Parliament to regulate and direct the general affairs of the empire." That did not mean, however, that Parliament could deprive a subject of essential constitutional privileges. Taxation without representation was intolerable to Johnson, since he did not believe America was even virtually represented in Westminster. He felt the indiscriminate application of parliamentary sovereignty could result in the annihilation of American rights, liberty, and property. Unlike Franklin, Garth, Burke, and De Berdt, Johnson preferred to stress constitutionality over practicality. He demanded complete repeal of the Townshend duties. If the administration retained a token tax on tea, Johnson asked, "do they imagine the Colonies will not see that it is still an actual exercise of the right of taxation which they claim, and constitutes a precedent against them in which the Colonies cannot consistent with their principles or rights acquiesce?"[31]

[29] Bollan to Samuel Danforth, March 18, 1769, *Bowdoin and Temple Papers*, p. 132.

[30] Bollan, *The Freedom of Speech and Writing upon Public Affairs, Considered with an Historical View* . . . (London, 1766), pp. 141, 148; *Succinct View*, pp. 10, 18; *The Free Briton's Memorial to All the Freeholders* . . . (London, 1769), pp. 20, 30; Bollan to Samuel Danforth, Jan. 28, 1771, to Mass. Council, Sept. 1, 1773, *Bowdoin and Temple Papers*, pp. 254, 314–315.

[31] Oscar Zeichner, *Connecticut's Years of Controversy, 1750–1776* (Chapel Hill, 1949), pp. 93–94; Johnson to William Pitkin, May 25, 1769, "Letters of William Samuel Johnson to the Governors of Connecticut," MHS *Collections*, ser. 5, IX (Boston, 1885), 350.

Arthur Lee's position typifies that of the American radical growing in hostility as the decade unfolded. In 1769 he asserted that North Americans were not subject to every law made by the British legislature. Colonists would recognize the crown as their executive and Parliament in some instances as their legislature, particularly for the regulation of trade and direction of military operations, but *not* the exercise of taxation. In 1770, as Junius Americanus, Lee insisted that his compatriots did not oppose "the just authority of Parliament, which they revere." Four years later the Virginian would claim it was "an eternal law of Nature" that property cannot be taken without consent. America, he asserted, had always claimed and exercised the right to grant money voluntarily. Having rejected Parliament's power to tax the colonies, Lee also asked the superfluous question whether it was even expedient to do so? The answer, of course, was negative. By 1774 an ardent minority of American partisans shared Lee's total rejection of parliamentary sovereignty.[32]

Between 1766 and 1773 there was a growing consensus among moderate American Whigs, symbolized by the *Farmer's Letters* of John Dickinson, that Parliament could legislate for the colonies in general terms and regulate imperial trade, but not tax them.[33] This same consensus prevailed to a remarkable extent among the leading agents during these years. Jackson, Garth, Johnson, De Berdt, and Bollan all subscribed to this view with minor variations. Although Burke believed theoretically that Parliament *could* tax, he saw no reason to do so. After 1768, Franklin and Lee personally considered more radical applications of imperial theory; but they did not make these views public until the tea crisis began to boil.

THE PATRIOT AGENTS: A SPECIAL PERSPECTIVE

Lee, Johnson, Bollan, Franklin, and Henry Marchant regarded America with an intensity that set them apart from their colleagues. They also shared a vision of British political society which contrasted sharply with what they believed to be the relative purity of provincial

---

[32] Arthur Lee, *Observations on the Review of the Controversy between Great Britain and Her Colonies* (London, 1769), pp. 15, 29; *The Political Detection; or, the Treachery and Tyranny of Administration . . .* (London, 1770), p. 88; *An Appeal to the Justice and Interests of the People of Great Britain . . .* (London, 1774), passim.

[33] Crane, "Franklin's Marginalia," p. 168.

public life. William Samuel Johnson was thunderstruck by the electioneering he witnessed in 1768. He wrote to a friend that colonials accustomed to fair and honest voting could have no conception of an English election with its "Intriguing, Treating, Bribing, Buying, etc." [34] Such a seasoned observer as Franklin reported that "this whole venal nation is now at market, will be sold for about two millions, and might be bought . . . by the very Devil himself." [35] With the recurrence of parliamentary elections six years later, Arthur Lee found "public corruption at present, and public calamity for the future, are the dismal objects which incessantly fill my mind." [36]

During his stay in London, Henry Marchant never ceased marveling and morbidly reflecting upon an empire he believed destined for destruction. In the metaphor he devised, Britain was swelling like the head of a rickety child, while the body was fast wasting. "Thus the Head feeding upon the Body, without procuring any supplies to it, will sooner or later become all Head & no Body, when Louis Baboon & his Continental brothers will make a Foot Ball of it for their Cubs." Marchant responded to London like the fabled Puritan in Babylon. After visiting the Pantheon in Oxford Street he described its splendor and noted that "the whole is wonderfully adapted to raise every wanton Passion to distract the Mind and I think to destroy the Virtue." He altogether sickened at "the Grandieur of London, its amusements, Courts, Balls, Plays &c" and regretted "what a pity it is our Americans stay in England too long." [37]

To those agents who were truly colonials Britain seemed a fit place only for the "Man of Dissipation and Pleasure." They were confronted, for example, by the notoriety of two who presided over the

[34] Johnson to Jedediah Elderkin, Jan. 23, 1768, Emmet Collection, NYPL; Johnson to Joseph Chew, Sept. 12, 1767, to Jared Ingersoll, Aug. 18, 1769, Johnson Letter-book, Vol. I, Bancroft Transcripts, NYPL.
[35] Franklin to William Franklin, March 13, 1768, Smyth, V, 117. "The general Corruption and Servility of Parliament is now so generally seen & known to all the Nation, that it is no longer respected as it used to be. It is despis'd for its Venality, and abominated for its Injustice.—and yet it is not clear that the People deserve a better Parliament, since they are themselves full as corrupt & venal; witness the Sums they accept for their Votes at almost every election" (Franklin to Joseph Galloway, April 10, 1771, MFY).
[36] Lee to Francis L. Lee, April 2, 1774, Lee MSS, II, HLHU.
[37] Marchant to Ezra Stiles, May 14, 1772, Stiles MSS, YUL; Marchant's London diary, entries for Jan. 18 and 25, 1772, RIHS; Marchant to William Greene, Feb. 25, 1772, Peck MSS, Vol. III, RIHS.

Board of Trade—George Montagu Dunk, second Earl of Halifax, and Robert Nugent, Viscount Clare. Halifax spent lavishly on parliamentary elections, and his affair with Mary Anne Faulkner, a singer at the Drury Lane Theater, was the talk of the town in 1769. Clare, on the other hand, acquired his great wealth by marrying a succession of rich widows, though like Halifax he begat several bastards by his mistresses. Clare always supported the ministry in power, converted from Catholicism to Protestantism and back again, and was called the "most uninformed man of his rank in England." [38] With such statesmen responsible for colonial administration, the provincial agents understandably became alienated from the authority of imperial government. They developed a foreboding sense of doom, expecting shortly to witness the collapse of a decayed political organism too long infested by parasites. In search of historical precedent when attempting to articulate in print their apprehension, they recalled the deterioration of ancient Rome.

The agents' view of corruption in Britain had great importance in fortifying the American conviction that resistance was necessary. William Bollan contributed particularly to this impression. Between 1768 and 1770 he produced four pamphlets—all well-circulated in North America—devoted to "our unhappy divisions and debts, luxury and dissipation, violence and instability." Bollan aimed his attack especially at the unreformed electoral system—"that course of bribery which now takes place between candidates and electors." Initially he regarded suffrage reform as the panacea for Britain's troubles; but by 1770 he saw hope for rectification of the errors since 1763 only in "a state-revolution, that the constitution may be purified." [39]

In a variety of ways the agents' communications to their constituents contributed to the growing gap that divided the Empire by disaffecting its overseas members. Too often correspondence received in America exposed British apathy toward the colonies and their problems. After 1769 the lobbyists increasingly attributed unreasonable intentions to ministerial men, thereby contributing to the height-

---

[38] Marchant to Greene, Feb. 25, 1772, Peck MSS, Vol. III; "Dunk" and "Nugent," DNB.

[39] Bollan, *Continued Corruption, Standing Armies, and Popular Discontents Considered* . . . (London, 1768); *An Epistle from Timoleon, to All the Honest Free-Holders* . . . (London, 1768), p. 1; *Free Briton's Memorial*, pp. 1–2, 31; *The Free Briton's Supplemental Memorial to the Electors* . . . (London, 1770), pp. 45, 60.

ening of fears on both sides and intensifying what was fast becoming a psychological war of nerves. As Edmund Burke observed: "The Americans have made a discovery, or think they have made one, that we mean to oppress them: we have made a discovery, or think we have made one, that they intend to rise in rebellion against us. . . . We know not how to advance; they know not how to retreat." [40] Accusations of bad faith developed on both sides into the belief that the opposition was dishonest and that behind the facade of constitutionalism a plot was brewing—a plot on the one hand to impose tyranny on the colonies and on the other hand to dismember the Empire. The agents' correspondence clearly mirrors this mounting mistrust and served to convince Americans that their liberties were being schemed against.

As early as 1764, Bollan had suggested to Thomas Hutchinson that the new parliamentary legislation for the colonies represented an effort to fell the American "tree of liberty." Two years later Richard Jackson wrote Governor Pitkin a private letter indicating that the agent had "reason to think some ill designs by Persons are now at Work to spirit up ill will against us." By 1767 such reports began to reach the colonies with sufficient frequency to become alarming. William Samuel Johnson informed Connecticut that the administration's policy seemed to be to attack the colonies one by one. A few months later Franklin independently confirmed this judgment by warning Joseph Galloway that America's adversaries wished to render colonial assemblies useless and raise an independent revenue to support the bureaucratic establishment overseas. [41]

In 1768, Dennys De Berdt told Thomas Cushing of a plan "to provoke the Common people to some acts of violence" that would in turn elicit administrative punishment. The next year De Berdt's apprehensions became increasingly shrill. He cautioned his employers to beware of enemies who sought to cause "any Act of Treason or Rebellion" that would justify their seizing colonial lands "& thereby

---

[40] Lawrence H. Gipson, *The British Empire before the American Revolution*, XI (New York, 1965), 255; *Sir Henry Cavendish's Debates of the House of Commons during the Thirteenth Parliament of Great Britain*, ed. John Wright (London, 1841–1843), I, 398.
[41] Bollan to Hutchinson, Dec. 13, 1764, Dana MSS, 1674–1769, MHS; Jackson to William Pitkin, Nov. 8, 1766, CHS *Collections*, XIX (Hartford, 1921), 51; Johnson to Pitkin, May 16, 1767, MHS *Collections*, ser. 5, IX, 232; Franklin to Joseph Galloway, Aug. 8, 1767, Smyth, V, 43.

become proprietors of *your* Lands in America." His admonitions were continually "dark & discouraging [because] the Scheme of oppression runs very high & rains general discontent." [42]

By 1770 this anxiety had enlarged into a full-blown "conspiracy." Arthur Lee wrote his brother that North's ministry intended to dispense patronage in America to those who would prove themselves "active instruments of oppression." Bollan added similarly disconcerting information and Franklin advertised his alarm "at the late bold Attempt on the Liberties of our brave Fellow-Subjects in America." Burke especially became instrumental in disseminating the "plot" theory at this juncture. During the summer of 1770 he published his *Thoughts on the Cause of the Present Discontents*, claiming the court had revived its prerogatives through "influence" manipulated by a "junta" of persons in power behind the scene. Colonial radicals eagerly seized upon the notion of a secret and wicked court system, expanding it to include a tyrannical ministry. At the same time Burke's letters to James De Lancey in New York portrayed Hillsborough as an underhanded, untrustworthy martinet. [43]

While the colonists were absorbing and acting upon these alarms, the British too were spreading stories of their own, most of them warning that ungrateful and hostile provincials concealed excessive demands designed to dismember the Empire. Several of Franklin's London newspaper essays prior to 1768 were intended to counter these reports; but still they persisted. In 1768 and 1769, William Samuel Johnson remarked on the prevailing temper to Connecticut's leading politicians. "They affect to imagine, that, by giving way in any measure to the claims of the Colonies, they should hazard the loss of all their hold of them." The next year Johnson reported that the same misconceptions obtained, with the same unfortunate effects. Thereafter a simpler commonplace circulated. As McCulloh reported it, "The Enemies of America say it is aiming at Independence." Amidst

---

[42] De Berdt to Thomas Cushing, Oct. 5, 1768, Feb. 13 and Oct. 12, 1769, Jan. 1, 1770, to Richard Cary, Feb. 25, 1769, to James Otis, Nov. 17, 1769, Matthews, "Letters of De Berdt," pp. 346, 361, 381, 392, 365, 387.

[43] Lee to Richard H. Lee, Oct. 20, 1770, Lee MSS, I, 121, APS; Bollan to Samuel Danforth, March 8, 1770, *Bowdoin and Temple Papers*, p. 166; Crane, *Franklin's Letters to the Press*, p. 185; Charles R. Ritcheson, *British Politics and the American Revolution* (Norman, Okla., 1954), pp. 139, 150–151; Edmund Burke to James De Lancey, Dec. 4, 1771, Sutherland, *Burke Correspondence*, II, 290–291.

this climate of suspicion, it is little wonder colonial agents found lobbying as an art of persuasion increasingly difficult.[44]

After 1770 the agents were unable to divert these misconceptions. Franklin's "Rise and Present State of Our Misunderstanding," which first appeared in the *London Chronicle* and was later reprinted in the *Pennsylvania Gazette,* contended "that those writers who busily employ their talents in endeavouring to exasperate this nation against the Colonies, are doing it a very ill office." Such pleas went unheeded, and Franklin deplored the hasty handiwork of *"angry Governors, discarded Agents, or rash indiscreet Officers of the customs."* [45]

DEBILITATING EFFECTS OF IDEOLOGY

Inevitably the constitutional discussions and political recriminations of the Great Debate tended to make each side increasingly inflexible. As attitudes and emotions began to harden, opportunities for the agents to arrange a reconciliation diminished. As Franklin put it, "perpetual abuse and false representation may exasperate and alienate on both sides. It may divide. It can never unite." Consequently in his public writings Franklin deliberately minimized the more divisive issues. Despite his best intensions, however, Franklin was not altogether successful. Many of his more polemical pieces created an unfavorable impression in London and spurred on excitable colonists.[46]

Even the most significant colonial contributions to the literature of the Great Debate proved more antagonizing than persuasive. John Dickinson's *Farmer's Letters* were read widely, "but to little purpose," Arthur Lee reported, "though universally admired." De Berdt believed that some moderates might have been convinced by Dickinson, "tho' on the other hand warm spirits have been further irritated." Johnson informed William Pitkin that many in London found the

[44] Crane, *Franklin's Letters to the Press,* nos. 21, 51; Johnson to Jedediah Elderkin, Jan. 23, 1768, Emmet Collection; Johnson to Jonathan Trumbull, Dec. 5, 1769, Feb. 3, 1770, MHS *Collections,* ser. 5, IX, 383, 406; McCulloh to James Iredell, Oct. 2, 1775, Duke University Library.

[45] Crane, *Franklin's Letters to the Press,* pp. 215–220; Arthur Lee, *A True State of the Proceedings in the Parliament of Great Britain and in the Province of Massachusetts Bay . . .* (London, 1774), p. 23.

[46] Crane, *Franklin's Letters to the Press,* pp. xxxvi, 225, 228, 234, 239, 247, 252–254, 296, 316, 386.

Farmer's Letters a "treasonable, seditious paper."[47] Both De Berdt and Johnson found transoceanic tension mounting in 1768–1769. Massachusetts' agent feared that when "passions are once inflamed it's difficult to preserve them from outrage & outrage always widens the breach."[48]

Late in 1768, Charles Garth noted a subtle turn the debate was taking, a turn that exposed what would later become insuperable differences. At first the provincials, along with Chatham consistently and Franklin occasionally, differentiated between taxation and legislation; "yet from many Papers publish'd in America, it now appeared that the distinction was exploded by Men of Understanding in the Colonies, and that the objection to the Power of Parliament extended a great deal farther." The fact that so many petitions were directed to the crown solely, bypassing Parliament, seemed to confirm the deepest fears of British politicians.[49]

After 1767 the agents unsuccessfully warned their constituents not to neglect Westminster. "In consequence," Garth commented, "their Friends in Parliament are very much embarrassed." By 1770, Robert Charles and Franklin feared that "applying to Parliament to obtain Leave of the King to pass Colony Acts, would be a Novelty, and possibly be hereafter attended with disagreable Consequences." Two years later Franklin observed that "petitions came no more from [America] to Parliament, but to the King only. That the King appeared now to be the only Connection between the two Countries." Thereafter the agents divided on this problem according to their constitutional positions. Thus Arthur Lee encouraged Sam Adams to memorialize the throne, while Edmund Burke urged the necessity of "official Communication which all the Subjects of this Empire ought to hold with the Sovereign Legislature."[50]

[47] Lee to [Richard H. Lee?], Dec. 27, 1768, Lee, *Arthur Lee*, I, 189; De Berdt to Richard Cary, July 6, 1768, Matthews, "Letters of De Berdt," p. 335; Johnson to William Pitkin, July 23, 1768, MHS *Collections*, ser. 5, IX, 292.

[48] Johnson to Pitkin, March 23, 1769, *ibid.*, 324; De Berdt to Thomas Cushing, Aug. 16, 1768, Matthews, "Letters of De Berdt," p. 339.

[49] Crane, *Franklin's Letters to the Press*, p. 202 n.; Garth to S.C. CC, Nov. 10, 1768, *SCHGM*, XXX, 230–232.

[50] Garth to S.C. CC, Oct. 14, 1768, *SCHGM*, xxx, 229; Trecothick to Boston Selectmen, May 10, 1770, MS 224, Rare Book Room, BPL; Franklin to ?, April 12, 1770, MS in the possession of Mr. William C. Coles Jr., Moorestown, N.J.; Franklin to Thomas Cushing, Dec. 2, 1772, Smyth, V, 449; Arthur Lee to Sam Adams, April 7, 1772, Adams MSS, NYPL; Burke to N.Y. CC, May 4, 1774, Sutherland, *Burke Correspondence*, II, 533.

The more truculent and adamant attitudes maintained by the colonies as the Great Debate progressed proved dangerous for lobbyists whose sole concern was with practical achievements. On countless occasions the agents might have successfully pressured for repeal of undesirable legislation; but they were tightly bound by instructions sent by men who would only accept their goals under the rationale of "inalienable right." Once an issue fell into the polemical whirlpool of political theory it was pulled beyond reach and hope. William Knox summed up the dilemma lucidly at the close of 1768.

I have been told that the colony agents were sent for lately by Lord Hillsborough, and acquainted that if they would wave the point of right, and petition for a repeal of the duties as *burdensome & grievous,* Administration were disposed to come into it. The agents, however, declared they could not leave out the point of right, consistent with their present instructions, but should inform their respective colonies, and so it rests.[51]

Such had not always been the case. In fact ideology did not seriously complicate the lobbyists' operations until 1766. When the Massachusetts Committee of Correspondence instructed Jasper Mauduit in 1764 to remonstrate against pending measures, it assiduously avoided opposing parliamentary authority, though it quietly reserved to itself the taxing power. Similarly the first reaction in Georgia to the Grenvillite program was an instruction for agent Knox to oppose the new legislation, but to stress its adverse economic effects rather than deny its constitutionality. In opposing the Stamp Act the agents recognized early that such arguments "as tended to overturn the Power of Parliament would have" no weight. Therefore, in campaigning for repeal, the North American lobby emphasized the harm being done to the economy of the Empire and "the impracticability of enforcing this Law throughout the Continent without a Military Force."[52]

---

[51] Knox to George Grenville, Dec. 15, 1768, Add MSS 42086, f. 167. See also Thomas Allan to Lord Townshend, March 6, 1770, PRO, Northern Ireland, D.O.D. 572/3.

[52] Mass. CC to Jasper Mauduit, Nov. 3, 1764, *Speeches of the Governors of Massachusetts from 1765 to 1775 . . . ,* ed. Alden Bradford (Boston, 1818), p. 24; James Habersham to William Knox, April 15, 1765, *The Letters of Hon. James Habersham, 1756–1775* (*Collections of the Georgia Historical Society,* Vol. VI [Savannah, 1904]), p. 32; Jackson to Thomas Fitch, June 5, 1765, CHS *Collections,* XVIII, 350; Jared Ingersoll to Fitch, Feb. 11, 1765, to Conn. General Assembly, Sept. 18, 1765, NHCHS *Papers,* IX (New Haven, 1918), 306, 336–337; Lawrence H. Gipson, "The Great Debate in the Committee of

During the movement for repeal, however, there were portents of future trouble. Robert Charles received petulant petitions from New York's Assembly and could not prevail upon a single M.P. to present pleas so violent in tone. Likewise Charles Garth complained of remonstrances framed in America so offensive "that Members very well inclin'd to serve the colonies could not be prevailed with to offer them to the House . . . [and] that petitions could not well be drawn by those agents to the satisfaction of their constituents without suggesting a hint that the Colonies have hitherto been in the possession of the power of taxing themselves." [53]

Trouble loomed larger for the agents in the winter of 1767–1768, when the Townshend duties appeared. William Samuel Johnson and Garth promptly informed their employers that these grievances would not be repealed until the colonies waived the point of right. In March 1768, De Berdt hesitantly admitted to his constituents that he had drafted a "Representation" in which he "rather chose to argue from the disadvantages the late measures would bring both upon America and the Mother Country, because such arguments at present have by far the greatest weight." [54] Five months later the harried agent admonished the Bay colonists outright: "I wish, in all your applications, you had left the matter of right out of the question, and only applied for a repeal of the laws, as prejudicial to the colonies." At the opening of 1769 the new pall cast over lobbying in Georgian England by politics and political theory was illuminated by De Berdt's poignant comparison. "In the repeal of the Stamp Act it was a very different application from the present; in the former the whole Ministry were on our side; but now it is the reverse. When ever these Acts are repeal'd, the question of right must be kept out of sight . . . & the repeal must be on the foot of inexpediency." [55]

In February and March 1769 this particular contretemps achieved

---

the Whole House of Commons on the Stamp Act, 1766," *PMHB*, LXXXVI (1962), 19.

[53] John Watts to Robert Monckton, April 16, 1765, *Letter Book of John Watts* (NYHS *Collections*, Vol. LXI [New York, 1928]), p. 346; Garth to S.C. CC, Feb. 17, 1765, Namier, "Garth, Agent," p. 651.

[54] Johnson to Jared Ingersoll, Jan. 2, 1768, Johnson Letter-book, I; Garth to S.C. CC, Nov. 10, 1768, *SCHGM*, XXX, 230–233; De Berdt to Thomas Cushing, March 18, 1768, Matthews, "Letters of De Berdt," 331.

[55] William Tudor, *The Life of James Otis . . .* (Boston, 1823), p. 324; De Berdt to Richard Cary, Aug. 26, 1768, to Thomas Cushing, Jan. 2, 1769, Matthews, "Letters of De Berdt," pp. 339–340, 350–351.

its maximum vexation. The agents held three meetings and at the first two "unanimously agreed to Petition the House for a repeal of the obnoxious acts, leaving the matter of right quite out of the question." On the third occasion, however, several disclaimers arose, "the most material of which was, that our taking no notice of the matter of right was virtually giving it up." [56]

Remonstrances, &c. from America, having uniformly denied the right, it was not fit for the Agents to take upon themselves to waive it . . . without express instructions from their constituents. . . . These objections, with some others, appeared so insurmountable to several, that they declined being concerned in it, though such petition was drawn up and canvassed; whereupon those who would have taken that measure gave it up, and the project seems to be at an end. [57]

Thereafter the swelling of political ideas in America, bolstered by a century of experience with public institutions that were mutations of British originals, drove a wedge ever deeper into the Empire. "If they had chosen the nonimportation measure as the leading Card," Burke wrote, "they would have put themselves upon a par with us, and we should be in as much haste to negotiate ourselves out of our commercial, as they out of their constitutional difficulties." [58]

In a sense, the agents did themselves and their employers a disservice by minimizing the importance of the Declaratory Act in 1766. The door seemed to be wide open for the colonists to press their increasingly radical views, yet doing so would, in fact, have been hazardous for both lobbyists and their constituents. The Americans, in effect, were encouraged not to accept the principle of Parliament's right to tax them. After 1769 the major question in the Great Debate shifted from specific problems of taxes and the administration of government to the correct definition of a single concept—sovereignty. It is hardly a coincidence that after 1769 the agency underwent a marked decline. Institutions were being forcibly transformed by ideas. [59]

[56] De Berdt to Thomas Cushing, Feb. 25, 1769, to Delaware CC, March 9, 1769, Matthews, "Letters of De Berdt," pp. 364, 366; Franklin to Joseph Galloway, March 9, 1769, WCL.

[57] William Samuel Johnson to William Pitkin, March 23, 1769, MHS *Collections*, ser. 5, IX, 324–326.

[58] Burke to Rockingham, Sept. 18 and 25, 1774, Guttridge, *Burke Correspondence*, III, 30–31.

[59] Edmund S. and Helen M. Morgan, *The Stamp Act Crisis: Prologue to Revolution* (Chapel Hill, 1953), pp. 285, 295; *Pamphlets of the American Revolution, 1750–1776*, ed. Bernard Bailyn, I (Cambridge, Mass., 1965), 130.

CHAPTER 10

Undermined from Abroad: The
Agents and Their Constituents

The stability and strength of a pressure group depend greatly upon the support it receives from its employers. Yet in the decade before the American Revolution, colonists, however inadvertently, threw diverse obstacles in the path of their agents. They did not always select them prudently and failed to keep them adequately informed of events and changes in the provincial outlook. Too often the constituencies neglected and underpaid their representatives at the Court of St. James. Nevertheless, for a variety of reasons, men wanted and accepted agencies. Montagu and Burke, for example, needed the money. Burke and McCulloh felt it would bring them added political status without entailing very much work. Still others, such as McCulloh and Lee, hoped it would improve their influence and perhaps even lead to a seat in the Commons. For Lee, Bollan, and Franklin, an agency simply legitimized what they most wanted to do anyway.

Had their constituents endowed them with greater authority and responsibility, bickered with them less, and handled their communications from London more discreetly, the agents might have accomplished more. Instead the agency became an object of provincial factionalism, thereby rending the fabric of the institution as well as colonial solidarity. American insensitivity to British political life exacerbated these circumstances. The colonists failed to support the nonimportation boycott consistently. Combined with colonial acts of violence that alienated the most sympathetic Britons, and ingratitude for ministerial concessions, these conditions helped make the agents' task a trying one.

SOURCES OF FRUSTRATION

During the developmental decades, as we have seen, the American colonists had not been especially prompt or prescient about keeping their agents informed and fully authorized. The pace and pressure of imperial administration were then much more leisurely, however, so that delays and inconveniences never reached crisis proportions. After 1766 events moved more quickly and required ready reactions from those responsible for dealing with them. The agents, unfortunately, were not always in a position to act with dispatch; and the cause often lay across the ocean. Clearly, if the legislative committees charged with the duty of corresponding with the agents had promptly directed them to oppose vigorously any kind of colonial duties for revenue, the representatives would have executed their orders.[1]

In 1767, William Samuel Johnson observed that none of the northern agents had been instructed regarding repeal of the Currency Act. Hence none had taken action. Six months later Henry Eustace McCulloh remarked that America might be indulged with "emissions of their own Currency next Sessions . . . provided their Agents are duly impowered to appear & assent to them. —*without which nothing will be don.*" Garth summed up the attitude of many agents in feeling they should not waive "the Claim of Right without Instruction or Authority." Efforts at coordinated lobbying were consequently undermined, vindicating Franklin's contempt for "agents unimpowered and uninstructed." Men involved in British politics who were sympathetic to the colonists acutely recognized the pressing need for agents with clearly defined capacities for decision and responsibility. As John Wilkes urgently pressured Massachusetts, "proper powers . . . must be sent over to your agents here."[2]

Owing to a lack of direction from abroad, agents called before the

[1] Garth to S.C. CC, June 6, 1766, *SCHGM*, XXVIII (1927), 230–234; Bernhard Knollenberg, *Origin of the American Revolution, 1759–1766* (New York, 1960), p. 154.

[2] Johnson to William Pitkin, March 19, 1767, "Letters of William Samuel Johnson to the Governors of Connecticut," MHS *Collections*, ser. 5, IX (Boston, 1885), 219; McCulloh to Edmund Fanning, Sept. 12, 1767, Fanning-McCulloh MSS, No. 252, Southern Historical Collection, University of North Carolina Library; Garth to S.C. CC, March 12, 1769, *SCHGM*, XXXI, 52–54; Franklin to John Ross, Dec. 13, 1767, Smyth, V, 74; Wilkes to William Palfrey, Sept. 27, 1769, George M. Elsey, "John Wilkes and William Palfrey," CSM *Publications*, XXXIV (Boston, 1943), 415.

governmental boards often found themselves at a loss in contending with an issue presented to them. This happened on numerous occasions to Cuchet Jouvencel, Edward Montagu, William Bollan, William Samuel Johnson, and Thomas Life. The last-named, struggling with his colony's Susquehanna land claims, continually lacked instructions to guide his course of action. Garth's interviews with Lord Dartmouth became embarrassing when the agent's flexibility was constricted because he "had not received any Instructions . . . and therefore cou'd not say what the [Commons] House intended." [3]

The same sort of problem occurred concerning supporting information and documentary material the agents required for successful lobbying. Garth particularly lamented this problem, scolding his committee for failing to supply him with recently enacted laws, statements relating to provincial land disputes, affidavits, and Assembly journals. Franklin was obliged to remind Pennsylvania that a copy of the colony's laws would enable him to manage provincial business better, and that the Committee of Correspondence had not written for a very long time.[4] Joseph Sherwood had this same difficulty with Rhode Island—regularly after 1767. In August of that year he lamented his disadvantages in dealing with ministers when he lacked his constituents' account of events, especially since ministerial versions were so highly colored.[5]

Nor did most of the agents' financial relationships with their constituents improve markedly in these years. Johnson, paid £150 a year, was obliged to beg his colony for money to support his operations in the Mohegan case, a costly litigation to process. Connecticut always stood in arrears on her agents' expenses, often impeding their work for lack of funds. A few years before his death Thomas Life's salary was finally raised to £100 annually; but his account remained unsettled in

[3] *Journal of the Commissioners for Trade and Plantations from January 1768 to December 1775* (London, 1937), pp. 169, 197, 418; Life to Johnson, July 7, 1773, June 1, 1774, Feb. 1, 1775, WSJ MSS (bound), Vols. II, IV: Garth to S.C. CC, Feb. 25, 1773, Jan. 20, 1775, Garth Letter-book, pp. 146–147, 185–186, SCA.

[4] Garth to S.C. CC, Jan. 31, 1767, March 12, 1769, June 25, 1772, *SCHGM*, XXIX, 128–132, XXXI, 52–54, XXXIII, 243–244; Franklin to Joseph Galloway, Dec. 13, 1766, WCL; Cortlandt Skinner *et al.* to Franklin, Dec. 21, 1771, APS.

[5] Sherwood to Stephen Hopkins, Aug. 7, 1767, Jan. 13, 1768, Letters, VII, 52, 55, RIA; Sherwood to Moses Brown, July 21, 1769, Moses Brown MSS, I, 96, RIHS.

his lifetime, he died in "circumstances very scanty," and his wife continued to press Connecticut for her due as late as 1785.[6] Life's expenses arising from the Mohegan and Susquehanna proceedings were so considerable that Johnson, whose job included reimbursing his associate, had to consult a third agent to verify Life's bills. He referred Life's accounts to Joseph Sherwood—ironic because Sherwood had the unhappiest experience of any agent in dealing with his employers about money.[7]

De Berdt felt that the £200 he received as salary from Massachusetts in the later 1760's was not in keeping with his trouble and expense, nor equal to the dignity of the Assembly, "nor the importants of the state in which they have placed me." As late as 1771, William Bollan still demanded commissions dating from 1760. Characteristically, he looked into the fees other agents had received and informed his constituents of his findings: that lobbyists who came over from America gained more generous remuneration than those already in London; and that Montagu, Abercromby, Ingersoll, and Mauduit had been allowed percentages denied to him. The Council voted the fretful lobbyist £300 a year for the duration of his second agency.[8]

In theory Benjamin Franklin was the best paid of all the agents in these years. Yet the reality fell far short of his constituents' intentions. Pennsylvania paid him £500 annually until 1772 when a £300 raise gave Franklin the largest salary of any lobbyist. Georgia initially voted the Doctor £100 and later added another £50. He was never paid after 1773, though the Assembly finally compensated him with 3,000 acres of land. The General Court of Massachusetts intended to allow Franklin £300 per year. Thomas Hutchinson, however, managed to veto the Assembly appropriations continually after 1770. Hence the Doctor received none of the £1,200 owed him. Although instructed by the Bay Colony to keep a detailed expense account, Franklin found it impossible to separate the fees and gratuities each colony's business

[6] Johnson to William Pitkin, Nov. 13, 1767, to Jonathan Trumbull, Jan 20, 1770, MHS *Collections,* ser. 5, IX, 245, 396; Life to Johnson, July 6, 1774, WSJ MSS (bound), IV; Jackson to Trumbull, March 2, 1784, MS designation "War," X, 438a, CSL.

[7] Sherwood to Johnson, July 1771, MS designation "Indians," p. 282, CSL.

[8] De Berdt to Sam Adams, July 17, 1767, Sam Adams MSS, NYPL; Malcolm Freiberg, "William Bollan, Agent of Massachusetts," *More Books,* XXIII (1948), 170, 172, 177; Bollan's memorandum on his agency, Sept. 24, 1771, Dana MSS, 1770–1782, MHS.

required. He simply used his own money for such needs. Major outlays such as counsel and solicitor's bills he charged to the province.[9]

Insensitive provincials undermined the agents by neglecting to keep them adequately informed and subsidized—sins of omission. Simultaneously they indulged in an equally unfortunate sin of commission—publishing the lobbyists' confidential letters at inopportune moments. Such letters rebounded from the colonial gazettes into British public life, where they adversely prejudiced the agents' good names and political credit. As William Samuel Johnson noted, the British took alarm "at the frequent publication in America of extracts of letters from agents and others residing here, especially when they have taken the liberty to mention the names of great persons in or out of administration." Thus De Berdt underwent considerable anxiety in 1766 because some letters he had sent to New York were "imprudently printed there in the News, which coming back here may give offence, and thereby weaken my interest." Ironically, in 1769 the aged agent was in turn reprimanded for the very same crime by Speaker of the House Thomas Cushing. Despite this admonition, however, the Speaker continued to violate his own request. When Cushing received a confidential letter from De Berdt later that year, he opened it and began to reveal its contents in company that included such conservatives as Andrew Oliver. Only the discretion of John Adams, seated close by, prevented Cushing from disclosing the substance in full. When De Berdt learned of the Speaker's bad faith, he confided to a friend his stunned reaction: "I must be a little cautious what I write to him, for my first Letter relating to Governor Barnard Mr. Cushon opened in publick company and a Creature of Lord Hilsbourghs being present took a Coppy of a Parigraph or too which suted his purpose & sent it to his Lordship." [10]

[9] *Pennsylvania Archives,* ed. C. F. Hoban and Gertrude MacKinney (Philadelphia, 1852–   ), ser. 8, VII, 6427, VIII, 6899; Pa. CC to Franklin, Oct. 16, 1772, Franklin Papers, No. 86, LC; Ga. CC to Franklin, Feb. 24, 1774, Franklin Papers, pp. 234–242; Thomas Cushing to Franklin, April 20, 1773, Franklin Papers, No. 158; Franklin to Mass. CC, Jan. 13, 1772, Smyth, V, 351; *Benjamin Franklin's Autobiographical Writings,* ed. Carl Van Doren (New York, 1945), p. 288.

[10] Johnson to William Pitkin, April 11, 1767, to Jonathan Trumbull, Aug. 20, 1770, MHS *Collections,* ser. 5, IX, 228, 448; De Berdt to Joseph Reed, March 18, 1766, Matthews, "Letters of De Berdt," p. 443; Cushing to De Berdt, Jan. 19, 1769, "Cushing Letters," MHS *Collections,* ser. 4, IV (Boston, 1858), 353; De Berdt to Richard Cary, March 29, 1769, March 5, 1770, Matthews, "Letters of De Berdt," pp. 369, 406.

William Bollan was similarly disregarded. In 1770 he had to reiterate the same unheeded injunction for the benefit of Massachusetts'
overzealous council. Franklin realized fully that letters he sent to the
colonies which were subsequently published there made him an
anathema in London.[11] By 1773 the Doctor reached a point of exas-
peration that prompted an acerbic note to Speaker Cushing:

It is extreamly embarrassing to an Agent to write Letters concerning his
Transactions with Ministers, which Letters he knows are to be read in the
House, where there may be Governor's Spies, who carry away Parts, or
perhaps take Copies, that are echo'd back hither privately. . . . It is
impossible to write freely in such Circumstances, unless he would hazard
his Usefulness. . . . I speak this now . . . for your Consideration with
regard to future Agents.

Franklin's candid warning proved prophetic all too soon. Flagrantly
disregarding the agent's security, Cushing permitted this very same
letter, clearly marked "private," to fall into Thomas Hutchinson's
hands. The Governor immediately dispatched it to Lord Dartmouth,
Secretary of State for the Colonies. Six months later the pattern
recurred, except that this time Cushing's carelessness victimized Arthur Lee. The Speaker loaned Lee's letter to the same person who had
procured Franklin's for Hutchinson. Dartmouth thereupon instructed
General Thomas Gage to authenticate these two "scandalous" documents so that they might be "the grounds of a proper proceeding"
against the agents.[12]

The agents' vulnerability to provincial criticism seemed to grow
precipitously after 1766, hardly an auspicious sign for the stability of
their institution. Owing to the intense factionalism characteristic of
Massachusetts politics, an agent for that colony could expect suspicion
and even defamation almost as a matter of course. The Mauduits,
Bollan, Jackson, and De Berdt were all cut by the razor's edge of
disapprobation. In De Berdt's case, his age and ill-health were used in
Boston to deprecate his effectiveness. During his last fifteen months

[11] Bollan to Samuel Danforth, May 19, 1770, *The Bowdoin and Temple
Papers* (MHS *Collections*, ser. 6, Vol. IX [Boston, 1897]), p. 188; *The Letters
of Benjamin Franklin and Jane Mecom*, ed. Carl Van Doren (Princeton,
1950), p. 117. Verner W. Crane has suggested that the publication of such
letters in 1770 marked a turning point in Franklin's political reputation in the
colonies and Britain (3*WMQ*, VIII [1951], 287).

[12] Franklin to Cushing, July 7, 1773, Smyth, VI, 83; Hutchinson to Dartmouth, Oct. 19, 1773, March 30, 1774, Dartmouth to Thomas Gage, June 3,
1774, Dartmouth MSS, Vol. I, ii, nos. 897, 964, 982, WSL.

the agent was obliged to devote many of his letters to defending himself against misrepresentations. Nonetheless, mistrust of agents and their capacity for political intercession increased. "The Agents for America," Samuel Cooper wrote, "I am afraid have not thoroly done their Duty to their Constituents." [13]

Both Franklin and Jackson received a mild reproof in 1766 from the Pennsylvania Committee of Correspondence for failing to prevent a parliamentary act affecting colonial trade. In a similar but more acrimonious affair seven years later, Franklin was blamed in Massachusetts for not giving early warning of a deleterious clause in a new statute. This chiding occurred at a time when nearly two hundred acts passed and the agents were excluded from the gallery of the Commons. Since clauses were often clandestinely smuggled into bills, it would have been impossible, Franklin protested, for the lobbyists to know every detail of all pending legislation. He attributed this criticism to provincial factionalism and the covetousness of his rivals. Other agents, however, could not afford to be so cavalier. In 1768, Edward Montagu dealt with Lord Hillsborough under the shadow of portending execration by Virginia's burgesses, a fear that materialized for Charles Garth in 1774, when South Carolina's upper house "censured Mr. Garth's conduct, in presenting the petition of the Commons to the King." [14]

Beginning in about 1768 and continuing steadily thereafter, a new succession of colonial rumors and incriminations about Franklin appeared. One had it that he would shortly become Hillsborough's undersecretary of state. Another suggested that he "offer'd to desert [his] Constituents" in order to retain ministerial favor. A third, originating in Philadelphia, served to denigrate the entire North American pressure group.

As our agent has become post-master of half this continent, and obtained the government of New-Jersey for his son, in consequence of his having impressed our assembly and people of this province, with sentiments of

[13] De Berdt to Thomas Cushing, Dec. 7, 1768, to Richard Cary, 29 March 1769, Matthews, "Letters of De Berdt," p. 348, 369; Cooper to Thomas Pownall, Feb. 18, 1769, "Letters of Samuel Cooper to Thomas Pownall, 1769–1777," ed. Frederick Tuckerman, *AHR,* VIII (1903), 303.

[14] Pa. CC to Franklin and Jackson, Sept. 20, 1766, Franklin Papers, No. 58, LC; Franklin to Thomas Cushing, July 7, 1773, Smyth, VI, 84–85; Montagu to Hillsborough, Nov. 11, 1768, PRO CO 5/114, p. 213; John Drayton, *Memoirs of the American Revolution* (Charleston, 1821), I, 103.

submission to our superiors, if the agents of the other colonies had taken the same pains, they might have been as well provided for.[15]

The agents were hardly oblivious to such attacks. Both Jackson and Johnson grew anxious at the prospect of ill-favor in Connecticut: Jackson because he held a place at the disposal of administration; Johnson because his deceased brother-in-law's creditors hounded the agent's wife for funds; and both on account of their handling of the Susquehanna affair. In 1774, Charles Garth became angered upon discovering "a Carolina Gazette . . . in which the Agent of the Province appears so publickly and so injuriously treated." [16]

One of the main causes of this problem was the general disorientation of public life during the crisis decade, and particularly the fact that control of the agency increasingly became an issue in provincial politics. Each faction or party sought to discredit the candidate of its opponents. Joseph Sherwood's dismissal by New Jersey in 1766 grew out of the machinations of provincial politicians maneuvering for power. The pattern nearly recurred four years later in Rhode Island, where Sherwood's enemies in the Assembly attempted to snatch his office but failed.[17]

In 1774, Georgia's upper house formed a committee to inquire into Franklin's conduct as agent. A quarrel resulted within the Assembly, exacerbated by Governor Wright's strong antipathy for the Doctor. The Commons House, asserting that the agency should be exclusively the province of the people, made Franklin their agent alone and instructed him independently. The controversy was unresolved at the outbreak of hostilities. Such antagonisms almost became an accepted part of Georgia's political life. The 1760's were studded with a sequence of conflicts involving legislature and governor wherein the prize sought was the agency. Between 1766 and 1768, for example, Charles Garth's status remained uncertain. Wright threatened "that if his influence would effect it, Garth would not be received by any official in London." When British officials accordingly refused to

[15] Franklin to William Franklin, July 2, 1768, Smyth, V, 142–143; Samuel Cooper to Franklin, Aug. 23, 1771, King's MSS, No. 204, BM; Van Doren, *Franklin's Autobiographical Writings*, p. 338; *Boston Gazette and Country Journal*, Jan. 16, 1769.

[16] Johnson to Jackson, Aug. 31 and Sept. 17, 1770, WSJ MSS (box), Vol. I; Garth to S.C. CC, May 12, 1774, Garth Letter-book, pp. 172–173, SCA.

[17] William Franklin to Benjamin Franklin, Nov. 13, [1766?], APS; Sherwood to Moses Brown, Sept. 15, 1770, Moses Brown MSS, I, 115, RIHS.

recognize Garth, the Commons house found itself without an agent in London.[18]

More than simply the victims of provincial factionalism, the agents occasionally found themselves personally aligned as protagonists, especially against the governor. When Francis Bernard in 1768 had the temerity to write letters to Whitehall "wherein [he] injuriously aspersed [Boston] and its inhabitants," it fell to Dennys De Berdt to expedite the attempt by his constituents to remove the Governor. Unfortunately they failed to supply De Berdt with power of attorney to prosecute their complaint and failed to bolster their petition to the crown with supporting documents, thereby forcing De Berdt to beg the Privy Council for postponements of the necessary hearing. Early in 1770 that tribunal, grown impatient, decided to conclude the whole affair once and for all. De Berdt, still lacking "any Proofs of the Allegations," underwent a humiliating inquisition that eventuated in Sir Francis' acquittal and the depreciation of the agency.[19]

The conservatives had at their disposal ample means of retaliation against both the popular party and its lobbyists. Bernard's successor, Thomas Hutchinson, took revenge in 1770 "by refusing a Grant which they [the House] made to their former Agents of near Eight hundred pounds sterling and intimating to them that all their powers of Agency expired with the Session." The Governor played his hand well, for he successfully hampered Bollan and complicated Franklin's circumstances. Bernard, of course, was delighted. He informed Hutchinson from London that "the Agent has lost all his Importance, as an Agent he is Allowed none. The Agent of the House has been refused having his Appointment registered at the Board of Trade, the legality of it has been denied. So that without Admission to the public Offices or Pay their Use & Value will not be great." [20]

After John Wentworth had become governor in 1767, he relied on Rockingham, not Trecothick, to keep him in office. Thereafter the

[18] Alfred O. Aldridge, "Benjamin Franklin as Georgia Agent," *Georgia Review,* VI (1952), 171–173; W. W. Abbot, *The Royal Governors of Georgia, 1754–1775* (Chapel Hill, 1959), pp. 142–143.

[19] Bollan to Samuel Danforth, June 21, 1769, *Bowdoin and Temple Papers,* pp. 145–146; PRO PC 2/114, pp. 211–214; Francis G. Walett, "Governor Bernard's Undoing: An Earlier Hutchinson Letters Affair," *NEQ,* XXXVIII (1965), 217–226.

[20] Hutchinson to [Thomas Gage?], Nov. 26, 1770, MA, XXVII, 58–59; Bollan to Samuel Danforth, April 15, 1771, *Bowdoin and Temple Papers,* p. 266; Bernard to Hutchinson, Feb. 11, 1771, Bernard MSS, VIII, 159–163, HLHU.

erstwhile friends drifted steadily apart. In 1768 the Governor attempted to have his former coagent dropped. But the Assembly proved recalcitrant, expressed satisfaction with Trecothick, and rejected several candidates proposed by Wentworth. Against this background, Wentworth could not have been too disappointed in 1772–1773 that Trecothick failed to testify for him in London when Peter Livius nearly succeeded in having him ousted. A member of the provincial Council, Livius placed before the Board of Trade an assertion of maladministration and misappropriation of revenue by chief executive and Council. When the Governor's private secretary arrived in England supplied with refutations, he discovered Trecothick sick in bed. Nevertheless the agent did what he could, writing Dartmouth and John Pownall a dispassionate defense of Wentworth. He was eventually acquitted; but at first the case went against him. In May 1773 the Board of Trade found him guilty and all but recommended dismissal. Trecothick at this point retired into the background, leaving further organization of Wentworth's defense to Lord Rockingham. The Privy Council ultimately exonerated the Governor; but he always blamed Trecothick's indifference for the initial blot upon his honor.[21]

New York's agency remained an object of provincial politics during Burke's term, nearly causing him to resign. Moreover, members of the Cruger–De Lancey connection responsible for Burke's appointment believed they "acted on the same principles of conduct and politics that were represented by Burke in England." Therefore they expected him to serve as their personal instrument in London, a constricting concept of the agency indeed, and one Burke sensibly shied away from. Nevertheless his position was such that the picture he received of colonial needs was somewhat out of focus because his particular correspondents in New York were "largely unrepresentative of the mounting radical sentiments destined to produce the Revolution."[22]

[21] John Wentworth to Paul Wentworth, Dec. 13, 1768, to Nathaniel Rodgers, Dec. 19, 1768, John Wentworth Letter-book, pp. 166, 168, NHHS; Theodore Atkinson to Trecothick, Dec. 28, 1772, Trecothick to John Pownall, Feb. 1, 1773, *The State of New Hampshire: Miscellaneous Provincial and State Papers, 1725–1800,* ed. Isaac W. Hammond, XVIII (Manchester, N.H., 1890), 637–638, 645; John Wentworth to H. Bellew, April 8, 1775, *Provincial Papers: Documents and Records Relating to the Province of New Hampshire, from 1764 to 1776,* ed. Nathaniel Bouton, VII (Nashua, N.H., 1873), 344.

[22] Ross J. S. Hoffman, *Edmund Burke, New York Agent . . .* (Philadelphia, 1956), pp. 94–95, 97; N.Y. Assembly to Burke, May 31, 1774, Burke Papers, SCL; Edmund Burke, *Selected Writings and Speeches on America,* ed. Thomas H.D. Mahoney (Indianapolis, 1964), p. xiii.

Burke's circumstances were symptomatic of a **dangerous** tendency which became increasingly evident after 1766. A majority of the colonial agents were Englishmen whose familiarity with American conditions derived in large part from the views of their particular correspondents. Thus some of the lobbyists, especially after 1770, were in varying degrees out of touch with the rapidly changing views of their constituents. This was unfortunate, for the colonists themselves had only a vague and tenuous understanding of British politics, opinion, and colonial administration.

PROVINCIALISM AND MISUNDERSTANDING

An ocean's distance from the seat of empire, provincials had a very imperfect understanding of public affairs in London. Because communications were slow, colonial naïveté grew out of ignorance of the issues most vital to British politics.[23] More than that, however, until the Stamp Act crisis Americans did not realize how sensitive administrations could be to words and deeds issuing from North America. They failed to recognize consistently that for better or for worse, what they did might affect imperial government. In 1760, Richard Jackson reminded Connecticut's Jared Eliot that the colonies "have hitherto not been sufficiently acquainted with our Court & Ministry, particularly that part of our Administration that is most connected with the Interest of the Colonies."[24]

Had the colonists supported the agreements not to import British goods, their lobbyists would have stood on firmer ground in London. From the summer of 1765 until repeal of the Stamp Act eight months later, an effective boycott contributed significantly to the campaign. In 1769–1770, in response to the Townshend duties and appeals from the agents, the device was repeated.[25] This time, however, after a transitory success, it floundered. The agents were acutely affected and

[23] In his speech on conciliation, Burke observed that "three thousand miles of ocean lie between you and them. No contrivance can prevent the effect of this distance in weakening government. Seas roll, and months pass, between the order and the execution; and the want of a speedy explanation of a single point is enough to defeat a whole system" (*Burke's Politics:* ed. Ross J. S. Hoffman and Paul Levack (New York, 1949), p. 72.

[24] June 12, 1760, Eliot MSS, YUL.

[25] William Samuel Johnson was probably responsible for first proposing an anti-tea campaign in the colonies (Johnson to William Pitkin, June 9, 1767, MHS *Collections*, ser. 5, IX, 236).

complained bitterly to their constituencies. The economic reorienta-
tion of the Empire was partially responsible. Postwar depression had
given way to prosperity, and Britain looked to exciting prospects
eastward. While the Russo-Turkish War created a new demand for
manufactures, the East India Company had been exporting "prodi-
gious quantities to supply an extraordinary demand in that part of the
world." New sources of trade arose in France and Germany, "while at
home all the supernumary hands in the kingdom have . . . found full
employment in the vast works which are carrying on"—canal- and
road-building between the principal trading towns.[26]

Strengthening the solidarity of America's commercial ranks could
still influence Britain's receptiveness to colonial demands, however.
Early in 1770 intelligence arrived in London of "the revival of the
spirit of non-importation amongst the Boston merchants, which was
thought here to be almost at an end." With the firm resolve of the
Philadelphia community and a monolithic seaboard, Parliament was
pressured into revoking most of Townshend's invidious taxes. Nevertheless Franklin cautioned his employers to consume only domestic
manufactures until total repeal had been achieved. If the weapon
misfired it would never again be considered dangerous. As usual he
was quite accurate. Word trickled in that New York's merchants had
clandestinely broken the boycott. The rumor soon arrived that Pennsylvania's had done the same. Then William Samuel Johnson complained that the North American pressure group was undermined by
news that New York had overtly agreed to open the trade. Satisfied
with partial repeal, merchants there broke the agreement in July.
Whitehall received the news "with Exultation," for it "had found out
that the Non-importation Scheme itself was a meer Bravado." [27]

After that the deluge. Sherwood, Arthur Lee, and Henry Marchant
each grieved at this shortsightedness on the part of their employers.
Their enemies now firmly believed "the American opposition entirely

---

[26] Franklin to Joseph Galloway, Jan. 29 and March 9, 1769, WCL; Johnson
to Pitkin, Oct. 20, 1768, Sept. 18 and Dec. 5, 1769, MHS *Collections*, ser. 5,
IX, 298, 360, 384.

[27] Johnson to Jonathan Trumbull, March 6 and Aug. 20, 1770, MHS
Collections, ser. 5, IX, 426, 450; Franklin to Joseph Galloway, March 21, 1770,
Rosenbach Foundation and Gallery, Philadelphia; Johnson to Samuel Johnson,
April 14, 1770, Samuel Johnson MSS, III, 154, Columbia Univ. Library;
Franklin to Galloway, June 26, 1770, MFY; Thomas Whately to Jared Inger-
soll, Oct. 11, 1770, NHCHS *Papers*, IX (New Haven, 1918), 434.

Annihilated." John Temple told Johnson that colonials had lost their mettle in English eyes. The provincial honor was gone in 1770 when, "with everything at stake, they threw up the important game when they had all the trumps in their own hands, & like a Spaniel mearly cringed, & kiss'd the rod that whip'd 'em." [28]

Parallel to lack of enthusiasm in the colonies for economic sanctions, there existed a propensity to commit acts that could only succeed in alienating sympathetic British friends and intensifying the hostility of those who already regarded the provinces as *enfants perdus*. "Whatever may be the Rights of the Colonys," one lobbyist wrote, "this Country has at least hers also, and one of them is to be treated with Decency, by those people whom her Army so lately saved from slavery." The agents were invariably grateful when their employers drew memorials in a "temperate and unexceptionable manner," for no M.P. could be found to present unreasonable remonstrances. [29]

The lobbyists shuddered at the arrival of reports from the colonies of "sons of violence, who to redress particular grievances introduce far greater mischiefs." Aggressions by the Liberty Boys during the Stamp Act crisis were minimized in Britain and the law revoked. But in succeeding years colonial representatives found it increasingly difficult to disclaim outrages perpetrated by their constituents. Unhappily the agents too often bore the brunt of Whitehall's wrath for indiscretions committed by their employers. Franklin hoped to see the Currency Act repealed if "no further Imprudencies appear in America to exasperate Government here against us." [30]

Within a few months he would be disappointed. New York's Assembly refused to implement the Mutiny Act according to the pattern required by Parliament. Then several hundred New York merchants challenged the traditional navigation system, petitioning that the commercial regulations enacted by the Rockingham ministry in 1766 "instead of remedying, have increased the heavy burthen" under

[28] Sherwood to Moses Brown, Sept. 14, 1770, Moses Brown MSS, I, 115, RIHS; Marchant to Ezra Stiles, Sept. 5, 1771, Stiles MSS, YUL; Lee to Sam Adams, Dec. 31, 1770, April 7, 1772, Adams MSS, NYPL; *Bowdoin and Temple Papers*, pp. 280–282.

[29] Alexander Elmsley to Samuel Johnston, Dec. 2, 1774, Samuel Johnston MSS, N.C. Dept. of Archives and History, Raleigh; Dennys De Berdt to Richard Cary, Aug. 26, 1768, Matthews, "Letters of De Berdt," p. 340.

[30] William Bollan to Thomas Hutchinson, Dec. 26, 1765, MA, XXV, 43–43a; Franklin to Hugh Roberts, Feb. 27, 1766, Smyth, IV, 410; Franklin to Pa. CC, June 10, 1766, *PMHB*, V (1881), 353–354.

which colonial trade "already laboured." The document created a sensation, and stifled operations of the lobbyists.[31]

This storm had scarcely subsided when Massachusetts created a greater furor. In February 1768, the Assembly sent the other colonies its famous Circular Letter, avowing that Parliament had no right to impose duties for revenue in America. It also claimed the Townshend Revenue Act was unconstitutional, and denounced the principle of salaries for governors and judges independent of assembly authorization. These assertions touched off anew the General Court's running battle with Governor Bernard, alarmed the new customs commissioners at Boston, and electrified the Atlantic seaboard. In London the administration was infuriated. Once again the agents encountered sharp hostility to lobbying as Hillsborough in particular used the Circular Letter as an argument against making concessions.[32]

Unreasonable provincial behavior became notorious in London. Franklin had hoped the Americans would show proper appreciation when the Stamp Act was repealed, but remained disappointed. Barlow Trecothick apologized to Newcastle on behalf of the delinquent colonies who had not expressed any cognizance of his role in the movement for repeal. Lord Dartmouth admonished De Berdt for the unmindfulness of the Bay Colony, and Sherwood scolded his employers similarly.[33] In 1767 and 1768, the mercantile community felt very much provoked because it had spent nearly £1,500 in lobbying for an end to the Stamp Act and still had not received in return so much as a *"thank ye,"* except from Rhode Island. Their letters across the Atlantic, they complained, were either answered with "unkind reflections" or contemptuously ignored.[34]

---

[31] Jack M. Sosin, *Whitehall and the Wilderness: The Middle West in British Colonial Policy, 1760–1775* (Lincoln, Neb., 1961), p. 129; Dennys De Berdt to Thomas Cushing, March 14, 1767, MA, Letters, 1764–1774, p. 51; David Barclay to Israel Pemberton, March 3, 1767, Pemberton MSS, XIX, 57, HSP.

[32] Charles Garth to S.C. CC, March 12, 1767, Dec. 10, 1768, *SCHGM*, XXIX, 214–221, XXX, 233–235; William Samuel Johnson to Jonathan Trumbull, Sept. 29, 1768, Trumbull MSS, CHS.

[33] Franklin to Charles Thomson, Feb. 27, 1766, Smyth, IV, 411; Trecothick to Newcastle, Sept. 15, 1766, Add MSS 32977, f. 83; Sherwood to Samuel Ward, March 29 and May 15, 1766, Letters, VII, 38, 43, RIA.

[34] Benjamin Franklin to Joseph Galloway, June 13, 1767, Smyth, V, 28; William Samuel Johnson to William Pitkin, Oct. 20, 1768, MHS *Collections*, ser. 5, IX, 298.

The colonists' vision of their position in British political life was blurred by their misunderstanding of the mainsprings of power and opinion in London. In this respect they were sometimes casualties of their own unwise selections for the agency. Thomas Hutchinson reported that De Berdt "from time to time received *bona verba* from the ministry and fancied his constituents stood well with them, has wrote accordingly and by this means has encouraged them to go on in measures which must prove destructive." In 1768 even Barlow Trecothick informed the House of Commons that he regarded "America as deluded." As late as 1775, Burke informed Rockingham that "in America, they have scarce any idea of the state of men and parties here, nor who are their friends or foes." [35]

Because the constituencies were largely ignorant of the processes of colonial administration in London, they often expected of their agents impossible achievements. De Berdt informed Dedham's delegate to the Massachusetts House of Representatives that Americans had "no notion of the trouble there is in attending Ministers & Officers of State, & are as little sensible of the unavoidable expences which attend it for they can't be enumerated." In 1770, while Trecothick explained to the selectmen of Boston their ignorance of the proper channels of communication with the crown, Sherwood brooded over the failure of his Rhode Island employers to recognize the complexities of dealing with a tenacious Parliament and an equally hostile Exchequer. [36]

As serious as unfamiliarity with mechanical aspects of procedure in London was the simplistic view provincials held of the men who exerted authority there—politicians and bureaucrats who were the "hands of power" and "servants of power." [37] In Massachusetts, for example, there was a tendency to overestimate the capacity of Dartmouth as Secretary of State for the Colonies to calm the troubled

[35] Hutchinson to Israel Mauduit, June 6, 1767, MA, XXV, 183; *Sir Henry Cavendish's Debates of the House of Commons during the Thirteenth Parliament of Great Britain*, ed. John Wright (London, 1841–1843), I, 50; Burke to Rockingham, Aug. 23, 1775, *The Correspondence of Edmund Burke, 1774–1778*, ed. G. H. Guttridge, III (Chicago, 1961), 195.

[36] De Berdt to Samuel Dexter, Dec. 23, 1767, Matthews, "Letters of De Berdt," p. 328; Trecothick to Selectmen of Boston, May 10, 1770, MS No. 224, Rare Book Room, BPL; Sherwood to Moses Brown, Sept. 22, 1770, Moses Brown MSS, I, 115, RIHS.

[37] The phrases were coined by Jasper Mauduit in a letter to Samuel White, Feb. 19, 1765, *Speeches of the Governors of Massachusetts from 1765 to 1775 . . .* , ed. Alden Bradford (Boston, 1818), p. 31.

waters that divided Britain and America. Elsewhere colonials were unaware of the significant force such civil servants as John Pownall wielded in formulating policies and executing decisions. To compound the difficulty and the irony, many Americans firmly believed "that the [British] nation has been grossly misinformed with respect to the temper and behavior of the Colonists." [38] Some of the agents, undermined and inadequately supported by their employers, were partially responsible for this blindness to colonial circumstances. But much of political society in London seemed to cherish an insular ignorance of the North American colonies.

Given their provincial perspective of imperial government, as well as their unhappy experience with certain of the agents, it is hardly surprising that the colonists began to reappraise the institution in the later sixties, though not always systematically, thoughtfully, or consistently. Some Americans gradually began to realize the importance of the agency, but only after colonial sympathizers had strongly urged that the institution be treated with greater regard. William Bollan made his views very plain in 1771: "I wou'd advise the Province . . . to provide, if they can, an agent who has more learning & knowledge of the origin, nature, & rights of the Colonies than any of their adversaries, and to support him in season in a manner suitable to the dignity & difficulty of his office." Bollan's remarks, of course, were partially aimed at elevating his own stature. Such an objective observer as Thomas Hollis, however, also had a very clear conception of what the Massachusetts agent should be. He must always be a native of the province, born to a good family, "liberally bred," and trained in government and law. This ideal lobbyist would be sent to London for three years, maintained well there, and then recalled to either honor and emolument or contempt and infamy. Hollis even asked Andrew Eliot directly why someone of John Adams's caliber was not sent. [39]

Hollis' comments had been prompted by a letter from Eliot that referred to De Berdt's political naïveté. "Our Agent writes smooth

[38] Thomas Cushing to Arthur Lee, Sept. 1773, "Cushing Letters" MHS *Collections*, ser. 4, IV, 360–361; Mass. House of Representatives to De Berdt, Jan. 12, 1768, *The Writings of Samuel Adams*, ed. H. A. Cushing (New York, 1904–1908), I, 152.

[39] Bollan to Samuel Danforth, Jan. 28, 1771, *Bowdoin and Temple Papers*, pp. 255–256; Hollis to Andrew Eliot, May 10, 1769, Eliot-Mayhew-Hollis Papers, Bancroft Transcripts, p. 221, NYPL.

things to us," Eliot noted, "but I have long thought that good old gentleman knew very little of the matter." The New England minister wondered whether Thomas Pownall shouldn't be chosen "General Agent for all the Provinces"; for the former governor was "carrying on a secret correspondence with some leading men in this Province, and . . . in the other Colonies." Pownall himself informed James Bowdoin at this time that Massachusetts needed three agents properly commissioned and empowered. Two would come from America, according to Pownall's scheme, joined by a Briton who knew "the way of persons & things here." He suggested the third party to the agency ought to be an M.P.; and Pownall, having all the necessary qualifications, implicitly offered to fill the post without fee.[40]

Americans differed in various ways over what the agency should be. In 1768, James Habersham, speaker of Georgia's lower house, believed that lobbyists for the colonies could only be native Britons and not colonials in London on a temporary basis. Yet at the same time a colonial in London urged the speaker of Massachusetts' House that only an American devoted to the cause could serve adequately: "I know not one Briton that is thorough in his views in favor of America," he wrote; "they all have partialities & exemptions in their minds."[41]

Still others were beginning to have second thoughts about the value of agents altogether. At least until 1770 there remained a cluster of North American lobbyists who compared favorably in ability with those of Jeremy Dummer's day almost half a century before. But while the earlier group had been respected, the later one received considerable criticism. After the Stamp Act crisis, Americans expected the agents to perform in ways they never had before and to help resolve problems of greater magnitude. But instead of sending the most capable colonials to London, they grew disillusioned with the institution and proceeded to enervate it. Only between 1764 and 1768

[40] Eliot to Hollis, Jan. 29, 1769, "Letters from Andrew Eliot to Thomas Hollis," MHS *Collections*, ser. 4, IV, 439; Pownall to Bowdoin, July 21, 1770, *Bowdoin and Temple Papers*, p. 206. For a comparable proposal a generation earlier, see Lewis Morris to James Alexander, Feb. 24, 1735, Rutherfurd MSS, II, 113, NYHS.

[41] James Habersham to William Knox, May 7, 1768, *The Letters of Hon. James Habersham, 1756–1775* (*Collections of the Georgia Historical Society*, Vol. VI [Savannah, 1904]), pp. 64–65; Nathaniel Rodgers to Thomas Cushing, March 4, 1768, Sam Adams MSS, NYPL.

did they seem fully aware of the potential inherent in the 150-year-old mechanism.

It is ironical that the agents' success in London depended upon their relationships with placemen and politicians, as well as their generous use of money; for as the colonists grew increasingly disgusted with venality and influence, they would inevitably be obliged to repudiate the one extension of America that was part of and tainted by the British "system" of politics—the agency. To minds alienated from imperial authority, pressure groups seemed to be "the burdensome impedementa," in Bernard Bailyn's phrase, "the unfortunate but more or less inevitable details of public life which must be borne but need scarcely be dignified by a place in formal political thought." [42]

As early as 1767 a few colonials began to question the value of agents. At first the dissatisfaction was with provincial lobbyists, as opposed to those responsible solely to the elected house of the legislature. By the close of 1768, however, Andrew Eliot wondered "whether any Agent we could now choose, would be able to serve us." The next year several sources revealed a feeling shared by many in Massachusetts—that it would be best to appoint no agent whatever. The Bay Colony was disillusioned after a decade's experience; "there was little confidence in any of the agents," John Adams later recalled. "De Berdt, Mauduit, or Jackson. They could know nothing with certainty of London characters. . . . The legislature was, indeed, to be pitied. They knew not whom to trust." At this point the popular party relied chiefly on Thomas Pownall, Bollan, and De Berdt for political information and insight from London. "The first is capable enough of giving intelligence," Eliot told Thomas Hollis, "but unless I am greatly mistaken, he is a thorough modern politician. Mr. Bollan I have always esteemed a gentleman of learning and integrity. Good Mr. D'Berdt did as well as he could; he would not willingly deceive, but perhaps was often deceived." [43]

[42] *Pamphlets of the American Revolution, 1750–1776*, ed. Bernard Bailyn, I (Cambridge, Mass., 1965), pp. 170, 663.
[43] Francis Bernard to Shelburne, March 28, 1767, Bernard MSS, VI, 199–209; Eliot to Thomas Hollis, Oct. 17, 1768, "Letters from Eliot," MHS *Collections*, ser. 4, IV, 430, 451; John Erving to Bollan, July 26, 1769, *Bowdoin and Temple Papers*, pp. 149–150; Samuel Cooper to Thomas Pownall, Sept. 8, 1769, Jan. 1, 1770, Tuckerman, "Letters of Samuel Cooper," pp. 311–313; John Adams to William Tudor, March 11, 1818, *Works of John Adams*, ed. Charles F. Adams (Boston, 1850–1856), X, 197.

Elsewhere in the colonies this discontent began to spread after 1770. One Virginian wrote a merchant friend in London that "it seems to be the Resolution of the Country to employ a standing Agent no longer." To the south some Carolinians "joined in crying down the necessity of an agent unless on particular occasions and for special purposes." Others closer to the sources of power and better placed to judge could see beyond the colonists' political myopia. John Pownall "expressed his surprise, that [Virginia] had no Agent. He said they were constantly puzzled in reporting to his Majesty on the Acts of Assembly & other business for want of information which an Agent ought to give them." Arthur Lee, frankly anxious for the job, urged his Virginia brethren not to reject the institution as useless. "To say there never shall be an Agent, is not, in my opinion, wise. . . . As occasions do frequently arise in which he may be enormously serviceable & as a faithful one may be frequently so, why should you sacrifice one forever." [44]

Despite earnest admonitions from England, a number of agencies fell into disrepair and were abandoned after 1770. By 1773, when Rhode Island and Sherwood went their separate ways, the colony's legislature took a significant step. Instead of replacing the agent, it appointed a Committee of Correspondence to join those appearing rapidly along the seaboard. The Assembly thereby revealed disdain for an institution so replete with possibilities only seven years earlier. [45]

In 1768, Richard Henry Lee of Virginia suggested to John Dickinson of Pennsylvania that "not only select committees should be appointed by all the colonists, but that a private correspondence should be conducted between the lovers of liberty in every province." Colonists were already thinking less in terms of London correspondents and more in terms of intercolonial correspondence, less in terms of Anglo-American links and more in terms of forging American unity. New kinds of activist groups within the colonies were becoming skeptical of traditional London lobbying. What really seemed to be called for was direct action. It is hardly coincidental that the decline of the agency

[44] R. C. Nicholas to John Norton, Jan. 4, 1771, *John Norton & Sons: Merchants of London and Virginia*, ed. Frances N. Mason (Richmond, 1937), p. 150; Samuel Johnston to Alexander Elmsley, Sept. 23, 1774, *CRNC*, IX, 1071; *CRNC*, VII, 868; Arthur Lee to Richard Henry Lee, Feb. 14 and Oct. 20, 1773, Lee MSS, II, HLHU, and Lee-Ludwell MSS, VHS.

[45] See also E. I. Miller, "The Virginia Committee of Correspondence, 1759–1770," 1*WMQ*, XXII (1913), 18.

proceeded with inverse relation to the rise of intercolonial cooperation.[46] The agents, for their part, were not always acquainted with the
latest colonial sentiments, especially the most radical ones. Residence
in Britain had isolated them and desensitized them to some extent
from American opinion. Several, for example, saw no reason to anticipate a violent reaction to the Tea Act of 1773 and were stunned when
news of the Tea Party arrived. But for that matter, so was all of
Britain.[47]

[46] Lee to Dickinson, July 25, 1768, *The Letters of Richard Henry Lee*, ed.
James C. Ballagh (New York, 1911–1914), I, 29; see Michael Kraus, *Intercolonial Aspects of American Culture on the Eve of the Revolution* (New York,
1928), ch. 10; Lawrence H. Gipson, *The British Empire before the American
Revolution*, XII (New York, 1965), 155–156.

[47] Richard W. Van Alstyne, *Empire and Independence: The International
History of the American Revolution* (New York, 1965), p. 35; Lewis B.
Namier and John Brooke, *The History of Parliament: The House of Commons,
1754–1790* (London, 1964), I, 161.

CHAPTER 11

A Loss of Cooperation:
The Agents and Their Allies

During London's damp winter—the "season of business" when agents were most active—milk-girls, chimney sweeps, and vendors of brick dust went hurriedly about their business in the chilled streets. While hawkers of card matches and newsmen selling gazettes shivered out of doors, a cluster of men often sat comfortably inside around a fire examining newspapers. The agents and their associates were obliged to scrutinize the public press for attacks on the colonies that ought to be answered and items that should be forwarded to their constituents. In utilizing the fourth estate, however, success depended upon the lobbyists' relationship with the editors, publishers, and booksellers of London. Similarly the various communities of merchants and dissenters in Britain were equally important adjuncts to accomplished lobbying. A decline in cooperation among these groups would bring adverse consequences for the harried representatives of the North American interest.

COMMERCIAL REORIENTATION

The conditions and orientation of Britain's economic life changed during the decade prior to 1776. As new markets opened to the East, for example, and as prosperity returned after the spring of 1767, colonial commerce became less important, thereby reducing the strain created by American boycotts. While the Grafton-Chatham ministry was establishing itself in 1766, however, there was little reason to anticipate these shifts. As the parliamentary session of that year drew to a close, agent-merchant relations within the North American lobby seemed sound. Franklin commented to his employers that the merchants had been an invaluable asset, and in his operations placated and cajoled them in every way possible.[1]

In 1767 the two groups found various enterprises conducive to their cooperation. Franklin, Trecothick, and Jackson, with the support of the North American merchants, were able to dissuade the ministry from adopting a salt duty. The combined lobby also met with some frequency to discuss the management of Indian affairs and the new inland territories. Here again the three agents were in the vanguard, along with Edward Montagu of Virginia. Supplemented by Robert Charles, De Berdt, and Sherwood, they also spearheaded the drive to have the Currency Act repealed.[2]

Until the middle of 1767, Franklin felt optimistic about the coalition's chances. He argued before ministry and merchants that the latter could not be injured by repeal "provided a clause be inserted in the Act . . . declaring Paper Bills of Credit shall not be a legal Tender in Payment of any Sterling Debts or Contracts whatsoever already made or to be made." By June, however, speeches by Grenville and Townshend in the Commons coupled with shrewd ministerial maneuvers virtually ruined the possibility of repeal, much to Franklin's dismay. His role in winning over the merchants had been especially brilliant. At their request he responded to the Board of Trade's 1764 report against paper currency, arguing that it had been a blessing by providing colonials with a medium to facilitate the purchase of British manufactures. The merchants found this persuasive, but not the Board of Trade. Meanwhile Townshend ignited his bombshell on May 13, proposing to Parliament certain customs duties to be levied in the colonies. This development obliged the agents and merchants to

[1] Vincent T. Harlow, *The Founding of the Second British Empire, 1763–1793,* I (London, 1952), *passim;* A. H. John, "Miles Nightingale—Drysalter: A Study in Eighteenth-Century Trade," *Economic History Review,* ser. 2, XVIII (1965), 160–163; Franklin to Pa. CC, April 12, 1766, Rosenbach Foundation, Philadelphia.

[2] William Samuel Johnson to William Pitkin, May 16, 1767, "Letters of William Samuel Johnson to the Governors of Connecticut," MHS *Collections,* ser. 5, IX (Boston, 1885), 229; Trecothick *et al.* to Board of Trade, Oct. 30, 1767, PRO CO 323/24, pp. 321–323; Benjamin Franklin to William Franklin, Nov. 13, 1767, *Trade and Politics, 1767–1769,* ed. C. W. Alvord and C. E. Carter (Springfield, Ill., 1921), p. 104; *Benjamin Franklin's Letters to the Press, 1758–1775,* ed. Verner W. Crane (Chapel Hill, 1950), p. 79.

suppress their proposals for repeal, rather than abet a combination of circumstances that would siphon off more American money. The session ended inconclusively with Franklin acknowledging that the merchants' "friendship is worth preserving, as it may greatly help us on future occasions." By the time December and the new session arrived, however, he had begun to doubt whether the agents would have the merchant's full cooperation.[3]

So too had some of his colleagues. As early as March, William Samuel Johnson reported to Connecticut that the merchants had "grown very cool in their regard towards us." In September, Henry Eustace McCulloh wrote from London that "our Merchants throughout the Kingdom, have very lately entered into a firm Union, not only, not to form any new Connections in America, but not to ship to, or Answer the Order of their Old Correspondents till the Sins of past times are wiped off." [4]

These warnings continued through 1768, when Johnson's report was again discouraging. The most adamant enthusiasts pushed ahead with the campaign just the same. Franklin was astute enough to realize "that if the repeal was to be obtained at all, it must be proposed in the light of a favour to the merchants of this country, and asked for by them, not by the agents as a favour to America." Neither Whitehall nor Westminster was willing to concede an inch on any ground other than the expedient good of the kingdom. Even most members of the merchant community working with the agents had no sympathy for colonial constitutional claims.[5]

Franklin continued to confer with the merchants in 1768; but the repeal campaign never recovered the momentum it had achieved early the previous year. The ministry was so unsympathetic that the North American lobbyists decided it would be useless to attempt to bring their plea before Parliament. By this time imperial officials began to shield themselves behind the evasion that the matter had received full discussion and that it had been unanimously agreed upon that "Paper

[3] Extract of a letter from a merchant in London, April 11, 1767, *Virginia Gazette* (Purdie and Dixon), June 25, 1767; Crane, *Franklin's Letters to the Press*, p. 92; Franklin to Joseph Galloway, May 20, 1767, WCL; undated report from merchants to the administration, MFY; Franklin to Galloway, June 13 and Dec. 1, 1767, Smyth, V, 25–27, 72.

[4] Johnson to Jonathan Trumbull, March 14, 1767, MHS *Collections*, ser. 5, IX, 487; McCulloh to Edmund Fanning, Sept. 12, 1767, Southern Historical Collection, University of North Carolina Library.

[5] Johnson to William Pitkin, Oct. 20, 1768, MHS *Collections*, ser. 5, IX, 298; Franklin to Joseph Galloway, Feb. 17, 1768, Smyth, V, 97–100.

Currency with a legal Tender is big with Frauds, and full of Mischief to the Colonies, and to Commerce in general." By the turn of 1768–1769, the agents felt resigned to the futility of this cause.[6]

In 1768 and 1769, a smattering of issues suggested that the North American alliance was still intact, albeit less firmly than three years earlier. The agents and merchants met, for example, at the King's Arms Tavern in Cornhill to devise plans to encourage colonial trade. They agreed upon alterations in the Navigation Acts which they presented to Rockingham and his faction in hopes that they would bypass the bureaucracy by offering the proposal directly in the House of Commons. Despite cooperation and Trecothick's leadership, the comprehensive reform measure was stillborn, thereby heightening the lobby's sense of frustration.[7]

In 1769 the colonial press seemed to assume a close identity of interests between commercial figures and agents. As late as January 1770, Charles Garth noted with some satisfaction that the merchants "very heartily" joined him in applying for a remission of the high duty on imported rice. Garth persuaded twenty merchants to back that plea and another seventeen to bless the appeal to continue the bounty on indigo. Some of the commercial elements of London and Bristol backed the free importation of iron and the bounty on hemp. Concurrently, however, there appeared serious signs of discontent. Garth encountered difficulty enlisting opposition to a merchant-sponsored move to reduce the bounty on tar, pitch, and turpentine imported from America. Working on the same problem, McCulloh found the merchants sharply divided between the London community and those in the outports. Only some of the latter were sympathetic to the colonies and their London representatives. Anxiously the agents of the southern colonies memorialized the Board of Trade on this account.[8]

When the Townshend duties first appeared in 1767, the agents sought merchant cooperation toward repeal. But the prosperity resulting from ample crops and the Russo-Turkish War minimized the

---

[6] Jack P. Greene and R. M. Jellison, "The Currency Act of 1764 in Imperial-Colonial Relations, 1764–1776," 3*WMQ*, XVIII (1961), 501–502; Franklin to Lord Kames, Jan. 1, 1769, Smyth, V, 189.

[7] [John Almon], *Political Register* (1768), II, 89.

[8] *Boston Gazette and Country Journal*, April 24, 1769; Garth to S.C. CC, Dec. 10, 1769, Jan. 12, 1770, *SCHGM*, XXXI, 137–140; Ella Lonn, *The Colonial Agents of the Southern Colonies* (Chapel Hill, 1945), p. 345; *Journal of the Commissioners for Trade and Plantations from January 1768 to December 1775* (London, 1937), p. 88; Edward Montagu to Va. CC, March 3, 1770, *VMHB*, XII (1904), 166.

impact of the colonial boycott on merchants and manufacturers. Although the North American merchants were less enthusiastic than in past years, many did assist with petitions, parliamentary pressure, and conversations with politicians. Petitions, however, seemed to displease the House of Commons. Consequently the agents at this point were obliged to suppress them or search very hard for Members and Lords willing to serve as sponsors. The merchant-agent team pleaded that trade ought to be encouraged to its broadest extent, rather than constricted by regulations and taxes.[9]

As the tempo of the colonial nonimportation boycott intensified in 1769, a £700,000 drop in trade became apparent. Barlow Trecothick thereupon took action. Very soon a considerable number of petitions from America "and a great number of others from the City of London and almost all the Counties in England" were forthcoming, pleading for complete curtailment of the Townshend duties. One from the London merchants emphasized the danger of nonpayment of colonial debts. Nevertheless repeal failed in 1769, discouraging some of the merchants and causing others to lose interest. Yet De Berdt was confident of getting them "to make another effort in conjunction to add weight to that of the Agents." He was one of a committee of seven merchants appointed by the London group who had waited on Hillsborough early in 1769. They found the Secretary of State "very peremptory in his opinion that the Ministry would not consent to a repeal this Session." There was, De Berdt reported, "an obstinacy in the Administration not at present to be overcome, supported by them under the specious name of firmness." As a result of this condition, such leaders among the merchants as David Barclay were "very cool."[10] Others, like William Beckford and contacts of William Bollan, wanted to be helpful but were balked by the hostility of various Members of Parliament.[11]

[9] James J. Burns, *The Colonial Agents of New England* (Washington, D.C., 1935), pp. 142–143; *Letters and Papers of Benjamin Franklin and Richard Jackson, 1753–1785*, ed. Carl Van Doren (Philadelphia, 1947), pp. 22–23.

[10] De Berdt was not alone in using this phrase. John Fothergill wrote William Logan on August 5, 1769, that "your treatment of the North American merchants, having made them cool in your service, has given the Ministry the opportunity of representing all America as perfectly satisfied with the administration, a few fractious spirits excepted. I was in hopes that your agents would have joined together, as one man to have undeceived them" (Gilbert Collection, College of Physicians, Philadelphia).

[11] William Samuel Johnson to Jonathan Trumbull, Dec. 5, 1769, MHS *Collections*, ser. 5, IX, 384–385; De Berdt to Thomas Cushing, Feb. 1, 18, and

When the new ministry of Lord North appeared early in 1770, the agents regrouped their forces for another attack on the Townshend duties. Franklin busied himself among the merchants in the City, beseeching them to present the administration or Parliament with an account of the number of conditional orders they had received "in order to obviate an opinion industriously propagated here, that the trade still goes on covertly." Franklin felt unsure of the merchants' support, but hoped to capitalize on the factionalism prevalent within British politics. William Samuel Johnson found the merchants not altogether happy about the colonial boycott; but neither were they or the manufacturers "clamorous" for repeal.[12]

After several meetings late in January and early in February, the merchants "agreed to apply for the repeal of the whole act." Their petition was presented immediately, though they had slight hope for its success. That they sought *total* repeal came as a minor triumph for the agents' powers of persuasion; for the merchants bluntly informed their exhorters that only the improvement of trade conditions concerned them—"they had no other regard for America, *that* Concernd the Agents, and not the Merchants." The colonial lobbyists also managed to engage some merchants who were not members of the Society of Merchant Venturers in Bristol, thereby keeping part of the mercantile community of the West Country in line. Garth, Montagu, and McCulloh sent them a list of the colonies' strongest objections to the Townshend duties, so that they could and did incorporate this list into their petition presented to the chairman of the Board of Trade. Just enough leverage was brought to bear upon the new-born administration, so that in March all the Townshend taxes were abolished except that on tea. Complete success would have been remarkable, however, because the merchants saw with increasing clarity that the boycott dike across the sea was springing leaks. Reports from London in February and March also indicated that the North American pressure group was now losing its cohesiveness. Franklin remarked that the merchants "were at length prevailed on to present a petition, but they moved slowly, and some of them . . . reluctantly; perhaps from a

25, 1769, to Delaware CC, Jan. 9, 1769, "Letters of Dennys De Berdt, 1757–1770," ed. Albert Matthews, CSM *Publications*, XIII (1912), 355, 362, 364, 354; Bollan to Samuel Danforth, April 22, 1769, *The Bowdoin and Temple Papers* (MHS *Collections*, ser. 6, Vol. IX [Boston, 1897]), pp. 135–137.

[12] Franklin to Joseph Galloway, Jan. 11, 1770, WCL; Johnson to Jonathan Trumbull, Feb. 3, 1770, MHS *Collections*, ser. 5, IX, 406.

despair of success. . . . The manufacturing towns absolutely refused to move at all." [13]

Edward Montagu suggested to his Virginia constituents in 1770 that Wilkes and the Middlesex election squeezed out any competitors for political attention. Consequently "our Merchants in London have been extreme shy, & very unwilling to take the Lead in an Affair, as interesting to them as America." Franklin's correspondence from this time on scarcely mentions the merchants. [14] From the colonial standpoint a significant metamorphosis was in process. The merchants and manufacturers could no longer be counted on as during the Stamp Act crisis. It had been difficult to prevail upon London's commercial groups to protest against the Townshend Acts. Merchants of other communities now flatly refused assistance, asserting that they had enough trade without America's and that her nonimportation agreements could very soon be expected to disintegrate. Moreover support that the agents had hoped for from the East India Company now seemed to be withering as that organization was torn by dissension over its policies. By the autumn of 1771 even Bristol had forgotten its inclinations of 1769–1770. Indeed the Society of Merchant Venturers there steadily hardened in support of governmental policies between 1766 and 1774. Though individual merchants might urge elimination of the Townshend duties, the Society itself took no action. [15]

The years between repeal of those duties and the furor created by the Boston Tea Party were relatively calm, marked by neither notable cooperation nor conflict. A superficial repose fell over the several

[13] Dennys De Berdt to Thomas Cushing, Feb. 2, 1770, to Thomas McKean, Feb. 15, 1770, to ?, Feb. 24, 1770, Matthews, "Letters of De Berdt," pp. 396–397, 399, 405; *St. James's Chronicle*, Feb. 3, 1770; W. R. Savadge, "The West Country and the American Mainland Colonies, 1763–1783, with Special Reference to the Merchants of Bristol" (unpub. B.Litt. thesis; Oxford University, 1951), pp. 304, 309; *Boston Gazette and Country Journal*, May 7, 1770; Franklin to ?, March 18, 1770, Smyth, V, 253.

[14] Montagu to Va. CC, Feb. 6 and 8, 1770, *VMHB*, XII, 164–165; Charles R. Ritcheson, *British Politics and the American Revolution* (Norman, Okla., 1954), pp. 137–138; Verner W. Crane, "The Club of Honest Whigs: Friends of Science and Liberty," 3*WMQ*, XXIII (1966), 230.

[15] William Samuel Johnson to Jonathan Trumbull, Feb. 3, 1770, MHS *Collections*, ser. 5, IX, 406–407; Savadge, "West Country and American Mainland Colonies," p. 383; B. W. Labaree, *The Boston Tea Party* (New York, 1964), p. 24; *Politics and the Port of Bristol in the Eighteenth Century*, ed. W. E. Minchinton (*Bristol Record Society Publications*, Vol. XXIII [Bristol, 1963]), p. xxxi.

interest groups as North's ministry carefully sidestepped new controversies that might endanger its position by agitating America. "As in
nature," wrote William Samuel Johnson in 1771, "so in politics, a
dead calm has succeeded a most furious storm, and all are intent upon
repairing the losses they have sustained, or enjoying the acquisitions
they have made, while the tempest raged." [16]

In the spring of 1773 sectors of the merchant community, joined by
the agents, complained that the Currency Act of 1764 caused trade to
decline and forced self-sufficiency upon the Americans. Dartmouth
and the Board of Trade consented to induce Parliament to allow
colonial assemblies to issue notes that would be considered legal
tender at provincial treasuries for duties and taxes. This paper would
thereby circulate freely at face value as a reliable medium of exchange.[17] Yet for the most part the flourishing condition of British
trade tended to reinforce the merchants' lack of concern for the
colonies. Moreover, as George H. Guttridge has noted, by the 1770's
merchants trading to America were less prominent "in the innermost
circles of Whig policy." Some had become too radical, but most
"accepted the coercion of America as an inevitable method of enforcing their mercantile claims." [18]

DIVIDED DISSENTERS

Just before the Townshend duties were repealed in 1770, Franklin
sent an appraisal of the agents' informal and political allies to an
unknown correspondent. He complained that the merchants and manufacturers moved reluctantly; after noting the favor of Rockingham,
Shelburne, and Chatham, Franklin remarked that "besides these, we
have for sincere friends and well-wishers the body of Dissenters generally throughout England, with many others, not to mention Ireland."

[16] To Jonathan Trumbull, March 15, 1771, MHS *Collections,* ser. 5, IX,
477.
[17] Benjamin Franklin to Joseph Galloway, Aug. 3, 1773, Craven Street
Letter-book, Franklin Papers, LC; Jack M. Sosin, "Imperial Regulation of
Colonial Paper Money, 1764–1773," *PMHB,* LXXXVIII (1964), 197–198.
Altering the Currency Act was less of a triumph for the agents than Professor
Sosin suggests. Lord Dartmouth had decided to relax the act's restrictions, and
the Board of Trade, where Bamber Gascoyne and Richard Jackson handled the
matter, concurred.
[18] *English Whiggism and the American Revolution* (Berkeley, 1942), pp.
55–56.

By 1773 he still believed "the Dissenters are all for us;" [19] but if
Franklin was correct in feeling nonconformists were more sympathetic
than any other social group in Britain, he may nevertheless have
misled the colonists into expecting too much from British dissenters.
Members of those groups who were active in politics had pressing
concerns of their own during these years; and their strength was
perhaps less than hopeful colonials imagined. As Verner W. Crane
has remarked, Franklin "could entertain few illusions regarding their
influence on administration, and hence on the march of events." [20]

The most significant issue of mutual concern to the agents and
dissenters involved the possible creation of an Anglican bishop in the
colonies. This was already a venerable concern by 1769, when Franklin wished his constituents would end their "Squabbles about a
Bishop." A year later William Samuel Johnson echoed these sentiments, adding the reminder that "it has, indeed, been merely a religious, in no respect a political design. . . . More than this would be
thought disadvantageous rather than beneficial; and would be opposed, I assure you, by no man with more zeal than myself, even as a
Churchman." [21] Here perhaps lay the crucial point. Leading Anglicans were by no means convinced that an American bishop was
desirable. When the Society for the Propagation of the Gospel revived
the proposal in 1771–1772, the dissenters and agents, including Marchant, Life, and Franklin, roused themselves to oppose. But there was
little danger. The Church hierarchy was not especially concerned, and
North's ministry preferred not to add fuel to the intensely warm
colonial discontent.[22]

Other projects of less general but perhaps more genuine urgency
during these years caused a number of colonial sympathizers to wonder about the efficacy of political dissent in London. In 1769, New
York's Presbyterians sought incorporation as a means of relief from

[19] Franklin to ?, March 18, 1770, to Thomas Cushing, July 7, 1773, Smyth,
V, 251–254, VI, 78.

[20] Crane, "Club of Honest Whigs," pp. 230–231.

[21] Franklin to Jane Mecom, Feb. 23, 1769, *The Letters of Benjamin Franklin and Jane Mecom,* ed. Carl Van Doren (Princeton, 1950), p. 109; Johnson
to Jonathan Trumbull, Feb. 26, 1770, MHS *Collections,* ser. 5, IX, 412–413.

[22] Entry for March 13, 1772, Marchant's London diary, RIHS; Marchant to
Ezra Stiles, March 17, 1772, Stiles MSS, YUL; Thomas Life to ?, March 31,
1772, Trumbull MSS, III (2), CSL; Jack M. Sosin, "The Proposal in the
Pre-revolutionary Decade for Establishing Anglican Bishops in the Colonies,"
Journal of Ecclesiastical History, XIII (1962), 83–84.

legal disabilities; the Anglicans successfully blocked this move. A year later a futile dispute between Congregationalists and Baptists over religious liberty in Massachusetts Bay led the Baptists to appoint their own London agent, but to no avail. Despite Jasper Mauduit's position as chairman of the Protestant Dissenting Deputies, his conservative behavior and theirs continued to mystify Franklin. Notwithstanding the Deputies' prominence, in fact, Franklin had not associated himself with them during his agency. Early in 1772, Henry Marchant lamented to Ezra Stiles that the community of dissenters in London really had no spiritual life, and added that Stiles was much better off in Newport.[23]

Marchant would find more enthusiasm for the P.D.D. after meeting Thomas Lucas, the new chairman. Rhode Island's agent would also discover, however, that the various dissenting organizations were quite engrossed in their own urgent matters, particularly relief from subscription to some of the Thirty-nine Articles. In this they would not yet succeed, although North permitted them to push their request through the House of Commons in 1772 and 1773. He knew full well the Lords would kill the measure in each case, and left it to the bishops to organize a successful resistance.[24]

The fact remains that from 1767 until 1779, when the dissenters finally won relief from the Thirty-nine Articles, they lacked sufficient political influence. In 1767, Lord Mansfield declared that the City of London could not elect dissenters as sheriffs simply in order to collect the fines when they refused to serve. Thereafter the nonconformist cause ebbed, while the Church of England regained some of its strength. One reason rested with royal patronage for high ecclesiastical appointments. Between 1760 and 1770 a number of bishops continued to vote with the opposition; but their numbers dwindled steadily, from nine in 1763 to two by 1775. As one American wrote a year after repeal

[23] Herbert L. Osgood, "The Society of Dissenters Founded at New York in 1769," *AHR*, VI (1901), 498–507; Alice M. Baldwin, *The New England Clergy and the American Revolution* (Durham, 1928), 109, 114; Franklin to Robert Morris and Thomas Leech, March 5, 1771, Smyth, V, 308–309; Franklin to Noble W. Jones, July 8, 1771, APS; Henry Marchant to Ezra Stiles, Feb. 26, 1772, Stiles MSS, YUL.

[24] Marchant to Stiles, March 17, 1772, Stiles MSS; J. Steven Watson, *The Reign of George III, 1760–1815* (Oxford, 1960), p. 156; Richard B. Barlow, "Anti-subscription and the Clerical Petition Movement in the Church of England, 1766–1772," *Historical Magazine of the Protestant Episcopal Church*, XXX (1961), 35–49.

of the Stamp Act, "The Episcopalians confederate themselves with the Crown officers of every department, procure ecclesiastical revenues, [and] monopoly of all lucrative and honorary employments." During Burke's agency he remarked that the colonists' refusal to receive a bishop had been "urged in the House of Lords as a strong example against the spirit of the Dissenters and to show the danger of setting them too much at large." [25]

After 1767 the Protestant Dissenting Deputies and New England Company continued to meet regularly. Their interests and effectiveness, however, seemed quite removed from concerns most vital to the agents and their constituents. Whether the militia exercised on the Lord's Day, the procuring of rentals from property they owned, the construction of turnpikes across their provincial estates, and similar issues occupied much of their time.[26] It is well known that nonconformists in the colonies were in the vanguard of the revolutionary movement. Their willingness to sever ties with Britain, however, was strengthened by the cool treatment they received from dissenting organizations in London, most of which seemed conservative to their American brethren. The prominent careers of such men as Joseph Priestley, Richard Price, James Burgh, and Thomas Hollis have perhaps diverted historians' attention from a significant trend. Less famous but equally important dissenters steadily turned their backs on America during the later 1760's and 1770's. "The Quebec affair," a correspondent wrote to New York's agent in 1774, "has given an amazing turn within these three weeks to the tame dispositions of the Quakers and Dissenters, who before that time were fast asleep." [27]

---

[25] Mark A. Thomson, *A Constitutional History of England, 1642 to 1801* (London, 1938), Pt. IV, ch. 10; Norman Sykes, *Church and State in England in the XVIIIth Century* (Cambridge, 1934), pp. 51–52; Lewis B. Namier, *England in the Age of the American Revolution* (2nd ed.; London, 1961), p. 259; Ross J. S. Hoffman, *Edmund Burke, New York Agent . . .* (Philadelphia, 1956), p. 110.

[26] P.D.D. Minute Books, MS 3083, i, f. 515, ii, ff. 28–145, GLL; Minutes of General Court of the New England Co. MS 7920, 1770–1775, ff. 1–23, GLL; Carl Bridenbaugh, *Mitre and Sceptre: Transatlantic Faiths, Ideas, Personalities, and Politics, 1689–1775* (New York, 1962), pp. 281–282, 286, 326–330.

[27] Thomas Wilson to Burke, June 28, 1774, *The Works and Correspondence of . . . Edmund Burke* (London, 1852), I, 232; see also Burke to Rockingham, Sept. 14, 1775, *The Correspondence of Edmund Burke, 1774–1778*, ed. G. H. Guttridge, III (Chicago, 1961), 208.

POLITICS AND THE PRESS

The fourth estate also became less useful as an adjunct to North American lobbying after 1766, although like the merchants' and dissenters' their lessened cooperation was not immediately apparent: Despite hazards, the expanding London press offered a potentially splendid forum for influencing public opinion. By 1769 the *Gazetteer* printed 5,000 copies daily, and the *Public Advertiser* 3,000. Each copy, moreover, was read by individuals in coffeehouses, offices, and homes. Yet for political reasons agents found the publishers cautious. "I am not now concerned in any of the Public papers," John Almon wrote in 1767. "They are so often brought before the House of Lords & there is so little faith among the printers." In 1771, a victory for freedom of the press followed the struggle involving John Wilkes and the magistrates of the City of London. The House of Commons tacitly abandoned its antipathy toward a published record of its proceedings. Thereafter the several departmental undersecretaries continued their vigil over the London papers, but asserted more of a corrective than a punitive influence.[28]

Unfortunately only Franklin and (after 1768) Lee, among the North American agents, fully exploited the possibilities of these newspapers. While the government began to relax its intense vigil after the Stamp Act crisis, the rest of the agents did not particularly avail themselves of the opportunity to add volume to the American voice at "home." Nor did some of them even take the trouble to insert extracts of letters from the colonies, although this was almost as effective as writing original material and much less demanding. Because the fourth estate borrowed freely, an item could easily achieve wide circulation.

The colonists commonly sent their agents documents to reproduce in London for political effect. Virginia did so quite often. In 1769 and 1770, the burgesses prepared addresses to the crown against taxation without consent. They ordered their speaker to transmit them to Edward Montagu, "with directions to cause the same to be presented to his most excellent Majesty, and afterwards to be printed and

---

[28] Crane, *Franklin's Letters to the Press*, pp. xvi–xvii, xxx, 126; Almon to Wilkes, March 15, 1767, Add MSS 30869, ff. 106–107; P. D. G. Thomas, "The Beginning of Parliamentary Reporting in Newspapers, 1768–1774," *EHR*, LXXIV (1959), 623–636.

published in the English papers." [29] In 1769, Massachusetts' Council wanted Bollan to publish a certain letter in London. But he found

> the present publication of your late letter . . . does not appear to me advisable, 1. Because this letter now lyes before the King, and an appeal to the people in that case is improper; 2. In consequence of your having only partial information, it contains only a partial defence; 3. All, or most, of the principal persons, especially those who are likely to favor your cause, are dispersed & gone, and the freshness of a publication, made in season before the subsequent consideration of the subject matter of it by government, is frequently serviceable. [30]

In this case Bollan's advice was probably prudent; yet many of the lobbyists apparently lacked the inclination for this type of journalism, and sometimes aimed gibes at each other rather than against measures of the administration. When De Berdt and Lee condemned their colleagues publicly, they augmented the animus against the agents created by their common enemies. [31]

De Berdt made only few and undistinguished efforts after 1766. During the campaign for repeal of the Stamp Act, he published anonymously several open letters to Dartmouth about the perplexed state of Anglo-American commerce. Then, except for a piece advocating repeal of the Currency Act, he remained silent for three years. Finally, at the close of 1769, he exposed the letters of Governor Bernard. Early the next year, in an effort to expedite repeal of the Townshend duties, he "printed a letter . . . with some remarks . . . & am now puting it in to the Hands of the members of both Houses that it may make the deeper impression on there minds than by bare Conversation." [32]

[29] *Journals of the House of Burgesses of Virginia,* ed. H. R. McIlwaine and J. P. Kennedy (Richmond, 1905–1913), XII, 102; Va. CC to Montagu, July 5, 1770, *VMHB,* XII, 363; Hoffman, *Burke,* p. 179.

[30] Bollan to Samuel Danforth, *et al.,* June 23, 1769, *Bowdoin and Temple Papers,* p. 147.

[31] *Pennsylvania Journal,* May 17 and Sept. 18, 1766; William Franklin to Benjamin Franklin, Nov. 13, [1766?], APS.

[32] *Boston Gazette and Country Journal,* supps. Nov. 18 and Dec. 30, 1765; De Berdt to Thomas Cushing, Feb. 25, 1769, to Selectmen of Boston, Dec. 5, 1769, to Richard Cary, Feb. 2, 1770, Matthews, "Letters of De Berdt," pp. 363, 389, 397–398.

Other Massachusetts agents utilized newspapers even less. Jackson confessed that he "never could prepare anything for the press in any degree." Bollan rarely published in the dailies, only on such occasions as in 1768, when the venality of parliamentary elections outraged him, or 1774, when one of his petitions appeared in the *London Chronicle*. Garth used the fourth estate sparingly and not for propaganda purposes beneficial to the colonies as a whole. Thus one colonial governor worried needlessly that an Assembly agent might busily "insert Queries in London Chronicles." [33]

The notable exceptions, however, should receive due credit. Writing for the *Gazetteer* and the *Public Advertiser* as Junius Americanus in 1769 and 1770, Arthur Lee won wide admiration for his essays, though John Wilkes objected to Lee's "extreme verbiage." Junius himself thought his "American namesake is plainly a man of abilities, tho' . . . a little unreasonable." Therefore Junius hoped "since he has opposed me where he thinks me wrong, he will be equally ready to assist me, when he thinks me right." Lee's avowed ambition was to "bring the signature of Junius Americanus into estimation, and by that means to gain a more easy ear to the discussion of American grievances." He intermingled matters of popular interest with colonial complaints to make the latter more palatable in London. [34]

In 1768, Lee published two pieces in the *Gazetteer* giving an account and analysis of proceedings in Boston. In 1769 his "Monitor's Letters" appeared, followed by the Junius Americanus series. For some while after that he seems to have abandoned newspaper work. But in 1773 he set about reprinting letters from Boston, for as he told Sam Adams, "Lord Dartmouth should read the excellent admonition." (Through his departmental lieutenants Dartmouth knew perfectly well the source of these "objectionable paragraphs.") Hence Tory Peter Oliver later despised Lee as the agent of an extremist faction: "It is lucky for some Writers, that they have no Reputation to lose; if

---

[33] Jackson to Charles Jenkinson, Sept. 4, 1764, *The Jenkinson Papers, 1760–1766*, ed. Ninetta S. Jucker (London, 1949), pp. 329, 439; Bollan to Thomas Hutchinson, Feb. 18, 1768, MA, XXV, 254–255a; *London Chronicle*, April 30, 1774; Lewis B. Namier, "Charles Garth, Agent for South Carolina," *EHR*, LIV (1939), 636 n.; Crane, *Franklin's Letters to the Press*, p. 7 n. 6.

[34] Wilkes to Junius, Sept. 12, 1771, Junius to Wilkes, Nov. 6, 1771, Add MSS 30881, ff. 11–12, 26; Arthur Lee to [Richard H. Lee?], Dec. 3, 1769, Richard H. Lee, *The Life of Arthur Lee* (Boston, 1829), I, 193.

they had, even *Arthur Lee* would not have run the Risque of that small Proportion he might possess, for the Sake of gratifying the Malignity of his Correspondents." Lee's style and influence were not so slight as Oliver, in bitter retrospect, imagined. One group even suspected that Lee might be responsible for the writings of Junius.[35]

Among the agents Franklin alone fully exploited the potential of Fleet Street; and his efforts have been suitably acknowledged by his contemporaries and modern scholars. It was much to his advantage that he had a lifetime of experience in printing and journalism, as well as contacts with the publishing trade. He wrote most often in rebuttal to specious opinions about America. To keep his authorship secret, create the impression of a regiment of pro-American writers, and perhaps compensate for his colleagues' failure to write, he attached various signatures to his essays. But by 1774 the administration attributed all colonial propaganda to "Judas's office in Craven Street." Franklin shrugged at such abuses. "'Tis the fashion to roast one another," he wrote his sister, "and I sometimes take a little of that Diversion myself."[36]

In the decade before the final rupture, Franklin's output for the press flowed unevenly. In the year following repeal of the Stamp Act, 1767, his production declined, partially owing to his German excursion. He continued to submit colonial letters to the *London Chronicle* as well as refutations against those who opposed repeal of the Currency Act. In 1768 he made extraordinary use of the gazettes, perhaps his most vigorous year in that respect. He published a fabulous Indian hoax in order to reiterate the free trade principles expressed two years before in his letter "on the Price of Corn." Speaking through Canassatego, Franklin fiercely attacked English smugness. As Pennsylvania's agent, his publicity task was complicated until 1769 by the cautious

[35] Lee to Richard H. Lee, Dec. 27, 1768, Lee MSS, Vol. I, no. 16, APS; Arthur Lee to Sam Adams, Jan. 25, 1773, Lee, *Life of Arthur Lee*, I, 226; ? to Dartmouth, Aug. 2, 1773, Dartmouth MSS, Vol. II, no. 672, WSL; *Peter Oliver's Origins and Progress of the American Revolution*, ed. Douglass Adair and John A. Schutz (San Marino, Calif., 1963), p. 78; Bernard MSS, XII, 211–218, HLHU; Wilkes to Junius, Jan. 15, 1772, Add MSS 30881, ff. 32–33.

[36] Benjamin Franklin to William Franklin, Oct. 6, 1773, Smyth, VI, 145; Crane, *Franklin's Letters to the Press*, p. xxvii; Verner W. Crane, "Franklin's Political Journalism in England," *Journal of the Franklin Institute*, CCXXXIII (1942), 214; Benjamin Franklin to Jane Mecom, Nov. 9, 1770, Van Doren, *Franklin and Mecom*, p. 117.

course Philadelphia's merchants followed with respect to the colonial boycott. Once convinced that his province would participate, however, he undertook the role of press agent in Britain for the Non-importation League. Many of his letters to the press in 1769 and 1770 were related to this function.[37]

After relying on the *London Chronicle* so heavily for several years, Franklin did not use it at all in 1769 and seldom thereafter. After that date, in fact, the *Chronicle* grew less hospitable to American propaganda—another manifestation of the decline of American influence. Franklin turned instead to the *Public Advertiser* and put many pieces in its pages in 1770, including his finest political fables and the eleven Colonist's Advocate letters.[38] The latter, the only sustained series he attempted as agent, appeared between January and March, marking the climax of Franklin's drive for repeal of the Townshend duties. When partial revocation passed on March 5, the sequence abruptly ended. In December, he began to believe that "just at this Juncture here; perhaps 'tis more prudent to be quiet, to stir no Questions, to let Heats abate." For the next two years he wrote relatively little for the press.[39]

From 1773 until his departure two years later, Franklin again busied himself, channeling most of his work through Woodfall's *Public Advertiser,* which printed the Doctor's two great satires: "Rules for Reducing a Great Empire to a Small One" and "An Edict by the King of Prussia." Much of what he wrote in this period related directly to the Massachusetts agency and problems it created for him: the Hutchinson letters, the fiasco in the Cockpit, and the chain of crises that developed from the Tea Party. In his last twelve months in England, "he wrote less and reprinted more . . . than in the other great emergencies." Years later Joseph Priestley recalled that Franklin spent his last day in London "looking over a number of American

[37] Franklin to Charles Thomson, June 27, 1766, Smyth, IV, 463; Franklin to Joseph Galloway, April 14, 1767, WCL; Crane, *Franklin's Letters to the Press,* pp. xxxvi, 125; Alfred O. Aldridge, "Franklin's Deistical Indians," APS *Proceedings,* XCIV (1950), 398–410.

[38] Verner W. Crane, "Certain Writings of Benjamin Franklin on the British Empire and the American Colonies," *Papers of the Bibliographical Society,* XXVIII (1934), 14; cf. Oscar and Mary Handlin, "James Burgh and American Revolutionary Theory," MHS *Proceedings,* LXXIII (Boston, 1963), 40.

[39] Verner W. Crane, "Three Fables by Benjamin Franklin," *NEQ,* IX (1936), 499–504; Crane, *Franklin's Letters to the Press,* pp. 167–209; Franklin to Samuel Cooper, Dec. 30, 1770, King's MSS, 201, ff. 18–19, BM.

newspapers, directing me what to extract from them for the English ones." [40]

Franklin's essays reveal his practical awareness of political realities. He usually eschewed discussion of fundamental constitutional issues, and argued along lines of expediency. This same pragmatic judgment regulated his sense of timing in releasing his work. Most of his publications were printed while Parliament sat or when elections were pending. Hence many of Franklin's pieces can be found in January issues between 1766 and 1770. During the legislative session of 1770, he typically communicated a letter from America to some Members, who handed it about. "It had due weight with several," Franklin wrote, "and was of considerable use." He then published it in the *London Chronicle*.[41] By 1770, however, the Doctor informed an American correspondent that William Strahan, publisher of the *Chronicle*, "is grown a great Courtier." A month later Strahan too confessed that he and Franklin did not share similar views in commerce and politics. In 1774 the Doctor closed his account with the printer, who since 1770, like Richard Jackson, had been in the service of the crown.[42]

Franklin knew most of the other newspapermen of London, though the strength of his relationships varied. He grumbled to his son in 1768 that Griffith Jones, editor of the *Chronicle* and Strahan's colleague, "seems a Grenvillian, or is very cautious. . . . He has drawn the teeth and pared the nails of my paper, so that it can neither scratch nor bite. It seems only to paw and mumble." Charles Say, on the other hand, who printed and directed the *Gazetteer* when Franklin wrote for it, was very congenial to the colonial cause. In 1774, Say undertook a special publicity job on the Massachusetts agency account for

[40] Franklin to William Franklin, Oct. 6, 1773, Smyth, VI, 145; Crane, *Franklin's Letters to the Press*, pp. xxxvi–xxxvii; B. I. Granger, *Political Satire in the American Revolution, 1763–1783* (Ithaca, 1960), pp. 27–28, 74–75, 91–92; Franklin to Thomas Cushing, May 6, 1773, Smyth, VI, 48; *Monthly Magazine*, XV (Feb. 1803), 1–2.

[41] Verner W. Crane, "Benjamin Franklin and the Stamp Act," CSM *Publications*, XXXII (1937), 64; Crane, "Franklin's Political Journalism," pp. 205–224; Franklin to ?, March 18, 1770, Smyth, V, 251.

[42] Crane, *Franklin's Letters to the Press*, pp. xv, xxii, xlvi, li; Strahan to Charles Jenkinson, Nov. 7, 1769, Add MSS 38206, f. 155; Strahan to David Hall, April 7, 1770, "Some Further Letters of William Strahan," *PMHB*, LX (1936), 478; J. A. Cochrane, *Dr. Johnson's Printer: The Life of William Strahan* (Cambridge, Mass., 1964), pp. 114, 129, 172, 188–189.

Franklin—printing the *Accounts* and *Letters* on British trade compiled by Joseph Massie. These leaflets were widely reprinted in British and American newspapers.[43]

Not once after 1766 did a group of the agents collaborate to produce a pamphlet or book designed to sway British political opinion toward the colonial view.[44] Nonetheless there had been a number of noteworthy individual efforts, particularly by Franklin, whose talents with a quill placed him in a special category as a colonial publicist. Among his notable works were *The Examination . . . Relative to the Repeal of the American Stamp Act* (Almon, 1767), *The True Sentiments of America* (Almon, 1768), and the *Principles of Trade* (Brotherton and Sewell, 1774).[45]

Early in 1769 he found "a Pamphlet has lately been published here in our Behalf, which seems to make some Impression. As it contains many Sentiments and Arguments that I have occasionally thrown out in Conversation, I think I know the Author, one of the Rockingham Party, and I have distributed a Number of them where I thought they might do good, gratis." In 1773, Franklin's Massachusetts constituents sent him *The Votes and Proceedings of the Freeholders and Other Inhabitants of the Town of Boston,* an enumeration of all their grievances and discontents. He delivered copies to prominent politicians, wrote a preface, and had it published by John Wilkie.[46] The agents' failure to secure repeal of the Currency Act in 1767 prompted Franklin to prevail upon Thomas Pownall to incorporate the Doctor's land bank plan into the fourth edition of Pownall's *The Administration of the Colonies,* in hopes that provincial legislatures would adopt it to satisfy their currency needs. Because Pownall's soporific speeches— partial to America—were poorly attended in the Commons, Franklin helped introduce them to the public as pamphlets.[47]

In various ways he persuaded others to participate in the forensic

[43] Benjamin Franklin to William Franklin, Jan. 9, 1768, Smyth, V, 90; Crane, *Franklin's Letters to the Press,* p. xlix.

[44] See William Bollan to James Bowdoin, Sept. 29, 1773, *Bowdoin and Temple Papers,* p. 320.

[45] Crane, *Franklin's Letters to the Press,* p. xlix.

[46] Franklin to Joseph Galloway, Jan 9, 1769, WCL; Franklin to Thomas Cushing, March 9, 1773, Smyth, VI, 22.

[47] Crane, "Certain Writings of Franklin," p. 6 n. 8; Greene and Jellison, "The Currency Act of 1764," p. 505; Crane, *Franklin's Letters to the Press,* p. l.

dimensions of the Great Debate. Between 1770 and 1774 he employed
an economist, Joseph Massie, to write leaflets, print broadsides, and
provide manuscripts, books, and papers. He also encouraged Edward
Bancroft to answer a ministerial writer. The agent recommended his
young protégé as an analyst for the *Monthly Review,* "in which his
standing share was to review all publications relative to America."
John Adams recalled long afterwards "that Bancroft was the ostensi-
ble reviewer, but that Franklin was always consulted before the publication." [48]

Joseph Priestley wrote his *Address to Dissenters on the Subject of
the Differences with America* at Franklin's request. That same year
Franklin furnished the materials for Arthur Lee to compile *A True
State of the Proceedings in the Parliament of Great Britain, and in the
Province of Massachusetts Bay,* printed by William Bingley on the
Massachusetts account. And in 1774, Franklin also emboldened Lee
to write *An Appeal to the Justice and Interests of the People.* The
Doctor sent John Almon Lee's "M.S. which he [Franklin] has perus'd
and thinks well written, so as probably to be acceptable to the Publick
at this time. If Mr. Almon should be of the same Opinion, it is at his
Service." [49]

Lee did not require very much encouragement. Between 1769 and
1775, in addition to his newspaper work, he made four contributions
to the literature of the Great Debate. First Becket and De Hondt
handled his *Observations on the Review of the Controversy between
Great Britain and Her Colonies.* Then, in 1770, Almon brought out
*The Political Detection: Or, the Treachery and Tyranny of Adminis-
tration, Both at Home and Abroad.* This included not only the Junius
Americanus essays, but a volley directed at enemy pamphleteers as
well. Lee confidently assumed the public would regard with contempt
"the laboured sophistry of an impudently pretended Review of the
American Controversy, and the News-paper bable of an old Mentor.
Whether they are the virtuous lucubrations of a coxcomb Deputy [50] to

[48] "Massie," *DNB*; Franklin's MS Ledger, 1764–1775, f. 58, APS; "Franklin's Accounts against Massachusetts," ed. Worthington C. Ford, MHS *Proceedings,* LVI (1923), 97, 99, 118; *The Works of John Adams,* ed. Charles F.
Adams (Boston, 1850–1856), III, 141–142.

[49] R. H. Fox, *Dr. John Fothergill and His Friends* (London, 1919), p. 325;
Crane, *Franklin's Letters to the Press,* p. 1; Van Doren, *Franklin and Mecom,* p.
145; Franklin to Almon, Nov. 7, 1774, Lowell Collection, HLHU.

[50] William Knox.

a pedantic Secretary of S——e; [51] or of an envenomed *retailer* of *German* Considerations, from a Blanket-Ware house; [52] or of a cankered junto of discarded American Agents." [53] In 1774, Lee wrote his *Appeal.* Parliament lacked the right to tax the colonies, he contended, and to do so went against Britain's interest anyway. Edward Dilly refused to print the essay, claiming sales would be insufficient to defray expenses. Thereupon Franklin sent it to Almon. Thousands of copies circulated in Britain and America; at a shilling and six pence *An Appeal* quickly went through four editions. Heartened by the success, Lee and Almon followed with *A Speech Intended to Have Been Delivered in the House of Commons, in Support of the Petition from the General Congress at Philadelphia.*[54]

Despite his lack of interest in newspaper publications, William Bollan also produced a steady flow of pamphlet literature during these years. In 1768, the year Bollan became agent for Massachusetts' Council, William Owen and John Almon published two of his efforts, the first directed against the venality of English elections and the second against corruption and military garrisons in North America. Both were studded with classical allusions and pleas for unencumbered colonial commerce. In the next six years Bollan produced half a dozen new tracts. Early in 1769 he set out "to write & *publish* as soon as conveniency & propriety will admit *some farther account of the establishment, rights and merits of the Colonies.*" The outgrowth was *The Free Britons Memorial,* another attempt to expose "the whole *Grenvillian* system of revenue." Like Franklin, and to a lesser extent Lee, Bollan followed the tack that infringing American rights hurt the British at home. More immediately the essay attacked the Grafton ministry on account of its handling of the Middlesex election. In 1770, John Williams also issued a lengthy addendum, *The Free Britons Supplemental Memorial.* Here again Bollan deprecated restrictive legislation and corrupt ministers.[55]

[51] Hillsborough.   [52] Israel Mauduit.

[53] *Political Detection,* pp. 68–69.

[54] Burton J. Hendrick, *The Lees of Virginia* (Boston, 1935), p. 169.

[55] Malcolm Freiberg, "William Bollan, Agent of Massachusetts," *More Books,* XXIII (1948), 179, 215–216; Bollan, *An Epistle from Timoleon, to All the Honest Free-Holders* . . . (London, 1768); Bollan, *Continued Corruption, Standing Armies, and Popular Discontents Considered* . . . (London, 1768); Bollan to Samuel Danforth, March 23, 1769, *Bowdoin and Temple Papers,* p. 134.

In 1772, Almon handled Bollan's *Britannia Libera,* still another critique of corruption and plea for freedom of speech and the press. Two years later Bollan devoted much time to drafting petitions. The few remaining friends in Parliament who would offer these remonstrances urged Bollan to have them printed for wider impact. In a similar situation in 1769, Bollan had bypassed publication because Massachusetts had a memorial then under administrative consideration which the agent did not want to endanger. By 1774, however, there seemed to be nothing to lose, so he "resolved to prepare, and publish with all possible despatch," his recent petition to the crown, replete with illustrations.[56] The procedure Bollan followed demonstrates the operations of the lobbyist functioning as press agent. He

went into the city to the printer,[57] who, during some time past, had been employed in my intended vindication of the Colonies,[58] after collecting numerous proper materials, told him he must lay that aside for the present, and prepare for printing a short pamphlet, with all speed, promising to make proper allowance to the men who should work out of common hours, directing him to send the next morning for part of the copy; when, going about it, and attending to it without intermission, the copy was completed on *Tuesday,* before dinner; and, by my Clerk's attendance, and my going to the printer's in person, several times, and afterwards going late farther into the city, to two of the principal publishers, in consequence of Mr. *Almon's* telling me at the printer's it was too late for the next day's publication, I prevailed on them to publish it on *Wednesday* morning.[59]

With such promptness publication could be expedited.

Bollan and Franklin contributed more to the literature of the Great Debate than the other agents taken together. Both men knew when to place shots to make the most of their power—just prior to the opening of Parliament, as a rule. Both recognized when silence was more prudent than publication. And both acquired intimate working relationships with the liberal booksellers of London. In 1772, Hillsborough resigned on the very morning when Franklin's propaganda on behalf of the Grand Ohio Company was scheduled to appear.

[56] Bollan to John Erving, July 21, 1774, Misc. Bound MSS, MHS.

[57] John Almon.

[58] *The Rights of the English Colonies Established in America Stated and Defended* . . . (London, 1774).

[59] Bollan to John Erving, March 11, 1774, *American Archives,* comp. Peter Force (Washington, 1837–1846), ser. 4, I, 225.

Hillsborough being the chief obstacle to the land scheme, the essay would serve no purpose any longer; so the agent and Almon, coordinating closely, stopped sales of *Dr. Franklin's Observations* before five copies had been bought.[60]

The other agents, however, as well as many of the booksellers, were less effective and less willing to undertake this sort of activity. William Samuel Johnson's failure to utilize the press as part of his agency operations is baffling. A highly articulate provincial, he knew several of London's more liberal printers quite well. Soon after Johnson's arrival Franklin took him to meet John Almon at the bookman's printing house. Johnson did not return again to Almon's until twenty-two months later, when he went several times to look after some "American papers." Then in the spring of 1769, and for eight months thereafter, Johnson began to see a good deal of Henry Sampson Woodfall, publisher of Junius and the *Public Advertiser*. At the same time that Johnson and Woodfall were having tea, dining, and taking long walks together, the Connecticut agent began making frequent entries in his diary that he was "writing." Early in 1770, the rash of composition and conferences with Woodfall ended just as abruptly as it had begun, perhaps because the Mohegan case now began to occupy more of Johnson's time. The purpose of his activity is uncertain. Perhaps he was merely catching up with his voluminous correspondence. But his *furor scribendi* may have been given over to writing anonymously for the press.[61]

Otherwise Johnson can only be credited with two parochial efforts. One was Connecticut's case against the Mohegan land claimants, which Johnson and Jackson "dispersed great numbers of" in 1770 wherever they imagined it might be useful. The other involved Johnson's colleague, Barlow Trecothick, and Sir James Jay. While Jay raised funds in England for King's College, Trecothick suspected him of financial irregularities and informed the board of governors in New York. His reputation smirched, Jay attempted exoneration through publication. In the subsequent skirmish Johnson came to Trecothick's assistance. Altogether it only served to distract two capable agents

[60] Bollan to Samuel Danforth, Jan. 28, 1771, *Bowdoin and Temple Papers*, p. 251; Smyth, V, 465–466, 479; John Almon, *Biographical, Literary, and Political Anecdotes, of Several of the Most Eminent Persons of the Present Age . . .* (London, 1797), II, 238.

[61] Entries for Feb. 23, 1767, through Sept. 1, 1770, Johnson's London diary, WSJ MSS.

when issues of greater importance to the colonies hung in uncertainty.[62]

In 1769, Dennys De Berdt had *An Appeal to the World: or a Vindication of the Town of Boston* reprinted in London and distributed "to all the members that are of consequence as well as spread them all over the Town." For the opening of Parliament early in 1770 De Berdt organized a pamphlet around a letter he had received from his constituents. It appeared as an *Extract of a Letter from the House of Representatives of the Massachusetts-Bay, to their Agent Dennys De Berdt, Esq; with Some Remarks.* The agent had each of these pamphlets printed in editions of five hundred copies, as well as the same number of Lee's *Junius Americanus* letters in booklet form. Most of the essays of the period, in fact, were initially produced in that amount until their influence and popularity could be ascertained.[63]

Joseph Sherwood wrote very little, though he had *The Case of the Colony of Rhode Island* printed in 1769 to support his employers' claim for military expenses arising from the Crown Point expedition of 1756. Henry Eustace McCulloh neither wrote nor reprinted, and Charles Garth made little effort to incorporate the power of the press into his lobbying functions. He only did so in 1774, when Sir Egerton Leigh attacked Carolinian Henry Laurens in a tract. Garth agreed to furnish material for a rejoinder and consulted with Ralph Izard, a Carolina planter in London at the time. Laurens bore the expense and Garth provided the documents, but Arthur Lee actually wrote the reply, published in April 1774.[64]

How effective then were the exertions of those agents who did write and the booksellers who published them? Franklin and Lee wrote well and to the point. Yet Franklin doubted in 1770 whether "the Freedom I used in declaring and publishing these Sentiments had much Effect; I rather think the Apprehension of an approaching War, inclin'd Government to milder Measures." Bollan immersed

---

[62] [William Samuel Johnson], *Governor and Company of Connecticut, and Mohegan Indians, by Their Guardians* . . . (London, 1769); Johnson to Jonathan Trumbull, Oct. 12, 1770, MHS *Collections*, ser. 5, IX, 455.

[63] Add MSS 35912, ff. 158–175; De Berdt to Thomas Cushing, Jan. 4 and 26, 1770, Matthews, "Letters of De Berdt," pp. 393, 395.

[64] Sherwood to Moses Brown, Sept. 22, 1770, Moses Brown MSS, I, 115, RIHS; Namier, "Garth, Agent," pp. 465 n. 1, 466; Lonn, *Agents of the Southern Colonies,* p. 236.

himself too often in classical obscurity and lost his readers in obfuscation. Material from the provinces that the agents reprinted did not meet with unmitigated success either. Franklin's lengthy preface for the English edition of Dickinson's *Farmer's Letters* was reported to have "had great effect with every thinking person here, and Mr. De B——t tells me that the Board of Trade feels the weight of them more than anything that has been wrote on the subject, & he says, they have staggered them very much." Yet Arthur Lee believed Dickinson's essays were read widely and respected, "but to little purpose," because not translated into results. Characteristically the bureaucrats regarded the agents' work lightly. John Pownall responded to the first printed narratives of Lexington and Concord contemptuously: "The account (published by an agent of theirs sent on purpose) is, however, so evidently prepared to convey misrepresentation and create alarm that it has had little effect on public credit." [65]

The North American lobbyists failed to avail themselves adequately of the power of the pen. Particularly after 1770, when—however tenuously—freedom of the press became established, many of the agents ignored the opportunity offered by this new dimension in lobbying. Just when colonial influence in London should have increased, it diminished. A message sent late in 1769 from William Knox to Grenville epitomized the unpropitious trend.

The Printer or more properly the Editor of the St. James Chronicle who has hitherto been your sworn Enemy, from the time Lord Suffolk moved the Lords to impose on him; and who refused Two Guineas from me to insert an Extract from the American Controversy because it was in defence of your opinions. This very man has voluntarily made a large Extract from your Speech and introduced it with a general account highly commendatory of the performance. Another American writer who has published his spleen against you on the Colony topic, has declared to Almon that he was mistaken in his opinion, and that he shall ever honour you. [66]

Not only were once friendly editors becoming alienated; for a variety of reasons the publishers seemed less available or reliable. For producing No. 47 of the *North Briton* in 1768, William Bingley was

[65] Franklin to Samuel Cooper, Dec. 30, 1770, King's MSS, no. 201, BM; *Boston Evening Post*, Sept. 26, 1768; Arthur Lee to Richard H. Lee, Dec. 27, 1768, Lee MSS, Vol. I, no. 16, APS; Pownall to William Knox, June 2, 1775, "Correspondence of William Knox," HMC *Report on Manuscripts in Various Collections*, VI (Dublin, 1909), 118.

[66] Nov. 10, 1769, Add MSS 42087, f. 91.

committed to Newgate for seventy-two days, and then transferred to King's Bench prison. In 1770 he reprinted *A Short Narrative of the Horrid Massacre at Boston.* Bankrupt a year later, however, he left for Ireland.[67] Franklin and Arthur and William Lee saw a good deal of the Dillys during the seventies. They even discussed promoting a subscription for the Americans at Edward's place in the Poultry. Curiously, however, the Dillys did more with religious tracts from the colonies than with political polemics. Despite frequent social contacts and compatibility with the agents, the Dillys published almost nothing for them.[68]

Almon published Franklin in 1765, 1767–1768, 1772, and 1774;[69] Lee between 1774 and 1776; Bollan in 1768 and 1774; and such essays as Otis' *Vindication of the British Colonies* in 1769. Lobbyists were fortunate in their connection with Almon. As one of his rivals conceded, "There is not a bookseller in London that knows better how to touch up an eighteen-penny pamphlet. —Materials or no materials, right or wrong, for or against, it is all the same." By dint of this detached commercialism, however, Almon reduced his value to the radical cause. To the agents' dismay he brought to light the works of various anti-American authors, particularly Grenville's puppet, William Knox. Thus Almon's printing of an English edition of the *Farmer's Letters* in 1768 (with Franklin's new preface) was offset by his publication of Knox's reply to John Dickinson, the Farmer.[70]

The agents' declining influence with their informal and traditional allies was paralleled by a more precipitous decline of influence among British politicians and men responsible for colonial management. The dramatic disruption of these bonds, the loss of "interest" in these circles, would set the stage for a final crisis, when helpless agents could only wait and watch the Empire quite literally disintegrate.

[67] H. R. Plomer, *A Dictionary of the Printers and Booksellers Who Were at Work in England . . . from 1726 to 1775* (Oxford, 1932), pp. 25, 143–144.

[68] S. H. Bingham, "Publishing in the Eighteenth Century with Special Reference to the Firm of Edward and Charles Dilly" (unpub. Ph.D. diss.; Yale University, 1937), pp. 4, 7, 9, 100–101; entries for Nov. 20 and 23, 1774, "Journal of Josiah Quincy, Jr., during His Voyage and Residence in England," MHS *Proceedings,* L (1917), 438 n., 442.

[69] Including the famous examination before the committee of the whole House of Commons in 1766; Almon printed it anonymously in 1767, rather than risk prosecution.

[70] *A Letter to the Right Honourable the E[arl] T[emple]* (London, 1766), p. ix; Knox to Grenville, July 23, 1768, Add MSS 42086, ff. 70–71.

A Decline of Influence: The
Agents and British Politics

As we have noted in Chapter 6, the 1760's in Britain were characterized by a prolonged search for political stability. So long as public affairs and the men responsible for their management remained uncertain, the agents' operations would be adversely affected. Even more serious perhaps, statesmen would lack the time or desire to become well informed about the colonies. Instead the procedural warfare characteristic of factionalism in a parliamentary system dominated, and such issues as the Wilkes dispute distracted attention and precious time from American considerations. Resolving the search for stability required some common ground upon which cohesion could be established. After 1766, with the exacerbating intensification of Anglo-American constitutional issues, one basis for unity was found in fixing a firm position toward the colonies. In consequence a variety of hostile or repressive measures was directed at the agents, measures which quite literally contributed to a hardening of imperial arteries. The lobbyists were excluded from parliamentary galleries, their petitions not often heard, their credentials not always recognized, and their mail clandestinely read. Parallel to these forms of intimidation occurred a general decline of colonial influence in British politics as traditional connections were snipped off in Whitehall and Westminster, and as agent-Members found their dual role ambivalent and even embarrassing.

A SEARCH FOR STABILITY

The tumultuous disequilibrium in British politics—its dominant feature since 1757—had become an object of national concern by the later 1760's. Bitterly condemning a decade of exhausting instability, David Hume lamented that potential statesmen were repelled from governmental service, leaving only "Adventurers, of whom the Public is naturally distrustful. The pecuniary Emoluments are of no Consideration to Men of Rank & Fortune." When Chatham formed an administration in 1766, he brought together an assortment of men whose only bond of union was himself. When he became ill, the Duke of Grafton at the Treasury refused to act as effective Prime Minister in his place, thereby reducing the administration to a collection of independent departments without a head. "I found it so," wrote Lord North after he succeeded Chatham, "and had not the vigour and resolution to put an end to it." [1]

By 1768 there were signs of change, however, pointing in the direction of greater stability. The Bedford group agreed to join the ministry, increasing the support for government in both houses, but especially in the Lords. This augmented voting strength would shift the balance of power within the ministry, with important implications for America. Those who still believed Chatham's colonial policy was correct were now in the minority. Shelburne's influence especially was reduced. Almost immediately Grafton found himself captured by the Bedfordites' views. When they succeeded on several anti-American policy questions, Chatham resigned. Grafton's retirement two years later in 1770 marked the end of a peculiar and protracted era in British public life. But no contemporary then could know that stability, of a sort, was at hand. North's primary goal, in fact, for the next three years would be the maintenance of his ministry's precarious hold. He stood for no new departures in policy, lacked long-term plans, and intended to meet problems as they were forced upon him. His attitude toward the American question was one of quiet firmness. [2]

Once Chatham and Shelburne were removed from power in 1768, and once the Bedfords were included in administration, the distinction between ministerial policy toward the colonies and that of the opposition became far more clear than it had been for several years. Within the opposition ranks, relations between Rockingham and Chatham became the crucial and perennial question. When coopera-

[1] Hume to Sir Gilbert Elliot, Sept. 10 and 19, 1767, *The Letters of David Hume*, ed. J. Y. T. Greig (Oxford, 1932), II, 161–162; Piers Mackesy, *The War for America, 1775–1783* (Cambridge, Mass., 1964), p. 22.

[2] J. Steven Watson, *The Reign of George III, 1760–1815* (Oxford, 1960), pp. 129–130, 146–150, 153.

tion between the two failed altogether in 1772–1773, the Whigs reached low ebb. Between 1771 and 1774 opposition in general was sporadic. Even when it revived during the final crisis there was a remarkable consensus on American affairs. As G. H. Guttridge has observed, the crown and the Whigs "both sought to maintain the authority of parliament." [3]

The North American agents followed the search for stability with a sense of helplessness; indeed their response to that search had a poignant sort of immediacy. Rockingham and his followers made their exit during the summer of 1766, causing Franklin to comment that "all ministerial Dispositions are extreamly fluctuating. . . . All American Affairs, even the Granting of Lands, are now at a Stand." In August Chatham and Grafton headed a new government. The transition again slowed the mechanics of colonial administration and the operations of those charged with the duty of expediting such affairs. "These frequent changes are certainly detrimental to the public," Henry Wilmot believed. Grafton remained nominal leader of the ministry until North replaced him early in 1770; but his unwieldy coalition underwent continual vicissitudes. Late in 1766, Franklin reported "a Ferment at Court; every Day producing Changes or Resignations . . . so that little else has been attended to." The following April he found that "daily apprehensions of new changes make it extremely difficult to get forward with business." In May the Doctor reported that "the Ministry . . . has not been looked upon, either by itself or others, as settled, which is another cause of postponing every thing not immediately necessary to be considered." [4]

Late in 1767 a series of cabinet resignations and replacements brought about "a fluctuation in the Ministry, during which time no business was done." At this juncture Shelburne relinquished stewardship of the Southern Department. "All American affairs will now be thrown into an entire new channel," William Samuel Johnson ob-

---

[3] *English Whiggism and the American Revolution* (Berkeley, 1942), pp. 28, 46, 71; Archibald S. Foord, *His Majesty's Opposition, 1714–1830* (Oxford, 1964), p. 359.

[4] Franklin to Pa. CC, June 10, 1766, *PMHB*, V (1881), 355; Franklin to Joseph Galloway, Aug. 22, 1766, MFY; Wilmot to William Alexander, Sept. 25, 1766, William A. Duer, *The Life of William Alexander, Earl of Stirling* (NJHS *Collections*, Vol. II [New York, 1847]), pp. 84–85; Franklin to Galloway, Dec. 13, 1766, April 14 and May 20, 1767, WCL; Franklin to John Ross, April 11, 1767, to Cadwallader Evans, May 5, 1767, Smyth, V, 23, 25.

served; "all is to begin anew with Lord Hilsborough; new negotiations are to be commenced, new connections formed, &c., which is an unhappy delay to all who have any affairs of that country to solicit." Johnson had been on the verge of concluding some Connecticut business with Shelburne's Southern Department. Now the whole would have to be arranged again with Hillsborough. Hence the agent's pique: "Thus it is in all affairs. . . . When you have pursued them all to a Close & think you are pretty sure of your point, some change of System intervenes & oversets all your plans. So unsteady are their Counsels, so uncertain the Tenure of those in Power!" [5]

Simultaneously and for months past, the forthcoming parliamentary campaign had thrown the country into a frenzy. In December, Johnson warned Connecticut's governor not to expect American issues to be raised in a session of the Commons preoccupied with election preparations. As late as May, although the voting had been accomplished, De Berdt found it "a time of great confusion, the heats & animosities of Electing new Members of Parliament are not yet subsided." The agents all agree that "amidst these violent struggles of Party the true Interest of the Kingdom is not like to be very much attended to." [6]

So much uncertainty had effects beyond the obvious stoppage of political business. The agents began to regard these conditions as normal. Some developed a tendency to procrastinate in presenting petitions or delay applying for redress in anticipation of a governmental shift favorable to the colonies. Ministries, for their part, became "afraid of changing anything in settled measures," Franklin wrote, "lest something should go wrong, and the opposition make an advantage of it against them." This applied with particular validity in 1768 and 1769, when the agents observed "with care the various windings and turnings of those in power, and discover, as far as may be, their

[5] Dennys De Berdt to Samuel Dexter, Dec. 23, 1767, "Letters of Dennys De Berdt, 1757–1770," ed. Albert Matthews, CSM *Publications*, XIII (1912), 328; Johnson to William Pitkin, Dec. 26, 1767, "Letters of William Samuel Johnson to the Governors of Connecticut," MHS *Collections*, ser. 5, IX (Boston, 1885), 252; Johnson to Eliphalet Dyer, Jan. 22, 1768, *The Susquehannah Company Papers: Memorial Publications of the Wyoming Historical and Genealogical Society*, ed. Julian P. Boyd (Wilkes-Barre, Pa., 1930–1933), III, 8.

[6] Johnson to Jared Ingersoll, June 9, 1767, NHCHS *Papers*, IX (New Haven, 1918), 409; Johnson to William Pitkin, Dec. 26, 1767, MHS *Collections*, ser. 5, IX, 250; De Berdt to Thomas Cushing, May 16, 1768, Matthews, "Letters of De Berdt," p. 454; Johnson to Ingersoll, Feb. 18, 1767, WSJ MSS.

views, schemes, and designs, as well as the different mutations, combinations, connections, and struggles of the several parties here." Composed of incompatible and mutually mistrustful men, His Majesty's government was weak.[7]

Charles Garth lamented to his Carolina correspondents that the "fluctuation of Counsels and of Ministers in this Country is a truly unhappy Circumstance for the People in all Parts of the Dominions; The Ground of Yesterday is no longer to morrow." In 1769, William Samuel Johnson believed England was on the verge of "some very decisive political revolution. . . . In the very fluctuating condition we are now in, affairs are every day almost varying, and assuming new appearances." Johnson's alarm intensified as he stayed on in London, watching "their intestine divisions and party squabbles, which . . . actually seem to threaten a dissolution of the whole political system, and the ruin of the empire."[8]

If ministries were frail in these years, their fragmented opposition—relied on heavily by the colonists and their agents—was even more shaky. Early in 1769, Johnson learned that several factions then out of office wanted to raise the American question in Westminster, but were unable to agree on the best way. A year later they split completely on the question of Lord Mansfield's decision regarding the publishers of Junius. Thereafter the colonial pressure group suffered from the lack of a united opposition.[9]

The search for political stability had tremendous impact upon the burgeoning American question. One observer, William Strahan, placed considerable blame for the outbreak of Revolution in 1775 upon "our wicked Factions at Home, whose Struggles for Place and Power have by degrees carried them such daring Lengths." Without going so far as Strahan, there can be no doubt that so long as factionalism persisted, no politician would have time to devote to provincial

[7] Franklin to William Franklin, Nov. 13, 1767, *Trade and Politics, 1767–1769*, ed. C. W. Alvord and C. E. Carter (Springfield, Ill., 1921), p. 104; Benjamin Franklin to ?, March 18, 1770, Smyth, V, 251–253; William Samuel Johnson to William Pitkin, May 25, 1769, MHS *Collections*, ser. 5, IX, 356.

[8] Garth to S.C. CC, Aug. 14, 1768, *SCHGM*, XXX, 218–222; Johnson to William Pitkin, Sept. 18, 1769, to Jonathan Trumbull, Oct. 16, 1769, MHS *Collections*, ser. 5, IX, 362, 376.

[9] Johnson to Jared Ingersoll, March 8, 1769, WSJ MSS (box), Vol. I; Carl B. Cone, *Burke and the Nature of Politics*, I (Lexington, Ky., 1957), pp. 213–215.

administration.[10] Henry Eustace McCulloh complained that "the affairs of America seem very little understood & not at all attended to."
William Samuel Johnson "heard a respectable counsellor at law ask
Mr. Jackson gravely in the Hall whether Philadelphia was in the E. or
W. Indies and said he had a notion it was upon the coast of
Sumatra." [11] After Johnson returned to Connecticut, Thomas Pownall
warned him not to expect any action to be taken regarding America
"because few think & of those who do think on these matters 'tis by
piece meal & not upon system." The ultimate indictment came from a
frustrated Franklin in 1773: "The great Defect here is, in all sorts of
People, a want of attention to what passes in such remote Countries as
America; an Unwillingness even to read any thing about them if it
appears a little lengthy, and a Disposition to postpone the Consideration even of the Things they know they must at last consider." [12]

Exasperated by the ephemeral quality of politics, not always knowing where power lay (or would lie a week hence), some of the agents
became lax in supplying information to the politicians. There were
exceptions to be sure. De Berdt conveyed affidavits of misbehavior by
British troops to Shelburne and his successor Hillsborough.[13] Lee also
disbursed pamphlets and copies of petitions sent from America to
Shelburne, Barré, Rockingham, Chatham, and Catherine Macaulay,
the radical writer. In 1774, Franklin relayed a copy of Joseph Galloway's "Plan of Union" to Lords Camden, Chatham, and Dartmouth;
and the next year he sent David Hartley "the Pennsylvania Votes for
3 successive Years, wherein he will find the Form & Manner of
Requisitions"—an attempt to prove that Grenville's offer to the agents
on May 17, 1764, had been spuriously tendered.[14]

Nevertheless, after 1770 the lobbyists seemed to busy themselves
less with personally explaining their employers' views to the leaders of

[10] Strahan to Franklin, Oct. 4, 1775, J. A. Cochrane, *Dr. Johnson's Printer:
The Life of William Strahan* (Cambridge, Mass., 1964), pp. 200–201.

[11] McCulloh to John Harvey, July 15, 1768, CRNC, VII, 757; Johnson's
London diary, entry for Nov. 27, 1769, WSJ MSS.

[12] Pownall to Johnson, July 31, 1772, WSJ MSS (box), Vol. II; Franklin to
Samuel Cooper, July 7, 1773, Smyth, VI, 93.

[13] De Berdt to Boston Selectmen, Jan. 29, 1769, Matthews, "Letters of De
Berdt," p. 351.

[14] Richard Henry Lee to William Lee, April 9, 1770, E. J. Lee MSS, VHS;
Rockingham to Arthur Lee, Dec. 31, 1774, Fitzwilliam MSS, R 1–1533, SCL;
Franklin to Hartley, Feb. 26, 1775, Berkshire County Record Office, England.

British public life. Lee's campaign in 1772 to make Dartmouth receptive to Massachusetts' representations was conspicuous for its isolation. Unfortunately interested parties outside the agency were incapable of taking up the slack sufficiently, though some tried.[15] Few people seemed to bother very much about the state of ministerial knowledge of America. The colonial question was continually put off after 1770 because people in Whitehall "were perplext with different and opposite accounts of the State of things in our Country, and knew not which to rely on, or what steps to take in consequence." When Josiah Quincy Jr. arrived in London late in 1774, North and Dartmouth took the opportunity to learn provincial sentiments and plied the young colonial for several hours with questions and arguments. Unfortunately such interviews were rare by this time, and knowledgeable visitors with fresh perspectives were infrequent.[16]

By 1774 an impasse had been reached. The colonists were lax in transmitting information. Their agents, frustrated by rebuffs received in London, were reticent and dilatory in communicating what was available to them. Most members of British political society had closed their eyes and ears. In December, William Bollan tried to have Quincy heard before the House of Commons—but unsuccessfully. The ministry's irresponsible handling of dispatches from crown servants in America had nearly closed off that source since 1770. "They say they can now give no Information with Security," a Grenvillite reported, "& Government here must be satisfied with less Intelligence for the future." [17]

If private sources of colonial knowledge were slight, public commentary was surprisingly meager between 1770 and the end of 1773. The last eighteen months of Grafton's administration had been absorbed by John Wilkes and his controversies, so that "it was sometimes difficult to raise half the number among exhausted members to debate

[15] Lee to Sam Adams, Dec. 24, 1772, Richard Henry Lee, *The Life of Arthur Lee* (Boston, 1829), I, 225.

[16] Benjamin Franklin to Joseph Galloway, March 21, 1770, Rosenbach Foundation and Gallery, Philadelphia; "Journal of Josiah Quincy, Jr., during His Voyage and Residence in England," MHS *Proceedings*, L (1917), 439–443, 447, 453.

[17] Bollan to James Bowdoin, Dec. 6, 1774, *The Bowdoin and Temple Papers* (MHS *Collections*, ser. 6, Vol. IX [Boston, 1897]), p. 379; Thomas Whately to George Grenville, Nov. 24, 1769, Grenville MSS in the possession of Sir John Murray, London.

a purely American question." During those same eighteen months the reconstructed ministry began to redefine the role of colonial agents in British politics.[18]

HARDENING THE ARTERIES

At first glance the agents' relationship to politics after the accession of George III seems paradoxical. In the mid-1760's, when public life was so unsettled, the agents achieved their greatest successes. After 1769, when a degree of stability returned, lobbyists found themselves balked and their institution declining. The reasons are not hard to find. As the Great Debate unfolded, as positions polarized, one basis for ministerial unity was found in firmer colonial policies. A consensus emerged that permissiveness had gone far enough. The departure of Shelburne in 1768, creation of an American Department, and installation of Hillsborough as its first secretary were symptomatic.[19] Almost immediately the agents felt the full impact of these efforts to reinforce the formal structure of overseas government. In brief, in both the sixties and seventies—though for different reasons—British politics made communication between the agents and government difficult: in the sixties because ministries were so unstable, and in the seventies because the stability that was achieved was structurally and ideologically impervious to the colonists' influence.

Deterioration of Anglo-American communications after 1763 had forced upon Whitehall a willingness to work with the agents in shoring up the sagging foundations of empire. This new element of cooperation became most apparent with repeal of the Stamp Act early in 1766. In 1767 the Chatham administration still found it useful to consult the agents. A year later, however, Dennys De Berdt reported that the Grafton ministry regarded the concerted efforts of the North American lobby as "disagreeable." In 1769 he communicated to the same confidant Hillsborough's "disapprobation to all Agents"; and Franklin noted "the Plan here at present being, to have as little to do with Agents as possible." By 1771, early in North's government, Franklin related a still more serious development to his constituents.

Under the present American administration, [agents] are rather looked on with an evil eye, as obstructors of ministerial measures; and the Secretary

[18] B. W. Labaree, *The Boston Tea Party* (New York, 1964), p. 190; Watson, *Reign of George III*, p. 143.

[19] R. A. Humphreys, "Lord Shelburne and a Projected Recall of Colonial Governors in 1767," *AHR*, XXXVII (1932), 269–272.

would, I imagine, be well pleased to get rid of them, being as he has sometimes intimated, of opinion that agents are unnecessary, for that, whatever is to be transacted between the assemblies of colonies and the government here, may be done through and by the governor's letters, and more properly than by any agent whatever.[20]

Factions and coalitions hostile to the colonies had at their disposal various ways of making work difficult for the agents and effective lobbying all but impossible. The Grenvilles, for example, even while in opposition, could stir up a "general rage" against America that permeated Parliament. A politician's views on provincial questions became "one of the distinctions of party here," Franklin observed. Members of the opposition who stood against measures to tax the colonies would be "stigmatized as Americans, betrayers of Old England, &c." When Tories out of office seized upon reports of the disreputable "conduct of the Assemblies of New York and Boston . . . in order to distress the friends of America in the present ministry, nothing so little interesting to them as our application can get forward," Franklin wrote.[21]

The mildest means a ministry might employ was simply to ignore agents and unpleasant issues they raised. The Grafton-Chatham coalition squelched Jackson, De Berdt, and Johnson in this fashion in 1767, when they sought favor for the New England fishing interest. Again in 1768, Garth related, administration refusal to push repeal of the Currency Act brought lobbying to a halt: "Paper Currency they decline meddling with; the Agents dare not stir in it, unless the Ministry will adjust in promoting the Measure." As the imperial crisis grew in proportions, the North regime wanted most of all "to avoid moving momentous questions," especially relating to North America. Hence during the first three years of his stewardship, Parliament did not once engage in major debate on America.[22]

[20] Lawrence H. Gipson, *The British Empire before the American Revolution*, XI (New York, 1965), 133 n. 59; De Berdt to Richard Cary, Nov. 15, 1768, March 29, 1769, Matthews, "Letters of De Berdt," pp. 342, 370; Franklin to Joseph Galloway, Jan. 9, 1769, *Benjamin Franklin's Autobiographical Writings*, ed. Carl Van Doren (New York, 1945), p. 186; Franklin to Thomas Cushing, Feb. 5, 1771, Smyth, V, 295.

[21] Franklin to Galloway, May 20 and Aug. 8, 1767, WCL; Smyth, V, 41; Franklin to John Ross, April 11, 1767, Smyth, V, 23.

[22] Johnson to William Pitkin, March 19, 1767, MHS *Collections*, ser. 5, IX, 219; Garth to S.C. CC, Jan. 27, 1768, *SCHGM*, XXX, 183–184; Arthur Lee

Very soon after taking power in 1770, North's government attempted to intimidate the agents by warning them "that any further opposition to the Ministry will induce the Government to withdraw the several bounties paid for the encouragement of American produce or importation to Great Britain." The admonition was repeated whenever the situation seemed to warrant, and it undoubtedly put a damper upon overt harassment of North and his cabinet. In 1774 stories persisted that the administration unjustly persecuted friends of the colonies. A year later Arthur Lee reported the rumor in London

that if anyone is proceeded against here for corresponding with the people of America, or befriending them here, [the Continental Congress] will immediately seize upon all those in America who correspond with or act for the Ministry. Without such a declaration their friends, & especially their Agents here, will be at the mercy of the most unprincipled Administration that ever disgraced humanity.[23]

Apart from these pressures, ministerial politicians relied on four weapons to keep the agents in check. Parliament could exclude agents from the galleries and avoid hearing remonstrances they tried to present. Administrations could refuse to recognize the legitimacy of an agent's appointment and gain access to his mail through spies and control of the postal system. All four methods effectively undermined lobbying and were utilized simultaneously in an attempt to restrict the agents. Taken together they produced a degree of political frustration that discouraged the entire North American pressure group.

Members of Parliament were by tradition quite conscious of political observers in their gallery. Denying any distinction between internal and external taxation, Charles Townshend glared up at the agents and declaimed: "I speak this aloud, that all you who are in the galleries may hear me." While the Commons sat as a committee of the whole early in 1766 to consider repeal of the Stamp Act, "an Order was made that . . . no Strangers whatever shou'd be admitted within the House." This, however, was a general exclusion, aimed at the press, and not particularly harmful to the agents. Four of them then

to Sam Adams, Oct. 13, 1773, Lee, *Life of Arthur Lee*, I, 237. There were no debates on the American question between May 9, 1770, and March 2, 1774.

[23] *Boston Evening Post*, May 28, 1770, Nov. 1, 1773; Arthur Lee to Francis L. Lee, April 2, 1774, *American Archives*, comp. Peter Force (Washington, D.C., 1837–1846), ser. 4, I, 237; Arthur Lee to ?, Sept. 5, 1775, Lee MSS, Vol. II, HLHU.

held seats and many others testified before the committee personally, thereby gaining entry. But after 1767 a special attempt was made to keep the colonial lobbyists outside and consequently ignorant of debate on American issues.[24]

The agents had been explicitly turned away on occasions in March and April 1767, and were forced to collect scraps from various Members "who are of a communicative turn" in order to relate to their constituents the circumstances of an important session. On May 11 all but Members were excluded, "except the Agents of the Colonies, who had special Leave to be present at the Debates." The business of the East India Company dominated, however, and the colonial question was put off until the thirteenth. On that day the "agents were, by a fresh order, specially excluded." The perplexed lobbyists lingered outside from three until five, and then abandoned their vigil in favor of dinner, but returned and attended until midnight. Within the legislators sat until one o'clock in the morning discussing New York's resistance to billeting troops.[25]

Early in 1768 the agents began maneuvering for repeal of the Townshend duties. Feeling became so intense, however, that they were again excluded, although occasionally an agent arranged clandestine entry by bribing the doorkeeper. The winter session of 1768–1769—significant on account of the Wilkes affair—attracted considerable crowds and the rule was invoked again. Franklin prevailed upon an M.P. "to endeavour obtaining leave for the Agents from America," as colonial issues were at stake also; "but it was deny'd." Both Commons and Lords preferred to seal themselves off from scrutiny.[26]

This pattern recurred regularly during the remaining parliamentary sessions before the Revolution. Traditionally a single Member might demand the expulsion of strangers, but the custom had been neglected

[24] William Samuel Johnson to William Pitkin, Feb. 12, 1767, MHS *Collections,* ser. 5, IX, 215–216; *JHC,* XXX, 513.

[25] Johnson's London diary, entries for March 6, April 30, and May 13, 1767, WSJ MSS; William Strahan to David Hall, May 16, 1767, *PMHB,* X (1886), 322; Johnson to William Pitkin, May 16, 1767, MHS *Collections,* ser. 5, IX, 230; Johnson to Jared Ingersoll, May 16, 1767, NHCHS *Papers,* IX, 407; Garth to S.C. CC, May 17, 1767, *SCHGM,* XXIX, 229–230.

[26] Johnson's London diary, entries for Jan. 1 and 15, Feb. 9 and 29, Dec. 19, 1768, Jan. 31 and Feb. 2, 1769, CHS; Franklin to Joseph Galloway, Dec. 29, 1769, WCL; William Bollan to Samuel Danforth, *Bowdoin and Temple Papers,* p. 123.

for some years. One of North's criteria in choosing a new Speaker of the House in 1770 was that he be a man who would enforce this rule; thereafter North kept "strangers" from the galleries whenever he wished discretion on the subject of a debate. It is ironic that access to the galleries became much more difficult for the agents just at the moment when the press won its great battle for permission to cover parliamentary sessions. What was precisely denied to the North American colonies after 1769 was made available to the fourth estate! Infrequently might an agent manage to violate the restriction against attendance in the Commons' gallery by devious use of connections, as on March 8, 1775, when Franklin sat above the House "staring with his spectacles." The Lords administered their regulations just as faithfully.[27]

Parliament exerted its stringency toward the agents and their employers in a still more devastating way—one that became a public grievance of the First Continental Congress and was eventually embodied in the Declaration of Independence.[28] In eighteenth-century Britain only a county meeting convened by the gentry, or in London a meeting of the county council, could legally petition the government for public changes in church or state (at least twenty signatures were required). Although innumerable private petitions represented the grievances of individuals and institutions, this prohibition operated as an effective check on public remonstrances for more than two-thirds of the century. Only after 1769 with the Wilkite protest, and really not until the Yorkshire movement in 1779–1780, did the modern system of public petitions emerge.[29]

[27] J. Steven Watson, "Parliamentary Procedure as a Key to the Understanding of Eighteenth-Century Politics," *Burke Newsletter*, III (1962), 126; Watson, *Reign of George III*, p. 142; "Strangers in the House," *Blackwood's Edinburgh Magazine*, CVIII (1870), 484–485. Interestingly enough the people's right to know was self-consciously observed in America during the early years of independence and even before. When new statehouses were constructed, provision was made for adequate galleries so that the public could attend legislative debates; see J. R. Pole, *Political Representation in England and the Origins of the American Republic* (London, 1966), pp. 69–70.

[28] *Sources and Documents Illustrating the American Revolution, 1764–1788, and the Formation of the Federal Constitution*, ed. Samuel Eliot Morison (2nd ed.; New York, 1965), p. 119.

[29] Peter Fraser, "Public Petitioning and Parliament before 1832," *History*, XLVI (1961), 200–202; Foord, *His Majesty's Opposition*, pp. 352–353.

As J. Steven Watson has shown, the years from 1690 until 1780 constituted a century when "petty points of procedure were more stressed in Parliament than at any other time." This was especially true in the late 1760's and after with regard to colonial remonstrances—some of which were public and some private. Both houses of Parliament asserted the memorials were too informal, lacking in dignity, unconstitutional, contrary to (long neglected) precedents, or offered by improperly authorized lobbyists. Such pretexts were occasionally employed between 1763 and 1768, but without serious setback to the North American pressure group. After that Parliament began to wield them as a bludgeon upon the heads of agents already excluded from debates. "To refuse hearing complaints," Franklin observed, "from punctilios about form, had always an ill effect, and gave great handle to those turbulent, factious spirits who are ever ready to blow the coals of dissention." [30]

Late in 1768, Pennsylvania sent Franklin and Jackson petitions for crown, Lords, and Commons seeking repeal of the Townshend duties. They never reached their ultimate destination. At first "no member could be found . . . who would venture to offer" them; finally the agents prevailed upon John Huske to do so in the House of Commons. Realizing it would inevitably be denied, he withdrew it, remarking that "if this Petition was rejected, it would probably be the last ever offered them from any Colony on any Occasion." The memorial for the Lords was also obstructed. "Mr. Jackson had it a considerable time in his Hands . . . but finally return'd it to [Franklin], Saying he could not find any one Lord of his Acquaintance willing to present and support it." Pennsylvania's request exceeded the bounds of her royal charter and minimized parliamentary sovereignty. Therefore the Assembly could not have been overly disappointed at its failure. Virginia prepared a tripartite distress signal similar to her northern neighbor's, "in which they say, they do not ask the Repeal of the Acts as a Favour, they claim it as a Right. No Lord or Commoner has yet been found hardy enough to offer either the Memorial or Remonstrance," Franklin reported.[31]

[30] Watson, "Parliamentary Procedure," p. 110; Watson, *Reign of George III*, p. 149; Franklin to William Franklin, Nov. 9, 1765, MFY; Dennys De Berdt to Boston merchants, March 9, 1767, Matthews, "Letters of De Berdt," p. 451.

[31] Franklin to Joseph Galloway, Jan. 9, 1769, *Franklin's Autobiographical Writings*, pp. 186–187; *Letters and Papers of Benjamin Franklin and Richard Jackson, 1753–1785*, ed. Carl Van Doren (Philadelphia, 1947), p. 23.

On January 25, 1769, a great debate arose in the House of Commons following the introduction of resolutions condemning Massachusetts' Circular Letter. It began when William Beckford requested permission to present Bollan's petition from the Massachusetts Council for repeal of the Townshend duties. The House consented to its being read, which Barlow Trecothick did, but divided heavily against referring it to committee. Thereupon the infuriated Trecothick scolded his colleagues roundly. "The practice of refusing to receive petitions from America is, it seems, to be continued. Small things ought to give way to great. Shall we stickle at a little want of form, in a matter where substance is so materially concerned? You throw out of doors the first movement made towards a reconciliation with our colonies." [32] The next day Sir George Savile sought to present another Bollan petition, this time asking the Commons not to concur in resolutions passed earlier by the Lords censuring Massachusetts' General Court, civil magistrates, and inhabitants of Boston. The Members would not receive such an unusual petition any more than its predecessor. It was not even allowed to lie on the table. In March, American affairs again arose. Trecothick moved for permission to lay before the House a petition from New York's Assembly opposing both the Townshend duties and the Restraining Act of 1767. Trecothick and Bollan had conferred in advance, and assumed "the whole matter was couch'd in very decent terms, & granted all the power of government that could be desired, save that of taking money out of their pockets." Nevertheless the ministerial members would not hear the document on grounds that it questioned the parliamentary power of taxation. "Thus, all the applications of the Colonies are rejected or ineffectual," William Samuel Johnson wrote. [33]

The comparable session a year later was equally fruitless. Beckford presented a petition from Bollan opposing the entire revenue system and asking to be heard personally. The House questioned the propriety of Bollan's authority as agent for the Council exclusively, but

[32] *Sir Henry Cavendish's Debates of the House of Commons during the Thirteenth Parliament of Great Britain*, ed. John Wright (London, 1841–1843), I, 185; Bollan to Samuel Danforth, Jan. 30, 1769, *Bowdoin and Temple Papers*, pp. 122–124.

[33] F. J. Gray, "The Parliamentary Career of Sir George Savile, Bart., 1759–1783" (unpub. Ph.D. diss.; Fordham University, 1958), p. 78; *JHC*, XXXII, 151; Johnson to William Pitkin, Feb. 9 and March 23, 1769, MHS *Collections*, ser. 5, IX, 319, 324.

finally agreed to receive the memorial if Bollan's name as agent was stricken. He was then given to think he would be heard and waited outside through seven hours of debate. The Commons eventually adjourned without even calling the lobbyist in, and tabled his petition. Lord North, meanwhile, uttered protestations about always being glad to accept any petition worth hearing. Trecothick again warned the legislators against using flimsy excuses to avoid bringing vexatious colonial questions into the open. "More than one attempt has been made," he said in the Commons, "to bring the distracted state of America before the House; but they all proved abortive." [34]

While Parliament scrutinized its galleries and remonstrances scrupulously after 1767, Whitehall had its own wiles—chiefly harassing the agents by attacking the validity of their credentials. In 1768, Dennys De Berdt complained that as agent of the entire province he could "go with more weight to the Ministry, than [as] the Agent of one House only." Hillsborough, newly entrusted with American affairs, had already told the infirm merchant that he "was in reality no Agent at all." [35] Later in the year De Berdt reported that "his Lordship has made objections of the like nature to several other Agents." At this time Hillsborough first began to use the question of legitimacy to stifle the colonists' efforts to be heard in London through their lobbyists. In his high-handed way he meant to enforce upon the colonies the officially preferred method of choosing agents. Robert Charles was one of his earliest targets. Hillsborough warned Governor Moore that irregularities were frowned upon; and in 1769 he suggested to Moore that petitions submitted to the crown through Charles rather than the governor were considered "irregular and disrespectful." [36]

In 1769, Hillsborough decided to recognize Henry Eustace McCulloh only in matters specifically concerning North Carolina's lower house, thereby forestalling lobbying against the proposed regulations

[34] Bollan to Samuel Danforth, March 6, 1770, *Bowdoin and Temple Papers*, p. 164; *JHC*, XXXII, 745; Wright, *Cavendish's Debates*, I, 552.

[35] De Berdt to Edward Sheafe, Oct. 21, 1767, to Thomas Cushing, June 27, 1768, to Samuel Dexter, June 27, 1768, Matthews, "Letters of De Berdt," pp. 327, 333, 334.

[36] De Berdt to Cushing, Sept. 16, 1768, *ibid.*, p. 341; Hillsborough to Francis Bernard, Feb. 16 and April 4, 1768, Bernard MSS, XI, 137–139, 163–165, HLHU; Hillsborough to Moore, Nov. 15, 1768, March 24 and June 7, 1769, *Documents Relative to the Colonial History of the State of New York*, ed. Edmund B. O'Callaghan (Albany, 1856–1887), VIII, 108, 156, 171.

upon the importation of pitch, tar, and turpentine from America. McCulloh's situation prodded the minister into rationalizing and formalizing his position. This simply obstructed the agents even more and cast a shadow of uncertainty over prospects for future operations. No lower house could of itself appoint a colony agent, Hillsborough dictated—only a personal agent if it wished.[37]

The pressure on Massachusetts increased now, and even more on Bollan as agent for the council. When Parliament seized upon this excuse for not hearing the agent's petition in March 1770, Bollan reflected upon the way arteries connecting the Empire had hardened since 1755. In that year, when an issue came before the Commons, some Members asked that Bollan's authority be shown. He simply answered that his instructions were a private matter between him and his employers and that public inspection would be improper. He insisted, moreover, that power to appear did not depend on such instructions, a point determined earlier by the King in Council. A Member so informed the House and all objection ceased. This may serve as a measure of how much governmental flexibility had tightened in fifteen years, constricting the colonies and their agents in the coils of procedural pretexts designed to choke off the growth of principles disagreeable to the administration.[38]

Early in 1771, Bollan continued to find his position uncertain. The Board of Trade, that is, Hillsborough, denied the validity of his authority again, but reluctantly consented to register him as a duly appointed agent. Bollan knew that if colonial questions came before Parliament he would be hamstrung and warned his constituents that they needed a man backed by the corporate whole. Meanwhile Hillsborough arranged for the colonial governors to veto legislative arrangements for salaries of agents appointed by only one house. When Bollan complained in April, John Pownall informed him that "the agencies of the Colonies had been attended with great uncertainty &

---

[37] *Journal of the Commissioners for Trade and Plantations from January 1768 to December 1775* (London, 1937), p. 88; McCulloh to N.C. CC, July 4, 1769, CRNC, VI, 55; Ella Lonn, *The Colonial Agents of the Southern Colonies* (Chapel Hill, 1945), pp. 142–144.

[38] Thomas Hutchinson to John Pownall, Dec. 28, 1769, MA, XXVI, 423; Francis Bernard to Hutchinson, March 10, 1770, Bernard MSS, VIII, 75–76, HLHU; Bollan to Samuel Danforth, March 8, 1770, *Bowdoin and Temple Papers*, pp. 165–166.

irregularity, so that sometimes it cou'd not be known who had good right to appear; wherefore it was judged proper that the appearance shou'd be made by persons appointed by acts of the several Colonies." Hillsborough regarded the now radical Council of Massachusetts as a group of private persons "who might have an agent if they pleased & pay him themselves." [39]

Franklin and Burke were subjected to similar pressures at the same time, though with less damaging results. Although Burke's name was never registered officially at the plantation office, his transactions as agent were not blocked on account of defective credentials. Admittedly he never had to give official consent to a "public act terminated here in the name of the Province." When Hillsborough attempted to intimidate New York's Assembly into acknowledging the nature of Burke's appointment, the agent threatened to resign rather than become an object of contention between colonial governor and legislature. Franklin's personal prestige protected him somewhat, but he feared the ministerial campaign would "put an end to Agencies, as I apprehend the Assemblies will think [that] Agents under the ministerial Influence that must arise from such Appointments, cannot be of much Use in their Colony Affairs." [40]

In addition to these overt weapons at the disposal of the ministry, there remained a covert device in its arsenal—access to the mails. Court spies and scribes for the *Gazette* commonly attended meetings of radical London organizations. Lacking a centralized intelligence agency, however, the government relied heavily on the post office to open, detain, and even copy correspondence, sending interceptions to the secretaries of state. The Post Office Act of 1711 provided the practice with sufficient legal justification. Suspicious mail might be opened freely, or specifically designated letters searched out. In this way the administration secured copies of letters written by opposition

---

[39] Bollan to Danforth, Jan. 28 and April 15, 1771, *Bowdoin and Temple Papers*, pp. 249–253, 266–267; Bollan to Hillsborough, March 30, 1771, Bowdoin-Temple MSS, Vol. II, MHS; *Royal Instructions to British Colonial Governors, 1670–1776*, ed. Leonard W. Labaree (New York, 1935), I, 387; Thomas Cushing to Franklin, April 20, 1773, Franklin Papers, no. 158, LC.

[40] Ross J. S. Hoffman, *Edmund Burke, New York Agent . . .* (Philadelphia, 1956), p. 107; Cone, *Burke and the Nature of Politics*, I, 254; Franklin to William Franklin, Jan. 30, 1772, Smyth, V, 380.

leaders. The foreign secretary supervised inspection of arcane correspondence, which was then immediately relayed to the crown. After
1766 security arrangements tightened appreciably. The bureaucracy
prepared "plant" letters for foreign courts or agents and searched
suspected letters with special "liquors" for invisible ink.[41]

The lobbyists were particularly affected by these measures; and
until they became aware of such practices they were easy victims. An
agent sending a letter to his constituents commonly placed it in an
open bag hanging in each coffeehouse, waiting for a packet to sail.
After this proved unwise, important communications were frequently
sent with some discreet colonial crossing the Atlantic. But most letters
still had to pass through conventional channels. By the time rebellion
erupted, American mail was being seized on board the packets "and
opened on general warrants on arrival at the Inland office." Late in
1766, Franklin reported to Joseph Galloway that a Pennsylvanian in
London had surreptitiously been reading their letters at the Pennsylvania coffeehouse. Franklin also observed that correspondence he received by a certain packet seemed clumsily opened and resealed.
Hence he warned his confidant to take precautions. Thereafter Franklin began excluding certain political news from his own communications to America. Just when a greater exchange of information might
have fostered a lift in relations, the agents and their correspondents
were forced to guard against repercussions that would result from
exposure of impolitic letters.[42]

In 1769, Dennys De Berdt wrote Speaker Cushing "under cover to
Mr. Cary, as we are timorous of our Letters being open'd." The
following year William Samuel Johnson reported that

all the correspondence with America is now so narrowly watched, and so
much umbrage is taken at the communication of anything, either in point
of fact or opinion, that they are pleased to call improper, that it is become
more than ever necessary for all on this side to request of their friends the
utmost degree of caution with respect to whatever they write . . . lest . . .
they occasion their being so guarded against as to render it impossible for
them to obtain the intelligence they would wish to have communicated.

[41] Henry Marchant's diary, entry for Sept. 9, 1771, RIHS; Kenneth Ellis,
The Post Office in the Eighteenth Century (London, 1958), pp. 62–65, 70;
William Knox to George Grenville, Nov. 1, 1768, Add MSS 42086, ff.
161–162.

[42] Ellis, *Post Office*, pp. 64–65; Franklin to Galloway, Sept. 27, 1766, April
14, 1767, MFY, WCL.

Some imprudences of this kind in some of the other Colonies have been very prejudicial.[43]

In 1771, Franklin warned Cushing that letters from Boston arrived badly sealed, as though they had been opened and crudely closed. "I suspect this may be done by some prying Persons that use the Coffee-house here," he wrote, and asked Cushing to send letters by way of a responsible merchant. Late in 1772 a letter from Franklin's son, the governor of New Jersey, also arrived in London patently examined. The Doctor thought it appeared messier than the usual official job. Instead he suspected "the Letter-Carrier might be corrupted and the Business done between the Office in Lombard Street" and his house. Franklin believed "the Rubbing them open may possibly have been the Ingenuity of Mr. Secretary Knox," Dartmouth's deputy in the American Department. In 1773 the incidence of letters rubbed open increased, and Franklin became even more positive that his reader was Knox and his spy the bellman. By 1775 the administration did not even bother in many cases to forward intercepted letters, but simply kept the originals.[44]

At first enterprising agents might have taken advantage of this situation intentionally to convey facts and sentiments designed for Whitehall's attention. But after 1773 indiscreet and abusive letters from such partisans as Arthur Lee fell into the hands of the colonial office, many of the letters uncomplimentary to Dartmouth himself. In 1775, Burke's report to the New York Assembly on the status of their remonstrance was intercepted, along with many highly political colonial letters. These could only serve to antagonize rather than inform.[45]

As the breach grew wider, North's administration attempted to obscure issues behind picayune points of procedure. This merely placed a chafing bandage over undressed lesions, with not so much as

[43] De Berdt to Cushing, Feb. 13, 1769, Matthews, "Letters of De Berdt," p. 361; Johnson to Jonathan Trumbull, Aug. 20, 1770, MHS *Collections*, ser. 5, IX, 448.

[44] Franklin to Cushing, June 10, 1771, Sept. 15, 1774, Smyth, V, 328, VI, 244; Franklin to William Franklin, Dec. 2, 1772, *ibid.*, V, 462, VI, 31; John Pownall to Arthur Lee, Dec. 23, 1775, PRO CO 5/154 (2), f. 206.

[45] Lee to ?, Dec. 22, 1773, Thomas Hutchinson to Dartmouth, March 30, 1774, Dartmouth MSS, Vol. I, ii, nos. 922, 964, WSL; HMC *14th Report, Appendix, Part X, The Manuscripts of the Earl of Dartmouth*, II (*American Papers*) (London, 1895), 347.

a little balm to keep the bandage itself from becoming a dangerous irritant to the festering sores it covered. Whitehall's effort to avoid the real problems by silencing the colonial agents had the effect of frustrating both constituents and lobbyists, so that when the ultimate crisis occurred, inertia replaced the quickened impulses of 1765–1766. Conditioned to expect failure, many felt powerless, and inaction resulted. Until 1768 the colonists assumed "that humble dutiful Remonstrances may yet have their Effect." During the parliamentary session of 1768–1769, the first serious signs of discouragement were discernible. Some agents communicated this privately in letters to America. John Huske asked his fellow Members in the House of Commons outright: "What will be the consequence of paying no attention to petitions from America?" [46]

Franklin wrote the Georgia legislature not to bother sending petitions questioning Parliament's right to tax the colonies. They would not be received. Even John Wilkes informed his Boston correspondents in 1769 that petitions to both Whitehall and Westminster were useless albeit necessary as *pro forma* gestures. The colonials responded accordingly. As Samuel Cooper wrote, "many among us are of opinion that it would be best for the Colonies to have no Agent and concern ourselves no more about Remonstrances and Petitions, which have had hitherto so little effect." Nevertheless several among the North American lobby remained undaunted and continued in 1770 to submit memorials for consideration, particularly Trecothick and Bollan. The latter still had faith in the petitioning process, even though friends told him his own efforts would be "fruitless." [47]

Early in 1773, Franklin wrote his son that he grew weary of endless obstacles to lobbying. He wanted to return to Philadelphia. A year later the Doctor poured out his irritation to Thomas Cushing.

When I see that all petitions and complaints of grievances are so odious to government, that even the mere pipe which conveys them becomes obnox-

[46] William Samuel Johnson to William Pitkin, Nov. 18, 1768, Jan. 3, 1769, MHS *Collections*, ser. 5, IX, 303, 309; Bollan to Samuel Danforth, Jan. 30, 1769, *Bowdoin and Temple Papers*, p. 123; Wright, *Cavendish's Debates*, I, 84.

[47] Franklin to Noble W. Jones, April 3, 1769, *Colonial Records of the State of Georgia*, ed. A. D. Candler (Atlanta, 1904–1916), XV, 26; Wilkes to William Palfrey, Sept. 27, 1769, George M. Elsey, "John Wilkes and William Palfrey," CSM *Publications*, XXXIV (1943), 415; Cooper to Thomas Pownall, Sept. 8, 1769, "Letters of Samuel Cooper to Thomas Pownall, 1769–1777," ed. Frederick Tuckerman, *AHR*, VIII (1903), 311.

ious, I am at a loss to know how peace and union are to be maintained or restored between the different parts of the empire. Greivances cannot be redressed unless they are known; and they cannot be known but through complaints and petitions. If these are deemed affronts, and the messengers punished as offenders, who will hence-forth send petitions? And who will deliver them? It has been thought a dangerous thing in any state to stop up the vent of griefs. Wise governments have therefore generally received petitions with some indulgence, even when but slightly founded. Those who think themselves injured by their rulers are sometimes, by a mild and prudent answer, convinced of their error. But where complaining is a crime, hope becomes despair.[48]

The agents found equally annoying a tendency in Britain to ignore or minimize the importance of colonial questions. As early as 1765 such a well-placed official as Thomas Whately informed Grenville that the antagonisms aroused in America "will prove only a popular cry of the day, not attended with any consequences." Four years later William Samuel Johnson cautioned his constituents that the administration had "long listened to the flattering, fallacious representations of their interested, wretched sycophants, and persuaded themselves that the opposition in America was no more than a petty, desperate, dying faction, not worth their notice." During the session of 1770, Burke loudly deplored "Parliament's having done nothing to keep its promise to take American affairs into serious consideration." When a general election occurred in 1774, not a single campaign was influenced to any marked extent by the situation abroad. Even in Bristol, where Burke and Henry Cruger were candidates, the contest involved little discussion of American issues. Charles Garth's Wiltshire constituents returned him unanimously, conspicuously ignoring his connection with South Carolina and various overt acts of partisanship toward North America.[49]

Ministries that held power after 1766 underestimated the significance of the imperial crisis and the extent of provincial patriotism.

[48] Franklin to William Franklin, March 15, 1773, to Cushing, Feb. 15, 1774, *The Complete Works of Benjamin Franklin,* ed. John Bigelow (New York, 1887), V, 116–117, 302–303.

[49] Whately to Grenville, Oct. 25, 1765, Grenville MSS in the possession of Sir John Murray, London; Johnson to Jonathan Trumbull, Oct. 16, 1769, MHS *Collections,* ser. 5, IX, 375; Hoffman, *Burke,* p. 68; Lewis B. Namier, *Skyscrapers and Other Essays* (London, 1931), p. 36; P. T. Underdown, "Henry Cruger and Edmund Burke: Colleagues and Rivals at the Bristol Election of 1774," 3*WMQ,* XV (1958), 14–34; Garth to S.C. CC, Dec. 7, 1774, Garth Letter-book, pp. 181–182, SCA.

They did not believe the uneasiness in America was general, but rather that only a factious few questioned Parliament's sovereignty. Even after news of the Boston Tea Party reached London, Burke observed that "any Remarkable Highway Robbery at Hounslow Heath would make more conversation than all the disturbances of America." North's government took no notice of this affair for two full months, keeping a stony silence all the while.[50]

THE DECLINE OF INFLUENCE

Between 1766 and 1775 the strength of colonial influence in London declined, first gradually and then precipitously. The fortunes of the agents are symptomatic of this declension and provide a rough measure by which its progress can be determined. Their experiences and observations reveal with notable clarity what the process of imperial deterioration meant at the center of government in England.

The Rockinghams' departure from office in August 1766 did not seem to cause the agents undue apprehension, though Dennys De Berdt observed that the colonies had "lost several Good friends by the Change." The forthcoming session seemed promising. By the following March, however, William Samuel Johnson wrote his constituents that the colonies had lost allies during the winter, particularly among the merchants and freeholders. He repeated the disappointing message that summer when the Townshend duties were enacted. Charles Garth then informed the South Carolina Committee of Correspondence that "the Friends of America are too few to have any share in a Struggle with a Chancellor of the Exchequer." From July 1765 until January 1768, Henry Seymour Conway, essentially sympathetic to the colonies, served as leader of the House of Commons. His replacement, Lord North, remained in that capacity for fourteen years. In October 1768 both Chatham and Shelburne resigned. In consequence America lacked a strong friend in the cabinet.[51]

---

[50] William Samuel Johnson to Jared Ingersoll, March 8, 1769, WSJ MSS (box), Vol. I; Burke to Rockingham, Feb. 2, 1774, *The Correspondence of Edmund Burke, 1768–1774*, ed. Lucy S. Sutherland, II (Chicago, 1960), 524; Cone, *Burke and the Nature of Politics*, I, 258.

[51] De Berdt to Thomas Cushing, Sept. 2, 1766, Matthews, "Letters of De Berdt," p. 325; Johnson to Jonathan Trumbull, March 14, 1767, to S. Gray, June 9, 1767, WSJ MSS; Garth to S.C. CC, July 5, 1767, SCHGM, XXIX, 298–300.

As the session of 1769 progressed, Franklin, De Berdt, and Johnson lamented abuses the colonies were receiving; "but how must we be surprised to reflect that some of that very administration were once, viz. at the Repeal of the stamp act, our warmest advocates, and even got their places in some degree by espousing our Cause." De Berdt gave one correspondent a detailed rundown: "Several of your old friends are gone into Ministerial measures, particularly Lord Camb-den who now sees clearly the right of taxing America; General Con-way is grown old & indifferent; Lord Chatham now lies quite aside, & Mr. Onslow, son of the late great commoner, is in the treasury, & the Duke of Grafton at the head of it." [52]

In 1770, Franklin complained to several friends that no one in North's new cabinet was favorably disposed towards the colonies. The winter sitting seems to have been a turning point. At first the cabinet had been divided almost equally between those who would repeal all the Townshend taxes and the followers of Hillsborough who advo-cated only a partial repeal. When Grafton, Conway, and Camden left office, the Bedford faction swung the balance toward partial revoca-tion. [53] Subsequent cabinet changes would be even more damaging to the North American interest. In 1771, Lord Suffolk, new leader of the Grenvillites, came in along with another figure hostile to the colonies, Alexander Wedderburn. Soon Lord Rochford, prominent among those urging firmness, would shift from the Northern to the Southern Department. With the ambivalent exception of Dartmouth, who suc-ceeded Hillsborough as American secretary in 1772, the cabinet was clearly going to stand firm in the event of an American crisis. [54]

Simultaneously the agents also came to realize that their "friends" among the opposition minorities were often motivated by principles and pressures quite removed from any intrinsic sympathy for colonial aspirations. In 1769, Arthur Lee wrote his brother that Shelburne was the "only one attached to us from principle." Chatham, Rockingham, and the radical Duke of Richmond were merely "against opposing us." During the legislative session that year William Samuel Johnson

[52] Franklin to Joseph Galloway, Jan. 29, 1769, WCL; Johnson to R. Walker, March 12, 1769, WSJ MSS (box), Vol. I; De Berdt to Richard Cary, Feb. 2, 1769, Matthews, "Letters of De Berdt," p. 358.
[53] Franklin to Joshua Babcock, Feb. 26, 1770, MFY; Franklin to ?, March 18, 1770, Smyth, V, 252; Franklin to Joseph Galloway, March 21, 1770, Rosenbach Foundation, Philadelphia.
[54] Watson, *Reign of George III*, 150–151, 154.

cynically but astutely observed that the Rockinghams really did not seem so very enthusiastic to repeal the Townshend Revenue Act, "but rather that it should remain to embarrass the present Ministers, and as a means of their destruction, to whom they hope to succeed. They had rather have the honor of doing it themselves, and mean in their turn to govern the Colonies, though in a different way." [55]

Burke's criticism of the administration during these debates was directed at the bungled management of American affairs that discredited British authority. He had no particular brief to argue on behalf of the beleaguered colonists. In 1770, Franklin recognized that any of the opposition leaders in power would uphold the concept of parliamentary sovereignty, though probably not implement it in practice. Early in 1774, when the Coercive Acts were being considered in Parliament, "great disappointment took place by the principal persons, men of the greatest weight in the opposition, not speaking at all." [56]

Disillusioned with the opposition, colonists and agents did not know where to turn for support. In desperation they clung to Chatham; but that statesman, ravaged by gout and chronic fits of mental depression, had little prospect of power—either ministerial or as a dispassionate voice of authority above politics. Nevertheless, the lobbyists faithfully kept him abreast of every whisper and remonstrance loosed by the colonists, seeking his favor and hoping for his return to governmental activity. [57] The agents' pilgrimages to his country seat, Hayes, became known in London, and were incorporated into anecdotes full of significance despite their distortion. An English Tory took delight in relating one of these to a friend.

Now remember I do not write this to you as gospel, but take it as I got it, as you may the following droll anecdote of that charlatan in politicks, Lord Chatham. It seems Dr. Franklin and some other of the agents waited upon him and told him they were instructed by the Congress to wait upon his Lordship to know if he approved of what they had done and in everything to be directed by him. They have done extremely right and just what they ought, answered his Lordship. But, my Lord, what steps shall we next take

[55] Lee to [Richard H. Lee?], Sept. 18, 1769, Lee, *Life of Arthur Lee*, I, 191; Johnson to William Pitkin, April 11, 1767, April 26, 1769, MHS *Collections*, ser. 5, IX, 226, 338–339.

[56] Hoffman, *Burke*, 71, 189–190; Franklin to ?, March 18, 1770, Smyth, V, 252; Bollan to John Erving *et al.*, March 15, 1774, Force, *American Archives*, ser. 4, I, 228.

[57] Bollan to Chatham, Sept. 29, 1774, PRO 30/8/20, f. 78.

should neither the King or Parliament attend to their petition but proceed
to coercive measures as is suspected? At this instant my Lord was seized
with a violent gouty pain. Oh! Oh! that cruel tormenting disease that
seizes me always when I apply my mind intensely to business. . . . I am
in such agony. Come some other day. O no, I shall send to let you know
when I am able to confer with you; and so dismissed them without any
answer to that very important question, and as yet has not sent for them.[58]

While courting Chatham's favor, the lobbyists neglected the Rockinghams, a faction with sounder prospects and a greater willingness to
participate in political skirmishing. By failing to supply the Marquess
faithfully in the 1770's with news of the colonies, the agents allowed
Thomas Hutchinson to slip into the role of Rockingham's authority on
American affairs. As interpreter of the provincial situation, Hutchinson presented His Lordship with an unfavorable view of the course of
colonial radicalism.[59]

Apart from specific losses in influence among the ministries and
their opposition, the agents encountered a general decline in sympathy
for America at Parliament. Many memorials that would have been
submitted to the governmental boards under normal conditions had to
be offered to Parliament instead during these years. Hence the composition and inclination of its membership became vitally important to
lobbyists. Unfortunately the outlook of the imperial legislature turned
increasingly hostile to the colonies and their agents after 1766. In
April 1767, De Berdt reported "a strange temper prevailing" in the
Commons, one that made it difficult for the administration to achieve
aims unobtrusively for overseas possessions. Two years later Johnson
found it "surprising how few friends we have there [in the House of
Commons], who are so upon real principle. I fear I could not name
above five or six; but those who will be so upon the ground of
opposition may be pretty numerous." [60]

When the Massachusetts Circular Letter and *Liberty* affair became

[58] John Pringle to Walter Scott, Jan. 30, 1775, HMC *Report on the
Manuscripts of Lord Polwarth . . .* (London, 1961), V, 370.
[59] De Berdt to Edward Sheafe, Nov. 23, 1769, Matthews, "Letters of De
Berdt," 388; Stephen Sayre to Sam Adams, Sept. 18, 1770, Adams MSS,
NYPL.
[60] De Berdt to ?, April 10, 1767, MA, Letters, 1764–1774, 52–53; Johnson
to William Pitkin, Jan. 3 and May 25, 1769, MHS *Collections*, ser. 5, IX, 310,
346–347.

objects of debate in 1769, the friends of America—Thomas Pownall, Barré, Dowdeswell, Rose Fuller, Beckford, Burke, and Trecothick—would not exactly defend the Boston proceedings, but at least found ways to excuse them. By 1770 a colonial visiting London relayed depressing news to his father: "Parliament is composed of men who are out of the way of being affected by the Distresses of America." Thereafter the decline became headlong, causing the agents to reflect nostalgically upon the days when their institution carried weight.[61]

As a chill settled upon the colonial interest, it became increasingly difficult to find Members willing to espouse the American cause. During the Stamp Act crisis, Sir William Meredith had handled Montagu's memorial from Virginia; but Meredith cooled perceptibly as the decade progressed, and accepted a government post from Lord North in 1772. Arthur Onslow, formerly Speaker of the House of Commons, had been receptive to De Berdt in 1765–1766, and "very explicitly in the favour of America." But his long life ended in 1768. During the Stamp Act campaign, De Berdt's petitions were also handled by Conway and George Cooke, "our member for Middlesex, a man of considerable Influence in the House & Chairman of the American Committee." But Cooke, a friend of Richard Jackson's, also died in 1768.[62]

In 1768–1769, Jackson could find no peer willing to present Pennsylvania's protest against the Townshend duties to the House of Lords. John Huske, who handled it in the Commons, had worked for repeal in 1766 and collaborated with the agents until 1769, when he fled to France to escape prosecution for deficiencies in his accounts as deputy treasurer of the chamber. He died there in 1773. In 1769 De Berdt relied on Isaac Barré, follower of Chatham and Shelburne, to handle a remonstrance from Boston against Governor Bernard. Barré also befriended William Samuel Johnson by introducing him to English political society; and in 1771, Arthur Lee considered the colonel America's sincerest friend in London. By 1774, however, Barré voted

---

[61] William Samuel Johnson to William Pitkin, Feb. 9, 1769, *ibid.*, p. 313; Thomas Coombe, Jr., to his father, Oct. 3, 1770, Coombe MSS, HSP; Franklin to James Bowdoin, Jan. 13, 1772, Smyth, V, 358.

[62] "William Meredith," *DNB*; De Berdt to Samuel White, Jan. 16 and Feb. 15, 1766, Matthews, "Letters of De Berdt," pp. 310–312; "H. S. Conway," *DNB*; D. J. Turner, "George III and the Whig Opposition (1760–1794)" (unpub. Ph.D. diss.; University of Nottingham, 1953), p. 245.

with the administration in favor of the Boston Port bill and presented no colonial memorials thereafter.[63]

In 1769, Bollan found a parliamentary patron in Sir George Savile, a Rockingham Whig of vast wealth and the greatest of the independent country gentlemen. Savile remained a friend until 1774. He was by then tired of public life, frustrated by his political impotence, and ready to quit London altogether. When Bollan asked him to sponsor a petition in March against the Coercives, "he declined the presentation because he was in honour obliged various ways to apply himself closely to another business." Between 1768 and 1770, Bollan had also gained considerable support from William Beckford, Lord Mayor of London and one of the richest men in the British empire. His death in 1770 deprived the colonies of a warm and colorful friend.[64]

Early in 1774, William Dowdeswell, Lord Mayor Frederick Bull, and Sir Joseph Mawbey agreed to sponsor certain of Bollan's petitions in the Commons; their support proved ephemeral. The agent shortly found Savile unreliable. Dowdeswell was ill and near death, and Mawbey lost his seat in the parliamentary election. The Lord Mayor soon proved "less spirited for the business than before, and inclined to postpone the presentation." At best "the chief members in the House were more inclined to support than present" memorials. In the Lords, Bollan met a comparable situation. Only Camden and the radical Duke of Richmond, hated by George III, remained as patrons.[65]

The friendship or capacity of other politicians to help the colonies declined apace. The Earl of Northington, president of the Privy Council in 1766–1767, was "an old and infirm gentleman, not very able to attend the trial of causes, and is beside enough concerned in

[63] Lewis B. Namier and John Brooke, *The History of Parliament: The House of Commons, 1754–1790* (London, 1964), I, 159; Benjamin Franklin to Joseph Galloway, Jan. 9, 1769, Van Doren, *Franklin's Autobiographical Writings,* p. 188; De Berdt to Thomas Cushing, June 1, 1769, Matthews, "Letters of De Berdt," p. 375; memoirs of William Samuel Johnson, misc. box, WSJ MSS; Arthur Lee to Sam Adams, June 10, 1771, Lee, *Life of Arthur Lee,* I, 215; Alexander Elmsley to Samuel Johnston, May 17, 1774, *CRNC,* IX, 1001; "Isaac Barré," *DNB.*

[64] Bollan to Samuel Danforth, Jan. 30, 1769, March 6, 1770, *Bowdoin and Temple Papers,* pp. 123–124, 164; Gray, "Career of George Savile," pp. 128, 131–132; Bollan to John Erving *et al.,* Force, *American Archives,* ser. 4, I, 226.

[65] Bollan to John Erving, March 11, 15, and 23, 1774, Force, *American Archives,* ser. 4, I, 226–227, 230; Bollan to Erving, April 1 and May 2, 1774, misc. bound MSS, MHS.

the present disquietudes and cabals of the Court to engross all the attention he is able to give to business." Johnson, Jackson, and Life were particularly affected by Northington's disinterest because he would preside over the Mohegan hearings if his "distemper" permitted. It did not. Jeremiah Dyson, M.P. and Treasury lord, headed an important parliamentary committee and had considerable influence. In 1764 he had willingly expedited the passage of special legislation favorable to the colonies. Five years later, however, he joined North in opposing repeal of the Townshend duties. When Henry Marchant sought Dyson's favor in 1772 for Rhode Island's delayed claims, he proved amiable but did nothing to help the agent.[66]

Rose Fuller, an absentee West Indian planter and brother of Jamaica's agent, had vigorously opposed the Stamp Act. During the 1760's he remained friendly to the American position, presiding over the committee of the whole House of Commons when repeal of the Stamp Act was debated. According to Horace Walpole, Fuller's partiality for repeal governed his conduct in the chair. But by 1772 he was considered a "ministerial man." The Tea Party infuriated him so much that he proposed levying a £20,000 fine on Boston as punishment. Sir William Baker remained a warm exponent of colonial views until his retirement in 1768. He died two years later. His son, also William, participated actively in public affairs until the early seventies, when his interest waned. He gradually withdrew from both politics and the American trade his father had established. In 1774, Baker persuaded the merchants to present a petition seeking the restoration of colonial commerce. Soon thereafter he lost his parliamentary seat when his patron failed to support him in the general election.[67]

In 1774, Thomas Hutchinson wrote a colonial patriot that some who "formerly espoused your cause are now as forward as any in condemning you, particularly Governor Pownall." No figure in Brit-

[66] Richard Jackson to William Pitkin, Nov. 8, 1766, CHS *Collections*, XIX (Hartford, 1921), 49; Johnson to Jonathan Trumbull, March 14, 1767, to William Pitkin, March 23 and April 26, 1769, MHS *Collections*, ser. 5, IX, 328, 336, 488; *JHC*, XXXII, 895; Marchant's London diary, *passim*, RIHS.

[67] *Gentleman's Magazine*, XLVII (1777), 247; Horace Walpole, *Memoirs of the Reign of King George III*, ed. C. F. Bucker (New York, 1894), II, 78, 213, 300; *The Last Journals of Horace Walpole during the Reign of George III . . . 1771–1783*, ed. A. F. Steuart (London, 1910), I, 53; Lewis B. Namier, *The Structure of Politics at the Accession of George III* (2nd ed.; London, 1960), pp. 115–118; Turner, "George III and the Whig Opposition," pp. 245, 409.

ish political life reveals the decline of colonial connections more clearly than Thomas Pownall, governor of Massachusetts until 1760, M.P. from 1767 until 1780, and author of *The Administration of the Colonies.* He was one of the best informed men on American problems and very proud of that fact. In 1764, George Croghan found Pownall could not "bear any body to know any thing in North America So well as himself." Later that year, as soon as Franklin reached London, he conferred with "the Governor" about plans for a colonial paper currency. In six weeks' time, they submitted a carefully considered scheme to George Grenville. Failing in that, they tried again in December 1765, this time pressuring Rockingham. But other concerns took priority at that point. Pownall warmly befriended Johnson during his agency. Others among the North American lobby, however, looked upon "the Governor" less favorably. De Berdt, whose office Pownall coveted, mistrusted him, found him very officious, and wondered "whether he is a real friend to America or no." [68]

Pownall regarded many of America's lobbyists with contempt, considered them corrupt and ignorant, and "too apt to convert their powers to their own importance." In place of agents he recommended that a "patron" be employed in England to treat with the ministry. But by 1770 his integrity and influence had become uncertain as far as the colonies were concerned. Franklin wrote that "Mr. Pownall appears a warm and zealous Friend to the Colonies in Parliament, but unfortunately he is very ill heard at present." Whenever he rose to speak on behalf of America, the conservatives either left the House of Commons or else started a deafening din. Bollan, whom Pownall regarded as a hack, considered him a friend in 1769. At this time Thomas held somewhat different opinions on colonial issues from his brother John; they would soon coincide. [69]

At what point Thomas Pownall "went over" is difficult to ascertain.

[68] *The Diary and Letters of Thomas Hutchinson,* ed. Peter O. Hutchinson (Boston, 1884–1886), I, 220; John A. Schutz, *Thomas Pownall: British Defender of American Liberty* (Glendale, Calif., 1951), pp. 203, 223–224; Croghan to Sir William Johnson, March 10, 1764, *The Critical Period,* *1763–1765,* eds. C. W. Alvord and C. E. Carter (Springfield, Ill., 1915), p. 223; Franklin and Pownall to Grenville, Feb. 12, 1765, MFY; Pownall to Thomas Hutchinson, Dec. 3, 1765, MA, XXV, 112–113a; De Berdt to Thomas Cushing, Nov. 19, 1768, Matthews, "Letters of De Berdt," p. 345.

[69] Schutz, *Pownall,* p. 223; Joseph Harrison to John Temple, April 15, 1766, Bollan to Samuel Danforth, May 6, 1769, *Bowdoin and Temple Papers,* pp. 73, 137; Franklin to Samuel Cooper, Feb. 24, 1769, Smyth, V, 197.

Before 1770 one agent suspected his good faith—"as irresolute as the Wind, in one days debate a friend to America, the next quite with the Ministry." The effect of such vacillation earned him the opprobrium of both sides. By 1773 the apostasy was probably completed. "Mr. Pownall has, I hear, sayd the government are solliciting him to go over." In August Pownall and North discussed how best to employ the former's services. In 1774 he supported the ministerial policy of penal measures against America and accepted a position at the disposal of the crown.[70]

The speakers of the House of Commons provide another gauge (and a crucial one) by which to judge colonial fortunes. By the 1750's the speaker had taken command of the administrative machinery of the House. He supervised the fees taken by lesser officials and took responsibility for their actions. The clerk, sergeant at arms, messengers, housekeepers, and doorkeepers all answered to him. Thus his favor and influence were vital to the agents as parliamentary lobbyists. Sir Arthur Onslow, who served for decades until 1761 and transformed the office, had been a good friend of the colonists and of such agents as Jackson and De Berdt. Sir John Cust, elected in 1761, served until his death in 1770. He was not a success, largely because he allowed great license in debate and often lost control of the House. Nevertheless he was diligent and impartial; and as a member of the Privy Council, important for the agents to cultivate. Franklin, Jackson, and Johnson were on quite good terms with him. The lobbyists dined with him on occasion, and Franklin even received patronage recommendations from him.[71]

Cust's successor, Sir Fletcher Norton, was proposed by North in 1770 in order to have a firmer hand guiding (or repressing) constitutional debates on the American question. His selection was both deliberate and unfortunate for the colonies. An experienced lawyer, he had held places under Bute and Grenville, but was dismissed by

<hr/>

[70] De Berdt to Richard Cary, Jan. 3, 1769, Matthews, "Letters of De Berdt," p. 352; Frederick Vane to John Temple, [July 1773?], *Bowdoin and Temple Papers*, p. 307; Pownall to Dartmouth, Aug. 10, 1773, Dartmouth MSS, vol. II, No. 679, WSL; Turner, "George III and the Whig Opposition," pp. 244, 296.

[71] J. Steven Watson, "Arthur Onslow and Party Politics," *Essays in British History Presented to Sir Keith Feiling*, ed. H. R. Trevor-Roper (London, 1964), pp. 158–159, 165–166; Van Doren, *Franklin and Jackson*, p. 86; De Berdt to Samuel White, Jan. 16, 1766, to Thomas Cushing, Sept. 19, 1766, Matthews, "Letters of De Berdt," pp. 310, 326; "John Cust," *DNB*; Johnson to Jared Ingersoll, Feb. 18, 1767, WSJ MSS; Franklin to ?, June 6, 1766, MFY.

Rockingham in 1765. For the next five years he pleaded various cases boldly at the bar, where his greed earned him the sobriquet "Sir Bull Face Double Fee." From 1767 until his accession he served Connecticut as occasional counsel in the Mohegan case, and in that capacity saw a good deal of Jackson and Johnson. The latter admired Norton's legal abilities and relied on him for advice. The other agents, however, regretted Norton's acquisition of the speakership. (He had accused Pitt in 1766 of fomenting rebellion by siding with the colonies against the Stamp Act.") The Whigs tried but failed to prevent Norton's election in 1770. In the chair he ruled the Commons with greater firmness than Cust, even to the extent of wrangling with various Members. Rough, insolent, and a notorious bully, he sometimes used his position to browbeat minorities. His outlook became increasingly anticolonial. In 1774, William Bollan reported that "the Speaker had endeavoured to throw cold water upon my Petition." Norton served his patron, Lord North, well.[72]

Still another facet of declining parliamentary influence was reflected in the decreasing value of agent-Members. Burke did not consistently convert his membership to the specific advantage of his American employers. When the Quebec bill of 1774 loosely defined the boundaries of New York, he asked for greater precision and the amendments he proposed were accepted. More often Burke found his dual allegiance an unhappy burden. As a Member of the House of Commons he felt it was improper for him to appear there as the protagonist of a special interest. Only in 1775, when he offered New York's remonstrance on the floor of the Commons, did he actually discharge an agency assignment in Parliament, "and then his behavior was half-hearted and perfunctory."[73]

Along with the other agents holding House seats, Burke was subjected to criticism for his two offices.[74] Unlike Charles Garth, he avoided recognizing or resolving his pluralistic predicament until

[72] A. I. Dasent, *The Speakers of the House of Commons* (London, 1911), pp. 276–281; Johnson to William Pitkin, Feb. 12 and April 11, 1767, to Jonathan Trumbull, Feb. 3, 1770, MHS *Collections*, ser. 5, IX, 214, 222, 405; Bollan to John Erving, *et al.*, March 15, 1774, Force, *American Archives*, ser. 4, I, 227.

[73] Cone, *Burke and the Nature of Politics*, I, 255; Hoffman, *Burke*, pp. 179, 190.

[74] See Lewis B. Namier, "Charles Garth, Agent for South Carolina," *EHR*, LIV (1939), 645; Verner W. Crane, "Three Fables by Benjamin Franklin," *NEQ*, IX (1936), 502.

1774, and then he did so ambiguously. Early in 1766, Garth had written his constituents that

> the point in dispute between Great Britain and her Colonies is doubtless the only possible Point that could have been unpleasant to me in the Situation. I stand as a Representative in Parliament and an Agent for a Distinguished part of America. . . . This Situation of Mine had render'd it more than Ordinary incumbent upon me (even was it not a Duty in a particular manner owing to you) fully to inform my mind and Understanding upon so great a Question.[75]

Unfortunately the intellectual development of the Great Debate sooner or later imposed upon each agent so perplexed a moment of decision. The outcome always favored the supreme legislature, creating an invisible but recognizable distinction among the lobbyists.[76] When elections occurred, as in 1768 and 1774, the agent-M.P. had to protect his place. Campaigning not only diverted him from the steady continuum of effective lobbying, but raised embarrassing questions about allegiance as well.[77]

As individuals the agents outside Parliament found their points of contact ever diminishing. McCulloh remarked characteristically in 1767, "The Gentleman on whom I relied, has experienced the mutability of Fortune." Franklin and Arthur Lee suffered similarly in 1773, when John Temple's circumstances fell because of the Hutchinson letters he allegedly procured. Then surveyor-general of customs in England, the impulsive Temple had access to various parts of the bureaucracy and had thereby obtained extraordinarily useful information for the agents. In 1774, North dismissed Temple without explanation.[78]

Excessive chauvinism may have alienated some agents' connec-

---

[75] Burke to N.Y. CC, Feb. 2, 1774, Sutherland, *Burke Correspondence, 1768–1774,* II, 522; Garth to S.C. CC, Jan. 19, 1766, *SCHGM,* XXVI, 71–72; Namier, "Garth, Agent," 645.

[76] James Abercromby to ?, Jan. 6, 1764, Add MSS 38204, ff. 9–10; Richard Jackson to Jared Ingersoll, March 22, 1766, NHCHS *Papers,* IX, 383; Wright, *Cavendish's Debates,* II, 439; Namier and Brooke, *History of Parliament,* I, 162.

[77] Entry for March 25, 1774, Matthew Brickdale's parliamentary debates, MS minute book, No. 10, BUL; Franklin to Pa. CC, March 13, 1768, Smyth, V, 119.

[78] McCulloh to Edmund Fanning, Sept. 12, 1767, Fanning-McCulloh Papers, No. 252, Southern History Collection, University of North Carolina Library, Chapel Hill; Lee to Sam Adams, Dec. 22, 1773, Adams MSS, NYPL; Hutchinson, *Hutchinson Diary and Letters,* I, 192.

tions. Johnson admitted in 1767 that he had perhaps estranged several Britons by tactlessly making comparisons unfavorable to the mother country. His colleague De Berdt probably deluded himself into believing influence existed where there was none. Hence William Tudor's caustic observation: "The habitual deference of most persons of his [De Berdt's] standing in England, to mere titled rank, prevents the due exercise of the faculties in their presence; and the talking a '*whole hour with his lordship*,' seems to have prepared his mind for any belief whatever." [79]

Franklin had two medical friends in England whose political support was lost, in varying degrees, as a result of the Great Debate. He valued Dr. John Pringle, the royal physician, who remained a reliable contact for a decade, despite the controversy that electrified London between 1769 and 1772 over the merits of pointed as against round-knob lightning rods. George III ordered Pringle, president of the Royal Society, to support the merits of round knobs, which Franklin flatly opposed. When Pringle approved of pointed rods, the King forced his resignation. In any case Pringle became disillusioned with colonial behavior by 1775.[80] Dr. John Fothergill acquired political significance because he numbered among his patients Franklin, Dartmouth, Sir Fletcher Norton, and Grenville. But once when Fothergill attended Grenville, the latter, after listening for a while to his healer's views on America, gave him five guineas and dismissed him, saying "really, doctor, I am so much better that I don't want you to prescribe for me." In 1768, Fothergill wrote William Logan that "America will require all her friends to assist her. Many she has lost, others she has made ashamed to appear in her behalf." In the winter of 1774–1775, Fothergill and David Barclay served as the fulcrum for secret political negotiations between Franklin and the administration. When these proved abortive, even Fothergill recognized that colonial ideology had swept the provincials and their representatives beyond what he considered the bounds of reason.[81]

[79] Johnson to Eliphalet Dyer, April 10, 1767, WSJ MSS; De Berdt to Thomas Cushing, July 19 and Aug. 26, 1768, Matthews, "Letters of De Berdt," pp. 336, 338; William Tudor, *The Life of James Otis . . .* (Boston, 1823), p. 325.

[80] Leonard W. Labaree, "Benjamin Franklin's British Friendships," APS *Proceedings*, CVIII (1964), 425–426; John Fothergill to Benjamin Franklin, March 1775, Franklin Papers, No. 2217, LC.

[81] "An Account of Negotiations in London," Smyth, VI, 399; R. H. Fox, *Dr. John Fothergill and His Friends* (London, 1919), 317 n. 3, 320; B. D. Bargar, *Lord Dartmouth and the American Revolution* (Columbia, S.C., 1965), pp. 133–134, 137.

Finally, the various radical societies that were formed in England, and especially in London, during these years underwent internal disagreements that reduced their helpfulness to the agents. The Bill of Rights Society, for example, in which Arthur Lee participated, was riven by dissension, unable to settle on the best policies to pursue. If Lee sided with any group within the Society he alienated the rest.[82]

Altogether political instability and its consequences became the bane of Anglo-American cooperation during the decade before 1776. The most certain basis for equilibrium increasingly appeared to lie in a firmer colonial policy. North and Hillsborough took that view beginning in 1768 and acted upon it in ways that virtually ruined the agency as an effective institution. Their views, moreover, shaped those of men responsible for implementing policy through colonial administration. Their alienation from America remained the final blow to hopes for conciliation through the agents.

[82] Lee to Sam Adams, June 14, 1771, April 7, 1772, Adams MSS, NYPL; Henry Marchant to Ezra Stiles, Sept. 21, 1771, Stiles MSS, YUL.

CHAPTER 13

A Decline of Influence: The Agents and Imperial Administration

Departmentalism is one of the most characteristic of bureaucratic defects. Often it indicates a serious deterioration in the administrative system as a whole. In the absence of a joint sense of purpose, there will inevitably be chronic friction, a situation commonly caused by the expansion of existing organizational units. When new purposes have to be executed with insufficient preparation, the administrative centers of gravity shift and new men contest the authority of established leaders. This was precisely the situation in Britain between 1766 and 1775, especially owing to creation of the American Department. "It is surprising how little attention gentlemen here pay, and how slender intelligence they can give one relative to things not immediately within their departments," William Samuel Johnson lamented in 1768. William Bollan objected strongly when Hillsborough rejected his singular petition to the crown, suggesting instead that the agent make separate applications to the several governmental boards.[1]

In 1681 the lords of trade had refused to take action on the Massachusetts charter until that colony sent agents to London and they were heard.[2] After 1768 men responsible for managing colonial

[1] Eric Strauss, *The Ruling Servants* (New York, 1960), p. 56; J. Steven Watson, *The Reign of George III, 1760–1815* (Oxford, 1960), p. 126; Johnson to William Pitkin, July 23, 1768, "Letters of William Samuel Johnson to the Governors of Connecticut," MHS *Collections*, ser. 5, IX (Boston, 1885), 292; Bollan to Hillsborough, May 25, 1772, Dartmouth MSS, vol. II, no. 366, WSL.

[2] Philip S. Haffenden, "The Crown and the Colonial Charters, 1675–1688: Part I," 3 WMQ, XV (1958), 306.

policy in London did their utmost *not* to hear from the agents, and in fact tried to limit their usefulness. During the eight years before independence, American influence underwent a relentless decline in British administrative circles. In the process the most bureaucratic tendencies of imperial government were highlighted in ways invidious to the North American interest.

THE AMERICAN DEPARTMENT AND THE BOARD OF TRADE

For half a dozen years after 1766, Wills Hill became an extremely important person to anyone interested in the colonies. In 1751, at the age of thirty-three, he was made Earl of Hillsborough in the Irish peerage. Twelve years later his friend George Grenville installed him at the Board of Trade as president. When Rockingham took over in 1765, Hillsborough resigned. A year later, however, he returned as First Lord of Trade, with the stipulation that the Board be altered from one of representation to a board of report only. Preparatory to reshaping colonial policy, Chatham intended to reconcentrate control of American affairs in the Southern Department. Toward this end he insisted upon reducing the Board to the status it had had before 1752. Hillsborough responded by refusing to bear the burdens of a meaningless office. He decided not to handle the routine duties of reading correspondence and preparing colonial instructions. The right to make original representations to the crown had made the Board the originator of a large amount of colonial business. After 1766, however, their lordships no longer considered certain matters that had come before them as a matter of course. A new measure of responsibility for provincial supervision was given to Shelburne's Southern Department.[3]

After repeal of the Stamp Act as never before, American affairs were fragmented among the Board of Trade, both secretaries of state, the Privy Council, Treasury, Customs, and Admiralty boards. The Privy Council, however, did not appreciate being sent large numbers of colonial laws, referred them right back, and ordered the Board of Trade to proceed as it customarily had. Hence lobbyists petitioning on colonial concerns "were often at a loss to know where to conduct their

---

[3] Arthur H. Basye, *The Lords Commissioners of Trade and Plantations . . . 1748–1782* (New Haven, 1925), pp. 144, 146–148, 155, 158, 160–161; John Norris, *Shelburne and Reform* (London, 1963), pp. 26–27.

business," and passed from office to office until their money and patience were exhausted.[4]

In December 1766, Hillsborough left his truncated post in favor of Robert, Earl Nugent. The agents were unsure what policies the new First Lord would favor, and despaired of successfully promoting measures favorable to the colonies. "But here men often alter," Franklin rationalized. "One comfort is, that if he proves an Enemy, the Board has not the Power or Influence it had, being reduced to a meer Board of Reference, proposing or moving nothing of itself."[5] The routine of business at the Board of Trade, however, and its place in the machinery of government were only slightly changed. It remained important for lobbyists to maintain cordial relations there. In 1767, North American agents seeking repeal of the Currency Act labored tirelessly to convert their lordships. At first they reported making progress with Nugent himself, but no headway with his colleagues. The lords commissioners, being good organization men, were reluctant to see any act revoked which they had fathered. Later in the year Franklin persuaded Shelburne and Conway of the virtues of repeal. They led him to expect such action at the next session, "but they said there was some difficulty with others at the Board . . . ; for there was a good deal in what Soame Jenyns had laughingly said, when asked to concur in some measure, *I have no kind of objection to it, provided we have heretofore signed nothing to the contrary.*" The statute stood untouched, an illustration of administrative inertia.[6]

From 1766 until 1768 the Southern Department became a center of colonial activity. Once again the agents had to readjust points of contact and operational patterns. While Shelburne held sway over American affairs, Grafton sorely resented the concentration of so much power in the hands of his subordinate. Grafton's threatened resignation and the subsequent cabinet upheaval finally led to the creation of an American Department, necessary on account of the congestion caused by so much business in the Southern Department

[4] Norris, *Shelburne and Reform,* pp. 26–27; Thomas Pownall, *The Administration of the Colonies* (2nd ed.; London, 1765), p. 88.

[5] Claud Nugent, *Memoir of Robert, Earl Nugent* (Chicago, 1898), pp. 75–77; Franklin to Joseph Galloway, Dec. 13, 1766, April 14 and May 20, 1767, WCL.

[6] Montagu to Shelburne, Sept. 8, 1766, Shelburne MSS, CXI, 317, WCL; Basye, *Lords Commissioners of Trade,* pp. 162–166, 182; Franklin to William Franklin, Aug. 28, 1767, Smyth, V, 47.

as well as the difficulty of correlating the work of the secretary with that of the Board of Trade. Objectively considered this innovation was welcomed by the colonial agents, most of whom wished it had occurred years earlier. "It would have given greater dispatch," Henry Wilmot noted, "and lessened expense." [7]

On January 20, 1768, Hillsborough assumed the dual post: First Lord of Trade again and first Secretary of State for the Colonies. He now had control of American patronage; and the lords of trade became, in effect, his advisory council. The agents promptly recognized that the lords commissioners would henceforth be influenced by Hillsborough's opinions. Since these seemed none too favorable to the colonies, it disturbed William Samuel Johnson to think that such ideas had been "revolving in his mind ever since he was at the Board of Trade." [8]

As soon as Hillsborough became custodian of America's welfare, the agents began "feeling out the Avenues to his Ear, & endeavouring to catch his smile." They knew in advance, however, that the object of their concern was unsympathetic. Earlier he had told Stephen Sayre that "he would rather see every Man to 50 in America put to the sword than the Stamp Act repealed." When Johnson waited on the new minister to congratulate him, Hillsborough did not attempt to disguise his antipathies. He sourly reminded Johnson that his employers in Connecticut did not write with sufficient frequency to the administration. During the remaining years of his agency Johnson consistently found Hillsborough dogmatic and disinclined to do anything that might relieve America. [9]

Of all the agents, Franklin had the most unpleasant experience with Hillsborough. On January 16, 1771, the Doctor waited on him "to acquaint him" with his appointment as Massachusetts' agent. The porter initially told Franklin that Hillsborough was not at home; but

[7] Wilmot to William Alexander, Sept. 25, 1766, William A. Duer, *The Life of William Alexander, Earl of Stirling* . . . (NJHS *Collections,* vol. II [New York, 1847]), pp. 84–85; W. O. Simpson, "Lord Shelburne and North America," *History Today,* X (1960), 54–57.

[8] Basye, *Lords Commissioners of Trade,* pp. 166, 169; Johnson to William Pitkin, Feb. 13, 1768, MHS *Collections,* ser. 5, IX, 262–263.

[9] Johnson to Jedediah Elderkin, Jan. 23, 1768, Emmet Collection, NYPL; Sayre to Jackson and Bromfield, Dec. 24, 1767, Lee-Cabot MSS (1707–1773), MHS; Johnson to William Pitkin, Feb. 13, 1768, MHS *Collections,* ser. 5, IX, 253–262; Arthur Lee to [Richard H. Lee?], Dec. 27, 1768, Richard H. Lee, *The Life of Arthur Lee* (Boston, 1829), I, 189.

as Franklin's coach began to rumble out of Hanover Square "the coachman heard a call, turned, and went back to the door." This time the porter announced that his master would see Franklin and took him into the levee room where he found Sir Francis Bernard, among others. Undersecretary John Pownall soon summoned Franklin into Hillsborough's presence. The Doctor was frankly "pleased with this ready admission and preference, having sometimes waited three or four hours" for his turn. As soon as he explained his mission, Hillsborough cut him short by saying: "I must set you right there, Mr. Franklin, you are not agent." Franklin protested and insisted that he had his appointment in his pocket. The minister replied that Governor Hutchinson had vetoed the bill. Franklin thereupon informed his antagonist that "there was no bill, my Lord; it was a vote of the House." The embarrassed Hillsborough at this point called in John Pownall, who vindicated the agent. Franklin politely indicated he was ready to depart, and added that he would register his appointment with Pownall at the Board of Trade. Hillsborough retorted angrily:

No such paper shall be entered there, while I have any thing to do with the business of that Board. The House of Representatives has no right to appoint an agent. We shall take no notice of any agents, but such as are appointed by acts of Assembly, to which the governor gives his assent. We have had confusion enough already. Here is one agent appointed by the Council, another by the House of Representatives, Which of these is agent for the province? Who are we to hear in provincial affairs? An agent appointed by act of Assembly we can understand. No other will be attended to for the future, I can assure you.

When Franklin suggested that an agent of the people did not require the governor's assent, Hillsborough answered: "I shall not enter into a dispute with you, Sir, upon this subject." He thereupon returned the Doctor's appointment papers unread and repeated three times that he would continue to administer American affairs with firmness. Franklin now took his leave, observing "that an agent can [not] *at present* be of any use to any of the colonies." [10]

The Doctor irritably wrote Samuel Cooper that Hillsborough's character "is Conceit, wrongheadedness, Obstinacy, and Passion." Still Franklin and the colonies would have to wait another eighteen months to be rid of their bugbear. In the meanwhile, Franklin at-

[10] Franklin to Samuel Cooper, Feb. 5, 1771, Smyth, V, 300–304.

tended the minister on several occasions, each time being told by the porter that his master was not at home. Franklin knew that was untrue because a personal friend was inside with Hillsborough each time. Finally, arriving on a levee day when a number of carriages stood outside, the Doctor received the same negative answer. He never saw his hated enemy thereafter.[11]

In August 1772, Hillsborough resigned both his positions rather than accept the projected plan to settle the Ohio country. Out of office he continued to act with the court party in opposing concessions to America. He was succeeded by William Legge, Earl of Dartmouth.[12]

Through Hillsborough's tenure and Dartmouth's after him, the two senior secretaries of state looked upon their new colleague as merely a glorified First Lord of Trade. Only the persistence of undersecretary John Pownall finally halted attempts by Lords Rochford and Suffolk to force the colonial secretary to send his orders through their offices. After a point the bureaucrats themselves were uncertain what department held jurisdiction over various issues. Understandably lobbying in such a context was difficult. When Hillsborough resigned, Pownall suspected that the post might be discontinued, its powers reverting to the Board of Trade, or else "some new arrangement." During the confused months of transition late in 1772, colonial affairs suffered. Pownall reported business had so accumulated that "I tremble to look at it." Innumerable letters and papers were awaiting the new minister's "serious attention, and two or three needing the consideration of the Cabinet." [13]

Known as "the Psalmsinger" because of his attachment to the evangelicals, Lord Dartmouth lacked administrative ability. He remained Secretary for the Colonies and presided over the Board of Trade for three years because his step-brother, Lord North, and George III were devoted to him. He was scarcely interested in practi-

[11] *Ibid.*, pp. 298–299; Franklin to William Franklin, Jan. 30, 1772, APS; Benjamin Franklin to William Franklin, Aug. 19, 1772, July 14, 1773, Smyth, V, 413, VI, 99.

[12] *The Last Journals of Horace Walpole during the Reign of George III* . . . *1771–1783*, ed. A. F. Steuart (London, 1910), I, 346.

[13] Basye, *Lords Commissioners of Trade*, pp. 170–173, 182–183, 188–189; Margaret M. Spector, *The American Department of the British Government, 1768–1782* (New York, 1940), pp. 25, 66; Pownall to William Knox, Aug. 1 and Oct. 31, 1772, Knox MSS, I, 51, 56, WCL; Pownall to Dartmouth, Oct. 17, 1772, Dartmouth MSS, Vol. II, no. 435, WSL.

cal politics and incapable of taking a forthright position on the American issues that arose during his tenure. The agents responded to Dartmouth variously. Franklin, who had first met him in 1765, when he was Rockingham's First Lord of Trade, liked him. They cooperated from the onset of the movement to repeal the Stamp Act. By 1773, however, the Doctor's esteem had abated. He still regarded Dartmouth as a man of good intentions, "but [he] does not seem to have strength equal to his wishes." In 1775, Franklin wrote his son that Dartmouth had "in reality no Will or Judgment of his own, being with Dispositions for the best Measures, easily prevail'd with to join in the worst." [14]

In office Dartmouth disarmed the agents with evasions that left them uncertain where either he or they stood, as in 1773, when he informed Charles Garth that "he was only one among many Lords who generally attended His Majesty's Privy Council on Plantation Matters, but that . . . he should recommend all such Measures, as with Propriety he could." Other agents complained that Dartmouth was away from London so much that their petitions languished in his office. They soon realized with astonishment that high-level discussions of American affairs were commonly held in his absence. The nobility and gentry traditionally took lengthy holidays in autumn, and Dartmouth adhered unswervingly to the custom during even the most serious crisis. [15]

An agent entering the office of the American Department found himself in what had once been the Duke of Monmouth's bedchamber. On the ceiling the original stucco remained with the large cypher "JMB" denoting James, Duke of Monmouth and Buccleugh. Directly below at his desk sat John Pownall, departmental undersecretary and secretary to the Board of Trade. In both capacities he wielded considerable influence. Hillsborough delegated a great deal of authority and responsibility to him, so much that the subordinate came to be regarded by agents as the minister's "closet companion." Hence one lobbyist's caustic summary: "Hillsborough or Pownall, arbitrary, opin-

[14] Franklin to William Franklin, Nov. 9, 1765, Aug. 17, 1772, July 14, 1773, March 22, 1775, C. M. Smith MSS, II, HSP, and Smyth, V, 410, VI, 98, 369.

[15] Garth to S.C. CC, May 20, 1773, Garth Letter-book, p. 152, SCA; B. D. Bargar, *Lord Dartmouth and the American Revolution* (Columbia, S.C., 1965), ch. 7.

ionated, subtle and severe." Under Dartmouth the relationship be-
tween cabinet officer and undersecretary remained constant; Arthur
Lee felt that "one may judge of the Secretary of State from his
Deputy." [16]

When Dartmouth took over in 1772, Pownall wrote him quite
frankly: "I do not promise you that you will find it altogether a bed of
Roses." Pownall wanted to retire, but remained only to find the scope
of his work increased. While Dartmouth spent weeks at a stretch in
the country, his undersecretary was left to run the office. He took over
patronage and administrative business passing through his department
and board, even steering controversial papers away from the Privy
Council, "in which Channel a door might be opened to discussion
perhaps very disagreeable." Often Pownall did not have time to consult his superior before making a decision and simply sent word of the
fait accompli to his Lordship. By 1773, Dartmouth was usually guided
by the advice and preparatory work of his right-hand man. Late that
year, in conjunction with William Knox, Pownall undertook the task
of devising a settlement for the province of Quebec. [17]

Just when Pownall became estranged from the North American
interest is not clear. Franklin issued a strong indictment against him in
the winter of 1766–1767: "The Standing Secretary seems to have a
strong Bias against us, and to infect them [the lords commissioners]
one after another as they come to it." Several years later, William
Samuel Johnson confirmed his constituents' "apprehension that our
Plantation Secretary is no great Friend to the Colonies." [18] Nonetheless, Johnson, a moderate, found Pownall cordial between 1767 and
1772, while Burke and Bollan received an occasional favor from him
until 1773. His good graces, however, had increasingly tended toward
such conservative politicians as Governors Bernard and Hutchinson of
Massachusetts, Frederick Smyth, loyalist chief justice of New Jersey,
and Joshua Mauger, M.P. and formerly agent for Nova Scotia. [19]

[16] William Knox, *Extra Official State Papers* (London, 1789), I, 24; Lee to
?, n.d., to Sam Adams, June 10, 1771, Lee, *Life of Arthur Lee*, I, 200–204,
215; Lee to Richard H. Lee, Oct. 20, 1773, Lee-Ludwell MSS, VHS.

[17] Pownall to Dartmouth, Aug. 8 and Sept. 3 and 6, 1772, Dec. 18, 1774,
Dartmouth MSS, Vol. II, nos. 377, 408, 412, 1022, WSL; Pownall to Knox,
Sept. 26 and Oct. 3, 1772, Knox MSS, I, 54, 56, WCL.

[18] Franklin to Joseph Galloway, Dec. 13, 1766, WCL; Johnson to Robert
Walker, March 12, 1769, WSJ MSS (box), Vol. I.

[19] Johnson to Agur Thomlinson, May 6, 1769, Johnson Letter-book, vol. II,
Bancroft Transcripts, NYPL; Burke to N.Y. CC, May 6, 1772, *The Corre-*

Pownall devoted his attentions increasingly to his own political and pecuniary ambitions. He received lucrative commissions for managing Indian presents for North America, and accumulated sinecures to augment his fortune. In 1775 he acquired a seat in the Commons and became agent for the Virgin Islands a year later.[20]

Pownall's colleague at the American Department after 1770, William Knox, also exerted significant influence. During Pownall's protracted absences, the arrogant and self-assertive Knox managed their office. He had not always been politically conservative or well placed. When he sought Georgia's agency in 1762, he had "few friends to depend on" and was oriented more toward the colony's interest. By 1765–1766, however, he became closely associated with George Grenville. In 1770, Hillsborough offered Knox the junior undersecretaryship. Since Knox's political sympathies were well known, Thomas Pownall remarked that "this cannot but be a marking symptom." In succeeding years, Knox steadily increased the role he played. In 1774 he helped shape the Quebec Act and effect various measures antithetical to patriotic provincials.[21]

In 1772, Franklin had wondered whether Hillsborough's successor would be any more amenable, not through mistrust of Dartmouth but because "he has the same Secretaries, Pownall and Knox; probably they will remind him of the late Measures, and prompt him to continue them." Three months later Arthur Lee confessed to his brother that he had "as little interest with the present Secretary [Dartmouth], as with his Predecessor [Hillsborough]. Indeed his fa-

---

spondence of Edmund Burke, 1768–1772, ed. Lucy S. Sutherland, II (Chicago, 1960), 304; Bollan to Samuel Danforth, July 16, 1770, *The Bowdoin and Temple Papers* (MHS *Collections*, ser. 6, Vol. IX [Boston, 1897]), p. 204; John Pownall to Francis Bernard, July 9, 1768, Bernard MSS, XI, 215, HLHU.

[20] Spector, *American Department*, pp. 43, 60; *The Diary and Letters of Thomas Hutchinson*, ed. Peter O. Hutchinson (Boston, 1884–1886), I, 183, 461.

[21] Knox to W. H. Lyttelton, Feb. 10, 1762, "Correspondence of William Knox, Chiefly in Relation to American Affairs, 1757–1808," HMC *Report on Manuscripts in Various Collections*, VI (Dublin, 1909), 86; *The Grenville Papers*, ed. W. J. Smith (London, 1852–1853), III, 109–110; Thomas Pownall to James Bowdoin, July 14, 1770, *Bowdoin and Temple Papers*, p. 199; Knox to Dartmouth, Nov. 15, 1774, HMC *14th Report, Appendix, Part X, The Manuscripts of the Earl of Dartmouth*, II (*American Papers*) (London, 1895), 233.

vors are likely to run very much in the same channel." By then,
however, Dartmouth had begun to abdicate his responsibilities. Others moved quickly to grab for them, and in consequence authority over
the colonies was fragmented again. By 1773 the remaining agents
apparently were ignorant of the changing configuration of power.
Only the civil servants affected by the shift knew—and noted it with
bitterness. As Pownall wrote Knox:

Our business has hitherto been as light as you could wish, and I think it is
likely to continue so, for what can Lord Dartmouth have to do whilst
Bamber Gascoigne is minister for America at the Board of Trade and Lord
Suffolk at the Council Office, where they will not let us have anything to
say, all Councils for American business being in Lord Gower's absence
held by Lord Suffolk.[22]

Bamber Gascoyne seems to have been the most important member
of the Board of Trade during this period. He acted for the lords
commissioners in Parliament, laying such papers before it as were
requested. A member of the Board since 1763, he lost his seat in the
Commons that year to John Huske. Although Gascoyne later regained
a place in the Palace of Westminster, he never forgot his embarrassing
defeat by a colonial. His coming into a position of power over provincial affairs lowered the level of colonial influence in London that
much more at an unfortunate time.[23]

After 1773 both the Board of Trade and the American Department
declined. The former became less active, meeting less often and receiving fewer communications from America. In 1774 the coercive
legislation never came before the lords commissioners at any time.
The next year their activity picked up slightly, but hardly in proportion to the crisis. Dartmouth's American Department underwent a
similar loss of status, again measurable by John Pownall's pique: "I
have done nothing but play truant . . . for I found no body would do
anything. . . . I know nothing but what I read in those inestimable
State Papers that are published every day . . . and I am not ashamed

---

[22] Franklin to William Franklin, Nov. 3, 1772, Smyth, V, 445–446; Lee to
Richard H. Lee, Feb. 14, 1773, Lee MSS, II, HLHU; Pownall to Knox, July
23, 1773, "Correspondence of William Knox," p. 110. Granville Leveson, Earl
Gower, was Lord President of the Privy Council; the Earl of Suffolk was
Secretary of State for the Southern Department.

[23] Garth to S.C. CC, May 4, 1773, March 31, 1774, Garth Letter-book, pp.
151, 168–169, SCA; *Additional Grenville Papers, 1763–1765*, ed. J. R. G.
Tomlinson (Manchester, 1962), p. 17.

to say that they furnish me with better and earlier intelligence of what is doing in America than I receive through any other channel." [24]

Looking in on Pownall and Knox, Thomas Hutchinson found them "lownging," and remarked that "it is strange to see every office in a state of inaction." The permanent undersecretaries were themselves unhappy at being neglected. Pownall penned his colleague still another poignant note in 1775:

As to measures for America, I know nothing about them, for since I have been deserted by our principal [Dartmouth], that business is got into other hands, and my friend Eden knows a great deal more and does a great deal more of the American business than your faithful servant. In short, my dear friend, our office makes a most pitifull figure and is most thoroughly disgraced by a conduct in Lord North that I cannot understand. Whether this proceeds from any personal dislike to me or from some fascination in Lord Suffolk and his secretary I cant tell; but so it is that I am as ignorant of what is intended, tho' I know a great deal is in agitation.[25]

Bureaucrats have commonly sought to compensate for their declining status by taking advantage of opportunities to exert their waning power, often in trivial ways. An attitude of noncommunication became a convenient cloak to protect them from criticism and disguise their decline. An external facade of secrecy served to boost their own morale, put off the ever-present lobbyists, and hide from view changes in power behind the scene. As Charles Garth concluded in his last letter to South Carolina's Committee of Correspondence, "the Business and orders at Office are in General kept So private of late as to be Almost as Soon known in America as Suffer'd to Transpire here." [26]

Had the agents much to hope for from the new repositories of power? It is doubtful that they were even aware of the rapid ascent of William Eden, the object of Pownall's jealousy. This ambitious young man succeeded Thomas Whately in 1772 as Lord Suffolk's undersecretary at the Northern Department. Suffolk expected his protégé to promote "the credit of our department" by acting vigorously, even at the risk of encroaching upon other administrative bodies. Eden rapidly

---

[24] Basye, *Lords Commissioners of Trade*, pp. 190–192; Pownall to Knox, Aug. 31, 1774, "Correspondence of William Knox," pp. 114–115.

[25] Hutchinson, *Diary and Letters of Hutchinson*, I, 343; Pownall to Knox, Oct. 10, 1775, "Correspondence of William Knox," p. 122.

[26] Marshall E. Dimock, *Administrative Vitality* (New York, 1959), p. 104; Charles Garth to S.C. CC, May 27, 1775, Garth Letter-book, SCA.

acquired great responsibilities and through his friendship with Lord
North found colonial affairs passing increasingly through his hands.
In 1774 he gained a seat in the House of Commons and would shortly
be regarded by Horace Walpole as "the new confidential agent of
Lord North." When John Robinson, senior secretary to the Treasury,
fell ill early in 1775, Eden became North's temporary assistant in
Treasury business, although he continued his regular work at the
Northern Department. As the First Lord's closest adviser on American
affairs, Eden achieved enormous power for one so recently entered on
the political scene. Unfortunately he consistently and staunchly supported the administration that had hoisted him to prominence. In
1774 he considered "the Bostonians dirty dogs. . . . They thought
Hutchinson a tyrant—I met him on Thursday last, at the Attorney
General's—they might as well have taken a lamb for a tiger." [27]

IMPERIAL ADMINISTRATION UNDER STRESS

As the dimensions of the colonial crisis deepened, they placed even
greater stress upon the traditional system of imperial administration.
They also tended to intensify the bureaucratic tendencies that had
long been part of that system, as well as some of its other characteristics. The strain of continual crisis required a responsive and uncomplicated system capable of handling problems smoothly as they arose.
Instead the processing of colonial statutes, petitions, and litigation
involving the frustrated agents was delayed for months and even
years. Estrangement from the civil servants alienated many of them
from British authority altogether. "A man must have patience and
resolution," remarked John Wentworth, "to resist the endless delays of
Office; neither ought evasions or even Refusals to discourage him." [28]

To expedite their business the agents continually had to prod ap-

[27] Franklin B. Wickwire, *British Subministers and Colonial America,
1763–1783* (Princeton, 1966), p. 143; Leslie Scott, "Under Secretaries of
State, 1755–1775" (unpub. M.A. thesis; Manchester University, 1950), pp.
65–93; Eden to Pownall, Jan. 9, 1775, PRO CO 5/247, p. 225; North to
Eden, Aug. 12, 1775, Add MSS 34412, ff. 343–344; Richard W. Van Alstyne,
"Parliamentary Supremacy versus Independence: Notes and Documents,"
Huntington Library Quarterly, XXVI (1963), 203–204.

[28] Wentworth to Daniel Peirce, Jan. 15, 1766, Peirce Papers, Portsmouth
Athenaeum, N.H. I am indebted to Professor Jere Daniell of Dartmouth
College for this reference.

propriate persons in Whitehall. As McCulloh observed, "nothing will ever be done Without previous Application." All too often, however, such entreaties proved insufficient. The agents sometimes were informed that the public offices were too busy to hear American questions, at other times that an issue had been deferred owing to the failure of a certain lord or official to appear, and on still other occasions that a board was about to adjourn for some months. In the latter situation the agents were always advised not to press for consideration until the subsequent session. Even during the seasons of business, hearings before the great boards were infrequent and dockets crowded, obliging lobbyists to attend continuously at Whitehall and the Cockpit in hopes that their cases would be called.[29]

When Matthew Lamb, counsel to the Board of Trade, died in 1768, he left much colonial legislation unexamined. For two years subsequently there was no regularly commissioned legal adviser, although laws were sometimes referred to an outside solicitor. In 1770, when Richard Jackson finally assumed the post, Benjamin Franklin remarked that "this office having been Vacant near two Years, is the Reason that many Colony acts have lain so long here, not pass'd upon." Jackson was generally prompter with his reports than his predecessor had been, although he still required a certain amount of prodding by John Pownall from time to time. Occasionally Jackson's neglect became more serious still, as in 1773 when he simply forgot to examine documents from New Jersey.[30] Yet pressuring the official in question was not always the solution, as some of the agents recognized. "If I had hurried Mr. Jackson's report," Burke wrote, "I had run the risque of one that might be neutral; or perhaps not favourable. I have always observed that his report has, as it ought to have, great weight with the Board; and indeed in most cases is decisive." [31]

[29] McCulloh to Edmund Fanning, Jan. 26, 1768, Fanning-McCulloh Papers, no. 252, Southern Historical Collection, University of North Carolina Library; Franklin to William Franklin, July 2, 1768, Smyth, V, 143–145; Henry Marchant's London diary, entries for June 2 and 25, 1772, RIHS; Garth to S.C. CC, March 23, 1770, March 27, 1771, Dec. 20, 1772, *SCHGM*, XXXI, 239–240, XXXIII, 125–129, 231.

[30] Charles M. Andrews, "The Royal Disallowance," AAS *Proceedings*, XXIV (1914), 349–351; Franklin to Joseph Galloway, June 11, 1770, WCL; John Pownall to Jackson, April 30, 1770, PRO CO 324/21, ff. 325–326; Jackson to Dartmouth, March 26, 1773, Dartmouth MSS, Vol. II, no. 585, WSL.

[31] Burke to James De Lancey, Aug. 2, 1773, Sutherland, *Burke Correspondence*, II, 446–447.

Three illustrations encompass all the delays the agents found so exasperating after 1766; the Mohegan and Susquehanna cases and Rhode Island's claims for remuneration owing to the Crown Point expedition of 1756. The Mohegan dispute had begun in 1705, been laid to rest in 1743, and revived in 1766, eliciting William Samuel Johnson's arrival in England as special agent for Connecticut. The lobbyists found the Privy Council forever adjourned, however, on account of the "distemper" of its chairman, Lord Northington, or the failure of some other officer to be present. After four years of procrastination, Jackson remarked that "it is incredible with what difficulty a number of Privy Councillors who are to hear and a number of counsel who are to argue this cause can fix on a time when they can spare many days." Connecticut's agents were impeded on the one hand by the Master of the Rolls, "the principal Privy Councillor bred to the law," who blocked them "upon very narrow principles of mode and form," and on the other by Earl Gower, the Lord President of the Council. The latter, Johnson reported, arbitrarily resolved "as soon as the affairs of state will permit, to go down to his country seat in the North, and will not be detained by this cause." The Privy Council did not finally render a decision until 1773, after eight years of delay and postponement.[32]

Connecticut's dispute with the Penn family over the Susquehanna lands was still unsettled at the outbreak of Revolution in 1775. In this case the various legal counsel, solicitors, and officials of the American Department were responsible for the sequence of delays and a fantastic degree of incompetence. At one point a petty placeman sailed off to the West Indies with the most crucial documents of the case tucked away in his satchel.[33]

Rhode Island's claims against the Exchequer for military expenditures in 1756 remained unsettled throughout Joseph Sherwood's

---

[32] Jackson to Eliphalet Dyer, July 24, 1766, WSJ MSS (bound), Vol. III; Johnson to William Pitkin, March 19, 1767, June 28, 1770, MHS *Collections*, ser. 5, IX, 221, 439–440; Jackson to Jonathan Trumbull, Feb. 5–6, 1770, Trumbull MSS, III, 5b, 6a-d, 17c, CSL.

[33] Johnson to Committee of Susquehanna Co., March 10, 1769, to Eliphalet Dyer, Oct. 12, 1769, *The Susquehannah Company Papers: Memorial Publications of the Wyoming Historical and Genealogical Society*, ed. Julian P. Boyd (Wilkes-Barre, Pa., 1930–1933), III, pp. 89–90, 186; Johnson to Jonathan Trumbull, June 28, 1770, MHS *Collections*, ser. 5, IX, 443.

agency. Repeatedly he sought the stamps of approval required, and repeatedly the various offices "came to a Resolution to postpone giving an Answer thereto for the present." Hence Marchant was especially appointed in 1771 to prod the bureaucracy. He encountered the same obstacles that had plagued Sherwood for a decade—endless delays at the administrative offices. He complained bitterly to Ezra Stiles of this disconcerting inaction: "The Great Ones of the Earth being at their Seats in the Country or at Paris. And there is most certainly the greatest Inattention to the affairs of state you . . . possibly can conceive of. The Kingdom is like a Ship laying to in a Storm—Her Helm Eased, And the Mariners all below asleep." [34]

In part these issues dragged on because they were so expensive to prosecute. Johnson learned that large retaining fees to prominent lawyers handling the Mohegan case were not enough. It was necessary to tip the lawyers' clerks and footmen as well. While awaiting a decision on the Mohegan litigation at the Privy Council in 1771, Johnson made sure the head clerk would give Connecticut's papers a favorable shuffle by slipping him five guineas. Johnson's successor, Life, paid a shorthand writer two guineas to attend the House of Lords and record speeches. As Franklin's legal counsel, Life incurred interesting charges. In 1771 he handed Richard Jackson, counsel to the Board of Trade, five guineas for reporting out an act concerning the colony of Georgia and another ten shillings six pence to Jackson's clerk. Handling Franklin's affairs in 1774, Life paid the Lord Chancellor's clerk nearly as much as he gave the jurist for an attendance. Life never failed to reward the doorkeepers and messengers at the Cockpit; and Franklin himself allowed each messenger at the Board of Trade a guinea at Christmas. [35]

The legitimate fees as well as the supplementary inducements required to expedite American affairs rose rapidly in the four decades after they were formally established. In 1731, for example, it cost ten shillings to have a document copied at the plantation office. After repeal of the Stamp Act in 1766, the agents had to pay four, five, and

---

[34] Sherwood to Josias Lyndon, March 21, 1768, Feb. 4, 1769, Letters, VII, 65, 92, RIA; PRO T 29/39, f. 354 (April 20, 1769); Marchant to Ezra Stiles, Sept. 5, 1771, Stiles MSS, YUL.
[35] Johnson's "Bill of Costs" is printed in Joseph H. Smith, *Appeals to the Privy Council from the American Plantations* (New York, 1950), 672–684; for Life's Connecticut expenditures, see MS designation "War," X, 435a-r, CSL; Life's account with Franklin is in Franklin MSS, LXIX, 108, APS.

six times that much for the same service, if they could get it at all.[36] The growth of political tensions made lobbying an increasingly expensive proposition; but concurrently the rising cost of accommodation made provincial employers reluctant to pour needed funds into a soul of empire they regarded as rife with corruption. Caught in the middle, the agencies suffered. As never before their accounts were carefully scrutinized by assemblies reluctant to waste a shilling. At first the representatives simply complained to their constituents that "it is Impossible to transact the Provincial Business or appear in Character of Agent at the Publick offices without making large Gratuitys to the Secretarys, Clerks, &c." The agents soon found themselves with an ugly problem. If they curtailed expenditures in the name of economy, they ran the risk of reproof for ineffectually upholding their duty. If they spent more liberally in their constituents' behalf, they were in danger of not being reimbursed.[37]

Any petition to Parliament would be referred to a committee where legal counsel must be employed to attend. The smallest fee of each counsel was ten guineas per day. Hence several hundred pounds were required at the outset. Jackson, Johnson, Life, and De Berdt were continually strapped for funds and complained ceaselessly of the costly litigation they ran up against. Because of the sums required, both the agents and their constituents became highly disenchanted with the appellate system of carrying provincial cases across the ocean to tribunals that were financially unreasonable and juridically hostile.[38]

As one would expect of such a system, it also developed an exaggerated sense of administrative proprieties. Many deviations and means of circumventing standard procedures were accessible during the generations prior to the Seven Years' War. After that, however, all sorts of long-ignored regulations were invoked in order to suppress the provin-

---

[36] As a basis for comparison see Oliver M. Dickerson, *American Colonial Government, 1696–1765* (Cleveland, 1912), p. 72 n. 127, and O. C. Williams, *The Clerical Organization of the House of Commons, 1661–1850* (Oxford, 1954), pp. 301–303.

[37] Sir Lewis Namier and John Brooke, *The History of Parliament: The House of Commons, 1754–1790* (London, 1964), I, 77; De Berdt to Thomas Cushing, July 28, 1766, "Letters of Dennys De Berdt, 1757–1770," ed. Albert Matthews, CSM *Publications*, XIII (1912), 321.

[38] De Berdt to Thomas Cushing, Jan. 1 and Feb. 2, 1770, Matthews, "Letters of De Berdt," pp. 391, 396; Williams, *Clerical Organization*, app. 3.

cial voice.[39] A strong feeling grew within governmental circles that there was a "regular, official method" of effecting any business. Administrations frowned upon alternative methods as "irregular and disrespectful." Before 1766, for example, issues of prime political importance might be managed by the First Lord of Trade independently of his board. This system permitted the lobbyist to avoid excessive delays. After that date it became increasingly difficult to circumvent proprieties in search of prompt solutions to pressing problems. In fact it was not always clear where the "present Channel of Communication" lay. By 1775 the agents found they must operate only through the Secretary of State for the Colonies, "that being the regular official method, and the only one in which we might on occasion call for an Answer." Yet by that time responsibility for colonial administration had shifted from the ineffectual Dartmouth to other hands.[40]

To make operations still more difficult for the agents, their constituents were remarkably naïve where matters of protocol were concerned. As often as not they persisted in sending petitions that they expected would be delivered personally to George III. Sherwood, Montagu, Garth, De Berdt, and Johnson were particularly put upon in this way. The perplexed lobbyists could be faithful to the spirit of their instructions only by violating the letter. De Berdt obeyed his employers' directions but worried at having departed from "the common form of business, as Petitions delivered to the King in person are not liable to be call'd for in Parliament—to remove which inconvenience I left a Copy at Lord Hillsborough's House." [41]

Remonstrating with the crown directly served only to antagonize both Parliament and the bureaucracy. The agents had to placate pride

---

[39] Benjamin Franklin to Noble W. Jones, Aug. 3, 1772, Buffalo and Erie County Public Library, Buffalo, N.Y.

[40] Lord Hyde to Dartmouth, Aug. 13, 1765, Dartmouth MSS, Vol. II, no. 78, WSL; Franklin to Noble W. Jones, April 3, 1769, *The Colonial Records of the State of Georgia,* ed. A. D. Candler (Atlanta, 1904–1916), XV, 26; PRO PC 2/114, pp. 212–213, 225–226, 229, 234–235, 245–246, 248–249 (for Robert Charles's efforts to maneuver New York's paper money legislation through Whitehall in 1770); Franklin *et al.* to E. Biddle, Dec. 24, 1774, *Boston Gazette and Country Journal,* March 27, 1775; Franklin to Charles Thomson, Feb. 5, 1775, Smyth, VI, 303.

[41] Sam Adams to De Berdt, Sept. 22, 1768, *The Writings of Samuel Adams,* ed. H. A. Cushing (New York, 1904–1908), I, 247; De Berdt to Thomas Cushing, Sept. 15, 1769, Matthews, "Letters of De Berdt," p. 378.

and place within Whitehall. After submitting his documents to Hillsborough—"the proper channel"—William Samuel Johnson also presented his case to the President of the Privy Council, just "to stop every
avenue of prejudice." A proprietary colony such as Maryland appeared
doubly oblivious to the approved methods. The Assembly not only sent
memorials to be conveyed personally to the king, but did so by means of
an agent, thereby ignoring "the Proprietor or his Deputy in the
Government there, which His Majesty considers as the only proper
and constitutional channel." [42]

As formality and propriety became dominant considerations in Anglo-American administration, even the give-and-take characteristic of
the traditional levee also disappeared. On Tuesdays during the active
seasons of government, Hillsborough held levees at his residence in
Hanover Square. Designed to increase the administration's sensitivity
to imperial problems, these gatherings were usually attended by colonial officials, agents, and merchants. After 1771, however, levees gradually lost their usefulness as media for the exchange of information
and opinions. Following his squabble with Hillsborough in 1771,
Franklin informed his constituents that he no longer saw any value in
attending the mid-day assemblies. In 1772 a Boston newspaper
published a remarkable note under the byline "London news":

So extremely fond is that weak and vane *minister* (as he calls himself) of
seeing his dearly beloved name in Public Prints, that it is said a standing
order is left with the Publisher of one of the news Papers, weekly to insert
as follows: 'Last Tuesday there was a numerous and grand Levee at the
Right Hon. The Earl of Hillsborough's, Secretary of State for the American Department, at which many of the Colony Agents, Governors, Merchants &c. attended.' . . . So far, however, are the Colony Agents from
attending his Lordships grand *Ideal* Levees, that, it is said, they are all so
disgusted with his vain, supercilious, haughty and overbearing ignorance,
that scarce any of them ever appear at POMPOSITY HALL. [43]

Hillsborough's successor continued the practice of holding weekly
levees, though he changed the regular day to Wednesday. With
renewed hope Franklin resumed attendance at these affairs and was

[42] Johnson to William Pitkin, Oct. 20, 1768, March 23, 1769, MHS *Collections,* ser. 5, IX, 295, 323, 325; *Archives of Maryland,* ed. William H. Browne
et al. (Baltimore, 1883–), XIV, 552–553.
[43] *Boston Evening Post,* May 28, 1770; *Boston Gazette and Country Journal,*
June 25, 1770, July 8, 1771, Sept. 21, 1772; Franklin to Thomas Cushing,
April 13, 1772, Smyth, V, 392.

received warmly by Dartmouth.[44] But this device to facilitate Anglo-American communication soon became a casualty of rising political tensions. Lord North's levees, held in the Cockpit at noon on Thursdays, were not attended faithfully by any of the agents. On account of his dislike for the First Lord, Franklin boasted that he did not go to a single one; after January 1774 he "never attended the Levee of any Minister." The institution became opprobrious among opponents of the administration. Hence Burke's contempt for "the sight of half-a-dozen gentlemen from America, dangling at the levees of Lord Dartmouth and Lord North, or negotiating with Mr. [John] Pownall." [45]

At first glance it might seem that levees lost their importance because the focus of colonial lobbying shifted to Parliament after 1763. Actually, by the early 1770's, when levees declined in value, responsibility for American affairs had in several respects moved back to Whitehall. In 1767 one agent reported to his constituents that "a vast struggle for Power is expected this Winter." Henry Eustace McCulloh had heard there would be a concerted effort "to take the Affairs of the Colonies out of the hands of the Parliament and place them in their old Channel, that is, under the direction of the Crown, and the Great Boards,—by repealing the restrictive Acts." While Parliament by no means abandoned its new concern for colonial matters, a balance was restored between 1768 and the beginning of 1774. American affairs continued "to be under a necessity of being regulated by Parliament," De Berdt noted, "it being neither in the Ministrys power nor even the King himself either to dispense with the Laws or revoke them." Nevertheless creation of an American Department added a new center of activity, another arena where influence was sought.[46]

In one respect, readjustment suited the direction colonial political ideas were taking; but it also intensified the frustration of the agents.

[44] Benjamin Franklin to William Franklin, Nov. 3 and 4, 1772, to Thomas Cushing, Nov. 4, 1772, Jan. 5, 1773, Smyth, V, 444–446, 448, VI, 1 n.

[45] Henry Marchant's London diary, entries for Jan. 30, April 2 and 30, May 7, and June 11, 1772, RIHS; Benjamin Franklin to William Franklin, July 14, 1773, March 22, 1775, Smyth, VI, 96, 319; Burke to Rockingham, Sept. 18, 1774, *The Correspondence of Edmund Burke, 1774–1778,* ed. G. H. Guttridge, III (Chicago, 1961), 30–31.

[46] McCulloh to John Harvey, Sept. 13, 1767, CRNC, VII, 517; De Berdt to Thomas Cushing, Aug. 26, 1768, Matthews, "Letters of De Berdt," p. 337.

Their experience with petitions aimed exclusively at the crown had not been fruitful, for the appropriate channels were blocked by hostile vessels of unfriendly ministers. The agents continued placing a number of their requests for redress before the Privy Council. If the administration preferred, it could bring petitions into the Commons for debate. Hence ministerial support had to be cultivated in advance. Against the possibility that politicians would seek to shield American remonstrances from excessive publicity via an airing in Westminster, the agents usually took "care that it should be sufficiently known, both within and without doors, that such addresses have been presented." [47]

After 1769 memorials offered to the throne by way of Whitehall stood a very poor chance of success, especially when submitted by agents. Franklin reported that Hillsborough "seems to think Agents unecessary (perhaps troublesome)" and insists upon colonial applications being submitted only through the governors, any other channel being "irregular and disrespectful." This dictum immediately affected Robert Charles and Henry Eustace McCulloh. Hillsborough flatly informed McCulloh *"that Petitioning in* [McCulloh's] *Circumstances was foolish,"* and roundly discouraged North Carolina's lobbyist. Between 1771 and 1774, the agents' attempts were quashed; they found Dartmouth more polite but as disheartening as his predecessor.[48] In 1773, when Arthur Lee applied to the Secretary of State for the Colonies, he found Dartmouth had "no power to relieve us in *any thing*. The means of redress for the rest of our complaints, he [said], *only Parliament* can minister." [49]

In 1765–1766 the first imperial crisis had its primary locus in Parliament, where both sides found sufficient flexibility to resolve it. In 1774–1775 the final crisis would return the spotlight to Westminster again. During the intervening decade, significant changes occurred in Parliament's administrative operations—changes profoundly important to the agents and Anglo-American unity.

[47] De Berdt to Cushing, Feb. 1, Sept. 15, and Nov. 16, 1769, Matthews, "Letters of De Berdt," pp. 356, 378, 385; William Samuel Johnson to William Pitkin, Feb. 9, 1769, MHS *Collections*, ser. 5, IX, 321.

[48] Franklin to Noble W. Jones, April 3, 1769, Candler, *Colonial Records of Georgia*, XV, 26; Ross J. S. Hoffman, *Edmund Burke, New York Agent . . .* (Philadelphia, 1956), p. 94; McCulloh to John Harvey, July 24, 1769, *CRNC*, VIII, 58.

[49] Lee to Sam Adams, Dec. 22, 1773, Adams MSS, NYPL. Italics mine.

THE DECLINE OF INFLUENCE

When Increase Mather served as Massachusetts agent in the 1690's, clerical underlings at court had eased his task by procuring documents, arranging introductions, and preventing the issuance of deleterious dispatches and legislation. Until the later 1760's, career agents such as Bollan found parliamentary managers quite willing to cooperate. Political "men of business" would dovetail their operations with those of the provincial pressure group. In 1770, however, Bollan had difficulty getting documents relating to the Boston massacre "laid before the house of coṁons for consideration." By 1774 officials of the House passed inaccurate information to the lobbyists and ultimately refused them copies of pending bills that affected America. Upon inquiry they learned the clerks were prevented "by an order given that no person but the members shou'd have copies." Again the same rigmarole of passing from one desk to another reinforced the agents' revulsion against "dangling after the great, dancing from office to office, watching, peeping, prying, enduring Insolence, & cringing to Power." [50]

John Hatsell became clerk to the House of Commons in 1768. A close friend of many politicians, his views were conservative, and he dedicated his great study of parliamentary procedure to Jeremiah Dyson, his patron. Hatsell was inclined to obstruct the provincial agents after 1770, and regarded Lord North with contempt for losing the American colonies. [51]

Faced with adapting their techniques to the circumstances of parliamentary government, the agents found Westminster's internal machinery in disorder and transition, with scarcely a secure handle to grasp. Proceedings at committee hearings of the Commons were becoming highly irregular. Rules were ignored more than observed.

[50] *Narratives of the Insurrections, 1675–1690*, ed. Charles M. Andrews (New York, 1915), pp. 272, 277; Bollan to James Bowdoin *et al.*, May 11, 1770, *Monthly Bulletin of Books Added to the Public Library of the City of Boston*, VI (1901), 270–271; Bollan to Bowdoin *et al.*, March 22, 1774, Bowdoin-Temple MSS, Vol. III, MHS; William Samuel Johnson to Jedediah Elderkin, Jan. 23, 1768, Emmet Collection, NYPL.

[51] Williams, *Clerical Organization of the Commons*, pp. 65–66; accounts of De Berdt, entry for Oct. 1769, Dartmouth MSS, Vol. I, no. 974, WSL; Hatsell, *Precedents of Proceedings in the House of Commons* (4 vols.; London, 1776–1796).

Committees commonly disregarded their instructions and exceeded their powers to such an extent that one contemporary felt "the evil cannot go much farther for it would be difficult to imagine they can be worse than they are." Committees were supposed to examine witnesses separately, with each barred from the committee room except during his own *viva voce*. These and various other rules were not observed during the 1760's. Instead, "generally speaking every body is admitted and the Members are perpetually breaking in upon the Counsel or Agent." [52]

Because the lobbyists dealt with colonial legislation—trade regulated by law and boundaries determined by legal grants—they often required expert legal advice and aid. Barristers and solicitors were commonly employed to appear before the governmental offices, for as one agent stated, "in causes depending between party and party at the Council Board it is necessary according to the course of judicial proceedings, to employ a regular sollicitor." [53]

What manner of men did the agents usually hire to represent the colonies? Jackson, Johnson, and Franklin frequently called on Thomas Life before he became Connecticut's full-time agent; and Franklin still needed Life's services as late as 1774–1775. After 1771 Life employed Jackson and John Dunning in the Susquehanna case, even though the Penns had earlier paid Dunning against Connecticut. Also popular with Garth and Franklin, Dunning was a close friend of Shelburne and one of the chief legal advisers to the Whig opposition. He served as solicitor general between 1768 and 1770. Similarly, an earlier holder of that office, William de Grey (1763–1765), had been employed by Jackson, Charles, and Jasper Mauduit. During the latter's agency, he also relied on Charles Yorke, attorney general during Bute's administration. Later Massachusetts agents, particularly De Berdt, Franklin, and Lee, enjoyed good working relationships with Serjeant John Glynn, radical lawyer and M.P. for Middlesex after 1768, and John Lee, "another able man of the profession." Garth also

---

[52] Williams, *Clerical Organization of the Commons*, pp. 72–73, 165–169, 177; *The Liverpool Tractate: An Eighteenth-Century Manual on the Procedure of the House of Commons*, ed. Catherine Strateman (New York, 1937), pp. xxiv, xxix, 57, 71.

[53] Ella Lonn, *The Colonial Agents of the Southern Colonies* (Chapel Hill, 1945), pp. 225–226; Thomas Life to Jonathan Trumbull, Aug. 2, 1775, Trumbull MSS, IV (2), 143, CSL.

"called in Mr. Chamberlayne of Gough Square, a very able practising Solicitor." [54]

By the early 1770's the agents had grown disillusioned with London's legal profession. Henry Marchant found its members a dissipated group. By 1774, Bollan regarded lawyers as being "of little service. Those who are eminent, and hope to rise in their profession, are unwilling to offend the court." Thomas Life's lament was similar: "It is very difficult to get Counsel of great Eminence in their Profession to leave their respective Courts either in Law or Equity in the time of full Business to attend at any other place." These lobbyists had wasted countless hours waiting for their own and administration counsellors to appear at various hearings. As the ultimate crisis came on, both the attorney general and the solicitor general were strongly anti-American in outlook. Referring in 1774 to Franklin's castigation, Arthur Lee remarked that Weddeburn's "insult was offered to the [American] people through their agent." [55]

As civil servants in these years became more authoritarian and cautious, agents encountered mounting hostility toward American problems and lobbyists. They felt their influence waning as the hitherto loose apparatus of Anglo-American administration tightened at every level. The agents accustomed themselves to the fact that the great boards might summon them one day to attend a hearing the next, or even the same day. So long as matters of minor importance were at stake it did not matter that the lobbyist lacked time to familiarize himself with the problem and prepare his brief. He simply stalled or pleaded illness, and the hearing would be postponed until he

[54] *Journal of the Commissioners for Trade and Plantations from January 1759 to December 1763* (London, 1935), p. 109; *ibid.* (1764–1767), pp. 99, 331; *ibid.* (1768–1775), pp. 400, 428; Jackson to Jonathan Trumbull, Nov. 7, 1770, Trumbull MSS, III (1), 30a-b, CSL; Life to Johnson, March 3, 1773, WSJ MSS (bound), Vol. III; Franklin to Thomas Cushing, Feb. 15, 1774, *The Complete Works of Benjamin Franklin*, ed. John Bigelow (New York, 1887), V, 294, 297–299; De Berdt to Cushing, Nov. 16, 1769, Mathews, "Letters of De Berdt," p. 385; "John Glynn," *DNB*; Garth to S.C. CC, Dec. 27, 1773, Garth Letter-book, pp. 158–159, SCA.

[55] *The Literary Diary of Ezra Stiles*, ed. F. B. Dexter, (New York, 1901), I, 315; Benjamin Franklin to Thomas Cushing, Feb. 15, 1774, Bigelow, *Works of Franklin*, V, 293; Life to Jonathan Trumbull, July 5, 1775, MS designation "War," X, 4350-r, CSL; Lee to Sam Adams, Feb. 8, 1774, Lee, *Life of Arthur Lee*, I, 240.

notified the department of his readiness. This practice, however, was ill suited to overcoming the differences created by the presence of substantive issues that demanded serious consideration. Trecothick found this onerous in 1767. Two years later Arthur Lee complained that "only six days notice is given to the agent to summon his witnesses three thousand miles distant." In 1774, Bollan and Franklin received similar treatment on the eve of the latter's appearance in the Cockpit. "This very short notice seemed intended to surprise us," the Doctor observed. As a result Franklin arrived without legal aid, not expecting "to find counsel employed against the petition; [having] no notice of that intention till late in the preceding day." On other occasions, agents were chided by the Board of Trade or Privy Council for failing to appear when they "had not had any such notice" even to do so.[56]

Another avenue of communication gradually closed off to the lobbyists was the right to search the public offices for documents required as evidence in matters of colonial concern. Earlier in the eighteenth century no copies of documents at the Board of Trade could be given to any person without approval by the commissioners. When an agent requested materials or the right to search for information among the papers of the Board, he should have been refused; yet the clerks were allowed to procure the desired papers, which were given after their lordships had scrutinized them. Until the middle 1760's the agents generally had ready access to whatever their work required—for a fee. But by 1770, Bollan procured copies of documents only with hardship, and then "the clerk wou'd have had me receive the latter copies without his authentication, which with difficulty I obtain'd." Documents lacking the proper mark of legitimacy were almost worthless to the colonists and their delegates. Problems in procuring such authentication formed the prelude to having access to the papers denied altogether.[57]

[56] *Journal of the Commissioners for Trade, 1764–1767*, pp. 331, 424; Lee to [Richard H. Lee?], Nov. 9, 1769, Lee, *Life of Arthur Lee*, I, 193; Bollan to Mass. Council, Feb. 2, 1774, *Bowdoin and Temple Papers*, pp. 336–337; Franklin to Thomas Cushing, Feb. 15, 1774, Bigelow, *Works of Franklin*, V, 294–296; Trumbull MSS, IV (I), 45a-b, CSL.

[57] Edward P. Lilly, *The Colonial Agents of New York and New Jersey* (Washington, D.C., 1936), pp. 17–18, 105, 192; Jackson to Franklin, Dec. 27, 1763, *Letters and Papers of Benjamin Franklin and Richard Jackson, 1753–1785*, ed. Carl Van Doren (Philadelphia, 1947), p. 123; Bollan to Samuel Danforth, May 1, 1770, *Bowdoin and Temple Papers*, p. 180.

Jackson still had influence at the plantation office as late as 1767, but he began to encounter obstacles in locating the particular documents his work required. In 1766, Franklin could lay his hands on desired papers at the Board of Trade; but the following year he met with difficulty. Sherwood, acting with Franklin, was unconditionally refused documents at the Board and Secretary of State's office. Late in 1769, De Berdt still obtained copies of letters "properly attested." In 1770, however, he lamented to his employers that

it will be exceedingly difficult to fix directly on those papers which may be necessary for our purposes . . . —they must be obtain'd by order of the privy council, and this order cannot be made general unless the party is in favour, and you may suppose there is no reason to expect much assistance from the chief officers or Clerks of the public Boards.

In 1770–1771, Thomas Life was permitted to search the Privy Council and plantation office. Two years later he reported inconveniences in that respect to his Connecticut constituents. In 1768, Johnson applied "to the clerks of the Exchequer for copies of the usual writs," but those he received were "very general, and not grounded upon any particular fact or information." Two years later Connecticut's agent acquired a copy of the Susquehanna case report with very great difficulty, and in 1771 he was refused outright in a similar situation. In 1768, Garth feared that the Privy Council "are so cautious of granting Copies of Office Papers, that perhaps I may not be indulged there with." Until 1773 he received "liberty to inspect sundry papers relative to the constitution of the Council" by the Board of Trade.[58]

That office did not turn markedly against the colonies until after repeal of the Stamp Act. During Grenville's regime it had sponsored legislation favorable to America before the Privy Council and in Parliament. Regarding the Stamp Act itself, the Board played a passive role. It did little more than tabulate and copy letters, complaints, and memorials for the use of Parliament. Lobbying for settlement of the Illinois country in 1767, Franklin found that "there remained no

[58] Jackson to ?, Jan. 9, 1767, MA, Misc. Letters, 1763–1773, p. 146; Franklin to William Franklin, Nov. 25, 1767, Smyth, V, 67; Sherwood to Benjamin Franklin, July 21, 1767, APS; De Berdt to Thomas Cushing, Oct. 12, 1769, Jan. 1, 1770, Matthews, "Letters of De Berdt," pp. 381, 391–392; Life to Jonathan Trumbull, Agents Letters, 1742–1773, no. 73, CHS; Johnson to William Pitkin, July 23, 1768, Aug. 20, 1770, MHS *Collections*, ser. 5, IX, 292, 448; Garth to S.C. CC, Oct. 14, 1768, Dec. 27, 1773, *SCHGM*, XXX, 229, Garth Letter-book, p. 159, SCA.

obstacle but the Board of Trade, which was to be brought over privately before the matter should be referred to them officially." While the agents had begun to encounter difficulties at the plantation office, they still seemed surmountable. In 1768, however, Charles Garth reported to his constituents that he found the Board cordial but inflexible, tending to form opinions prematurely and arrive at hearings with closed minds. Montagu and Jackson also ran up against obstacles placed in their way by men infatuated with proprieties. The agents of necessity continued to press their causes at the Board of Trade, but with increasing futility and hostility, as Garth, Franklin, and Bollan informed their employers.[59]

By 1772 some of the agents no longer trusted information received at the Board of Trade and American Department—"the shallow arts, the guile-ful givings-out, of those contemptible creatures Hillsborough & his associate Pownall." The lobbyists seem to have broken communication with the lesser employees at the colonial office. Their correspondence never mentions William Pollock, chief clerk at the American Department, who had charge of office papers and preparing dispatches.[60]

Nor did they have much to do with Richard Cumberland, solicitor and clerk of reports to the Board of Trade—a strategically located person. Cumberland's work "consisted of taking minutes of the debates and proceedings at the Board, and preparing for their approbation and signature such reports, as they should direct to be drawn up for his Majesty, or the Council, and, on some occasions, for the Board of Treasury, or Secretaries of State." Because Cumberland received confidential information from Pownall, he was potentially a useful contact. By 1770, however, he took a dim view of such a radical organization as the Bill of Rights Society. He soon came to oppose the colonial patriots, believing they had been misled by the irresponsible opposition in Britain.[61]

[59] Basye, *Lords Commissioners of Trade*, pp. 137, 140, 143, 152; Franklin to William Franklin, Aug. 28, 1767, Nov. 3, 1772, Smyth, V, 46, 445–446; Garth to S.C. CC, Aug. 14, 1768, Dec. 17, 1771, *SCHGM*, XXX, 218–219, XXXIII, 123–124; *Journal of the Commissioners for Trade, 1768–1775*, pp. 29, 31; Bollan to Mass. Council, Feb. 24, 1774, *Bowdoin and Temple Papers*, p. 340.

[60] William Bollan to Mass. Council, Sept. 1, 1773, *Bowdoin and Temple Papers*, pp. 308–317; Arthur Lee to Sam Adams, April 7, 1772, Adams MSS, NYPL.

[61] William Samuel Johnson's London diary, entry for Dec. 8, 1770, WSJ MSS; "Richard Cumberland," *DNB*.

At the Treasury a similar situation obtained. In 1763, Jasper Mauduit found Jeremiah Dyson, secretary to the Board and later a member, amenable. So did William Samuel Johnson through the sixties, but not thereafter. Among subsequent secretaries to the Treasury the agents maintained worthwhile friendships until about 1768. Samuel Martin was succeeded by Thomas Whately, an important connection for the agents because he had access to Grenville. Ingersoll and Johnson developed good relationships with Whately; but he left the Treasury in 1765. In 1767, Johnson felt that he entertained "mistaken Principles & Ill Opinions with respect to the Colonies." By 1772, when Whately had become secretary to Lord Suffolk, Secretary of State for the Southern Department, the agents regarded him as "our arch foe." [62]

Benjamin Franklin was pleased in 1765 when an "old acquaintance," Grey Cooper, replaced Whately as secretary to the Treasury. Franklin even wrote one of his political essays at Cooper's country home, and their friendship remained strong until 1768. Thereafter there seems to have been less contact between them. The agents had almost no influence with Charles Lowndes, John Robinson, and Thomas Bradshaw, the Treasury secretaries who took office after repeal of the Stamp Act. [63]

In the Northern and Southern Departments the same pattern prevailed. While Lord Shelburne administered colonial affairs at the Southern Department, he had two subordinates of pivotal importance: Lauchlin MacLeane and Maurice Morgann. Formerly a Philadelphian, Undersecretary MacLeane was a political radical regarded as a "fortune hunter" by American speculators and "mad" by Shelburne himself. Between 1766 and 1768, Franklin, Jackson, and Johnson found MacLeane a reliable contact. But he departed shortly after Shelburne, lost his influence, and in 1771 accepted a sinecure from Lord North. Maurice Morgann served alongside MacLeane as Shelburne's deputy and principal adviser on colonial policy. During his

[62] Jasper Mauduit to Andrew Oliver, July 2, 1763, MA, CCLXXXVIII, p. 5; Johnson to William Pitkin, March 23, 1769, MHS *Collections*, ser. 5, IX, 328; Johnson to Ingersoll, Feb. 18, 1767, WSJ MSS; Arthur Lee to Sam Adams, June 14, 1771, Adams MSS, NYPL.

[63] Franklin to William Franklin, Nov. 9, 1765, MFY; Franklin to Jane Mecom, Dec. 24, 1767, *The Letters of Benjamin Franklin and Jane Mecom*, ed. Carl Van Doren (Princeton, 1950), p. 102; Franklin to Cooper, June 24, 1768, MFY; Franklin to William Franklin, July 2, 1768, Smyth, V, 143–144; Dora Mae Clark, "The Office of Secretary to the Treasury in the Eighteenth Century," *AHR*, XLII (1936), 22–45.

term of service Morgann exerted considerable influence and befriended Franklin, Jackson, and the De Berdt circle. By 1770, however, one colonial observer reported that "Mr. Morgann seems quite
dependent on Ministry, and what is a little unhappy, his patron, Lord
Shelburne, has little prospect of coming in again." [64]

Beginning about 1770 the agents found all levels of the hierarchy at
the Privy Council becoming progressively more intractable. Imitative
bureaucrats were not only acting upon orders, but following their
superiors in blocking American avenues of access. By 1771, Garth's
influence at the Cockpit seems to have been waning, as he grudgingly
admitted later to Lord Dartmouth. Jackson and Bollan also encountered procedural difficulties at the Privy Council. In 1771, Bollan
began to meet resistance there, particularly among the clerks. A year
later he reflected nostalgically upon the 1740's and 1750's, when his
relations had been so cordial with the personnel. By 1774 he found
lobbying at the Council office virtually impossible. The most pressing
business could not persuade the members to meet with sufficient
frequency to expedite imperial matters. Documents of colonial concern became stuck in some crevice and lay forgotten. Seeking an
appointment with Lord Gower, Bollan was evaded and rudely sent
from one bureaucrat to another. Each in his turn refused to cooperate,
talk, or permit inspection of the minute books to determine whether
anything had been done or was intended regarding American affairs. [65]
In June 1774 the Privy Council's committee on plantation problems
established new rules governing its operations in an attempt to increase efficiency. By adhering inflexibly to patterns unfamiliar to the

[64] Scott, "Under Secretaries of State," pp. 264–273, 288–309; J. N. M.
Maclean, *Reward Is Secondary* (London, 1963); Jack M. Sosin, *Whitehall and
the Wilderness: The Middle West in British Colonial Policy, 1760–1775*
(Lincoln, Neb., 1961), pp. 60, 143, 146–147, 151–152, 157, 184; Joseph
Reed to ? Pettit, May 7, 1770, William B. Reed, *The Life of Esther De Berdt*
(Philadelphia, 1853), p. 148. Franklin B. Wickwire has demonstrated that, by
1774, Morgann was unsympathetic to American problems (*British Subminis-
ters*, p. 152).

[65] De Berdt to Thomas Cushing, Nov. 16, 1769, Matthews, "Letters of De
Berdt," p. 386; Garth to Dartmouth, July 25, 1774, Dartmouth MSS, Vol. II,
no. 933, WSL; Bollan to Mass. Council, Jan. 28, 1771, Feb. 2, 1774, *Bowdoin
and Temple Papers*, pp. 249–250, 338; Bollan to Hillsborough, May 25, 1772,
to Dartmouth, Feb. 5, 1774, Dartmouth MSS, Vol. II, nos. 366, 818, WSL;
Bollan to James Bowdoin *et al.*, Feb. 28, 1774, Bowdoin-Temple MSS, Vol. III,
MHS.

agents, the Council simply accentuated the declining possibility of trans-Atlantic accommodation. Incessant changes in administrative form made the lobbyists' relationship to government inscrutable.[66]

The agents responded to these conditions in two ways. Some were alienated, as we have seen, and looked with hostility upon a bureaucracy they regarded as grossly ignorant of America. They publicly chided the civil servants for their "inferior knowledge." Others, however, capitulated to the administration's concerted pressures. The "servants of power" had become altogether less hospitable to the American interest. Their attitude was manifest in their behavior—the performance of traditional functions poorly, reluctantly, and finally not at all. In part they merely reflected the growing inflexibility they saw at the highest levels of government. Yet they were also undermined by the departmental autonomy and authority of British imperial administration.[67]

[66] Smith, *Appeals to the Privy Council,* pp. 276–277 and ch. 5; Benjamin Franklin to David Hartley, Feb. 26, 1775, Berkshire Country Record Office, England.

[67] See Karl Mannheim, *Ideology and Utopia* (New York, 1936), pp. 105–106.

CHAPTER 14

The Agents and the
Final Crisis, 1774–1775

"The fack can't be no longer disgised that a Krysis is onto us."
—ARTEMUS WARD

Late in 1774 the secretary to the Continental Congress prepared a roster of agents in London who might receive and handle American petitions. He listed the colonies geographically from north to south. Beside Rhode Island, Delaware, Maryland, Virginia, and North Carolina he inscribed "None." Five of the thirteen colonies lacked representatives altogether. Four of the others had entrusted themselves to Franklin's hands. Half of the agents were disaffected by the direction colonial political ideas had taken. Thus David Barclay lamented on New Year's Eve, 1774, that "if Deputies had been sent hither from the Congress it would have been of considerable Advantage." Months earlier Burke exaggerated for effect in chiding the House of Commons for continually frustrating the colonists by refusing to admit their agents' petitions: "You have not now one left in England to be heard in behalf of any of the colonies." Concurrently Esther De Berdt Reed wrote her brother that "agencies at present are not very desirable." [1]

THE AGENCY IN PROFILE: A FINAL GLANCE

Among the few new agents at this time, Paul Wentworth, who obtained New Hampshire's agency during the winter of 1773–1774, can

[1] Herbert Friedenwald, "The Journals and Papers of the Continental Congress," *PMHB*, XXI (1897), 448; Barclay to J. Gipson, Dec. 31, 1774, American Revolution box, NYPL; *PHE*, XVII, 1182 (March 15, 1774); William B. Reed, *The Life of Esther De Berdt* (Philadelphia, 1853), p. 195.

scarcely be considered an asset to the declining institution. In 1770 he had been commissioned as a private agent by people living west of the Connecticut River (in what is now Vermont) who wanted their disputed homesteads confirmed in London against the claims of New York speculators. He did nothing to help these settlers, but used their needs as a pretext to get himself the New Hampshire agency, ostensibly in order to urge their remonstrance. When the issue finally came before the Board of Trade in 1775, Wentworth acted feebly in behalf of his constituents, no action eventuated, and the Revolution curtailed litigation.[2]

In 1773 he warmly advocated Thomas Hutchinson's cause to Rockingham and continued to present the Marquess with a hostile version of colonial conditions. In 1774, Wentworth refused to join his fellow agents in presenting the petition of the Continental Congress, a memorial which he told John Pownall "is an assertion of all their Claims in a very high Tone & with very offensive expressions." He even leaked the agents' lobbying strategy to his friends in the bureaucracy.[3] He was clearly a wretched choice for agent. In 1775, Edmund Burke accused him of collusion with the administration, whereupon Wentworth wrote his apologia to Rockingham, claiming that "to my knowledge I am wholly unknown, name & face, to every Person, High or low, in the present administration—except for Lord Dartmouth—Mr. Cooper [4]—& Mr. Pownal, by official Communications merely." Perhaps he protested too much. When the colonies broke free this *chevalier d'industrie* became a loyalist and British spy.[5]

When North Carolina's agency fell vacant in 1774, the colony appointed Alexander Elmsley and Thomas Barker as special agents to secure crown approval of provincial legislation. Barker was an influential lawyer and assemblyman and had been treasurer of the northern district of North Carolina until 1761, when he emigrated to England.

---

[2] Wentworth to William Samuel Johnson, Jan. 8, 1771, WSJ MSS (box) II; Matthew B. Jones, *Vermont in the Making, 1750–1777* (Cambridge, Mass., 1939), pp. 176, 182–185, 254; *Journal of the Commissioners for Trade and Plantations from January 1768 to December 1775* (London, 1920–1938), p. 421.

[3] Wentworth to Rockingham, Aug. 7, 1773, R1–1438, Fitzwilliam MSS, SCL; *The Diary and Letters of Thomas Hutchinson*, ed. Peter O. Hutchinson (Boston, 1884–1886), I, 186, 339; memo by Pownall, Dec. 20, 1774, Dartmouth MSS, Vol. I, ii, no. 1088, WSL.

[4] Grey Cooper, secretary to the Treasury.

[5] June 2, [1775?], R1–1563, Fitzwilliam MSS, SCL; petition of sundry American Loyalists, PRO T 1/518.

The Assembly elected him to replace Jouvencal in 1765, but the Council vetoed the selection. Elmsley, a London merchant who had lived in North Carolina, had also been a member of its Assembly. He very much wanted McCulloh's agency; and his letters to friends in the colony form a candid commentary on contemporary politics. This duet scored a triumph of sorts when they won exemption for North Carolina from the bill of 1775 restricting colonial trade to Britain and the British West Indies. Their action in this case was a breach of colonial unity, however; not surprisingly, they did not assist the other agents during the desperate winter negotiations of 1774–1775.[6]

Although Benjamin Franklin remained in London until March 1775, his effectiveness was much reduced thirteen months earlier by the famous confrontation with Alexander Wedderburn in the Cockpit. In 1773, Franklin had procured private letters written by Thomas Hutchinson to Thomas Whately, a Grenvillite, and letters of Andrew Oliver, lieutenant governor of Massachusetts.[7] The "oligarchs" had explicitly cautioned their correspondents "to Keep their contents from the *Colony Agents*, who the writers apprehended might return them, or copies of them, to America. That apprehension was, it seems, well founded; for the first agent who laid his lands on them, thought it his duty to transmit them to his constituents." The epistles touched off a scandal of considerable proportions on both sides of the Atlantic. Franklin wanted his role in the affair kept quiet. He had sent the letters to half-a-dozen prominent Massachusetts patriots with the stipulation that no copies would be made. They were to be shown confidentially to a few friends and then returned to England. But "Franklin was setting a dinner before hungry men and forbidding them to eat." They ignored his instructions by having the letters read to the Massachusetts House. That body promptly ordered them printed. The aftermath is well known. The General Court impeached the two

[6] William Tryon to Dartmouth, June 24, 1765, Dartmouth MSS, Vol. II, no. 78, WSL; Ella Lonn, *The Colonial Agents of the Southern Colonies* (Chapel Hill, 1945), 137, 210, 282, 371.

[7] How the agent obtained these documents became the focus of much frenzy in England and remains a mystery to this day. John Temple, the obvious link, denied culpability, and Franklin supported him, perhaps owing to a greater regard for honor than for truth (John Almon, *Biographical, Literary, and Political Anecdotes* . . . [London, 1797], III, 237, 240, 242–243, 247). See also *The Last Journals of Horace Walpole during the Reign of George III* . . . *1771–1783*, ed. A. F. Steuart (London, 1910), I, 243 n.; and Franklin to Thomas Cushing, July 7, 1773, Smyth, VI, 81.

villains and sent petitions to London requesting their removal. Franklin conveyed the documents for Lord Dartmouth to present to George III.[8]

January 29, 1774, was appointed for a hearing before the Privy Council. Israel Mauduit represented Hutchinson and Oliver as their agent, and Solicitor General Wedderburn appeared in their behalf. Franklin stood isolated. Arthur Lee was at Bath. His Majesty's councillors refused to hear Bollan because he represented the upper house, whereas the memorial originated in the lower. Wedderburn took the opportunity to vilify Franklin and seized again upon the agent's appointment to obtain leverage.

The rank in which Dr. Franklin appears, is not even that of a Province Agent: he moves in a very inferior orbit. An Agent for a province . . . is a person chosen by the joint act of the Governor, Council, and Assembly. . . . Such a real Colony Agent . . . will think it his duty to consult the joint service of all the three, and to contribute all he can to the harmony . . . of the whole. This at least is what I learn from the copy books of two Gentlemen, who at different periods were Agents for this very Colony. But Dr. Franklin's appointment seems to have been made in direct opposition to all these. . . . [He] therefore . . . not only moves in a different orbit from that of other Colony Agents, but he gravitates also to a different center.[9]

Franklin, of course, remained mute throughout the long attack.

Although the petition was denied, Massachusetts' radicals ultimately won the battle. Later in the year, after passage of the Boston Port Act, General Thomas Gage replaced Hutchinson. The fiasco in the Cockpit, however, effectively curtailed Franklin's agency. He became an object of popular abuse in England; and his remaining fourteen months in London form an epilogue of covert operations. His usefulness as a public lobbyist was at an end. One month after the dramatic hearing David Hume hoped that William Strahan could give him some "justification, at least in alleviation of Dr. Franklyn's

---

[8] Franklin's public letter, Dec. 25, 1773, reprinted in the *Boston Gazette and Country Journal*, March 7, 1774; John C. Miller, *Origins of the American Revolution* (2nd ed.; London, 1959), p. 331; for Franklin's account see his letter to Cushing, Feb. 15, 1774, *The Complete Works of Benjamin Franklin*, ed. John Bigelow (New York, 1887), V, 292–305.

[9] *The Letters of Governor Hutchinson and Lt. Governor Oliver* . . . (London, 1774), pp. 99–100; Franklin to Cushing, April 2, 1774, Smyth, VI, 224.

Conduct. The factious Part he has all along acted must be given up by his best Friends. . . . What pity, that a man of his Merit shoud have fallen into such unhappy Circumstances!" [10]

Following his humiliation Franklin's New Jersey and Georgia agencies ended. He also wrote to Massachusetts that he could not continue; but just when Arthur Lee should have been available to take over, he was persuaded by Paul Wentworth to visit Italy instead. Wentworth even furnished Lee with £300 to make sure of his departure! [11] Franklin was therefore obliged to retain the now awkward role of agent for the Bay Colony. Fortunately, when Lee returned from the continent he had matured as a political man. He cooperated with the remaining agents and procured the introduction of American grievances into the famous Middlesex Petition. When William Bollan received the addresses of the Continental Congress late in 1774, Lee had them extensively circulated. When the Lord Mayor, aldermen, and livery of London wished to offer George III a remonstrance in 1775, the Common Hall asked Lee to write it. [12]

The character of Franklin's association with Burke during these years is unclear, but they were not notably close. New York's agent paid little more attention to the Doctor than he did to the other agents. By 1774 their estimates of the scope of parliamentary authority had diverged. The only instance of joint effort between these two figures occurred a few days before Franklin left London in March 1775. They spent several hours in conference, and three days later Burke delivered his memorable speech on conciliation. Perhaps the Doctor had been influential. Ironically, despite his own disinterest in cooperation, Burke recognized the deleterious effects of its absence. He carefully suggested to the House of Commons that his plan for conciliation with America did not "propose to fill your lobby with

[10] Franklin to Jane Mecom, Sept. 26, 1774, to Joseph Galloway, Oct. 12, 1774, Smyth, VI, 246, 254; *The Letters of David Hume,* ed. J. Y. T. Greig (Oxford, 1932), II, 287–288.

[11] Franklin to Thomas Cushing, Feb. 24, April 2, and June 1, 1774, Smyth, VI, 224–225, 232; Alfred O. Aldridge, "Benjamin Franklin as Georgia Agent," *Georgia Review,* VI (1952), 171–173; Hutchinson, *Diary and Letters of Hutchinson,* I, 434.

[12] Lyon G. Tyler, "Arthur Lee, a Neglected Statesman," *Tyler's Quarterly Historical and Genealogical Magazine,* XIV (1932), 70–76; *The Revolutionary Diplomatic Correspondence of the United States,* ed. Francis Wharton (Washington, D.C., 1889), II, 63, 78–80.

squabbling colony agents, who will require the interposition of your mace at every instant to keep the peace among them." [13]

Despite his public stature Burke was not consistently valuable to New York or America during the final crisis. In 1774 he gave the Assembly a peculiarly belated account of the Quebec Act, and even remarked that the bill could not materially affect the rights of New York. In December 1774 and August 1775 he flatly refused to cooperate with the other agents in presenting the petitions of the Continental Congress.[14] Burke's efforts to present New York's remonstrance in 1775 lacked vigor, for he placed distinct limits upon colonial autonomy. He believed in parliamentary supremacy in all cases except for the practice of taxation. Burke had formed these views during the Stamp Act crisis and did not alter them until after war in America had begun.[15]

Like Burke, Charles Garth found himself paralyzed by uncertainty as the breach widened. When the petition of the Continental Congress arrived in December 1774, Garth was conveniently out of touch in Wiltshire, where Franklin's message could not readily reach him. Six weeks later Thomas Hutchinson attended a dinner party at which Garth was present. The Governor observed to his diary that South Carolina's agent had been in opposition, "but speaks not in favour of American measures in Parliament." On February 26, 1775, the Lord Chancellor provided a *repas* at which Garth condemned the proceedings of the Continental Congress and advocated an act declaring that body illegal in order to incapacitate anyone who attended from holding public office. Three months later he gracefully concluded his

---

[13] Ross J. S. Hoffman, *Edmund Burke, New York Agent . . .* (Philadelphia, 1956), pp. 127, 132; Dixon Wecter, "Burke, Franklin and Samuel Petrie," *Huntington Library Quarterly*, III (1940), 318.

[14] Burke scarcely ever acted in concert with the other agents. None of their names appears in his letters to New York (P. T. Underdown, "Edmund Burke as a Member of Parliament for Bristol . . ." [unpub. Ph.D. diss.; University of London, 1955], p. 195).

[15] Carl B. Cone, *Burke and the Nature of Politics: The Age of the American Revolution*, I (Lexington, Ky., 1957), pp. 252, 283. For criticisms of Burke on account of his handling of New York's land dispute with New Hampshire settlers, see Hoffman, *Burke*, pp. 147, 167, 175–177, 179–181, 186–188, 191–193. For Henry Cruger's general complaint, see H. C. Van Schaack, *Henry Cruger, the Colleague of Edmund Burke* (New York, 1859), pp. 19–20.

thirteen-year agency by writing Charleston that "I shall probably have little more to Trouble you with for Some time. . . . If any Thing occurrs which I can come at the Knowledge of, as Intended by or Towards America, & I can with Authenticity Transmit, I shall not Neglect So to do." [16]

Still another agent whose office became nominal at this time was Thomas Life. He also would not cooperate with Franklin late in 1774. When the latter confronted Life with his instructions, the agent pleaded that he lacked sufficient authorization from Connecticut's Governor or Assembly, "and as my attending to present the Petition might very well be dispensed with and I did not think myself justified in so doing I begged to be excused which I was informed some other of the agents had done—I saw no real Benefit that could arise to the Colony. . . . If I have erred it has been thro' Caution." Although Life disapproved of the violent proceedings in New England, he continued to attend the Susquehanna case until the end of 1775. [17]

Clearly the agents were in a weakened condition as the winter crisis early in 1774 came on. They lacked, as Bernard Donoughue has shown, "a substantial and rooted interest in the Community and in Parliament; and without it they became an isolated band of agitators. Moreover, the British Government which they hoped to influence was at this time totally and inflexibly committed to its policy of coercion." So far as the agents were concerned this policy seemed even to extend to themselves; for as one wrote, "the active Americans here stand in daily peril of their lives." [18] Arthur Lee's statement may have been extreme, but there was every indication that the administration intended to muzzle the agency. At the time of Franklin's denunciation in the Cockpit—January 1774—Bollan's status as agent for only the Council was used to exclude him from speaking on behalf of his coagent. Thereafter the administration and Parliament repeatedly seized upon this same excuse to shut themselves off from hearing colonial grievances. Such action in the House of Commons prompted Burke's rebuke to the assembled members: "We are resolved not to

[16] Garth to S.C. CC, Jan. 20 and May 27, 1775, Garth Letter-book, SCA; Hutchinson, *Diary and Letters of Hutchinson*, I, 376, 396.

[17] Life to Franklin, Dec. 19, 1774, Franklin MSS, Vol. V, HSP; Life to William Samuel Johnson, Feb. 1, 1775, WSJ MSS (bound), II.

[18] Bernard Donoughue, *British Politics and the American Revolution: The Path to War, 1773–1775* (London, 1964), pp. 156–161; Arthur Lee to ?, Feb. 20, 1774, Richard H. Lee, *The Life of Arthur Lee* (Boston, 1829), I, 266.

hear the only person we *can* hear; but are mighty ready to hear anyone else. Pray observe how this argument runs; a general agent you will not admit, and a particular agent you cannot conceive." In the privacy of his correspondence with New York, Burke notified his employers that "few colonies have [an] agent properly authorized to communicate your desires in that character to Parliament." [19]

OPPOSING THE COERCIVES, SPRING 1774

News of the Boston Tea Party struck London like an incendiary bomb. It seemed the ultimate act of violence. One London observer wrote William Samuel Johnson that refusing to accept the tea had caused the biggest frenzy and strongest anticolonial feeling in England he had ever seen. The newspapers roundly abused America daily. Richard Jackson cautioned Connecticut not to participate in such public outrages defying parliamentary authority. But Franklin and Bollan, as guardians of the wayward colony, were most embarrassed by the reckless act. The Doctor candidly reprimanded Speaker Cushing for the unwise and unnecessary destruction of private property. Franklin hoped the General Court would repair the damage by compensating the East India Company. No amount of money, however, could win back the Britons permanently estranged by this impetuous affair. When Bollan approached Henry Seymour Conway in 1774 about presenting a remonstrance, the General complained "that violence and disorders in the Colonies laid difficulties in the way of their friends obtaining the relief they wanted." Hence the Rockingham Whigs sat nearly mute while the Coercive Acts passed. Even Burke approved singling out and punishing the persons who had committed the crime.[20]

The Tea Party seemed a gross violation of authority to moderates as well as extreme conservatives in North's cabinet. In February and March 1774, irrespective of personal feelings and previous constitutional commitments, all were united—from North and Dartmouth to

[19] *Boston Evening Post*, July 18, 1774; Hoffman, *Burke*, p. 134.
[20] Nicholas Ray to Johnson, April 4, 1774, WSJ MSS (bound), Vol. II; Jackson to Johnson, April 5, 1774, *ibid*. (box), Vol. II; Franklin to Cushing, Feb. 2, 1774, Smyth, VI, 179; Bollan to John Erving *et al.*, March 11, 1774, *American Archives*, comp. Peter Force (Washington, D.C., 1837–1846), ser. 4, I, 226; Hoffman, *Burke*, pp. 128–129.

Sandwich and Suffolk—in wishing to assert an undivided British sovereignty over the colonies. Several recent scholars have related the emergence of punitive measures in London: the early vigor and sudden demise of the proposal to prosecute the Boston activists on charges of treason; the proposal to move the customs house and Assembly from Boston; the legislative measure to alter the Massachusetts constitution. While the story of the Coercives is familiar, the agents' difficulties in opposing them are less well known and symptomatic of the deepening crisis.[21]

From the outset in considering what measures should be taken, it was clear that no one in the ministry was willing to deal with the North American agents—either for advice or for accounts of grievances submitted by the colonies. Letters from London reprinted in colonial newspapers announced that "the Evidence before the Privy Council was suppressed, the agents refused a hearing at the bar, and no member for Boston or America in either House." [22] Most important, in March 1774 the petition as a means of redressing Anglo-American distress began to gasp its last breaths. Bollan battled to find someone to handle a petition designed "to ascertain the rights of the Colonies." On the fourteenth Sir Joseph Mawbey attempted to present it, but without success. A comical sequence of conferences ensued, with Mawbey scurrying back and forth from chamber to lobby seeking support and advice from Bollan. From the Treasury bench North "ridiculed the Petition," not thinking it worth a division. So it was allowed and tabled, "where it would lie ready to be taken up when any prejudicial measure should require it." On the twenty-first Mawbey moved that Bollan should be heard in support of his petition, "which being opposed by Administration, was refused," chiefly on grounds that it was not strictly relevant to the pending punishment.[23]

Bollan then prepared a second, different remonstrance, unequivocally opposing the Boston Port bill. Again there were difficulties in

[21] Donoughue, *British Politics and the American Revolution*, chs. 3–4; Benjamin W. Labaree, *The Boston Tea Party* (New York, 1964), ch. 9; cf. Jack M. Sosin, "The Massachusetts Acts of 1774: Coercive or Preventive?" *Huntington Library Quarterly*, XXVI (1963), 235–252.

[22] Lawrence H. Gipson, *The British Empire before the American Revolution*, XII (New York, 1965), 110; *Boston Gazette and Country Journal*, May 23, 1774.

[23] Bollan to John Erving *et al.*, March 11, 15, and 22, 1774, Force, *American Archives*, ser. 4, I, 226–227, 229–230; *JHC*, XXXIV, 561.

finding a sponsor; again Mawbey consented to undertake it. Sir Joseph intended to present it before the House went into committee to consider the bill; but the speaker, clerk of the Commons, and several friends agreed that the petition could not then be presented "because the Bill itself might be lost in the Committee." They decided the objections would only be admissible before the third reading. When that opportunity came Mawbey "was gone out of town." This time the search for a sponsor turned up Alderman Brass Crosby. But the results remained the same. Bollan's authority was called into question, his petition was undermined, and the House refused to hear it. At the close of this debate Burke reminded his fellows that "Criminals are a part of a Court & therefore should be heard & asked Guilty or not guilty." [24]

Frustrated by the Commons, the agent turned to the peers for a hearing. There the same struggle to find a patron recurred, and Bollan bounced from one noble's doorstep to another and back again. Finally Lord Stair "determined to support it." Debate ensued within the chamber on March 30. Just as Bollan prepared to quit the lobby in disgust, "the proper officer came out of the House," led the agent inside, and introduced him: "The Lords had agreed to hear me; and . . . observed it was necessary for me to confine myself to the matter in question; . . . I [then] proceeded to set forth the great importance of the port of *Boston*." When he paused to catch his breath, "a noble Lord stood up and observed" that Bollan had petitioned as agent for the Council, but did not confine himself to their concerns solely. Another peer, seated near Bollan at the bar, cried out with others, "go on, go on." Bollan completed his testimony and left. The bill passed regardless. [25]

Concurrently the sheriffs of London, Sayre and Lee, met with twenty-seven others at the Thatched House Tavern to prepare a similar protest to the House of Lords. Among the company were Franklin, Arthur Lee, Edward Bancroft, a group of South Carolina merchants, some West Indians, and representatives of several other colonies. Considering "the interposition of Parliamentary power to be

[24] Bollan to John Erving *et al.*, March 23, 1774, Force, *American Archives*, ser. 4, I, 230; Bollan to Erving, April 1, 1774, misc. bound MSS, MHS; *JHC*, XXXIV, 595–596; entry for March 25, 1774, Matthew Brickdale's parliamentary debates, MS minute book, no. 10, BUL.

[25] Bollan to Erving *et al.*, April 1, 1774, Force, *American Archives*, ser. 4, I, 233–234; Garth to S.C. CC, March 31, 1774, Garth Letter-book, pp. 168–169.

as unnecessary, as it is arbitrary & unjust," the petition was presented, read, tabled, and ignored. The Port of Boston would be closed.[26]

On April 28, William Dowdeswell offered the Commons another petition from Bollan, "the Prayer of which was that the House would not pass the Bill . . . depriving . . . Massachusetts of the Constitution they enjoyed under their Charter, without Being heard in Support of their Government." To no one's surprise Jeremiah Dyson repudiated the agent's authority. But Dowdeswell was prepared. He counteracted by producing Bollan's credentials from the Council and noting that the Lords had received Bollan's petition and heard him a month before. Dyson pressed his charge that a legitimate lobbyist must be the creature of governor, council, and assembly jointly. Burke at this point, full of wrath, rose to denounce the continual suppression of the colonial voice.

We have acted very inconsistently relative to this gentleman & have Changed him oftener than any Metamorphosis of Ovid. He was the same man the 14th of March last when we read his Petition as the 25th of the same month when we rejected one. . . . If we do not admit an agent it is at all times to deny Justice. By whom shall we hear the colonies, if not by agents —If William Bollan is not *properly* appointed agent—Let us settle how an agent is *properly* to be appointed. Its said a Special attorney may be appointed—but not a general one. Is it not strange that a set of persons shall be capable of being accused & not capable of appointing an agent to defend? No Court but ourselves would dare to refuse such an agent as Bollan —The receiving a petition is always less dangerous than rejecting one. We should fix & let America know how an agent that we will receive shall be appointed—as it is not intended to proceed against the Americans as Rebells—they should not be called so. We are more likely to drive them to arms by refusing to hear them than by any other means.

After three hours of debate the Commons voted against hearing the petition. The next day Sir George Savile unsuccessfully fought the bill regulating the Massachusetts judiciary. On May 2 he presented a petition to the House, signed by the Americans then in London, declaring it unconstitutional to deprive a province of its rights without a hearing. The document was tabled. Later in the day Isaac Barré castigated the House for ignoring Bollan's pleas, citing the fact that Bollan's credentials had been accepted and approved at the various

[26] Richard H. Lee, *Memoir of the Life of Richard Henry Lee and His Correspondence* . . . (Philadelphia, 1825), I, 268–269; Arthur Lee to Sam Adams, May 16, 1774, Adams MSS, NYPL.

public offices. The London press joined in exposing the sham and pretense of the imperial legislature.[27]

In May the pattern recurred in the House of Lords. Once more various peers kept Bollan dangling in uncertainty for days and weeks on end. Who would present his protest? When? Would the agent be heard again at the bar? Finally the Duke of Richmond offered and the clerk read it. Debate followed and the peers rejected it. This time hardly anyone even questioned the agent's status. It was candidly admitted all around that the Lords urgently wanted to pass the bill regulating government in Massachusetts and would not be stopped.[28]

The routine resumed at year's end when the Continental Congress sent its remonstrances to the London lobbyists. But as Franklin had anticipated in 1772, "the slighting, evading, or refusing to receive Petitions from the Colonies on some late Occasions, by the Parliament, had occasioned a total loss of Respect for, & Confidence in that Body . . . & brought on a Questioning of their Authority." Hence petitions would no longer be directed to Westminster, "but to the King only: . . . the King appeared to be now the only Connection between the two Countries." Franklin warned Dartmouth that he "thought it a dangerous Thing for any Government to refuse receiving Petitions, and thereby prevent the Subjects from giving vent to their Griefs."[29]

Those agents who attempted to forestall the Coercives were particularly hurt by the response of the merchant community, which "acted on this important occasion as in every other matter of this nature heretofore." Bollan felt certain that the West Indian merchants and manufacturing interests would unite with the North Americans in

---

[27] Garth to S.C. CC, April 30, 1774, Garth Letter-book, pp. 171–172, SCA; entry for April 28, 1774, Brickdale's parliamentary debates, MS minute book, no. 10, BUL; *PHE*, XVII, 1279, 1289–1300, 1306; *JHC*, XXXIV, 689; Bollan to John Erving *et al.*, April 30, 1774, misc. bound MSS, MHS; North to George III, April 28, 1774, *The Correspondence of King George III, 1760–1783*, ed. John Fortescue (London, 1927), III, 99; F. J. Hinkhouse, *The Preliminaries of the American Revolution as Seen in the English Press, 1763–1775* (New York, 1926), pp. 166–167.

[28] Bollan to Mass. Council, May 12, 1774, *The Bowdoin and Temple Papers* (MHS *Collections*, ser. 6, Vol. IX [Boston, 1897]), pp. 367–369; *A Complete Collection of the Protests of the Lords . . .* , comp. J. E. T. Rogers (Oxford, 1875), II, 141, 146; Bollan to John Erving *et al.*, May 31, 1774, misc. bound MSS, MHS.

[29] Franklin to Thomas Cushing, Dec. 12, 1772, Smyth, V, 449.

defense of unimpeded commerce. But he was disappointed. Both
groups declined opposition to the Coercives. Even David Barclay,
apparently cynical of his colleagues' chances, was discouraged about
petitions originated among the merchants. A group of concerned
manufacturers asked Franklin to dine with them in April; but this
only produced an exchange of viewpoints over the new duty on
foreign linens. According to William Lee, the various commercial
interests that would have preferred to see the Coercives quashed were
incapable of organizing effectively.[30]

Once these punitive measures became statutes, the agent-merchant
entente became even more tenuous. Pleading with his countrymen to
adhere to their boycott, Franklin knew too well that the provincial
representatives had lost one of their most important allies. He advised
the Continental Congress that no petition would receive attention
without the proper support in England, and told the Philadelphia
assemblage they "must make the merchants *feel,* before they will stir
for you, as their conduct respecting the Boston Port Bill sufficiently
evinces." [31]

Nevertheless, in the autumn of 1774 another projected boycott
simply brought vast orders from the New World in anticipation. Lee
and Franklin continued until the very end to urge their colonial
correspondents to hurt Britain through her influential merchants and
manufacturers. But the agents failed to realize that this class was less
vulnerable than before and that the administration had assurances
from America that no embargo would be effectively abided. In late
September 1774, Burke found that "the insensibility of the Merchants
of London is of a degree and kind scarcely to be conceived. Even those
who are the most likely to be overwhelmed by any real American
confusion are amongst the most supine." [32]

Burke, his fellow agents, and the few interested merchants were

[30] Franklin to Joseph Galloway, Aug. 3, 1773, Craven Street Letter-book,
Franklin Papers, LC; Force, *American Archives,* ser. 4, I, 230–231; Bollan to
John Erving *et al.,* April 1, 1774, misc. bound MSS, MHS; Franklin to
Thomas Cushing, April 2, 1774, Smyth, VI, 225; William Lee to ?, June 1,
1774, PRO CO 5/118, ff. 26–27.
[31] *Benjamin Franklin's Letters to the Press, 1758–1775,* ed. Verner W.
Crane (Chapel Hill, 1950), 266–267.
[32] Franklin to Bishop Shipley, Sept. 28, 1774, MFY; Arthur Lee to Richard
H. Lee, Dec. 13, 1774, Force, *American Archives,* ser. 4, I, 1040; Burke to
Rockingham, Sept. 18, 1774, *The Correspondence of Edmund Burke,
1774–1778,* ed. G. H. Guttridge, III (Chicago, 1961), 31.

only a shade more successful in opposing the Quebec Act during the early summer. Pennsylvania and New York, the two colonies most affected by the projected boundaries, both had traditional claims to all the land west of their settlements. Hence Burke and William Baker led the protests and managed to have certain territories originally included in Quebec attached to upstate New York and Pennsylvania. These negotiations with Lord North, who left the House doing nothing for thirty minutes while he met with the lobbyists upstairs, were accomplished on June 10. Burke's success in this case was one of his more solid achievements on New York's behalf.[33]

THE CLIMATE OF OPINION, 1774

On April 19, 1774, Burke delivered his great speech on "American Taxation," wherein he told the House that "for nine long years, session after session, we have been lashed round and round this miserable circle of occasional arguments and temporary expedients." By the following March it seemed to him as though "every principle of authority and resistance has been pushed, upon both sides, as far as it would go." Concurrently Charles Garth reported that the English protagonists felt "it was not the Power of Taxation that was now only questioned; the Power of restricting and regulating the Trade of the Colonies for the Benefit and Welfare of the British Manufacture and Commerce was now brought into Doubt in many Writings." Apathy had given way to hostility as "the Midling Rank of people and Gentry in the Country appear rather adverse [to the colonies] from a Notion that the proceedings in America have arisen from a Spirit of Independence." Both sides were aggravating the situation by grossly distorting the facts and issues in the public press, as Thomas Life observed to Jonathan Trumbull.[34]

During the middle third of 1774 the climate of opinion in both Britain and America grew somber with the stillness of expectancy. In April, during parliamentary debates on the Coercive Acts, Lord North

---

[33] Donoughue, *British Politics and the American Revolution*, pp. 122–124; Jack M. Sosin, *Agents and Merchants: British Colonial Policy and the Origins of the American Revolution, 1763–1775* (Lincoln, Neb., 1965), p. 184.

[34] Edmund Burke, *Speeches and Letters on American Affairs*, ed. Hugh Law (London, 1908), pp. 2, 97; Garth to S.C. CC, Dec. 7, 1774, Garth Letterbook, pp. 181–182; Life to Trumbull, July 5, 1775, MS designation "War," X, 4350-1, CSL.

had referred to "the evil disposition, the turbulant Conduct, and the
dark designs of many in the Colonies." Burke's report to New York of
this speech indicated the First Lord's emphasis upon American
schemes to end colonial "dependence on the parent Country." North
had the shrewdness to convert a political rumor into a test of national
allegiance by asserting that opponents of punitive measures were
abetting provincial efforts at autonomy. This effectively embarrassed
various British liberals into silence or actual support of the administration.[35]

The agents, or at least some of them, helped to heighten their
employers' sense of impending crisis. Yet for the most part their shrill
reports and warnings from London were sincere manifestations of
their own apprehensions. Franklin insisted that North's administration wanted to drain America's treasuries. The Doctor was convinced
in 1774 that "the decrying and vilifying the people of [Massachusetts]
and . . . their agent among the rest, was quite a Court measure." The
entire episode in the Cockpit seemed a "preconcerted" plot, Franklin
informed his employers. Later in 1774 he reported the possibility that
£60,000 in specie had been sent to America to bribe the leading
patriots. By then such rumors ran rampant. Arthur Lee warned that
crown and Parliament were determined to take up arms, and the
administration equally prepared to "destroy" America.[36]

The general election campaign which took place in October 1774
gave the colonists no reason to relax their watchfulness. The newly
elected Parliament remained as hostile and determined as its predecessor, perhaps more so—"the patriots (except in London and Bristol)
being every where unsuccessful." In April, Edmund Burke had found
"the popular current, both within [Parliament's] doors and without, at
present sets strongly against America." Men who spoke "in opposition,
did it, more for the acquittal of their own honour . . . than from any
sort of hope they entertained of bringing any considerable Number to
their opinion; or even of keeping in that opinion several of those who
had formerly concurred in the same general Line of Policy with

[35] Burke to N.Y. CC, April 6, 1774, *The Correspondence of Edmund Burke,
1768–1772*, ed. Lucy S. Sutherland, II (Chicago, 1960), 527–529.
[36] Franklin to John Huske, Sept. 6, 1772, APS; *Benjamin Franklin's Autobiographical Writings*, ed. Carl Van Doren (New York, 1945), p. 328; Franklin
to Jonathan Williams, Sept. 28, 1774, Williams MSS, Indiana University
Library; Lee to Richard H. Lee, Dec. 6, 1774, Lee-Ludwell MSS, VHS.

regard to the Colonies." [37] The election brought in about one hundred sixty new Members; but the moderates among these, Burke noted, were not "much more considerable in this Parliament than in the last." The number favorable to punitive legislation for the colonies "have been raised to near three hundred. Such is the State of Parliament." [38]

Among the erstwhile friends of America, especially within the opposition, 1774 was a year of serious losses by estrangement. Most followers of Chatham and Rockingham clearly approved of the Boston Port bill as a necessary punishment. In fact the opposition did not even try to divide the Commons against the port bill and the quartering bill. So long as this continued, North's ministry would be unhampered in its efforts to maintain a parliamentary majority for its American policies. In the House of Lords the government's margin was even stronger; and never more than two of the bishops opposed court policies in 1774–1775. As the year waned, such quondam allies as Thomas Pownall and Sir William Meredith were totally lost to the administration side—serious blows to the diminishing weight and numbers of the North American interest.[39]

By this time the ten-year debate had clearly reached an impasse that could no longer be reconciled by peaceful means. It would be difficult to judge by the agents at what point unbridgeable differences made rebellion inevitable; for it was not the lobbyists' place to issue publicly pessimistic pronouncements. As early as 1767, Franklin had doubted to Joseph Galloway whether British governments would ever "be satisfied without some Revenue from America, nor America ever satisfied with their imposing it; so that Disputes will, from this Circumstance besides others, be perpetually arising." [40] Similar sentiments were not yet widespread, however, among the provincial representatives. They would not be for six more years.

By 1774, Franklin was completely convinced that the ideological

[37] Lee to Thomas Cushing, Dec. 6, 1774, PRO CO 5/118, ff. 91–93; Burke to N.Y. CC, April 6, 1774, Sutherland, *Burke Correspondence*, II, 528.

[38] Burke to N.Y. CC, March 14, 1775, Sutherland, *Burke Correspondence*, III, 135; Donoughue, *British Politics and the American Revolution*, ch. 8.

[39] Donoughue, *British Politics and the American Revolution*, pp. 135, 141–142; G. H. Guttridge, *English Whiggism and the American Revolution* (Berkeley, Calif., 1942), p. 79.

[40] April 14, 1767, WCL.

problem constituted an impossible conundrum for the Empire, and expected conflict. America would never acknowledge the legislative or taxing power of Parliament. Secret negotiations between Franklin, Howe, and Hyde in the winter of 1774–1775 ended in February, when all three agreed that their positions were so far apart as to make further meetings futile. Just a few months before, Richard Jackson had conceded the point of no return was passed and hoped Britain would "take the first opportunity to close with [the colonies], as soon as it can be done with honour." Alexander Elmsley revealed similar sentiments to Samuel Johnston.[41]

For Edmund Burke the transition occurred during 1774. In his speech on "American Taxation," given April 19, he viewed "the imperial rights of Great Britain and the privileges which the colonists ought to enjoy under these rights to be just the most reconcilable things in the world." Yet in his address "On Conciliation with the Colonies" he saw that "things were hastening towards an incurable alienation." Two months later, in May 1775, he recognized that "all our prospects of American civilization are . . . over." [42]

As early as 1769–1770, however, the only basis for reconciliation had been clearly recognized. A new constitutional understanding of the allocation of powers within the Empire was required. Simultaneous with Franklin's realization of this fact came Lee's regret, shared by many, that ministries had exercised their authority in such a way that made redefinition of that authority imperative. Thereafter America's appeal became increasingly clear. To restore the old harmony Parliament would have to repeal all legislation passed since 1763 affecting America unfavorably. The demand for a complete return to the "old system" became a shrill colonial refrain echoed by the London agents in varying degrees of intensity.[43]

[41] Crane, *Franklin's Letters to the Press*, pp. 257, 271 and n. 6; Hutchinson, *Diary and Letters of Hutchinson*, I, 204; Elmsley to Johnston, April 7, 1775, Force, *American Archives*, ser. 4, II, 296–297.

[42] Burke, *Speeches and Letters on American Affairs*, pp. 59–60, 79; Burke to Charles O'Hara, [ca. May 28, 1775], Guttridge, *Burke Correspondence*, III, 60.

[43] Franklin to Joseph Galloway, Jan. 11, 1770, WCL; Lee, *Observations on the Review of the Controversy between Great Britain and Her Colonies* (London, 1769), pp. 34–35; *An Appeal to the Justice and Interests of the People of Great Britain . . .* (London, 1774), p. 49; Sam Adams to Arthur Lee, April 4, 1774, *The Writings of Samuel Adams*, ed. H. A. Cushing (New York, 1904–1908), III, 101. See also Burke's response to North's proposal of Feb. 27, 1775 (Burke, *Speeches and Writings on American Affairs*, p. 134).

To explain the catastrophe the Empire had undergone, most of the colonial representatives ultimately pointed to the related problems of taxation and representation. In Burke's mind "the public and avowed origin of this quarrel was on taxation." The Navigation Acts were of only secondary importance as a causal factor. In William Samuel Johnson's memoirs taxation "finally became the ground of the Revolution." Almost from the beginning, Arthur Lee argued that the biggest colonial grievance, "that on which the rest are grafted, *is the violated right of representation.*" Among the agents who saw the problem in wider perspective, William Bollan spoke with unaccustomed clarity: "Unlimited authority is the great fort which they appear determined to defend; . . . wherefore the existence of this boundless authority is the great question." [44]

The last pamphlet of Bollan's career, *The Rights of the English Colonies,* published in 1774, was symptomatic of the transformation of his thinking as well as of the more advanced students in America. Before resuming his agency in 1768, Bollan placed the colonies in a distinctly inferior position—politically and economically. Their function was to supply raw materials to enrich Britain and strengthen the empire. Provincial assemblies were clearly subordinate to Parliament. By 1774 the agent's thinking had altered appreciably. He no longer spoke of colonial subordination, but rather of an extended imperial system consisting of equal units. The British monarch stood atop that system, and to him alone was American allegiance due. Parliament, in this construct, was simply the law-making body for the British isles. [45]

In 1774, John Almon successively issued one of Bollan's long petitions, a collection of his memorials which the Commons had ignored, and finally *The Rights of the English Colonies* in time for the opening of the parliamentary session of December 1774. The agent "presented numerous copies to worthy persons," but in neither England nor America did his essay make a favorable impression. Many years later John Adams reflected sadly:

I scarcely ever knew a book so deeply despised. The English reviewers would not allow it to be the production of a rational creature. In America

---

[44] Burke, *Speeches and Writings on American Affairs,* p. 110; MS memoirs of Johnson, WSJ MSS (misc. box); Lee, *The Political Detection . . .* (London, 1770), p. 64; Bollan to James Bowdoin, Sept. 29, 1773, *Bowdoin and Temple Papers,* p. 320.

[45] *The Rights of the English Colonies Established in America Stated and Defended* (London, 1774), pp. 1, 49–51.

itself it was held in no esteem. Otis himself expressed in the House of Representatives, in a public speech, his contempt of it. . . .

All this I regretted. I wished that Bollan had not only been permitted, but encouraged to proceed. There is no doubt he would have produced much in illustration of the ecclesiastical and political superstition and despotism of the ages when colonization commenced and proceeded. But Bollan was discouraged, and ceased from his labors.[46]

A WINTER OF DISCONTENTS, 1774–1775

The winter of 1774–1775 was one of discontents, as hopes for reconciliation dimmed. Three attempts at accommodation involving the agents took place that winter, almost simultaneously: a petition from the Continental Congress, Franklin's secret negotiations, and final efforts at collaboration with the merchant community.

As 1774 drew to a close, colonists and agents regarded petitions as useless. Yet the first Continental Congress had no alternative in formalizing its search for conciliation. It drafted a "long, manly and respectful" plea for "relief from fears and jealousies occasioned by the statutes and regulations, adopted since the close of the late war." In December this document, addressed to the crown, reached the agents. Once again—with the formal structure of imperial government in collapse—an extraconstitutional device in America called upon the agents to congeal the fast-dissolving bonds of transoceanic union. Addressed to Bollan, Lee, Burke, Life, Garth, Wentworth, and Franklin, it was sent in care of the last-named, who was expected to gather his colleagues. Franklin promptly notified them all and requested a meeting at Waghorn's in the Old Palace Yard, adjoining the House of Lords, to consult on the best time and manner for presentation.[47] Burke, Life, and Wentworth[48] flatly refused to cooperate, each giving

[46] Bollan, *The Petition of Mr. Bollan, Agent for the Council of the Province of Massachusetts Bay . . .* , and *The Petitions of Mr. Bollan . . . Lately Presented to the Two Houses of Parliament . . .* ; Bollan to James Bowdoin, Dec. 6, 1774, *Bowdoin and Temple Papers*, p. 380; *The Works of John Adams*, ed. Charles F. Adams (Boston, 1850–1856), X, 355–356.

[47] Arthur Lee to Ralph Izard, Dec. 27, 1774, *Correspondence of Mr. Ralph Izard of South Carolina . . .* , ed. A. I. Deas (New York, 1844), I, 35–37; *Journals of the Continental Congress, 1774–1789* (Washington, D.C., 1904–1937), I, 115–124; all the memoranda are similar to the one Franklin sent Burke on Dec. 19, 1774, Burke MSS, 3/390+, SCL.

[48] Wentworth wrote Franklin that "without having any qualifications at all, that I know of, I should not only take a very exceptionable part in regard to Mr.

the same pretext, "viz: that they had no Instructions relating to it from their Constituents." Garth being out of town, only Bollan and Lee remained to handle the memorial with Franklin.[49]

At first they contemplated the possibility of having it published, but they were advised not to until it had been placed before Parliament, lest it be deemed disrespectful to the crown. Arthur Lee promptly took the petition to Chatham for the Great Commoner's approbation. "My object," Lee declared, "is to unite the heads of opposition under one uniform large ground." He failed. Rockinghams and Chathamites would only join in castigating the unwise policies of North's administration. Burke and his friends upheld the constitutional supremacy of Parliament "in all cases whatsoever"; whereas Chatham supported the American denunciation of parliamentary taxation.[50] Franklin, meanwhile, also in December, brought it to the American Department. John Pownall had already cautioned Dartmouth that the petition was written in "a very high tone and with very offensive expressions." Nevertheless he received the agents cordially, telling them the King would accept their remonstrance because "it was found to be decent and respectful." On Christmas Eve, Bollan, Franklin, and Lee were informed that His Majesty received it graciously and would lay it before Parliament when they met. Actually the colonial secretary was expressing a wish rather than a policy and deluded his interviewers into false optimism. His unwarranted encouragement made the eventual outcome even more bitter.[51]

When Parliament reassembled after Christmas recess, the petition was communicated to Westminster without any special recommendation from the crown. Instead it was included in a "heap of Letters of

---

Trecothick, who is still agent though he has withdrawn himself from all business; and of the [New Hampshire] legislature . . . from whom I never had any authority" (Jan. 13, 1775, *The State of New Hampshire: Miscellaneous Provincial and State Papers, 1725–1800*, ed. Isaac W. Hammond, XVIII [Manchester, 1890], 658–659).

[49] Franklin to Charles Thomson, Feb. 5, 1775, Smyth, VI, 303; Garth to Franklin, Feb. 1775, Franklin MSS, XLII, 30, APS.

[50] Franklin to Charles Thomson, Feb. 5, 1775, Smyth, VI, 304; Lee to Richard H. Lee, Dec. 26, 1774, Force, *American Archives*, ser. 4, I, 1058; Cone, *Burke and the Nature of Politics*, I, 280–281.

[51] Dennis De Berdt Jr. to Joseph Reed, Jan. 6, 1775, William B. Reed, *Life and Correspondence of Joseph Reed* (Philadelphia, 1847), I, 101; B. D. Bargar, *Lord Dartmouth and the American Revolution* (Columbia, S.C., 1965), ch. 15.

Intelligence from Governors and officers in America, Newspapers, Pamphlets, Handbills, &c. . . . the last in the List, and was laid upon the Table with them, undistinguished by any particular Recommendation of it to the Notice of either House." The agents' task was now to draw attention to the neglected petition. On January 25, Sir George Savile rose to tell the Commons that Franklin, Bollan, and Lee wished to be heard on behalf of the memorial referred to Parliament by the crown. After discussion this was denied. The House then prepared to divide, but Burke contemptuously said he "would not trouble the noble Lord [North] and his train, to walk out every five minutes in funeral pomp to inter petitions." The next day Savile again sought to have the agents explicate Congress' plea at the bar of Commons. The motion was rejected. On the same day a remonstrance from London's community of merchants trading to America received comparable treatment. Franklin and his associates could only despair "that Petitions are odious here, and that Petitioning is far from being a probable means of obtaining redress." The Commons meanwhile shelved the memorial of the Continental Congress.[52]

In the past when merchants and agents cooperated it had been to correct circumstances unfavorable to the advantageous flow of trade. Not many of the merchants, however, sympathized with the alterations in colonial attitudes that developed after the Stamp Act crisis. An increasingly apparent anti-Americanism could be discerned among the commercial class. William Baker, Burke's liaison with the London merchants, reported late in 1774 that a recent gathering of those trading to America had indicated considerable partiality for the administration's punitive policies. Eventually this group agreed to present a petition stating the losses and dangers to British commerce likely to result from continued colonial tensions. But Burke called this document "cold and jejune." It was indeed mild compared with the urgent appeals of 1765–1766.[53]

As 1774 drew to a close, Franklin met with David Barclay to discuss the possibility of a merchants' meeting in order to petition Parliament. In addition Franklin inserted public letters in the press to stimulate

[52] *PHE*, XVIII, 74 ff., 181–183, 193–194; Franklin to Charles Thomson, Feb. 5, 1775, Smyth, VI, 304; *JHC*, XXXV, 81; "A Letter of Benjamin Franklin, 1775," *AHR*, IX (1904), 524–525.

[53] Charles R. Ritcheson, *British Politics and the American Revolution* (Norman, Okla., 1954), p. 181.

his erstwhile allies. During the third week of December a significant shift occurred. On the thirteenth, Arthur Lee remarked that the merchants would never be budged until their fears were alarmed "so strongly, as to make the cause their own." Nine days later Lee excitedly communicated news that the merchants had "advertised for a meeting, & every thing seems to promise a speedy accommodation." Lee's exuberance reached its peak five days later. He thought the resolves of the Continental Congress had moved many in Britain, including both merchants and the ministry. Franklin welcomed these improved prospects, but tempered his high hopes with the patience acquired through long experience in public affairs. Meetings with Barclay and the merchants seemed encouraging but unproductive.[54]

Under these conditions Burke was altogether skeptical. He told his merchant friend, Richard Champion, that

if the Merchants had thought fit to interfere last Winter [1773–74], the distresses of this might certainly have been prevented; conciliatory Measures would have taken place; and they would have come with more dignity, and with far better effect, before the Trial of our Strength than after it. . . . By Means of this reserve, the authority of the Mercantile Interest, which ought to have supported, with efficacy and power, the opposition to the fatal Cause of all this Mischief, was pleaded against us; and we were obliged to stoop under the accumulated weight of all the Interests in this Kingdom. . . . Now, as it was foreseen, they begin to stir, because they begin to feel. But still the same Influence which hindered them from taking any previous measures to prevent their disaster, will, I fear, hinder them from taking any effectual Measures to redress it. The meeting in London was large, and the Sense of their situation as lively as possible; but as far as I could find, they had nothing like the Sentiments of honest, free, and constitutional resentment, which Englishmen used formerly to feel, against the authors of any publick Mischief; and they seemd to entertain full as great apprehensions of taking any Steps displeasing to the authours of their Grievances, as they shewed desire of Redressing them.[55]

On the morning of January 4, about three hundred fifty merchants involved in American trade met at the King's Arms to discuss colonial

[54] Crane, *Franklin's Letters to the Press*, p. 270; Franklin Papers, nos. 265–267, 269, 272–274, 279; Lee to Richard H. Lee, Dec. 13 and 22, 1774, Lee MSS, II, VIII, HLHU; Lee to Ralph Izard, Dec. 27, 1774, Deas, *Correspondence of Izard*, I, 35–37.

[55] Jan. 10, 1775, Guttridge, *Burke Correspondence*, III, 95–96.

questions. They ultimately decided to petition Parliament; but Burke's report of their proceedings reveals scant new optimism. Their alarm did not yet seem strong enough to overcome "their habitual deference to administration." New York's agent was distressed by the commercial classes' apathy toward problems of American government. He found their petition lacking in purpose and vigor and wished the Coercives had been opposed "as being fundamentally unjust and impolitic," so that then "the merchants might come with great weight and propriety, to speak of their effect upon trade." [56]

Burke nevertheless sought to capitalize on this resurgence among the merchants. He took a leading part in instigating new mercantile petitions for conciliatory measures, but met with much less enthusiasm than a decade earlier. Franklin was also active in the same promotional capacity and by mid-February could report that petitions had been received from trading ports and manufacturing towns concerned with colonial commerce. Yet little notice had been taken of these, he lamented. [57] Moreover, not all of the provincial merchants, by any means, supported the North American interest. In January, for example, the merchants of Birmingham met to discuss related problems of trade and constitutionalism. Such leading figures as Matthew Boulton and Dr. John Roebuck attended "to prevent, if possible, some of my neighbours from running into unwise measures, [initiated] by the intrigues of American and minority agents, who I have reason to believe have been busy here, as in most of the other manufacturing towns in England." [58]

During January, February, and March, the London merchants met with some frequency at the King's Arms Tavern. They invited the provincial towns to join the agitation; and in the weeks after Parliament convened on January 19, twenty-six towns sent petitions deploring the stagnation of American trade and requesting remedial action. By the beginning of March, Arthur Lee grudgingly conceded that the merchants were finally in motion, but complained that they required continual prodding. Lee also catalogued a considerable number of

[56] Burke to Rockingham, Jan. 12, 1775, *ibid.*, pp. 97–98.

[57] Hoffman, *Burke*, p. 167; Burke to Rockingham, Jan. 24, 1775, to Mark Huish, Feb. 22 and March 9, 1775, Guttridge, *Burke Correspondence*, III, 106–107, 121–122, 130; Franklin to Samuel Tucker *et al.*, Feb. 14, 1775, Smyth, VI, 308.

[58] Matthew Boulton to Dartmouth, Jan. 12, 1775, Dartmouth MSS, Vol. II, no. 1099, WSL; Sosin, *Agents and Merchants*, p. 219.

merchants with American business who were completely unsympathetic. In mid-March Rockingham presented a petition supported by more than sixty commercial firms. It opposed restraints on colonial trade and even criticized those Intolerable Acts the colonists found so vicious. The West Indian interest, although stimulated to concurrent activity, was unable to coordinate its attack. This lack of concerted pressure on a determined administration proved fatal. Hence William Lee's lament to Thomas Adams: "Our applications have been treated as in great measure they deserved, because the Ministry knew well enough the Merchants, except 2 or 3 of us, were not at all serious; hence it is, that our petitions are almost all, but the last to the H. of Lords, little else than milk & water. The Glasgow Merchants played the same game but with less trouble." [59]

This failure in March marked the final disruption of joint agent-merchant activity. The merchants' interest in American affairs and the influence they could exert in behalf of the colonies had waned. As Burke noted, the commercial communities opposed to North's administration "have not been much regarded," while the "manufacturing parts of the Kingdom" urged that "the reduction by force of the disobedient Spirit in the Colonies is their Sole security for trading in future with America." [60]

During December 1774, while Franklin and Barclay met to arouse the merchants' sentiments, and in January when they helped prepare the great petition, Barclay hoped that confidential negotiations between Franklin and ministerial emissaries might heal the imperial sores. Near the end of November, Barclay and his friend Lord Hyde sought a compromise reconciliation with the colonies through Franklin. Although not an actual member of North's ministry, Hyde had access to it. He was joined in the covert talks by Rear Admiral Sir Richard Howe. Barclay's associate in conferences with Franklin was the latter's well-informed physician, Fothergill, in close touch with his patient Lord Dartmouth. During one of their meetings in Fothergill's Harpur Street study, Franklin produced his "Hints for Conversation"

[59] Lee to Sam Adams, March 4, 1775, Adams MSS, NYPL; the merchants' petition is in the HLRO, dated March 15, 1775; William Baker to Rockingham, [ca. Feb. 5, 1775], Fitzwilliam MSS, R1–1541, SCL; William Lee to Adams, March 10, 1775, *VMHB*, VI (1899), 30–31.

[60] Burke to N.Y. CC, March 14, 1775, Guttridge, *Burke Correspondence*, III, 135.

to preserve a durable union. Copies were communicated through the intermediaries to North's cabinet and Speaker Norton. Over a game of chess, Franklin learned that his terms were unacceptable.[61]

In January and February a sequence of meetings proved equally fruitless. The impasse held. During these negotiations Franklin was annoyed by Barclay's fulsome compliments and was obliged to remind both Barclay and Fothergill that his authority was much more restricted than they realized or wished to recognize. In February, Barclay produced a plan of permanent union proposing that the colonial agents petition for the opening of Boston Port, the colonies first having paid for the destroyed tea. Franklin by now regarded the whole petitioning process with great cynicism and replied that only Massachusetts' lobbyists could discuss the tea affair. Bollan being "a cautious, exact man, and not easily persuaded to take Steps of such Importance without Instructions or Authority," such a move would largely lie in Franklin's hands; and he would only settle for immediate repeal of all the Coercives. Upon this rock the accommodation floundered. Howe then suggested that he and Franklin sail for America as peace commissioners, dangling as bait the possibility that the administration would guarantee payment of his salary arrears as Massachusetts' agent. The Doctor rejected a proposition that would have destroyed his reputation in America: "They would be considered as so many Bribes to betray the Interest of my Country."[62]

Howe arranged one final meeting between Hyde and Franklin on March 1, even though all parties regarded the situation as hopeless. Franklin had intimated that Boston would probably require indemnification for having its port closed as compensation for tea reparations. Hyde and Howe mistook this private opinion for a *sine qua non*, and the misunderstanding contributed to a total breakdown. The interview ran aground and with it the negotiations. Barclay and Fothergill were unhappy with both parties, but stood helpless.[63] The curtain having closed on this tragicomic farce, the lead—Franklin—made his exit. He quickly passed through the wings and out of the theater

---

[61] R. H. Fox, *Dr. John Fothergill and His Friends* (London, 1919), pp. 326–334; B. C. Corner and D. W. Singer, "Dr. John Fothergill, Peacemaker," APS *Proceedings*, XCVIII (1954), 11–22.

[62] Franklin wrote a lengthy "Account of Negotiations in London for Effecting a Reconciliation between Great Britain and the American Colonies," March 22, 1775, Smyth, VI, 318–399; Donoghue, *British Politics and the American Revolution*, p. 245.

[63] See Fothergill to Franklin, Oct. 25, 1780, Franklin MSS, APS.

where he had performed almost continuously for seventeen years. The spotlight shifted with him to a new setting where the denouement would be enacted, with redcoats and ill-trained militia instead of chessmen, and campfires for footlights.[64]

"REJECTED WITH SCORN LIKE ALL THE REST"

In many respects David Barclay's dilemma early in 1775 was symptomatic of the larger imperial crisis. Devices, arguments, and personnel that had worked so well for him in 1765 failed utterly in 1775. On both occasions he worked through Lord Hyde; only once was he successful. On February 28, 1775, Barclay was permitted to testify before the House of Commons, appearing as agent for the committee of North American merchants. With the House sitting as a committee of the whole, Barclay was even allowed to examine three witnesses in support of their petition, but all to no avail.[65] The traditional channels of communication were being frozen by political controversy and insurrection.

The great irony, in fact, was that while British opinion converged upon the need to uphold parliamentary supremacy, essential attributes of parliamentary government were being suppressed: the petitioning process, "strangers" in the gallery, and other facets of open debate. On January 20, 1775, Chatham intended to speak in the House of Lords on the American question and wanted Franklin present. At two o'clock in the afternoon the two gout-ridden statesmen met in the lobby of the House of Lords. The Great Commoner dramatically took Franklin by the arm and led him along the passage leading to the throne. Thereupon a doorkeeper reminded Chatham of the order that "none were to be carried in at that door, but the eldest sons or brothers of peers"; so the pair walked slowly back to the door near the bar where a cluster of men had gathered. "This is Dr. Franklin, whom I would have admitted into the House," Chatham announced boldly. Amidst the buzzing crowd the door opened. Chatham slowly limped into the chamber followed by his friend and proposed that the King be asked to withdraw the troops from Boston. His motion was rejected.[66]

---

[64] For another attempt at informal negotiation at this time, see Herbert A. Meistrich, "Lord Drummond and Reconciliation [1775]," NJHS *Proceedings*, LXXXI (1963), 256–277.

[65] Barclay to Hyde, Dec. 13, 1765, Grenville MSS in the possession of Sir John Murray, London; *PHE*, XVIII, 383–385.

[66] Carl Van Doren, *Benjamin Franklin* (New York, 1938), pp. 508–509; Gipson, *British Empire before the American Revolution*, XII, 278–279.

Undaunted, Chatham intended to offer his plan of reconciliation in the Lords on February 1. Before doing so, however, he consulted with two people—Lord Camden, the legal expert, and Franklin. In this connection Franklin went to Chatham's country estate on January 27; two days later Chatham came to Craven Street for two hours in order to discuss details of the plan; and on the thirty-first still another four-hour meeting took place. Among Franklin's many suggestions was the withdrawal of the royal instruction requiring that colonial agents be appointed by the assembly with the consent of the governor and council. His efforts were in vain, however, as Chatham's proposals were repudiated. During the debate Lord Sandwich even declared "he could never believe it to be the Production of any British Peer." Turning then toward Franklin, who was leaning on the Bar of the House, Sandwich added that "he had in his Eye the Person who drew it up, one of the bitterest and most mischievous Enemies this Country had ever known." [67]

By this time the entire petitioning process seemed to be in disarray. Franklin, Bollan, and Lee wrote the speaker of every colony that "the Treatment the Petitions already presented have hitherto received, is such as in our Opinion can afford you no Reliance on any present Relief through their Means." The colonies, for their part, submitted memorials which caused the agents embarrassment and great pains. Elmsley and Barker, for example, received one from North Carolina "which contained, besides strange inaccuracies, indirect reflections on the Parliament, or the Ministry at least." They took it upon themselves to ignore this document and instead "drew up a Memorial in more decent terms," because it "would have been preposterous to have presented a petition, which, amongst other things, set forth that the petitioner, from past experience, did not doubt of having his petition rejected." Their substitute won Carolina exemption from the act restricting colonial trade to England and the British West Indies. But their affront to the provincials won them obloquy rather than endearment. In addition to violating their instructions by sacrificing principle for expediency, they had informed the Committee of Correspondence that it used such grammar as "might have passed from a poor, ignorant criminal begging his life." [68]

By spring the colonists no longer held any hope for redress through petitions. Hence the Continental Congress sent memorials to the

---

[67] *Ibid.*, ch. 11, esp. pp. 282–283.

[68] Franklin *et al.* to speakers, Feb. 5, 1775, Franklin Papers (1754–1790), no. 1027, LC; Elmsley to Samuel Johnston, April 7, 1775, CRNC, IX, 1209.

agents with instructions to have them printed "and Disperced thro' every Town in England." In April 1775, when New York's Assembly sent Burke its remonstrances for presentation, it instructed him to have them printed. He gave ones for Parliament to the newspapers, but withheld New York's petition to the crown because John Pownall advised against publishing a paper addressed to the throne. The agent informed his employers that he "did not think it right to do anything against office, without absolute necessity." [69] In mid-May, Burke delivered the set to Dartmouth, who suggested to the agent that he present one in the Commons and find a sympathetic peer to do so in the Lords. The Duke of Manchester's effort was rejected without a reading. On May 15, Burke, quite ill, offered his employers' plea, but his fellows decided not to hear it because it rejected parliamentary taxation as a constitutional right. [70]

In July, Arthur Lee proposed to various colonial leaders an enterprising project—a collection of unheard petitions culled from the journals of the several colonial assemblies. "It will be of great use in proving the propriety of our proceedings to state the number of Petitions from all the Provinces which have been presented in vain. . . . There will be a moment, I am sure, when stating the repeatedly rejected petitions of America here, will bring down vengeance upon the heads of her inveterate enemies." [71]

By this time the agents and their employers had no cause to hope for assistance from any group in British politics, even the opposition. During the summer, weaknesses in Whig organization became manifest. The Rockinghams, consistent as always, hoped to prevent the complete entanglement of Parliament in the ministerial policy of coercion. "By striving to keep responsibility centered in the administration," G. H. Guttridge has written, "and by thwarting the union of king and parliament in the new tory system, the whigs might hope to preserve for parliament that independence which still appealed to the country gentlemen, and which would also provide a basis for the defeat of the ministry as soon as opportunity offered." While Rockingham, Burke, and the Cavendishes wished to keep Parliament disso-

[69] *Journals of the Continental Congress, 1774–1789,* II, 27, 171–172; N.Y. Assembly to Burke, April 5, 1775, photostat in Burke collection, SCL; Hoffman, *Burke,* p. 179.

[70] Burke to Dartmouth, May 11, 1775, Dartmouth MSS, Vol. II, no. 1264, WSL; *PHE,* XVIII, 643 ff.; *Journals of the House of Lords,* XXXIV, 461.

[71] Lee to Franklin, July 6, 1775, *PMHB,* XXVII (1903), 155; Lee to Sam Adams, July 8, 1775, Adams MSS, NYPL.

ciated from an American war, the means to that end were not at all clear. Hence they planned simply to wait until Parliament had rejected their plea for conciliation, and then mount a protest.[72] Assisting the agent or supporting colonial quests for redress did not fit into their program of detached aloofness.

"It is a capital mistake of our American friends to expect insurrections here," wrote Samuel Curwen from London. "The manufactories are in full employ, and one of the warmest of the friends of America told me that letters from Manchester expressed joy that no American orders had been sent; otherwise their must have been disappointment somewhere." In July, Colonel John Maunsell observed that "England was never in a more flourishing state—new doors opened to commerce; manufacturers fully employed; stocks as high as before the dispute." Burke perhaps uttered the most bitter commentary: We look to the Merchants in vain. They are gone from us, and from themselves. They consider America as lost, and they look to administration for an indemnity. Hopes are accordingly held out to them, that some equivalent for their Debts will be provided." [73]

In August, Richard Penn arrived in England as a special agent bearing the Olive Branch petition of the second Continental Congress for the remaining agents to present to the king.[74] Once again Arthur Lee invited Burke to meet with Penn and Bollan prior to waiting on Lord Dartmouth about the plea. As before, Burke would not budge, on the ground that he lacked the authorization of his New York employers. Immediately upon learning of Burke's abstention, William Baker wrote his friend an incisive and embarrassing inquiry:

You are the agent of New York alone. Is Mr. Garth agent for any other colony but Carolina? Mr. Bolland and Mr. Lee for any but Massachusetts-Bay, and Virginia? Is Mr. Penn the agent for any province whatsoever? And yet to them equally with yourself is the letter of the congress addressed. Can an assembly so formed have any agent here at all, one of the constituents of that character being his reception here under it? It is not, then nor can it be, under that description, that the letter of the

[72] *English Whiggism*, p. 83.

[73] Lewis B. Namier, *England in the Age of the American Revolution* (2nd ed.; London, 1961), pp. 254–255; Burke to Rockingham, Aug. 23, 1775, Guttridge, *Burke Correspondence*, III, 191.

[74] Penn's commission was inscribed jointly to Burke, Bollan, Lee, and Garth. The latter would have nothing to do with it (Guttridge, *Burke Correspondence*, III, 188).

congress is addressed to you. . . . Consider further, that Mr. Garth (a dependent of the ministry,) will hardly attend. Mr. Bolland is ill;—so that the presenting of the petition will rest with Mr. Penn and Mr. Lee alone. Is this a thing to be desired, when every engine is at work to convince the world that the people of this country are anti-Americans? [75]

Burke was unmoved. He replied by citing Hamlet, feebly denying any "craven Scruple of thinking too precisely on the Event." He implied that he would have taken vigorous action had the document been sent him in any capacity other than that of agent. Actually his earlier frustrations as a lobbyist had caused him to anticipate failure. He was certain the "paper . . . will be rejected with Scorn like all the rest." [76]

And he was correct. Dartmouth, improving upon his actions during the winter, this time was a model of directness. When Penn and Lee executed their mission, the retiring secretary simply told them "no answer would be given." In September the two Americans published their burden prefaced by a general notice that it had been ignored. In November the House of Commons did actually consider the Olive Branch, and ordered those Members who were also privy councillors to present it to His Majesty. But the time for that had passed. "The horrid tragedy," as Stephen Sayre called it, had already commenced.[77]

On August 23 the crown issued a proclamation for suppressing rebellion and sedition in America. This formally ended what Franklin considered "an odd State, neither in Peace nor War, neither dependent nor independent." With the collapse of this effort at conciliation the North American agency ended, and with it a 168-year colonial relationship.[78] William Bollan retired to ill health and obscurity, while Arthur Lee soon accepted the secret agency of the Continental Congress, leaving London for Paris and a new chapter in the history of American lobbying and diplomacy.

[75] Lee to Burke, Aug. 21, 1775, Burke MSS, no. 490, SCL; Burke to Lee, Aug. 22, 1775, Guttridge, *Burke Correspondence*, III, 188–189; Baker to Burke, Aug. 22, 1775, *Correspondence of Edmund Burke*, ed. Earl Fitzwilliam (London, 1844), II, 44–46.

[76] Burke to Baker, Aug. 23, 1775, Guttridge, *Burke Correspondence*, III, 196–198.

[77] Bargar, *Dartmouth and American Revolution*, pp. 154–155; Lee to Rockingham, Sept. 2, 1775, Fitzwilliam MSS, R150–157, SCL; *PHE*, XVIII, 896; *JHC*, XXXV, 455; Sayre to Chatham, May 29, 1775, PRO 30/8/55, f. 134.

[78] John to Abigail Adams, July 23, 1775, *Adams Family Correspondence*, ed. L. H. Butterfield (Cambridge, Mass., 1963), I, 253.

CHAPTER 15

A Summing Up

Until the later 1750's, public life in Georgian Britain had been notable for its stability. Crown ministers usually enjoyed tenure marked by security if not always serenity. For two political generations, a cloud of Whig inertia had blanketed the Hanoverian island. Where opposition ambition was not stifled, it lacked the impetus to upset the relentless tedium of administrations that survived by ignoring or muffling potential disturbances to the status quo. For a period after 1760, this lethargy and calm gave way to turbulence. Ministries rose and fell in rapid succession, and with them tumbled parts of the bureaucratic hierarchy that administered the concerns of the kingdom. These were years of transition. Four and a half decades of Whig preponderance were giving way to nearly half a century of Tory reign. Seething in between was a cauldron of bubbling change for which the reagent was the American problem.

The accession of George III in 1760 and consequences of the Seven Years' War imposed a twofold strain upon the Anglo-American political system. Administrative and financial necessities made changes essential at a time when British politics was in transition and consequently unable to supply and support those changes wisely or forcefully. In retrospect the British Empire after 1763 seems to have resembled a balloon suddenly inflated beyond capacity. Expansion exposed dangerous points of weakness, and the whole became susceptible to bursting.

Ever since the latter part of the seventeenth century, there had emerged in America "an entire apparatus of local politics, unconnected in origins with the overarching imperial structure, but to which it came gradually to accommodate itself." [1] The forms this accommodation took were essential ingredients of eighteenth-century colonial life, and the disruption of these forms by the alterations that followed 1760 created a revolutionary situation. When the transient ministries in Whitehall tightened a system of colonial administration that had been lax for many years, the colonists responded by presenting a united front—a hitherto unprecedented force.

Subjected to such conditions of stress, the formal and traditional mechanisms of imperial government began to give way. As Francis Bernard, Governor of Massachusetts, remarked in 1766, "the present disunion has broke thro' many respectable forms." [2] Under these pressing circumstances informal factors would have to play a major role in averting a breach. Until politics in London stabilized and a satisfactory trans-Atlantic relationship materialized, an extraconstitutional institution, such as the colonial agencies, might have served as an adhesive element. This in fact happened in 1765–1766, the high-water mark of the agencies.

Despite his veneer of unabashed whiggery, one of the first (and finest) historians of the American Revolution, David Ramsay, recognized the value of agents, especially as they were among the best-informed people in London on colonial affairs. "But while the lust of power and of gain," wrote Ramsay, "blinded the rulers of Great-Britain, mistated facts and uncandid representations brought over their people to second the infatuation. A few honest men properly authorised, might have devised measures of compromise, which under the influence of truth, humility and moderation, would have prevented a dismemberment of the empire; but these virtues ceased to influence, and false hood, haughtiness and blind zeal usurped their places." [3]

Ramsay had struck upon several crucial problems. There were a number of agents of high caliber during the 1760's. But the colonists were not uniformly willing to send their most capable men and reward them accordingly. This is surprising, since many Americans, at least between 1764 and 1768, recognized the high importance of the institution. Instead, disillusionment set in and many of the agencies were

[1] Bernard Bailyn, "Becker, Andrews, and the Image of Colonial Origins," *NEQ*, XXIX (1956), 531.
[2] To Henry S. Conway, June 28, 1766, Bernard MSS, IV, 228, HLHU.
[3] *History of the American Revolution* (Philadelphia, 1789), I, 349.

permitted to atrophy. The colonists came to place more faith in the efficacy of boycotts than in the proper choice and support of American personnel in London. While the British have commonly been blamed for a lack of statesmanship in handling the imperial question, the colonists have not borne their proper responsibility for the lack of qualified and authorized London agents.

For their part British politicians, particularly Grenville, Townshend, Hillsborough, and North, lacked the judgment and generosity needed to resolve the crisis that began in 1764. When their tempers were set on edge by the prolonged tension, they vented their anger on America's agents, closed their avenues of access, and made them unacceptable. Reports of intemperate and antagonistic ministerial behavior reached the colonies and fixed their will to resist that much more firmly. Britain's politicians were not then notable for their tact and discernment. Even George III declared that he did "not know of a man of less judgment than Lord Hillsborough." [4]

After 1766 mutual mistrust and differences in political theory between Britain and her colonies aggravated the instability of English public life. It became more difficult than ever for the colonies to negotiate their needs in London; and the agents—caught between their constituents and the imperial government—were hamstrung by the attendant inflexibility on both sides. Many of the reasons for their failure originated in problems beyond their control. Yet the triumphs they achieved during the brief Rockingham regime produced in some quarters unwarranted expectations that would soon be disappointed. Like other components of the old imperial system, the agencies underwent a gradual decline.

One of the most important causes of that decline is to be found in the factional nature of contemporary politics. Whereas the existence of stable ministries prior to 1760 had eased the task of political "men of business" in London, the swiftly shifting sands of fortune after that date complicated matters for lobbyists. This was especially true between 1763 and 1770, a period the late Sir Lewis Namier called "the seven years of confusion." [5] Toward the close of 1766, Benjamin Franklin complained that "these frequent Changes are extreamly discouraging to all who have Business to transact with the Government." Nearly four years later William Samuel Johnson could still observe

---

[4] "Wills Hill," *DNB*.

[5] *Crossroads of Power: Essays on Eighteenth-Century England* (London, 1962), p. 75.

that "in this ferment, or rather paroxysm of politics, the symptoms vary almost every twenty-four hours." [6]

Just when this mutability exerted a controlling influence over public affairs in Britain, the agents found themselves in positions of responsibility, sometimes to such an extent that it unnerved them. From time to time during the Seven Years' War they had cooperated with the Treasury lords in handling the apportionment of parliamentary funds for colonial military expenses. Perhaps on the basis of this experience, Grenville indicated that he might work through the agents in 1764–1765 as an alternative to more orthodox channels of communication. By the same token, the provincial representatives, for instance, undertook to commit their constituents to a compromise affecting colonial currency in 1764. The Stamp Act crisis, above all, showed that the lobbyists were critically needed and revealed their potential value.

As the character of American radicalism became transformed after 1766, however, many of the agents who were British found themselves out of sympathy with the constitutional claims of their employers. Others who were ardently procolonial suddenly realized the devastating impact political controversy could have on their attempts at expedient mollification and adjustment. As colonists in certain cases became disenchanted with their agents, the latter in turn lamented that they were inadequately supported by their employers. Realizing that they lacked authority, instructions, and funds, the lobbyists found their effectiveness sharply reduced.

As arguments over the allocation of power within the Empire reached a crescendo in the later 1760's, a parallel phenomenon took place in imperial politics, coinciding by no accident with the tenure of the first Secretary of State for the Colonies. Antagonized by colonial recalcitrance and intransigence, Hillsborough, some of his colleagues, and a number of Members of Parliament cracked down on the wayward Americans by making life difficult for their representatives. Ministries became less willing than their predecessors to consult the agents on pending legislation affecting the colonies and less willing to heed colonial petitions presented by the agents. Under these conditions the lobbyists understandably began to lose confidence in their own ability to bridge the growing gap. When Hillsborough refused to

[6] To Joseph Galloway, Oct. 11, 1766, WCL; to Jonathan Trumbull, Feb. 3, 1770, "Letters of William Samuel Johnson to the Governors of Connecticut," MHS *Collections*, ser. 5, IX (Boston, 1885), 407.

recognize the authority of agents chosen by assemblies alone, Edmund Burke lamented to his New York employers the "destruction of one of the most necessary Mediums of Communication between the Colonies and the parent Country. The province ought in my opinion to have *a direct* intercourse with Ministry and Parliament here, by some person who might be truely confidential with them who appoint him." [7]

After 1770 the new North ministry sought anxiously to settle into power. To achieve this end it became critically important to bypass American questions that might be upsetting. By 1770, moreover, the constitutional problem had almost been reduced to its most essential form—either Parliament was sovereign or it was not. Exposing this dilemma to public attention also threatened to disquiet and disrupt. Hence the administration preferred to keep the ideological issue suppressed. It did so with success for three and a half years. [8]

After 1770 colonial nonimportation agreements lost their potency as political and economic weapons. It became apparent that the American commercial groups could not sustain the boycott without breaches that undermined its effectiveness. By this time British trade no longer depended on North America, as it had earlier. New markets had recently opened to the East. The dark economic clouds that hovered over Britain after the Seven Years' War had blown away and prosperity had returned. The same wind that dispatched depression also tore apart the briefly joined West Indian–North American alliance and dampened the agents' relations with the merchant community. Therefore the ultimate crisis initiated by the Boston Tea Party late in 1773 found most of Britain's merchants unresponsive to efforts by their erstwhile allies to activate them.

By the early seventies, colonials on both sides of the Atlantic had begun to recognize a problem succinctly evoked in a letter to John Adams from a relative in London. "I agree with you, sir, absolutely that America suffers to an inexpressible degree for want of proper connections in England. But when you ask me to procure you a friend or an acquaintance here, you put me, sir, to a very difficult task indeed. This is the worst place in the world, perhaps, to form connections that are of real service." [9] This dilemma is central to the coming

---

[7] To James De Lancey, Dec. 4, 1771, *The Correspondence of Edmund Burke,* ed. Lucy S. Sutherland, II (Chicago, 1960), 291.

[8] Arthur Lee to Sam Adams, Oct. 11, 1773, Richard H. Lee, *The Life of Arthur Lee* (Boston, 1829), I, 237.

[9] Isaac Smith Jr. to Adams, Sept. 3, 1771, *The Adams Family Correspondence,* ed. L. H. Butterfield (Cambridge, Mass., 1963), I, 79–80.

of the Revolution; and the plight of the agents is clearly a significant manifestation of the problem. Through them it is possible to observe and gauge the waning influence of America and Americans in London.

Similarly those agents who stood by the colonists throughout underwent a deepening disaffection from imperial authority that typified a parallel reaction by their constituents. The provincial representatives were both frustrated and disgusted by what Franklin considered "the extream Corruption prevalent among all Orders of Men in this old rotten State." [10] The agents vocally conveyed such sentiments to their correspondents, and by injecting them into the hostile climate of colonial opinion, they reinforced the agitated provincials' sense of alienation from Parliament and the Empire.

A number of the London lobbyists personified and intensified a sense of separateness that comprised part of the rapidly growing colonial patriotism. Their letters provided colonists with a primary source of news and analysis of the deepening crisis. This information fed the hungry discontented with provocative and sometimes distorted views that seemed to vindicate their own deepest suspicions. "Happily America is capable of working her own salvation," Arthur Lee wrote, "or the influence of corruption & dissipation here would render her escape from the hand of Tyranny extremely doubtful." [11]

The agents commonly began to report that the English "Nation is against us, that we cannot depend upon any Support of any kind from thence, that the Merchants are very much against us," and so forth. [12] Even the few friendly factions such as Rockingham's, it was noted, supported the colonists out of self-seeking political expediency rather than any inherent intellectual sympathy. Simultaneously some agents began to urge their constituents to look to their own strengths and be self-sustaining in every way. As James Bowdoin put it, incessant rejection of American petitions "induced them to think that they had nothing to hope for but from themselves." [13]

The moderate or conservative agents—Richard Jackson, Edward

[10] To Joseph Galloway, Feb. 25, 1775, Smyth, VI, 311–312.

[11] To Benjamin Franklin, July 6, 1775, Franklin MSS, IV, 57, APS.

[12] Relying on information from New York based on Edmund Burke's letters, John Adams entered this note in his diary on Aug. 22, 1774 (*The Diary and Autobiography of John Adams*, ed. L. H. Butterfield [Cambridge, Mass., 1961], II, 107).

[13] To Alexander MacKay, Nov. 29, 1770, *The Bowdoin and Temple Papers* (MHS *Collections*, ser. 6, Vol. IX [Boston, 1897]), p. 243.

Montagu, Charles Garth, the Mauduits, and others—are extremely important because the differences that separated them from their colleagues demonstrate many of the cleavages that divided political society on both sides of the Atlantic. Similarly the patriot agents are significant because they embodied in microcosm the evergrowing difficulty of reconciling American Whigs and radicals to a polity from which they both felt estranged. Prodded by their representatives, the colonists looked inward, their backs up and wills stiffened. Henceforward they would cultivate the seeds of independence that had been stimulated, if not planted, by a group of North American agents.

Through one of those touches of irony that makes history endlessly fascinating, the expiring agency was nourishing its own progeny—the foreign service of a new nation. The beginnings of American lobbying are not to be found in the national period, but before the Revolution, when lobbying and diplomacy were intimately related. Just as Samuel was simultaneously the last of the biblical judges and the first of the prophets, so Arthur Lee was the last of the colonial agents and the first national diplomat. As the agencies became consolidated into the hands of a few, these patriots ceased to be parochial "men of business" and became in embryo exactly what Whitehall had proclaimed eighty years earlier they must not be, namely, "plenipotentiaries from a sovereign state." In 1771, Franklin had notified his Massachusetts constituents that when the colonies "come to be considered in the light of *distinct states*, as I conceive they really are, possibly their agents may be treated with more respect, and considered more as public ministers." Eighteen months later the Doctor proudly confided to his son Europe's most recent deference to him. "Several of the foreign ambassadors have assiduously cultivated my acquaintance, treating me as one of their *corps*, partly I believe from the desire they have, from time to time, of hearing something of American affairs, an object become of importance in foreign courts." Early in 1774 the Earl of Buckinghamshire remarked that Franklin "was here, not as an agent of a province but as an ambassador from the states of America. That he could not compare his embassy to anything but that sent by Louis XIV to the republic of Genoa, commanding the doge to come and prostrate himself at Versailles, to appease the resentment of the grand monarque." [14]

[14] MHS *Collections*, ser. 1, IX (Boston, 1804), 273; Franklin to Thomas Cushing, Feb. 5, 1771, to William Franklin, Aug. 19, 1772, Smyth, V, 295,

In the penultimate year of provincial subordination to Britain, Bollan, Franklin, and Lee realized that nearly half the colonies lacked agents and that most of the remaining lobbyists refused to participate in the negotiations between Britannia and her offspring. The recognition then came that each must serve as liaison with all, and not just his own disparate colony. America was now their constituency, not merely Massachusetts or Pennsylvania. Therefore they reproduced their letters so that every colony received a copy and would be apprized of proceedings in Westminster and Whitehall.[15] When the Olive Branch collapsed in the late summer of 1775, Arthur Lee became the confidential correspondent in London of the Continental Congress, and later their secret envoy in Paris. The irony turned back on itself following American independence. When an exchange of ministers was proposed to George III, he rejected the suggestion outright. "As to the question whether I wish to have a Minister accredited from America, I certainly can never say that it will be agreeable to me, and I should think it wisest for both parties if only Agents were appointed." [16]

414; Arthur Lee to Sam Adams, Dec. 22, 1773, Lee, *Life of Arthur Lee*, I, 241.

[15] See their general letter to the speakers of the colonial assemblies, dated Dec. 24, 1774 (Franklin's draft is in his papers, no. 268, LC). The agents' circular letter of Feb. 5, 1775, was given similar distribution. For an anticipation of this development, see De Berdt's letter to George Wyllys, Jan. 16, 1766, "Letters of Dennys De Berdt, 1757–1770," ed. Albert Matthews, CSM *Publications* XIII (Boston, 1912), 311.

[16] To Charles James Fox, Aug. 7, 1783, *The Correspondence of King George III, 1760–1783*, ed. John Fortescue (London, 1927), VI, 430. See also Richard B. Morris, *The Peacemakers: The Great Powers and American Independence* (New York, 1965), p. 439.

APPENDIX,
SELECTED BIBLIOGRAPHY,
AND INDEX

Dramatis Personae
1755–1775

ABERCROMBY, JAMES (1707–1775). Barrister (Lincoln's Inn, 1726); attorney-general of South Carolina (1730–1745). Private agent to Governor James Glen; North Carolina agent (1748–1757); North Carolina Assembly agent (1758–1760); Virginia agent (1754–1759); Virginia Council agent (1759–1774). Deputy auditor general of plantations (1757–1765). M.P. 1761–1768.

BARCLAY, DAVID, JR. (1728–1809). Quaker merchant and banker in London. Delaware agent (1760–1765); Pennsylvania financial agent (1762–1764). Leader and sometime agent of the Committee of North American Merchants.

BARKER, THOMAS (1733–1787). Attorney, merchant, North Carolina assemblyman, treasurer and sometime agent of the northern district of North Carolina (Albemarle) until 1761. North Carolina special agent (1774–1775).

BOLLAN, WILLIAM (ca. 1710–1782). Attorney; advocate general of Massachusetts (1743–1767). Massachusetts agent (1745–1762); Massachusetts Council agent (1768–1775).

BURKE, EDMUND (1729–1797). Politician and writer; M.P. 1765–1794. Private secretary to First Lord of the Treasury (July 1765–July 1766). New York agent (1771–1775).

CHARLES, ROBERT (1706?–1770). Placeman; to Pennsylvania from England in 1726 as private secretary to Governor Patrick Gordon; returned to England in 1739. New York agent (1748–1770); Pennsylvania assistant agent (1751–1754); Pennsylvania agent (1754–1761). Sometime commissioner of the lottery; Post Office comptroller (1763–1765).

DE BERDT, DENNIS, JR. (ca. 1742–1817). Merchant; New Jersey Assembly agent (1775).

DE BERDT, DENNYS (1694–1770). Dissenting merchant in London; associated in trade with Wright, Burkitt & Sayre. Massachusetts special agent (1765–1766); Massachusetts agent (1766–1770); Delaware agent (1765–1770).

ELMSLEY, ALEXANDER. Merchant. North Carolina assemblyman (1762–1768). North Carolina special agent (1774–1775).

FRANKLIN, BENJAMIN (1706–1790). Printer, scientist, politician and diplomat; clerk of the Pennsylvania Assembly (1736–1751), member for Philadelphia (1751–1764), deputy postmaster general for the colonies (1753–1774). Pennsylvania agent (1757–1762, 1764–1775), Georgia agent (1768–1774), New Jersey agent (1769–1774), Massachusetts agent (1770–1774).

GARTH, CHARLES (ca. 1734–1784). Barrister (Inner Temple, 1752). Commissioner of the salt office (1763); M.P. 1765–1780; recorder of Devizes (1765–1784); received secret service pension (1777–1780); commissioner of excise (1780–1784). Georgia crown agent (1763–1765); South Carolina agent (1762–1775); Maryland Assembly special agent (1765–1766); Georgia Assembly special agent (1765–1766).

INGERSOLL, JARED (1722–1781). Attorney. Connecticut agent (1758–1761, 1764–1765). Connecticut stamp distributor (1765); Vice-admiralty court judge, Philadelphia (1768–1776). Loyalist.

JACKSON, RICHARD (1721?–1787). Barrister (Lincoln's Inn, 1739); secretary to Chancellor of the Exchequer (1763–1765); counsel to South Sea Company (1764–1767); counsel to Board of Trade (1770–1782); counsel to Cambridge University (1771–1787). M.P. 1762–1784. Connecticut agent (1760–1770); Pennsylvania agent (1763–1769); Massachusetts agent (1765–1766).

JOHNSON, WILLIAM SAMUEL (1727–1819). Attorney, politician, and educator. Connecticut agent (1766–1771). Connecticut assemblyman, councillor, judge, delegate to Congress, and Senator. First president of Columbia College (1787–1800). Anglican.

JOUVENCAL, PETER CUCHET (?–1786). Clerk and placeman; clerk in offices of secretaries of state (1761–1767); private secretary to Lord Grafton (1765) and Chatham (1767). North Carolina agent (1761–1765).

KELLET, ALEXANDER. Georgia councillor and provost marshall. Georgia special agent (1756), especially for the lower house.

KNOX, WILLIAM (1732–1810). Civil servant and placeman; crown agent for East Florida (1764–1770), undersecretary at American Department (1770–1782). Georgia councillor and agent (1762–1765).

LEE, ARTHUR (1740–1792). Lawyer, politician, and diplomat. Abandoned medicine for law (Lincoln's Inn, 1770; Middle Temple, 1773). Returned to England from Virginia in 1768; wrote Junius Americanus essays. Massachusetts assistant agent (1770–1774); Massachusetts Assembly agent (1774–1775). Secret agent of the Continental Congress (1775–1779).

LIFE, THOMAS (ca. 1720–1777). London barrister. Connecticut deputy agent (1760–1770); agent (1771–1775).

LITTLE, WILLIAM. Politician; sometime private secretary to Governor John Reynolds; clerk and speaker of the Georgia Assembly and commissary for Indian affairs. Georgia special agent to present address from Georgia to Board of Trade (1757).

McCULLOH, HENRY EUSTACE (1739?–1788+). Planter and politician; equally at home in London and North Carolina. Admitted Middle Temple (1757). North Carolina councillor and customs collector for the Port of Roanoke (1761–1767). North Carolina agent (1768–1773). Unsuccessful candidate for Parliament (1774). Loyalist.

MARCHANT, HENRY (1741–1796). Lawyer and dissenter. Rhode Island special agent (1771–1772). Rhode Island attorney general (1771–1776); delegate to the Continental Congress (1777–1779); assemblyman (1784–1790); and United States judge (1790–1796).

MARTYN, BENJAMIN (1699–1763). Writer and civil servant; secretary to the Society for Establishing the Colony of Georgia. Georgia agent and crown agent, then a hybrid office (1753–1763).

MAUDUIT, JASPER (1697–1772). London woolen draper and dissenter; treasurer of the New England Company (1748–1765) and governor (1765–1772). Massachusetts agent (1762–1765). Occasionally assisted by brother ISRAEL MAUDUIT (1708–1787), pamphleteer, customer of Southampton, factor at Blackwell Hall, Indian agent for Newfoundland, and private agent for Thomas Hutchinson.

MONTAGU, EDWARD (ca. 1720–1798). Barrister. Virginia [burgesses] agent (1759–1770); Grenada agent (1775–1776); English agent for the King of Poland (1765–?). Occasionally represented the Thomlinsons as New Hampshire agent.

PARTRIDGE, RICHARD (1681–1759). London merchant, Quaker, and career agent: Rhode Island (1715–1759); New York (1731); New Jersey (1728–1759); Massachusetts (1737); Pennsylvania Assembly (1740–1759); Connecticut Assembly (1750–1759); sometime parliamentary agent for the London Meeting for Sufferings. Left New Hampshire for London in 1701; brother-in-law of Jonathan Belcher.

PINCKNEY, CHARLES (1699–1758). Planter and lawyer. South Carolina assemblyman and speaker; special agent in London (1754–1756).

SARGENT, JOHN (1715–1791). London merchant and banker; director of the Bank of England (1753–1767). M.P. 1754–1761, 1765–1768. Pennsylvania financial agent (1762–1764); New York special agent (1765–1766). Associated with Grand Ohio Company.

SHERWOOD, JOSEPH (ca. 1708–1773). London attorney and Quaker;

informal assistant to Richard Partridge in 1750's. New Jersey agent (1759–1766); Rhode Island agent (1759–1773).

SMITH, SAMUEL. London merchant and attorney. Sometime solicitor to Governor Arthur Dobbs of North Carolina. North Carolina Council agent (1759–1764). Crown agent for St. John (1773).

THOMLINSON, JOHN (?–1767). London merchant associated with Apthorp & Trecothick; commercial interests in New Hampshire and Jamaica. New Hampshire agent (1734–1767; ill after 1761).

THOMLINSON, JOHN, JR. (1731–1767). English provincial politician and attorney (Lincoln's Inn, 1752). M.P. 1761–1767 (dependent on Newcastle). New Hampshire agent (1763–1767).

TRECOTHICK, BARLOW (1718?–1775). Merchant trading to North America and the West Indies; associated with Charles Apthorp and the Thomlinson firm. London alderman (1764–1774); sheriff (1766); lord mayor (1770). New Hampshire agent (1766–1774). M.P. 1768–1774.

WENTWORTH, JOHN (1737–1820). Politician. New Hampshire special agent (1765–1766); governor (1767–1775); surveyor general of the king's woods (1767–1775); admiralty judge (1767–1775); lieutenant governor of Nova Scotia (1792–1808). Loyalist.

WENTWORTH, PAUL (?–1793). Adventurer; relative of John; stockbroker in London and Paris; plantation owner in Surinam. New Hampshire agent (1774–1775). M.P. 1780.

WILMOT, HENRY (1709–1794). Solicitor and placeman. Private secretary to Lord Chancellor Camden. Leeward Islands agent (1749–1781); private agent to the Proprietors of Pennsylvania (1760–1775), William Alexander, and the East Jersey Proprietors; New Jersey agent (1766–1769). Examiner of the letters patents (1774).

WRIGHT, JAMES (1716–1785). Attorney and politician. Born in London; taken to Charleston, South Carolina, as a child. South Carolina attorney general (1739–   ), agent (1757–1760); lieutenant governor of Georgia (1760–1761); governor (1762–1776).

Selected Bibliography

A more nearly complete record of the sources for this study appears in the footnotes to the text. What follows is intended as a selective guide to the primary sources and secondary literature bearing most directly on the history of the agencies. The official and personal papers of the agents have been scattered throughout more than forty repositories in Great Britain and the United States. A great many have been printed, but a considerable number remain still in manuscript. I have used these documents in conjunction with the great variety of evidence relating to British imperial politics in the eighteenth century: state papers, newspapers, speeches, pamphlets, journals, and letters.

For the vast amount of material in print pertaining to the history of Anglo-American relations between 1755 and 1775, there are four excellent and recent bibliographical studies: Lawrence H. Gipson, *The British Empire before the American Revolution*, Vol. XIV (New York, 1968); Jack M. Sosin, *Whitehall and the Wilderness: The Middle West in British Colonial Policy, 1760–1775* (Lincoln, Neb., 1961), pp. 269–292; Franklin B. Wickwire, *British Subministers and Colonial America, 1763–1783* (Princeton, 1966), pp. 195–216; and Jack P. Greene, "The Plunge of Lemmings: A Consideration of Recent Writings on British Politics and the American Revolution," *South Atlantic Quarterly*, LVII (1968), 141–175.

MANUSCRIPTS

Great Britain

The BRITISH MUSEUM has a number of well-known collections of considerable size in which scattered letters to and from the agents can be found. The best of these collections is the Newcastle series. The Hardwicke, Egerton, and Stowe manuscripts are less valuable. The Grenville manuscripts are extremely important; most of them have now been edited and published by W. J. Smith and J. R. G. Tomlinson. William Knox's letters to Grenville are very helpful. The King's Manuscripts contain four volumes of letters that passed between Franklin, Thomas Pownall, and Samuel Cooper. The papers of two printers, Almon and Strahan, are extensive and useful though in limited ways. John Wilkes' manuscripts, especially his diary, reveal the extent of certain agents' involvement in London politics.

The PUBLIC RECORD OFFICE has four groups of documents with material pertinent to the agents. Chatham's manuscripts reveal his increasing inability to intervene effectively on behalf of the colonies. The Colonial Office and Treasury Board papers include many petitions submitted by the agents, along with the recommendation or action taken by a particular administrative office. The Privy Council papers and minutes are useful for memorials presented in the Council and for land grants sought by colonial lobbyists.

The GUILDHALL LIBRARY in London is useful for its Noble Collection of newspaper clippings relating to the history of London, especially its aldermen. The manuscripts of the Protestant Dissenting Deputies and the New England Company reveal the political commitments of those groups. Jasper and Israel Mauduit, Richard Jackson, and Dennys De Berdt are referred to frequently in these papers.

The BRISTOL UNIVERSITY LIBRARY has Matthew Brickdale's parliamentary diary—eleven small notebooks covering the period from 1771 until 1774. The reports of Burke's speeches are excellent. The HOUSE OF LORDS RECORD OFFICE has the remarkable minute books of the committees of the House which form the basis for the printed *Journals*. The minute books reveal the great amount of time consumed by petty, domestic, or private considerations. The Main Papers constitute a running chronology of the American question as considered by the upper house.

The SCOTTISH RECORD OFFICE in Edinburgh has a few letters from Franklin to Lord Kames. The SHEFFIELD CENTRAL LIBRARY has the extremely valuable Fitzwilliam collection from the Wentworth-Woodhouse Estate. In addition to Edmund Burke's correspondence, there are letters from a number of agents in Rockingham's papers: Bollan, Arthur Lee, John and Paul Wentworth. The WIGAN CENTRAL PUBLIC LIBRARY in Lancashire has George Folliott's diary. Folliott was an American merchant who visited London in 1765–1766 and interviewed Rockingham. His impressions of the agents at work are informative. The Dartmouth manuscripts at the WILLIAM SALT LIBRARY, Stafford, are of the highest importance, particularly for Dartmouth's term as Secretary of State for the Colonies. A number of agents' letters are included, notably De Berdt's. Many items in this collection have been calendared and excerpted in HMC *14th Report, Appendix, Part X, The Manuscripts of the Earl of Dartmouth*, Vol. II (*American Papers*) (London, 1895), and *15th Report, Appendix, Part I*, Vol. III (London, 1896).

LORD MALMESBURY, Christchurch, Hampshire, owns the parliamentary notes taken by his ancestor, James Harris. These are less complete than Brickdale's, but treat the earlier period of the Stamp Act crisis. There are references to Garth's activities in the House of Commons. SIR JOHN MURRAY, London, owns some twenty boxes and additional portfolios with letters from, and relating to, George Grenville. These are helpful in illuminating the role played by Grenville's underlings, especially Thomas Whately.

United States

The AMERICAN ANTIQUARIAN SOCIETY in Worcester, Massachusetts, has a few letters from Jasper Mauduit to his Massachusetts constituents. Seventy-six volumes of Franklin's manuscripts, including his accounts, ledgers, bank records, and voluminous letters, are in the library of the AMERICAN PHILOSOPHICAL SOCIETY in Philadelphia. Unfortunately many of the letters Franklin wrote during the years of his agencies (1757–1762, 1764–1775) have been lost. Only one of ten letter books from this period survived. The loss of Franklin's letters to Isaac Norris in Philadelphia is particularly lamentable. There are a number of significant letters from Arthur Lee in a separate two-volume collection.

The Rare Book Room of the BOSTON PUBLIC LIBRARY has a few letters from Bollan, the Mauduits, and Trecothick. The Bortman Collection of the BOSTON UNIVERSITY LIBRARY includes correspondence between the Mauduits, Thomas Hollis, and Jonathan Mayhew. There are several important letters from Franklin in the BLUMHAVEN LIBRARY, Philadelphia, the ROSENBACH FOUNDATION AND GALLERY, Philadelphia, and the BUFFALO AND ERIE COUNTY PUBLIC LIBRARY, Buffalo. Eight letters from Joseph Sherwood may be found in the BROWN UNIVERSITY LIBRARY special collections.

The WILLIAM L. CLEMENTS LIBRARY in Ann Arbor, Michigan, has four helpful groups of manuscripts: the Shelburne Papers, particularly for the period from 1766 until 1768, when Shelburne was Secretary of State for the Southern Department; the superb Franklin-Galloway correspondence; the Knox letters—valuable for insights into the functioning of colonial administration; and the less useful Clinton Papers.

WILLIAM C. COLES JR. of Moorestown, New Jersey, owns two letters from Franklin during his second agency. A splendid commentary on the agents by Dr. John Fothergill is in the Gilbert manuscripts of the COLLEGE OF PHYSICIANS in Philadelphia. There are a few letters from William Samuel Johnson in the COLUMBIA UNIVERSITY LIBRARY.

One of the finest repositories for documents bearing on the agents is the CONNECTICUT HISTORICAL SOCIETY in Hartford. There are eighty-two documents from an earlier period grouped under the heading "Agent's

Letters." All but one antedate 1761. The letters to, and drafts of, letters
from William Samuel Johnson form a running commentary on Anglo-
American politics from the Stamp Act through the advent of revolution.
Altogether there are about 1,250 items in the Johnson manuscripts. Johnson's London diary is complete for the four and one-half years he acted as
agent. Although it chronicles the weather as faithfully as it does the
activities of the agents, the diary supplements Johnson's long letters perfectly. A small group of Trumbull manuscripts is also preserved in the
Historical Society. The bulk of Trumbull's papers (thirty volumes), however, are in the CONNECTICUT STATE LIBRARY in Hartford. Letters from
Richard Jackson and Thomas Life, as well as their accounts, are included.
Miscellaneous reports from Connecticut's agents, especially financial documents bearing on the Mohegan and Susquehanna cases, are in the manuscript categories designated "Finance and Currency" (Vols. IV–V), "Indians" (Vol. II), and "War" (Vol. X).

Various letters relating to political problems of English and American
dissenters are in the DARTMOUTH COLLEGE LIBRARY; but very few of these
bear directly on the agents, except for several by De Berdt and some which
mention Jasper Mauduit. A number of Henry Eustace McCulloh's letters
are in the Iredell manuscripts of the DUKE UNIVERSITY LIBRARY. There is
a letter from Joseph Sherwood in the Roberts Collection of the HAVERFORD
COLLEGE LIBRARY. The splendid resources of the HISTORICAL SOCIETY OF
PENNSYLVANIA are invaluable for a study of the agents. In addition to six
volumes of Franklin manuscripts, there are Jackson, Life, Barclay, Charles,
and Sherwood letters in the Coombe, Dreer, Gratz, Pemberton, Penn, and
Smith manuscripts, as well as comments on the agents by political observers.

Thirteen volumes of the correspondence of Sir Francis Bernard are in
the Sparks Collection of the HOUGHTON LIBRARY, HARVARD UNIVERSITY.
A number of Richard Jackson's letters are included, as well as a running
commentary, from the Governor's viewpoint, on the agency's role in
provincial politics during the 1760's. Most of Arthur Lee's letters in
Houghton have been published.

A typescript of Thomas Hollis' diary is preserved in the INSTITUTE OF
EARLY AMERICAN HISTORY AND CULTURE in Williamsburg. Hollis had
several meetings with agents and other lobbyists in the London coffeehouses. A substantial body of Franklin manuscripts is in the LIBRARY OF
CONGRESS in Washington, D.C., notably the exchange between Franklin
and Barclay during the negotiations of 1774–1775. Transcripts of letters
found in various English and American archives are also preserved in that
library.

One of the finest and least used collections rests in the MASSACHUSETTS
ARCHIVES in the Boston Statehouse. Incoming and outgoing correspond-

ence has been voluminously preserved and microfilmed. For the period between 1762 and 1775, see reels 22, 56, 104, and 287–288. (Reels 25 through 27, the Hutchinson manuscripts, are more easily read in transcription at the MASSACHUSETTS HISTORICAL SOCIETY.) In addition, letters to and from the Mauduits, De Berdt, Jackson, Bollan, Trecothick, and Franklin can be found in a set of manuscript letter-books labeled according to their inclusive years: 1701–1763; 1763–1773; 1763–1775; 1764–1774; 1765–1773.

A great many of Bollan's very detailed letters and a lesser number written by the other Massachusetts agents are located in several collections owned by the MASSACHUSETTS HISTORICAL SOCIETY: the Andrews-Eliot, Bowdoin-Temple, Dana, Knox, Lee, Lee-Cabot, Large, Price, and Savage manuscripts. The photostat collection also contains letters concerning the agents, including the Thomlinsons of New Hampshire.

THE NEW HAMPSHIRE HISTORICAL SOCIETY in Concord has a fine set of transcripts of John Wentworth's letters. The NEW JERSEY HISTORICAL SOCIETY in Newark has several dozen Sherwood letters (most of which have been printed), as well as a few scattered items of value in the Bamberger Autograph Collection. The New York—New Jersey Boundary Papers in the NEW-YORK HISTORICAL SOCIETY include some agents' letters. The Reed manuscripts there are rich in letters concerning Dennys De Berdt, Stephen Sayre, and Arthur Lee. There are a few Henry Wilmot items in the Alexander manuscripts.

The NEW YORK PUBLIC LIBRARY has scattered pieces of value in the American Revolution manuscripts and the Emmet Collection. The Sam Adams manuscripts are a mine of information; particularly valuable are the letters from Arthur Lee and Sayre. The Bancroft Transcripts include letters of William Samuel Johnson to be found nowhere else, Garth letters, and a set of Mayhew-Hollis-Eliot correspondence. A few stray Franklin letters are located in the PIERPONT MORGAN LIBRARY in New York City.

Letters from Alexander Elmsley are in the Johnston manuscripts located in the NORTH CAROLINA DEPARTMENT OF ARCHIVES AND HISTORY in Raleigh. A half-dozen good letters from Henry Eustace McCulloh are among the Southern Historical Collection in the UNIVERSITY OF NORTH CAROLINA LIBRARY at Chapel Hill.

A superb group of agents' letters exists in the RHODE ISLAND ARCHIVES in the Statehouse in Providence. Joseph Sherwood's letters spanning the sixties are in Volumes VI and VII of the "Letters" series. The accounts of the agents are categorized as such. In addition, a few stray items of interest appear in the Clark manuscripts and the Military Papers, 1730–1765. Sherwood letters are also to be found in the Brown manuscripts of the RHODE ISLAND HISTORICAL SOCIETY in Providence. Some of Henry Marchant's London correspondence is in the Peck manuscripts there. His

London journal, owned by Miss ALICE CLARKE, is on loan and is very revealing for the period 1770–1771.

Charles Garth's communications with the South Carolina Committee of Correspondence from 1766 through 1775 are in the SOUTH CAROLINA ARCHIVES in Columbia. The letters written during 1773–1775 remain unpublished. A limited number of Arthur Lee's dispatches are in the Lee and Lee-Ludwell manuscripts of the VIRGINIA HISTORICAL SOCIETY, Richmond. James Abercromby's letter book is in the VIRGINIA STATE LIBRARY in Richmond. But most of these drafts are illegible.

There are a few Franklin letters for this period in the UNIVERSITY OF PENNSYLVANIA LIBRARY. The YALE UNIVERSITY LIBRARY has the superb Mason-Franklin Collection—a considerable number of the Doctor's manuscript letters, related documents, photostats, engravings, and rare volumes. The Eliot, Sharpe, and Stiles manuscripts contain some very useful letters from Ingersoll, Bollan, and Marchant.

PRINTED DOCUMENTS

Benjamin Franklin's published writings, public and private, alone constitute a considerable chronicle of the agents' fortunes. His letters and some of his occasional pieces are published in *The Writings of Benjamin Franklin*, ed. A. H. Smyth (10 vol.; New York, 1907). A definitive edition of *The Papers of Benjamin Franklin*, ed. Leonard W. Labaree *et al.* (New Haven, 1959–) is in progress; ten volumes covering the period 1706–1763 have appeared to date. These must be supplemented by more specialized collections, several of them compiled by Carl Van Doren: *Benjamin Franklin's Autobiographical Writings* (New York, 1945), invaluable for the Franklin-Galloway letters; *Letters and Papers of Benjamin Franklin and Richard Jackson, 1753–1785* (Philadelphia, 1947); and *The Letters of Benjamin Franklin and Jane Mecom* (Princeton, 1950). Other Franklin letters relating to his agency can be found in *PMHB*, V (1881), 353–355, and *Franklin, Jonathan Williams and William Pitt: A Letter of January 21, 1775*, ed. by Bernhard Knollenberg (Bloomington, Ind., 1949). Verner W. Crane has brought the polemical essays together splendidly in *Benjamin Franklin's Letters to the Press, 1758–1775* (Chapel Hill, 1950). The agent's accounts have been edited by G. S. Eddy in "Account Book of Benjamin Franklin Kept by Him during His First Mission to England as Provincial Agent, 1757–1762," *PMHB*, LV (1931), 97–133, and poorly by Worthington C. Ford, "Franklin's Accounts Against Massachusetts," *MHS Proceedings*, LVI (1923), 94–127.

Franklin's predecessors in the Massachusetts agency also left remarkably full records. The "Letters of Dennys De Berdt, 1757–1770," ed. by Albert Matthews, are in *CSM Publications*, XIII (1912), 293–461. A great many of William Bollan's letters can be found in *The Bowdoin and*

Temple Papers (MHS *Collections*, ser. 6, Vol. IX [Boston, 1897]). A selection of Jasper Mauduit's papers, as well as some of Bollan's, appear in MHS *Collections*, Vol. LXXIV (Boston, 1918). Scholars should also consult "Letters from Jasper Mauduit, 1763–64," MHS *Collections*, ser. 1, VI (Boston, 1800), 189–195. Excerpts from Richard Jackson's correspondence with Francis Bernard appear in *Speeches of the Governors of Massachusetts from 1765 to 1775 . . . ,* ed. Alden Bradford (Boston, 1818).

Communications between Connecticut and her agents can be found in *The Fitch Papers . . . 1754–1766* and *The Pitkin Papers . . . 1766–1769* (CHS *Collections*, Vols. XVIII–XIX [Hartford, 1920–1921]). "A Selection from the Correspondence and Miscellaneous Papers of Jared Ingersoll," ed. F. B. Dexter, has been published as Volume IX of the NHCHS *Papers* (New Haven, 1918), pp. 201–472. Many documents of singular importance are included. William Samuel Johnson's "Letters to the Governors of Connecticut" is in MHS *Collections*, ser. 5, IX (Boston, 1885), 213–490. Johnson wrote copiously, reporting the changing circumstances, the decline of colonial influence, and the growing alienation and frustration of the lobbyists. Consequently these letters are one of the best sources for the period 1767–1771. Some of Johnson's private letters for these years are among *The Susquehannah Company Papers: Memorial Publications of the Wyoming Historical and Genealogical Society* (4 vols.; Wilkes-Barre, Pa., 1930–1933), ed. Julian P. Boyd.

Edmund Burke's correspondence with New York during his agency has been edited by Ross J. S. Hoffman as part of *Edmund Burke, New York Agent . . .* (Philadelphia, 1956), pp. 194–272. Other letters bearing upon Anglo-American politics during the crisis years are superbly presented in *The Correspondence of Edmund Burke*, ed. T. W. Copeland *et al.* (6 vols.; Cambridge, Eng., and Chicago, 1958–   ), especially Volumes II and III. Also useful is *Burke's Politics: Selected Writings and Speeches of Edmund Burke . . . ,* ed. Ross J. S. Hoffman and Paul Levack (New York, 1949).

A selection of Joseph Sherwood's letters with New Jersey has been published in the NJHS *Proceedings*, V (Newark, 1851), 131–153. Correspondence of Sherwood and Richard Partridge with Rhode Island, as well as agency accounts, are scattered through *The Correspondence of the Colonial Governors of Rhode Island, 1723–1775*, ed. G. S. Kimball (2 vols.; Boston, 1902–1903). The controversy over the agency in Maryland can be traced in *Remarks upon a Message, Sent by the Upper to the Lower House of Assembly of Maryland*, 1762 (Philadelphia?, 1763), pp. 26–29, and *An Answer to the Queries on the Proprietary Government of Maryland . . . Also, an Answer to Remarks upon a Message . . .* (Annapolis, 1764), pp. 13–17, 29–59. For Charles Garth's letters to Maryland during the Stamp Act crisis, see *MHM*, VI (1911), 282–305.

Some of the letters that passed between Virginia and Edward Montagu appear in "Proceedings of the Virginia Committee of Correspondence, 1759–1767," *VMHB*, X (1903), 337–356; XI (1903–1904), 1–25, 131–143, 345–355; and XII (1904–1905), 1–14, 157–169, 225–240, 353–364. Materials pertaining to the North Carolina agency will be found in *The Colonial Records of North Carolina*, ed. W. L. Saunders (30 vols.; Raleigh, 1886–1914), *passim*. The "Correspondence of Charles Garth" has been partially published in Volumes XXVI–XXXIII of *SCHGM*. Sources for the Georgia agency, and particularly that of William Knox, have been printed in three collections: "Correspondence of William Knox, Chiefly in Relation to American Affairs, 1757–1808," HMC *Report on Manuscripts in Various Collections*, VI (Dublin, 1909), 81–296; *The Letters of Hon. James Habersham, 1756–1775* (Collections of the Georgia Historical Society, Vol. VI [Savannah, 1904]); and "Letters to the Georgia Colonial Agent, July 1762 to January 1771," ed. Lilla M. Hawes, *Georgia Historical Quarterly*, XXXVI (1952), 250–286.

Documents pertinent to several of the agencies and Anglo-American politics generally can be found in "William Allen–Benjamin Chew Correspondence, 1763–1764," ed. David A. Kimball and Miriam Quinn, *PMHB*, XC (1966), 202–226; "An Account of a Conference Between the Late Mr. Grenville and the Several Colony Agents, in the Year 1764, Previous to the Passing the Stamp Act," MHS *Collections*, ser. 1, IX (Boston, 1804), 268–275; and *The Diary and Letters of Thomas Hutchinson*, ed. Peter O. Hutchinson (2 vols.; Boston, 1884–1886), an invaluable source for the years 1774–1775, when Hutchinson was in London dealing with Rockingham, Dartmouth, Jackson, Garth, Montagu, and others; the index is inadequate. For a sympathetic view of Americans in London during the same period, see "Journal of Josiah Quincy, Jun., during His Voyage and Residence in England . . . , MHS *Proceedings*, L (1917), 433–496.

SELECTED PAMPHLET LITERATURE BY THE AGENTS

Bollan, William. *The Ancient Right of the English Nation to the American Fishery; and Its Various Diminutions Examined and Stated with a Map of the Lands.* . . . London, 1764.

——. *Britannia Libera, or a Defence of the Free State of Man in England.* . . . London, 1772.

——. *Coloniae Anglicanae Illustratae: or the Acquest of Dominion, and the Plantation of Colonies Made by the English in America, with the Rights of the Colonists Examined, Stated, and Illustrated.* London, 1762.

——. *Continued Corruption, Standing Armies, and Popular Discontents Considred; and the Establishment of the English Colonies in America.* . . . London, 1768.

——. *An Epistle from Timoleon, to All the Honest Free-Holders, and Other Electors of Members of Parliament.* . . . London, 1768.

——. *An Essay on the Right of Every Man in a Free State to Speak and Write Freely, in Order to Defend the Public Rights, and Promote the Public Welfare.* . . . London, 1772.

——. *The Free Briton's Memorial, to All the Freeholders, Citizens and Burgesses, Who Elect the . . . British Parliament, Presented in Order to the Effectual Defence of Their Injured Right of Election.* London, 1769.

——. *The Free Briton's Supplemental Memorial to the Electors of the Members of the British Parliament.* . . . London, 1770.

——. *The Freedom of Speech and Writing upon Public Affairs, Considered with an Historical View.* . . . London, 1766.

——. *The Mutual Interest of Great Britain and the American Colonies Considered with Respect to an Act Passed Last Sessions of Parliament for Laying a Duty on Merchandise.* . . . London, 1765.

——. *The Petitions of Mr. Bollan . . . Lately Presented to the Two Houses of Parliament: with a Brief Introduction Relating to the Law of Nature.* . . . London, 1774.

——. *The Rights of the English Colonies Established in America Stated and Defended.* . . . London, 1774.

——. *A Succinct View of the Origin of Our Colonies.* . . . *Being an Extract from an Essay Lately Published Entitled the Freedom and Writing.* . . . London, 1766.

Burke, Edmund. *Speech on American Taxation.* London, 1775.

——. *The Speech . . . on Moving His Resolutions for Conciliation with the Colonies.* London, 1775.

——. *Speeches at His Arrival at Bristol, and at the Conclusion of the Poll.* London, 1775.

——. *Thoughts on the Cause of the Present Discontents.* London, 1770.

Franklin, Benjamin. *The Causes of the Present Distractions in America Explained: in Two Letters to a Merchant in London.* N.p., 1774.

——. *The Examination of Doctor Benjamin Franklin Relative to the Repeal of the American Stamp Act in 1766.* London, 1767.

——. *The Interest of Great Britain Considered.* This first appeared in London in 1760; in January, 1766, during the campaign to repeal the Stamp Act, Franklin brought out an influential second edition.

Knox, William. *The Claim of the Colonies to an Exemption from Internal Taxes Imposed by Authority of Parliament Examined.* London, 1765.

[——?]. *A Letter to a Member of Parliament, Wherein the Power of the British Legislature and the Case of the Colonists are Briefly and Impartially Considered.* London, 1765.

Lee, Arthur. *Answer to Considerations on Certain Political Transactions of the Province of South Carolina.* London, 1774.

Lee, Arthur. *An Appeal to the Justice and Interests of the People of Great Britain in the Present Disputes with America by an Old Member of Parliament.* London, 1774.

——. *Observations on the Review of the Controversy between Great Britain and Her Colonies.* London, 1769.

——. *The Political Detection: or, the Treachery and Tyranny of Administration, Both at Home and Abroad. . . .* London, 1770.

——. *A Speech Intended to Have Been Delivered in the House of Commons in Support of the Petition from the General Congress at Philadelphia.* London, 1775.

——. *A True State of the Proceedings in the Parliament of Great Britain and in the Province of Massachusetts Bay. . . .* London, 1774.

The Letters of Governor Hutchinson, and Lt. Gov. Oliver Printed at Boston and Remarks Thereon with the Assembly's Address and the Proceedings of the Lords Committee of Council. . . . London, 1774. Franklin's letters are printed on pp. 65, 72–73; Israel Mauduit's remarks are on pp. 45–64 and his petition on p. 71.

Mauduit, Israel. *A Memorial to the Lords Commissioners of His Majesty's Treasury.* N.p., 1764.

——. *Mr. Grenville's Offer to the Colony Assemblies to Raise the Supply Themselves, Instead of Having It Done by a Parliamentary Stamp Act.* London, 1765.

——. *A Short View of the History of the Colony of Massachusetts Bay, with Respect to Their Original Charter and Constitution.* London, 1769.

SECONDARY SOURCES

More than half a century ago, Charles M. Andrews wrote that "no adequate study has been made of the colonial agents" ("Some Neglected Aspects of Colonial History," NJHS *Proceedings* for 1901–1905, IV [Paterson, 1907], 9). Since then a good deal has been written about the agents, much of it painfully inadequate. Most of the literature has been concerned with the agents' relationship to provincial rather than London politics, a preoccupation that has led to a distorted view of the institution's effectiveness and usefulness during the decade prior to Revolution.

The fullest and most recent treatment of the agents in the revolutionary era is by Jack M. Sosin, *Agents and Merchants: British Colonial Policy and the Origins of the American Revolution, 1763–1775* (Lincoln, Neb., 1965). I have expressed my disagreement with Professor Sosin at length in 3WMQ XXIII (1966), 492–495. General studies include Edwin P. Tanner, "Colonial Agencies in England during the Eighteenth Century," PSQ, XVI (1901), 24–49; Beverly W. Bond Jr., "The Colonial Agent as a Popular Representative," PSQ, XXXV (1920), 372–392; and William L. Sachse, *The Colonial American in Britain* (Madison, Wis., 1956).

The best regional studies of the agencies have concentrated on the southern and island colonies. Ella Lonn's thorough examination of *The Colonial Agents of the Southern Colonies* (Chapel Hill, 1945) is complemented by chapter 13 of Jack P. Greene's *The Quest for Power: The Lower House of Assembly in the Southern Royal Colonies, 1689–1776* (Chapel Hill, 1963). Lillian Penson's excellent pioneering study, *The Colonial Agents of the British West Indies* (London, 1924), should be read along with her article, "The Origin of the Crown Agency Office," *EHR*, XL (1925), 196–206, which covers the period from the Seven Years' War through the Napoleonic era. For a case study of this new institution, see Robert R. Rea, "The King's Agent for British West Florida," *Alabama Review*, XVI (1963), 141–153, useful for its discussion of the career of John Ellis (1764–1776).

Other regional studies include Marguerite Appleton, "The Agents of the New England Colonies in the Revolutionary Period," *NEQ*, VI (1933), 371–387, which peculiarly omits the Mauduits; James J. Burns, *The Colonial Agents of New England* (Washington, D.C., 1935), which fails to use unpublished sources, overlooks the political importance of John Pownall, and incorrectly dates many of the agencies; and Edward P. Lilly, *The Colonial Agents of New York and New Jersey* (Washington, D.C., 1936), which overemphasizes local politics and does not carry the story beyond the Stamp Act crisis.

Provincial groups of agents are discussed by Harold W. Currie in "Massachusetts Politics and the Colonial Agency, 1762–70" (unpub. Ph.D. diss.; University of Michigan, 1960); Mabel P. Wolff, *The Colonial Agency of Pennsylvania, 1712–1757* (Philadelphia, 1933); E. I. Miller, "The Virginia Committee of Correspondence, 1759–1770," *1WMQ*, XXII (1913), 1–19; Samuel J. Ervin, "The Provincial Agents of North Carolina," *Sprunt Historical Publications*, XVI (Chapel Hill, 1919), 63–77; and William R. Smith, *South Carolina as a Royal Province, 1719–1776* (New York, 1903), ch. 4. An unusual but valuable essay by D. H. Watson is "Barlow Trecothick and Other Associates of Lord Rockingham during the Stamp Act Crisis, 1765–66" (unpub. M.A. thesis; Sheffield University, 1957). Watson provides sketches of Trecothick, John Wentworth, William Baker, George Aufrere, Henry McCulloh, William Bollan, and Paul Wentworth, based heavily on the Rockingham manuscripts in the Sheffield Central Library.

Among individual agents, Franklin's career, of course, has been most closely scrutinized. Verner W. Crane's exhaustive monographs are models of scholarship: *Benjamin Franklin, Englishman and American* (Baltimore, 1936); "Certain Writings of Benjamin Franklin on the British Empire and the American Colonies," *Papers of the Bibliographical Society*, XXVIII (1934), 1–27; "Benjamin Franklin and the Stamp Act," *CSM Publications*, XXXII (1937), 56–77; "Three Fables by Benjamin Franklin,"

NEQ, IX (1936), 499–504; "Franklin's Political Journalism in England," *Journal of the Franklin Institute*, CCXXXIII (1942), 205–224; and "Franklin's Marginalia and the Lost 'Treatise' on Empire," *Papers of the Michigan Academy of Science, Arts and Letters*, XLII (1957), 163–176.

J. J. Zimmerman's "Benjamin Franklin: A Study of Pennsylvania Politics and the Colonial Agency, 1755–1775" (unpub. Ph.D. diss.; University of Michigan, 1956), is complemented by William S. Hanna, *Benjamin Franklin and Pennsylvania Politics* (Stanford, 1964), which emphasizes Pennsylvania politics more than Franklin's agencies. Special studies of importance include Leonard W. Labaree, "Benajmin Franklin's British Friendships," APS *Proceedings*, CVIII (1964), 423–428; Alfred O. Aldridge, "Benjamin Franklin as Georgia Agent," *Georgia Review*, VI (1952), 161–173; James H. Hutson, "Benjamin Franklin and the Parliamentary Grant for 1758," 3*WMQ*, XXIII (1966), 575–595; G. S. Wykoff, "Problems concerning Franklin's 'A Dialogue Between Britain, France, Spain, Holland, Saxony and America,'" *American Literature*, XI (1940), 439–448; and B. C. Corner and D. W. Singer, "Dr. John Fothergill, Peacemaker," APS *Proceedings*, XCVIII (1954), 11–22.

Five general and related studies of Franklin shed light in diverse ways on his years in Britain. The fullest biography is Carl Van Doren's *Benjamin Franklin* (New York, 1938). The most interesting analysis of Franklin's political ideas is Paul W. Conner's *Poor Richard's Politicks: Benjamin Franklin and His New American Order* (New York, 1965). *Benjamin Franklin in Scotland and Ireland, 1759 and 1771*, by J. B. Nolan (Philadelphia, 1938), contains some helpful social history, especially for Franklin's London. Specialists should also consult J. P. Gleason, "A Scurrilous Colonial Election and Franklin's Reputation," 3*WMQ*, XVIII (1961), 68–84, and Nicholas Hans, "Franklin, Jefferson and the English Radicals at the End of the Eighteenth Century," APS *Proceedings*, XCVIII (1954), 406–426.

The literature for Edmund Burke is almost as extensive as for Franklin. Ross J. S. Hoffman has written a full monograph on *Edmund Burke, New York Agent . . .* (Philadelphia, 1956), but readers will also wish to consult *Burke and the Nature of Politics: The Age of the American Revolution* (Lexington, Ky., 1957) by Carl B. Cone. P. T. Underdown's *Bristol and Burke* (Bristol, 1961) and his "Henry Cruger and Edmund Burke: Colleagues and Rivals at the Bristol Election of 1774," 3*WMQ*, XV (1958), 14–34, shed light on Burke's notions of constituency and his political activities while serving as agent. Two excellent articles which should be read together are by Lucy S. Sutherland, "Edmund Burke and the first Rockingham Ministry," *EHR*, XLVII (1932), 46–72, and Thomas H. D. Mahoney, "Edmund Burke and the American Revolution: The Repeal of the Stamp Act," *Burke Newsletter*, VII (1965), 503–521. Less valuable are Calvin Stebbins, "Edmund Burke: His Services as Agent to the Province of New York," AAS *Proceedings*, N.S., IX (1893), 89–101, and Dixon Wecter, "Burke, Franklin, and Samuel Petrie," *Huntington Library Quarterly*, III (1940), 315–338.

The best treatment of "Barlow Trecothick," is by D. H. Watson in the *Bulletin of the British Association for American Studies*, N.S., I (1960), 36–49, and II (1961), 29–39, though specialists will also consult T. D. Jervey, "Barlow Trecothick," SCHGM, XXXII (1931), 157–169. John Wentworth's biographer is L. S. Mayo (Cambridge, Mass., 1921). Malcolm Freiberg has made a useful study of "William Bollan: Agent of Massachusetts," in *More Books*, XXIII (1948), 43–54, 90–100, 135–146, 168–182, 212–220. Bollan's activities, as well as Dennys De Berdt's, are discussed by Francis G. Walett, "Governor Bernard's Undoing: An Earlier Hutchinson Letters Affair," NEQ, XXXVIII (1965), 217–226. A unique source of information about De Berdt is William B. Reed's *The Life of Esther De Berdt* (Philadelphia, 1853). There is no biography of Jasper Mauduit, but Robert J. Taylor has written "Israel Mauduit," NEQ, XXIV (1951), 208–230, and Worthington C. Ford has examined "The Mauduit Pamphlets" in MHS *Proceedings*, XLIV (1911), 144–175.

Jared Ingersoll by Lawrence H. Gipson (New Haven, 1920) and *William Samuel Johnson* by G. C. Groce (New York, 1937) are both valuable, though neither concentrates on the agencies. Marguerite Appleton's "Richard Partridge: Colonial Agent," NEQ, V (1932), 293–309, is a fine but general essay. D. S. Lovejoy stresses the American's negative and moralistic response to London in "Henry Marchant and the Mistress of the World," 3WMQ, XII (1955), 375–398. Nicholas Varga has gathered all the scattered information on Charles in "Robert Charles: New York Agent, 1748–1770," 3WMQ, XVIII (1961), 211–235. *A History of the Barclay Family* has been compiled by C. W. Barclay (3 vols.; London, 1924).

Richard H. Lee's *Life of Arthur Lee* (2 vols.; Boston, 1829), is invaluable for the letters included as appendixes. Lyon G. Tyler has contributed "Arthur Lee, a Neglected Statesman," in *Tyler's Quarterly Historical and Genealogical Magazine*, XIV (1932), 65–77, 129–138, 197–216. One of the best sources for Henry Eustace McCulloh's life is G. J. McRee's *Life and Correspondence of James Iredell . . .* (2 vols.; New York, 1857–1858). Background on McCulloh will be found in Charles G. Sellers, "Private Profits and British Colonial Policy: The Speculations of Henry McCulloh," 3WMQ, VIII (1951), 535–551, and in John Cannon, "Henry McCulloch and Henry McCulloh," 3WMQ, XV (1958), 71–73. Lewis B. Namier's "Charles Garth, Agent for South Carolina," EHR, LIV (1939), 443–470, 632–652, is a model of its kind and includes long passages from letters now unavailable to scholars.

Valuable comparisons emerge from studies of the prerevolutionary agents. Among the most interesting are Raymond P. Stearns, *The Strenuous Puritan: Hugh Peter, 1598–1660* (Urbana, Ill., 1954), ch. 7, on the years 1641–1645; Kenneth B. Murdock, "Increase Mather's Expenses as Colonial Agent," CSM *Publications*, XXVII (1932), 200–204; Charles L. Sanford, "The Days of Jeremy Dummer, Colonial Agent" (unpub. Ph.D. diss.; Harvard University, 1952); and Leonard W. Cowie, *Henry Newman: An American in London, 1708–1743* (London, 1956), ch. 9, which treats the New Hampshire agency, 1709–1737.

Among the general volumes on British politics before the American Revolution, perhaps a half-dozen works require special mention. Lawrence H. Gipson's monumental examination of *The British Empire before the American Revolution* (13 vols.; New York, 1936–1967) covers the years 1748–1776 in great detail. While I have differed with Professor Gipson on some points (see *NEQ*, XXXIX [1966], 550–554), his series will long stand as the definitive narrative history of this period. The best one-volume treatment of the subject is Charles R. Ritcheson, *British Politics and the American Revolution* (Norman, Okla., 1954), in many ways a pioneering study. An excellent book of narrower compass is *British Politics and the American Revolution: The Path to War, 1773–1775* (London, 1964), by Bernard Donoughue. A parallel work by B. D. Bargar, *Lord Dartmouth and the American Revolution* (Columbia, S.C., 1965), exploits the Dartmouth papers to good advantage. In "The Committee of the Whole House to Consider the American Papers (January and February, 1766)," (unpub. M.A. thesis; Sheffield University, 1956), B. R. Smith contends effectively that Barlow Trecothick's examination before the House of Commons was as influential in procuring repeal as Franklin's more famous inquisition. Richard W. Van Alstyne, *Empire and Independence: The International History of the American Revolution* (New York, 1965), chs. 1–3, places the prologue to revolution in the broad context of "interest politics."

Index

341

About the Author

MICHAEL G. KAMMEN is a graduate of George Washington University, and he received his M.A. and Ph.D. degrees from Harvard University. He taught at Harvard before coming to Cornell University, where he is Associate Professor of History.

His articles and reviews have appeared in numerous scholarly periodicals, and his books include *Politics and Society in Colonial America: Democracy or Deference?* Professor Kammen won the Bowdoin Prize in 1964 for an essay based upon *A Rope of Sand,* and he was one of the first recipients—in 1967—of a research fellowship from the National Foundation on the Arts and the Humanities.

VINTAGE POLITICAL SCIENCE
AND SOCIAL CRITICISM

VINTAGE CRITICISM,
LITERATURE, MUSIC, AND ART

VINTAGE BIOGRAPHY AND AUTOBIOGRAPHY

R 775.

R 67